T0238269

Lecture Notes in Artificial Intelligence (LNAI)

Lecture Notes in Artificial Intelligence

Subseries of Lecture Notes in Computer Science
Edited by J. Siekmann

Lecture Notes in Computer Science

Edited by G. Goos and J. Hartmanis

Editorial

Artificial Intelligence has become a major discipline under the roof of Computer Science. This is also reflected by a growing number of titles devoted to this fast developing field to be published in our Lecture Notes in Computer Science. To make these volumes immediately visible we have decided to distinguish them by a special cover as Lecture Notes in Artificial Intelligence, constituting a subseries of the Lecture Notes in Computer Science. This subseries is edited by an Editorial Board of experts from all areas of AI, chaired by Jörg Siekmann, who are looking forward to consider further AI monographs and proceedings of high scientific quality for publication.

We hope that the constitution of this subseries will be well accepted by the audience of the Lecture Notes in Computer Science, and we feel confident that the subseries will be recognized as an outstanding opportunity for publication by authors and editors of the AI community.

Editors and publisher

Lecture Notes in Artificial Intelligence

Edited by J. Siekmann

Subseries of Lecture Notes in Computer Science

465

A. Fuhrmann   M. Morreau   (Eds.)

The Logic of Theory Change

Workshop, Konstanz, FRG, October 13–15, 1989
Proceedings

Springer-Verlag

Berlin Heidelberg New York London
Paris Tokyo Hong Kong Barcelona

Editors

André Fuhrmann
Zentrum Philosophie und Wissenschaftstheorie, Universität Konstanz
Postfach 5560, W-7750 Konstanz, FRG

Michael Morreau
Seminar für natürlich-sprachliche Systeme, Universität Tübingen
Biesingerstraße 10, W-7400 Tübingen, FRG

CR Subject Classification (1987): I.2.3, F.4.1

ISBN 3-540-53567-5 Springer-Verlag Berlin Heidelberg New York
ISBN 0-387-53567-5 Springer-Verlag New York Berlin Heidelberg

© Springer-Verlag Berlin Heidelberg 1991
Printed in Germany

Printing and binding: Druckhaus Beltz, Hemsbach/Bergstr.
2145/3140-543210 – Printed on acid-free paper

Preface

The logic of theory change can be traced back to Tarski's investigations into consequence operations in the 1930s. A consequence operation, in the sense of Tarski, may be seen as a special case of the simplest kind of theory change operation: *expansion*. To expand a theory T by some sentence A, one simply closes the union of T and A under logical consequence.

Expansion is appropriate where the sentence to be added is consistent with what has previously been accepted. However, if *not-A* is accepted in a theory, then expanding by A would change the old theory to an inconsistent one. Thus, when coming to know that A, it is more likely that we should want to change our theory such that we can take in A consistently: instead of simply expanding by A we should want to *revise* the theory to include A. A third kind of belief change operation—one which, in a sense, mirrors revision—is *contraction*: the removal of a sentence from a theory.

Half a century after Tarski´s investigations of consequence operations, revisions and contractions of theories came into focus from three initially very different directions.

- Peter Gärdenfors (1978) was trying to develop an epistemic semantics for *conditional sentences*. According to this theory a conditional *if A then B* is accepted in a theory T just in case B would be accepted on revising T so as to accommodate A (the so-called Ramsey test).
- Carlos Alchourrón was mainly interested in a particular kind of theory change: the *derogation of laws*. Together with David Makinson he published in 1980 a paper on the contraction of systems of norms.
- Inquiry proceeds by replacing one corpus of belief by another. Much of Isaac Levi's theory of inquiry revolves around the question as to when such transitions from one theory to another should qualify as rational. Levi's work has inspired much—and he has remained a critical commentator—of Alchourron, Gärdenfors and Makinson´s approach to theory change.

The first three authors, Alchourrón, Gärdenfors and Makinson, soon combined their efforts and published a seminal paper in 1985. The cluster of postulates and models presented in this paper is now—somewhat loosely—referred to as the AGM theory. Gärdenfors (1988)—to date the most comprehensive presentation of that theory—provides ample evidence that the logic of theory change is one of the most fecund research programmes in philosophical logic to have emerged in recent years. Apart from throwing new light on old problems and generating interesting problems of its own, it has quickly established important links with research in artificial intelligence. The present volume charts out some of these problems and connections.

Much of the work on theory change may be read as contributions towards a unified theory of *database updating*. Some of the models for theory change—such as those based on relations of epistemic entrenchment (see the contributions by Schlechta, Lindström and Rabinowicz, and Rott)—provide algorithms for the design of update programs. Conversely, some update programs may be interpreted as models for a theory of contraction and revision operations (see, for example, the contribution by Martins in this volume).

One of the initial motivations for studying the formal aspects of contractions and revisions was the quest for an epistemic semantics of *conditional sentences* based on the Ramsey test. Gärdenfors (1986, 1987) has shown that the Ramsey test clashes with certain natural assumptions about change operations; a similar result is presented in this volume for the negative Ramsey test (concerning the *rejection* of conditionals). In two further contributions Lindström and Rabinowicz, and Rott propose to weaken—in very different ways—the assumptions leading to Gärdenfors' original impossiblity observation. In Fuhrmann's contribution logics of conditionals are related to update logics, that is, modal variants of the AGM theory of revisions and contractions.

Revision of theories is a nonmonotonic operation: in the process of revising a theory so as to include *A* some of the original theory may get lost. This observation suggests connections to *nonmonotonic reasoning*. A start to relating the logic of theory change to theories of nonmonotonic inference is made in the contributions by Makinson and Gärdenfors, Brewka, Rott, and Schulz.

Finally, under the heading "Reformulations and Extensions" we have brought together four papers which give further evidence of the range of issues connected with theory change. Topics treated here include alternative semantics for propositional calculi (Pearce and Rautenberg), a recasting of the AGM theory as a modal logic (Fuhrmann), the dynamic aspects of Kamp's discourse representation theory (Asher), and an extension of the AGM theory to cover contractions by sets of sentences rather than single sentences at a time (Niederée).

The contributions by Doyle and Hilpinen were read at a conference in Lund, Sweden, in August 1989. Most of the other papers collected here were presented in October 1989 during a workshop at the *Zentrum Philosophie und Wissenschaftstheorie*, University of Konstanz. We should like to thank Prof. Jürgen Mittelstraß without whose generous support the workshop would not have been possible. Thanks are also due to Harald Borges, Erika Fraiss and Maria Schorpp for helping to organise the workshop.

Konstanz and   *André Fuhrmann*
Tübingen, August 1990   *Michael Morreau*

References

Alchourrón, C. and D. Makinson (1980), Hierarchies of regulations and their logic, in *New Studies in Deontic Logic*, ed. R. Hilpinen, Dordrecht (Reidel); pp. 123-148.

Alchourrón, C., P. Gärdenfors and D. Makinson (1985), On the logic of theory change: Partial meet functions for contraction and revision, *Journal of Symbolic Logic*, 50; pp. 510-530.

Gärdenfors, P. (1978), Conditionals and changes of belief, *Acta Philosophica Fennica*, 30; pp. 381-404.

Gärdenfors, P. (1986), Belief revisions and the Ramsey test for conditionals, *Philosophical Review*, 95; pp. 81-93.

Gärdenfors, P. (1987), Variations on the Ramsey test: More triviality results, *Studia Logica*, 46; pp. 319-325.

Gärdenfors, P. (1988), *Knowledge in Flux*, Cambridge/Mass. (MIT Press).

Levi, I. (1980), *The Enterprise of Knowledge*, Cambridge/Mass. (MIT Press).

Tarski, A. (1930), Fundamental concepts of the methodology of the deductive sciences, in *Logic, Semantics, Metamathematics*, ed. Woodger, Oxford (Clarendon), 1956.

Contents

Foundations

Inquiry, Argumentation and Knowledge[1]

Risto Hilpinen

University of Turku and University of Miami

> "Floyd Vance is Amy Denovo's father," he said.
> Wolfe nodded. "As I surmised. How do you know that?"
> "Damn you, I'm telling you! I know because ... I have personal knowledge.
> That's the information you say you have been hired to get."
> "It is indeed. But as I said, I must have answers that satisfy me."
>
> Rex Stout, *The Father Hunt*, Bantam Books, New York, 1969, p. 147.

I

The purpose of this paper is to discuss the ways in which inquiry and argumentation can change people's opinions, and the conditions which make people's opinions susceptible to change by inquiry and argumentation. I shall use as my basic epistemic concept the concept of an *information system*. By an information system I understand a set of propositions, together with a system of evidential relationships among the propositions; in other words, an information system is a potential description of what some person might *accept as true* in some situation or at some time. The expression "information system" is (approximately) synonymous with the expression "belief system" often used in contemporary epistemology, and in the following I shall occasionally use the latter expression. However, the expression "belief system" may be slightly misleading for my purposes, because philosophers tend to regard beliefs as mental or psychological states, as something located in a person's head or

[1] This paper is based on research supported by Finnish State Council of the Humanities grant No. 09/053. Earlier versions of this paper have been presented at the conference "The Dynamics of Belief and Knowledge", Lund University (Lund, Sweden), August 24 - 26, 1989) and in philosophy colloquia at the University of Otago (Dunedin, New Zealand, May 1989) and the University of Miami (Coral Gables, Florida, November 1989). I wish to thank the participants of these meetings for comments and discussion, and Mrs. Rita Luoma for assistance in the preparation of the paper.

"mind".[2] This conception of belief, together with the view that it is the business of epistemology to study beliefs and belief systems, has recently led to an unfortunate assimilation of epistemology to cognitive psychology. People have been highly successful in designing artificial representation and information systems which overcome many of the limitations of psychological or "mental" representations. (I want to make a distinction between representation systems and information systems: the latter are produced by means of the former.) All sign systems in which information is stored and which can be used for conveying information are information systems in my sense: they include pictures and diagrams, information files (which may have electronic or paper replicas), books, maps, etc. Such systems may be called belief systems as long as one remembers that they need not be in a person's head. We could say (metaphorically) that they are in a person's "mind", but then the word "mind" is used in such a way that my mind can be said to include the address book which I am carrying in my pocket. It is epistemologically irrelevant whether I keep my address book in my head or in my pocket. I take this to be the valid point of Karl Popper's criticism of what he calls the "belief philosophy" or "subjectivist epistemology".[3]

One advantage of the use of the expression "information system" is that it makes it clear that the system has (normally) been created intentionally, for a certain purpose, and is therefore a proper subject for evaluation and criticism: an information system may be satisfactory or unsatisfactory relative to the purpose for which it has been designed. Information systems can be regarded as artificial objects, as *artifacts*.

What is the function or purpose of an information system? Such systems are created and used for many different purposes, but the general purpose of any information system is, of course, to give information. Artificial information systems are usually created for the purpose of giving information about some specific area or about questions of a certain kind --- for example, the business of a telephone book is to give information about the telephone numbers of the

---

[2] Cf. Alvin Goldman , *Epistemology and Cognition*, Harvard University Press, Cambridge, Mass. 1986, pp. 13 - 17.
[3] See Karl R. Popper, 'Epistemology without a Knowing Subject', in *Proceedings of the Third International Congress of Logic, Methodology and Philosophy of Science*, ed. by B. van Rootselaar and F. Staal, North-Holland, Amsterdam 1968, pp. 333 - 73; reprinted in K. Popper, *Objective Knowledge: An Evolutionary Approach*, Clarendon Press, Oxford, pp. 106 - 152.

inhabitants of a certain city or area. (My phone book is my "belief system" as regards the telephone numbers of the inhabitants of the city where I live, because I use it in a certain way, viz. to make telephone calls. It is a part of my "extended mind".)

We can make here a distinction between *specialized* or *special purpose* information systems which are created for the purpose of giving information about questions of a certain kind (e.g., about telephone numbers) and *general purpose* or *multipurpose* information systems which are expected to give information about many different kinds of questions. The difference between special purpose and multipurpose information systems is a matter of degree; for example, different sciences can be regarded as multipurpose information systems since they should provide answers to many different questions (and kinds of questions), but they are nevertheless restricted to questions about certain kinds of phenomena. A person's total system of beliefs (the set of all propositions accepted by a person) is a multipurpose and a "global" information system: it should (ideally) cover all questions which are of interest to the person.

Under what conditions can an information system be said to "give" an answer to a question? A system gives an answer to a question if it *contains* an answer -- this may be called the "strict" interpretation of "giving an answer". But in a wider sense, an information system can be said to give an answer to a question if it has a consistent subset which (possibly together with some "background knowledge") entails an answer to the question.

II

Let us denote an information system used by a person a by 'B(a)' (or simply 'B' when reference to the person is unnecessary). B(a) is fully satisfactory relative to a set of questions QS = {$Q_1,...Q_n$} if and only if B(a) gives a satisfactory answer to each $Q_i \in$ QS. What is a satisfactory answer to a question? As was pointed out above, at least the following condition is necessary:

(C1)   A proposition is a satisfactory answer to a question only if it is sufficiently *informative* relative to the question, that is, gives all the information required by the question.

According to this requirement, an information system is unsatisfactory relative to QS if it does not give any answer to some Q in QS or if the answers given are incomplete or uninformative. This requirement may be termed the information requirement - or requirement of *informativeness*.

An information system should give information, but this is not enough: the information in the system should presumably also be correct or *true* (i.e., the system should not give *mis*information). Thus we get the following condition:

(C2)   A proposition is a satisfactory answer to a question only if it is *true*.

The second requirement reflects the importance of truth as an epistemic value. This condition may also be formulated as a requirement of *error avoidance*, in other words:

(C2')   A belief system is unsatisfactory relative to QS if it contains false answers to some questions Q ∈ QS.

The present conception of the epistemic virtues of information systems is an extension of the traditional view that information and truth (avoidance of error) are the fundamental objectives of belief formation.[4]

Conditions (C1) and (C2) differ from each other in the following respect: Usually it is possible to decide whether an information system gives the information requested by a certain question (or questions in the set QS) simply by inspecting the system and the members of QS: informativeness is understood here as a relation between a proposition and a question. We might say that condition (C1) is "epistemically transparent". This does not hold for (C2): usually the incorrectness or falsity of an answer cannot be "read off" from the answer itself; the correctness of an answer is not a relation between a question and an answer, but a relation between an answer and some external criterion of correctness (for example, "the facts" or "the world").

---

[4] For these requirements, see Risto Hilpinen, 'The Semantics of Questions and the Theory of Inquiry', *Logique et Analyse* 29 (1986), pp. 523 - 539. (See pp. 529 - 535.)

However, the requirement of error avoidance entails an internal criterion which can be used as a negative condition of satisfactoriness: if an information system gives inconsistent or conflicting answers to a question, it contains false answers, and is therefore (according to (C2')) unsatisfactory. A system which does *not* give conflicting or inconsistent answers to a question Q ∈ QS (or to different questions in QS) may be said to be *apparently error-free with respect to Q* (or QS). Thus condition (C2') entails the following "internal" condition of satisfactoriness for information systems:

(C2.1)   An information system B is satisfactory relative to QS only if it is apparently error free with respect to QS.

Inconsistency is an internal sign of error and the fact that a proposition included in B is inconsistent with other members of B makes B unsatisfactory. But is B satisfactory if it contains all the necessary information requested by QS and is also free from inconsistency and other forms of implausibility? If the *only function* of an information system is to give error-free answers to a specific set of questions, then such an information system seems perfectly satisfactory in the sense that its owner has no "internal" reason to revise it, i.e. take anything away from it, add new propositions to it, or replace its members by new propositions. However, many interesting information systems have other functions as well, and are used for other purposes. A person may also be interested in having *reasons* for accepting the answers which his information system gives to certain questions, and giving such reasons may be regarded as an additional function of the system. This requirement corresponds to the following condition on information systems:

(C3)   A proposition is a satisfactory answer to a question only if it is justified within the information system, that is, supported by other propositions in the system.

According to the classical justificationist account of the concept of knowledge, condition (C3) separates genuine knowledge from (mere) true belief. This requirement follows from the view that questions are not merely requests for true information, but requests for *knowledge*, understood in the traditional justificationist sense. An information system whose members satisfy the justification condition (C3) for a set of questions QS may be termed a *knowledge system* for QS. I shall assume here that if B gives conflicting answers to a question Q, then neither answer satisfies the justification requirement: B can give a justified answer to Q only if it is apparently error-free with respect to Q.

Conditions (C1) - (C3) correspond to the three conditions included in the classical justificationist analysis of knowledge. According to this analysis,

(DK)   a knows that p if and only if
        (i) a accepts p or believes that p
        (ii) p is true, and
        (iii) a is justified in believing that p.

The first condition is the condition of informativeness (C1); the second condition is the requirement of error-freedom (C2), and the third requirement is equivalent to (C3).[5]

III

According to (C1) - (C3), an information system B can be unsatisfactory relative to a question Q in three different ways: it may fail to contain the information requested by the question, it can give conflicting answers to a question, or the information provided by the system may fail to be supported by the other beliefs in B. In the latter two cases the answer provided by B is not justified within the system. If a question Q can have a correct answer only if a proposition p is true, p is called a *presupposition* of Q.[6] If the presuppositions of Q do not hold in B (are not true according to B), the information system cannot give satisfactory *or* unsatisfactory answers to Q; in this case we can say that the question does not *arise* (or cannot arise) in B. Consequently we can distinguish the following

---

[5] Recent discussion has shown that these conditions are not always sufficient for knowledge, and that additional conditions, for example, some requirement of "epistemic indefeasibility", may be necessary; see Risto Hilpinen, 'Knowledge and Conditionals', in *Philosophical Perspectives 2: Epistemology*, ed. by J. Tomberlin, Ridgeview Publ. Co., Atascadero, Ca., 1988, pp. 157 - 182. This requirement will be discussed below.

[6] For the concept of the presupposition of a question, see Risto Hilpinen, 'The Semantics of Questions and the Theory of Inquiry', p. 525.

possible relationships between an arbitrary question Q and a information system B:

R0:   Q does not arise in B; the presuppositions of Q do not hold in B.

R1:   Q arises in B, but B does not contain the information required by Q.

R2:   Q arises in B, and B contains an informative answer to Q, but the answer is not justified within B.

R3:   B contains a satisfactory answer to Q.

As mentioned earlier, I assume here that case R2 includes the case in which B gives conflicting or inconsistent answers to Q; in such a case none of the answers is justified within B. In R1 and R2, B(a) is unsatisfactory relative to Q: in these cases the information system does not give a satisfactory answer to the question. We can say that B(a) is in these cases *internally unsatisfactory*, i.e. B(a) can be seen to be unsatisfactory by inspecting the system itself (or by studying the relationship between B and Q), independently of any external standard. In this case the person a himself is able to judge B(a) to be unsatisfactory, and he has therefore a reason to try to improve the system, make it more satisfactory. A process by which the person a attempts to make B(a) more satisfactory is called an *inquiry*. An inquiry is an attempt to change one's information system deliberately in order to improve it. This can be done by presenting questions to some external source of information, and by adding the answers received to B(a). Questions of this kind may be termed *secondary questions* or research questions; they should be distinguished from the questions which determine the satisfactoriness of an information system (an inquirer's *primary questions*). The external source of information used by the inquirer may be his own senses, some measuring instrument, or any *prima facie* reliable source which is external to the system B(a).[7]

The case R2 can be divided into two subcases, viz.

---

[7] For the distinction between primary and secondary questions, see Risto Hilpinen, 'On Experimental Questions', in *Theory and Experiment*, ed. by D. Batens and J. van Bendegem, D. Reidel, Dordrecht 1988, pp. 15 - 29.

(R2i) B contains two conflicting answers to Q (i.e., two answers such that according to B, at least one of them is false).

(R2ii) B contains an informative answer to Q which is not supported by the other propositions in B.

If we assume that one purpose of an information system is to give *reasons* for (or *justify*) one's answers to the questions Q ∈ QS, then (R2ii) is an example of unsatisfactory information system. A person's answer to a question is not knowledge unless it is both true and justified by his other beliefs.

Recently some philosophers have argued that B need not be unsatisfactory in case (R2ii); i.e., that the justification requirement, in the sense of positive support, is not a necessary condition of an epistemically satisfactory information system. In his book *Change in View* Gilbert Harman argues that it is not always necessary or even reasonable to try to keep track of the justifications of one's beliefs.[8] Harman compares two theories of belief formation, which he calls "the coherence theory" and "the foundations theory", and characterizes them as follows:

> The foundations theory says one is justified in continuing to believe something only if one has a special reason to continue to accept that belief, whereas the coherence theory says one is justified in continuing to believe something as long as one has no special reason to stop believing it.[9]

It should be observed that Harman's use of the expression "justified" differs from its use in the present paper. Here justification is understood as a relationship between a proposition p and a set of propositions which support p, but Harman seems to use the expression "justified in continuing to believe" to indicate that one's information system is satisfactory with respect to p, i.e., that the system does not require revision in this respect. The difference which Harman sees here between the coherence theory and the foundations theory is that the foundations theory accepts requirement (C3) for information systems, but the coherence theory does not. (This is of course an unusual interpretation

---

[8] See Gilbert Harman, *Change in View*, The MIT Press, Cambridge, Mass. 1986.
[9] Harman, op. cit., p. 32.

of the difference between the two theories; normally they are regarded as competing theories about the structure of epistemic justification.)

Harman notes that since people rarely "keep track" of their reasons (I take this to mean that they rarely keep their reasons in their information systems), the foundations theory implies that people are unjustified in almost all their beliefs - which in my terminology can be expressed by saying that people's information systems are almost invariably unsatisfactory - which is, according to Harman, an absurd result.

It is not very interesting or illuminating to declare that it is necessary (or unnecessary) to have positive reasons for one's opinions - that one's information system should contain or need not contain reasons for the propositions which belong to the system. Sometimes it is useful to have supporting reasons in one's information system, but in other situations this may be unnecessary. The interesting question here is, of course, "necessary for what purpose?". For what purpose (or under what conditions) is it necessary, important or useful to include the reasons for one's opinions in one's information system? It is possible to imagine all sorts of purposes for which the inclusion of such reasons would be convenient. If we think that some of the propositions in our information system might be incorrect, we may be interested in including in the system reasons for our answers to some very important questions to convince ourselves that the answers are indeed correct. In this way the owner of an information system can use the system to convince himself that his answers are correct. One function of reasons is to allay doubts about the information system. But perhaps an even more important ground for including and keeping reasons in one's information system is that then the system can be used for convincing *other persons* that the system gives correct information about the questions in which they are interested. This may be called the *argumentative function* of an information system. Now we are assuming that the function of an information system is not just to give answers to a specific set of questions (QS), but that it can also be used for presenting arguments by which one can convince other people that a certain answer to a certain question is correct (or incorrect, as the case may be.)

Information systems have of course other important uses as well. The basic function of any information system is to provide answers to certain questions, but it is a special virtue of an information system to give answers or *resources for finding answers* to *possible* questions and problems, questions which *may arise in the future.* This feature of an information system might be called its *predictive capacity.* This end can be achieved by including general laws and explanatory principles in one's information system.

The last-mentioned desideratum for an information system suggests that an information system may be evaluated indirectly on the basis of the significance of the questions which it is capable of answering. Our beliefs can be evaluated in terms of their informativeness with respect the certain questions, but the questions themselves can be evaluated in the same way: not all questions are equally significant or important. It seems natural to define the importance or value of a question in terms of its informativeness. The more informative a given question is relation to the other questions in which a person is interested, the more important or significant the question is. The informativeness of a question Q_1 relative to another question Q_2 can be measured in terms of the expected value of the (amount of) information transmitted by a complete answer to Q_1 about a complete answer to Q_2.[10] Investigators are interested in general questions and explanation-seeking questions partly because such questions are potentially informative about many other interesting questions -- and also about questions which the investigator's information system may face in the future.

IV

On the basis of the relations R0 - R3 we can define 16 information change types with respect to a single question: let us assume that B1 is a person's original information system, and B2 the system resulting from the change.

---

[10]   This concept of transmitted information has been discussed in Risto Hilpinen, 'On the Information Provided by Observations', in *Information and Inference,* ed. by Jaako Hintikka and P. Suppes, D. Reidel, Dordrecht 1970, pp. 97 - 122 (cf. pp. 115 - 116).

		B2			
		R0	R1	R2	R3
	R0	R00	R01	R02	R03
B1	R1	R10	R11	R12	R13
	R2	R20	R21	R22	R23
	R3	R30	R31	R32	R33

Which of these belief change types are improvements of the information system, and thus possible aims of inquiry? From the *internal* stand-point, the changes Rii (i=0,1,2,3) are clearly neutral, neither progressive nor regressive. In a change of type R10, a question which has no answer in B_1 "disappears" as a result of the change, i.e., B_2 does not satisfy the presuppositions of the question. B_1 is internally unsatisfactory relative to Q, but B_2 cannot be said to be unsatisfactory because the question does not even arise in it. Even though a change of type R10 may thus be regarded as an improvement, it is not a possible *objective* of an inquiry: the purpose of an inquiry is to find a satisfactory answer to a question, not the falsification of its presuppositions. In the same way, changes of type R20 improve an information system in the sense that they dispose of a question to which no fully satisfactory answer has been found by falsifying its presuppositions. A change of type R30 eliminates a question in a situation in which it has a seemingly (i.e., internally) satisfactory answer. These changes can result from an inquiry, but they cannot be its basic objectives. The same holds for changes of type R0j (j=1,2,3).

We can say that an information change Rij is *internally progressive* if and only if B_2 is internally more satisfactory relative to Q than B_1. Changes R12, R13 and R23 are clearly internally progressive changes, and their reversals R21, R31 and R32 are internally regressive. Moreover, the former three changes are legitimate objectives of inquiry. They can be described as follows:

R12: to accept an answer to a question;
R23: to find justification (support) for an answer;
and
R13: to find a satisfactory answer to a question.

According to the hypothetico-deductive view of science, scientific investigation usually consists of R12 - R23 sequences: the former stage represents the *discovery* of a theory or a hypothesis (an answer), and the latter the *testing* of a hypothesis (and, in the positive case, its confirmation or justification).[11]

V

Above I have discussed the *internal* judgments concerning a person's information system, the judgments based on the information system itself. A information system can also be judged *externally*, from the stand-point of another information system - for example, a's information system may be considered from the stand-point of another person's (b's) information system - and this is of course the way in which b looks at B(a). This is also the way a person looks at his own earlier opinions: he considers them from the stand-point of his current view. Here we may consider a person's present and past selves as if they were different individuals or cognitive agents. If a's opinions fail to satisfy his own (a's) proper cognitive objectives (including the requirement of error avoidance) according to b's information system B(b), b may try to improve a's system by argumentation. Thus the *internal* judgments on a person's information system are apt to generate *inquiries*, whereas *external* judgments lead *arguments* or *debates*. Below I shall call the participants of an argumentation situation "the inquirer" (a) and "the critic" (b).

Of course, the critic may argue with the inquirer about some question even if the inquirer's system satisfies his own cognitive aims (according to the critic), if the critic is interested in misleading the inquirer. But I shall not consider such situations here. I am here interested in situations in which b is willing to argue with a, and change a's views, because he, b, takes them to be unsatisfactory from the point of view of a's own cognitive objectives. Again we can distinguish 16 relationships between the two information systems; now the relations Rij do not represent different belief changes but rather different relationships between B_1 and B_2 with respect to a question Q, and hence different *occasions for argumentation*: in each case B_1 is considered to be satisfactory or

---

11 Charles S. Peirce termed these two stages the *abductive* stage and the *inductive* stage of inquiry; see *The Collected Papers of Charles Sanders Peirce*, vol. 7, ed. by Arthur Burks, Harvard University Press, Cambridge, Mass. 1958, §§ 7.218 - 7.219.

unsatisfactory according to B_2 relative to Q. Here I assume that B_1 is the inquirer's (a's) information system and B_2 is the critic's information system.

Some cases in which B_1 and B_2 are *internally* equally satisfactory (and in which no progress occurs according to the internal criteria of cognitive progress) will now look different. Let p(i) be the answer given by B_i to question Q (if B_i contains such an answer). If both B_1 and B_2 are related to Q by R3, but p(1) is inconsistent with p(2), B1 is externally unsatisfactory because it contains (according to B_2) a false answer to the question, and the critic has a reason to argue against p(1). When an information system is judged by external criteria, the avoidance of error or the interest in truth means avoidance of conflict or disagreement with the external criterion (the critic's information system, B_2), not only the avoidance of internal inconsistency, as in the case of the *internal* evaluation of a system.)

Situations of type R0i and Ri0 (i > 0) may also be occasions for argumentation, even though the corresponding information change types cannot be intended objectives of inquiry. For example, if b's information system B_2 is related to Q by R1, and b wants to find an answer to the question and turns to the inquirer for information, a situation in which Q does not arise within B_1 is utterly unsatisfactory for b, because the inquirer would reply to b's question only by saying that the question does not "make sense" (for him, the inquirer). In such a situation b might wish to argue with a and defend the presuppositions of Q against a's beliefs.

In the case R10, in which the question Q does not arise for b, b seems to have less reason to argue against the inquirer than in the previous case -- at best he might argue that the question is not a meaningful or reasonable question if (for example) the inquirer is willing to spend a lot of time and other resources in order to find an answer to Q. In this case the argument would be that the question does not make sense, and a's information system is externally unsatisfactory with respect to Q because it contains false presuppositions.

VI

R12 and R13 represent argumentation situations in which a has no answer to question Q but b has an answer -- either an unjustified answer (R12) or a well-justified answer (R13). In this case the purpose of b's argument is to convince a about the truth of p(2). In the second situation, R13, he can do this successfully if p(2) is justified by $B_1 \cap B_2$. If p(2) is supported by B_1, b may be able to present a rhetorically convincing argument for p(2) even though such an argument may not be sound from b's own point of view. (This is the case if the argument has some essential premises in B_1 which b does not accept himself.) I call an argument based on premises accepted by the inquirer (a) *rhetorically convincing*, because the inquirer is likely to assent to such an argument, and an argument based on the premises accepted by the critic *sound* (from the critic's point of view), because the critic takes the premises of such an argument to be true.

There can be situations in which the critic can present for a certain thesis or conclusion a rhetorically convincing argument and a sound argument without being able to find for that conclusion an argument which would be both. If p(2) is justified within B_2, the critic can offer a sound argument for p(2) - an argument whose premises are true according to the critic. R13 is an occasion for *justification arguments*. This argument type shows the significance of the justification condition of the traditional analysis of knowledge: a person can present a sound argument for the truth of a proposition if and only if the proposition is internally justified within his information system.

If B_1 and B_2 are related by R33, but p(1) is inconsistent with p(2), the situation calls (on b's part) for an argument which refutes p(1) and convinces the inquirer about the truth of p(2). It is clear that under these circumstances the critic can convince the inquirer about the truth of p(2) only if the latter is willing to accept new beliefs and give up some of his earlier beliefs. As in the previous case, b can present a successful argument of this kind only if p(2) is internally justified in his information system. Thus the traditional justified true belief account of knowledge, where the concept of justification is understood internally, as a relation within a person's information system, may be termed an *argumentative* conception of knowledge. According to this view, one of the main characteristics of knowledge (as opposed to merely true belief) is that it provides the resources for successful argumentation: a person who knows is able to present convincing arguments for his opinion, and also able to defend it successfully against objections. This is an old view: the thirteenth-century philosopher Siger of Brabant expressed it as follows:[12]

> Finding truth presupposes the ability to solve any objection or dubitation against the proposition accepted as true. For if you do not know how to solve the objections that may arise, you are not in possession of the truth, since in that case you have not assimilated *the procedure of finding* truth and thus will not know whether or when you have arrived at truth.

Even reliable beliefs (beliefs caused by reliable processes) which are not internally justified within a person's information system are argumentatively ineffective. An epistemological theory in which the justification condition for knowledge refers exclusively to the reliability of belief or to the causal conditions of belief acquisition cannot do justice to our argumentative practices.

Insofar as the objections presented against a person's (the inquirer's) opinion may be based on evidence which is not part of his belief system, argumentative success as a condition of knowledge does not only require that the opinion should be justified within the person's belief system, but also that the justification (and the opinion in question) should not be defeasible by new evidence. Thus Siger of Brabant's condition of argumentative success resembles an indefeasibility condition of epistemic justification.[13]

VII

If the external perspective is applied to a person's opinions over time, we can see how judgments of progress are *revised* on the basis of empirical evidence. Let us consider a's beliefs at three different points of time or on three occasions, and let the corresponding information systems be B_1, B_2 and B_3. Now the inquirer may

---

[12] Quoted from Anthony Kenny and Jan Pinborg, 'Medieval Philosophical Literature', *The Cambridge History of Later Medieval Philosophy*, ed. by N. Kretzmann et al., Cambridge University Press, Cambridge 1982, p. 27. The reference is to Siger of Brabant, *Quaestiones super librum de causis*, ed. by A. Marlasca, Publications Universitaires de Louvain, 1972, p. 35.

[13] For a discussion of this requirement, see Risto Hilpinen, 'Knowledge and Conditionals', in *Philosophical Perspectives 2: Epistemology*, ed. by J. Tomberlin; see also note 5 above.

look at the *change* Rij from B_1 to B_2 with respect to a question Q *externally*, from the stand-point of B_3, and in so doing he may revise his earlier judgments of cognitive improvement or progress. For example, suppose that B_1 and B_2 are related by R13: in B_2 the inquirer has found an internally justified answer to the question. This looks progress. But suppose that B_3 is also related to Q by R3, but $p(3)$ $p(2)$: let us assume that $p(3)$ is inconsistent with $p(2)$. Then we would no longer say that the change from B_1 to B_2 was a progressive one, because the information received about the question was false. (It may have been progress with respect to other questions.)

If we consider a special case in which $B_3 = B_2$, i.e. if we look at the change from B_1 to B_2 "externally" from the stand-point of B_2, we get the result that every change of type R33 in which $p(1)$ is inconsistent with $p(2)$ is judged to be a cognitive improvement, that is, a replacement of error by truth (even though B_1 and B_2 may be *internally* equally satisfactory relative to Q). And this is of course as it should be: we do not change our opinions unless we think we have made a mistake. If B_1 and B_2 are "global" information systems (belief systems) which consist of all the propositions accepted by an inquirer at times t_1 and t_2, B_2 should presumably also be *internally* more satisfactory than B_1 with respect to *some* questions. If B_2 is a deliberate revision of B_1 and a result of some process of inquiry, it contains answers to certain "secondary" or research questions about which B_1 is silent; thus B_2 is more informative than B_1 (at least) with respect to such questions.[14] The judgment that one's current information system is better than its predecessors is often based on this increase in the informativeness of the system.

But even though the view that one's current beliefs are better than one's earlier beliefs (if the latter do not agree with the former) is almost analytic, in the sense that its denial would be self-defeating (pragmatically inconsistent, one might say), such a view is not infallible, because later external judgments may lead one to revise this view about the beliefs in question in particular cases.

---

14 For the concept of a secondary question (or research question), see section III above and Risto Hilpinen, 'On Experimental Questions', in *Theory and Experiment*, ed. by D. Batens and J. van Bendegem, D. Reidel, Dordrecht 1988, pp. 15 - 29.

Rational Control of Reasoning in Artificial Intelligence*

Jon Doyle[†]
Massachusetts Institute of Technology
Laboratory for Computer Science
545 Technology Square
Cambridge, Massachusetts 02139, USA

Abstract

In contrast to the idealized rationality formalized in decision theory, artificial intelligence studies agents of limited cognitive resources and abilities. These limitations require the agent to economize on its memory usage and reasoning effort, and to be able to deliberate and act in spite of incomplete and inconsistent beliefs and preferences. We discuss some of the means by which artificial reasoners tolerate and even exploit these limitations in carrying out basic cognitive tasks, focusing on the underlying notions of progressive and conservative reasoning and constitutional and constructive representation. We show how these means may all be viewed as species of rationally guided or controlled reasoning, or more generally, as forms of rational self-government.

1 Introduction

Logic has long been viewed as the theory of ideal or rational thinking. For example, when people criticize someone who asserts both a proposition and

---

*This paper is based on a talk presented at the Conference on the Dynamics of Belief, held in Lund, Sweden in August 1989. A shorter, earlier version of this paper appeared under the title "Reasoning, Representation, and Rational Self-Government" in *Methodologies for Intelligent Systems, 4*, (Z. W. Ras, editor), Amsterdam: North-Holland 1989, pp. 367-380. Copyright © 1990 by Jon Doyle.

†Jon Doyle is supported by National Institutes of Health Grant No. R01 LM04493 from the National Library of Medicine.

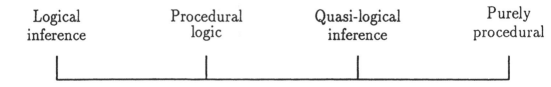

Figure 1: The spectrum of inference techniques

its contrary as being irrational, they refer to a logical sense of rationality. Traditionally, much work in artificial intelligence has adopted this view of what good thinking is by supposing that logical rationality is what is desired of intelligent agents.

The logical view of thinking has considerable attraction, since logic offers valuable insight into the relation between rationally held beliefs. Unfortunately, it does not cover all such relations. Its most striking omission is any consideration of the *purpose* (or purposes) of reasoning. That is, the logical view of thinking ignores questions of whether one should or should not draw some inference, and whether one inference is better or more appropriate than another. Such questions are presumed to be pragmatic, outside the realm of the theory of thinking proper. Indeed, requiring effective agents to know something about the value of information goes against the long, but traditionally esteemed effort to construct general-purpose reasoning systems. But if such systems are to work, success in reasoning must be unrelated to subject or knowledge. But in fact, domain-independent methods of reasoning are usually irrational, since worthwhile inferences in one domain may be of the same logical form as worthless inferences in another. With no way of preferring one path of reasoning to another, the usual result is that effort is wasted making easy but worthless inferences. (See also [20].)

The inability of ordinary logic to convey any information about what inferences should be performed, as opposed to what inferences are sound, has led artificial intelligence to employ a variety of techniques for making inferences. Pure logical inference ("if it seems sound, do it") forms one end of this spectrum (see Figure 1). Pure procedural manipulation of beliefs ("if it seems useful, do it") forms the other. Mixed methods also are employed, including procedural interpretations of logic (as in PROLOG) and various quasi-logical schemes of nondeductive inference (such as nonmonotonic logic, default logic, and circumscription).

In this paper, we explore a theory of thinking, called *rational self-government*, based on the view that thinking is an activity, not a purely theoretical relation between premises and conclusions (see [4] for a more complete treatment). Rational self-government uses decision-theoretic rationality instead of logical rationality as the standard by which to judge the choices made in reasoning and representation activities. Decision-theoretic rationality is the ideal theory of the other everyday sense of rationality, the one to which people refer when they criticize someone for irrationally making worse choices than he might, for example, when he wastes all his time on trivial chores unrelated to his most important purposes. Besides providing a precise standard for the procedural view of reasoning—that each step of reasoning should be of maximal expected value to the agent with respect to the agent's expectations and preferences—this notion of rationality provides a common intellectual framework with which to frame, communicate, and use expert and common knowledge in activities of reasoning, searching, planning, problem-solving, and learning. It also helps make ideas in artificial intelligence intelligible to readers from other fields (e.g., philosophy, logic, statistics, decision theory, and economics) for whom rationality is a central concept.

More specifically, instead of asking whether the conclusions reached in reasoning are sound (i.e., follow logically from the reasoner's hypotheses), rational self-government asks whether the selected reasoning steps and resulting conclusions efficiently serve the reasoner's purposes. Here we think of states of mind in terms of the sets of beliefs, desires, intentions or other attitudes held in them, and view steps of reasoning (including learning, deliberating, and planning) as changes of view, to adopt Harman's [12] term, as changes in the attitudes held by the reasoner (see Figure 2). Thus in each step of rational reasoning the agent uses its knowledge of its own powers and limitations and its preferences about its own mental states and activities to choose how it would like to change its beliefs, preferences, and plans, to change how it represents and formulates things, or to change how it does things, so as to maximize the expected value of the resulting state of mind.

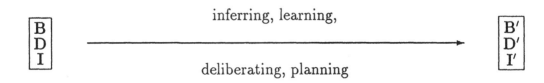

Figure 2: Reasoning as changing the sets **B**, **D**, and **I** of beliefs and likelihoods, desires and preferences, and intentions and priorities.

We begin by reviewing the decision-theoretic notion of rationality and some difficulties that arise in trying to use it to formulate the notion of rational thinking. We then use this conception to reconsider several standard sorts of reasoning studied in artificial intelligence. These include assumption making, learning, planning, and deliberation—all cases of what we call "progressive" reasoning—as well as belief revision and other forms of what we call "conservative" reasoning. We then use this notion of rationality to reconsider several ideas about representation, examining the notions of constraints on permissible mental states or "constitutional" representation and the structure of explicit belief or "constructive" representation.

2   Theories of rationality

The notion of rationality addressed by decision theory concerns right action given expectations and preferences. In the usual formulation, a choice is said to be rational for an agent if it is of maximal expected utility with respect to the agent's beliefs and preferences. Here the agent's beliefs in state S are described by a probability measure p_S over possible states of the world, and the agent's preferences are described by a utility function u_S which assigns a numerical utility to each possible state of the world. When choosing among different states of affairs, such as those corresponding to taking different actions, one compares the the expected utilities of each alternative. The expected utility $\hat{u}_S(a)$ of an action a is defined to be the average, over all possible states of the world, of the utility of the state of the world weighted by the probability of its occurrence given that action a is taken. (See, for example, [26].)

2.1 Qualitative theories of rationality

For thinking about artificial intelligence, a somewhat different formulation of decision theory is more useful. Rather than beginning with quantitative numerical measures of probability and utility over propositions, it is better to view expectations and preferences qualitatively as partial orders over propositions. This view is the most appropriate foundation for decision theory (see [26], [31]), since one cannot distinguish the actions of one agent from another whose utility function is an increasing linear transform of the first agent's utility function. In the partial order formulation, each partial order expresses preferences that may be compatible with several different numerical measures, each of which "represents" the ordering information explicit in the partial order. In contrast, the usual assumptions made in decision theory entail that the partial order expressing expectations has a unique representation as a probability measure. According to this formulation of decision theory, an action is rational if it is of maximal expected utility according to every choice of probability and utility functions compatible with the agent's expectation and preference partial orders.

2.2 Limited rationality

Even if decision-theoretic rationality is a proper standard for the conduct of reasoning, it is not easy to apply it sensibly in the design of artificial intelligence systems because artificial intelligence and decision theory take different stands on the nature of the agent to which the theory of rationality is applied. Artificial intelligence is concerned with agents whose rationality is limited, for example, by beliefs and preferences which may be less complete in terms of the probability and utility measures they determine than decision theory. Thinking of expectations and preferences as given by axiomatizations of the orders, this means more incomplete, possibly inconsistent sets of axioms about beliefs and preferences. In such cases there might be several different probability measures compatible with the beliefs of some artificial agent, and some of the utility functions compatible with its preferences might rank the same conditions in opposite orders. We can still define an action to be rational if it is of maximal expected utility according to every choice of probability and utility functions compatible with the agent's expectation and preference partial orders, but since these orders are less complete, there need not be any rational choices.

Another limitation faced in artificial intelligence is that of computational limitations on the ability to calculate and compare alternative courses of action. For example, agents with limited time or space with which to calculate may not be able to make all the necessary comparisons to reach a decision. Conclusions whose derivations take longer to compute than the time available or which consume more memory than the space available will not be available as beliefs of the agent. If resource limitations are not taken into account when organizing the reasoning of the agent, senseless and stupid behavior can result from computations terminated bluntly by exhaustion of resources. Reasoners organized in this way can miss obvious inferences in a haphazard fashion, succeeding on one problem but failing or making errors on simpler ones or seemingly identical ones that few people would distinguish. The difference is that people appear to prudently *manage* the use of their knowledge and skills to solve problems and make decisions, taking into account their own powers, limitations, and reliability. By anticipating limits they achieve much more reasonable behavior (what the Greeks called *sophrosyne*) than by simply suffering limits. Accordingly, much research on limited rationality has concentrated on the problem of allocating mental resources in effective ways (see [29,13,25]). For example, Russell and Wefald [25] describe how to use decision theory to guide search in playing chess. They use accumulated statistics about the results of past play from similar board positions to decide whether investigation of potential moves can be expected to yield moves better than the ones currently contemplated. This allows focusing of the search on those paths which might reveal significantly better moves, and helps avoid wasting time examining paths which produce moves of worse or similar value. Agents which recognize their own limitations and purposes and guide their reasoning accordingly are said by Good [11] to exhibit "Type 2" rationality

Decision Theory	AI
Ideal rationality	*Limited rationality*
Complete knowledge	Incomplete beliefs Incomplete preferences
Consistent knowledge	Inconsistent beliefs Inconsistent preferences
Unlimited resources	Limited resources

Figure 3: Differences between assumptions in decision theory and artificial intelligence

and by Simon [28] to exhibit "procedural" rationality, as opposed to "Type 1" or "substantive" rationality, which is the ordinary sort where the costs of reasoning are ignored and rationality is judged purely on the external ends of the agent.

We summarize these differences between the assumptions of decision theory and the assumptions of artificial intelligence in Figure 3. The most striking difference between the notions of ideal and limited rationality is that while there is fairly broad agreement that there is a normative ideal for rationality, there does not seem to be any corresponding normative ideal for limited rationality. Of course, there are some disputes about what constitutes ideal rationality. But the central fact about limited rationality is that there seem to be numerous different ways of limiting rationality, yielding incomparable degrees of rationality rather than a single continuum of approximations to ideal rationality. These incomparable degrees or dimensions of rationality correspond to multiple ways of governing reasoning, and as in the theory of human governments, there seems to be no way to get all the desirable properties of governments into one system. If that is the case, one cannot expect to find a generally accepted normative theory of limited rationality.

2.3 Selective rationality

One of the difficulties in making rational guidance of reasoning a practical ideal is that it asks too much, even when applied to cognitive tasks like allocation of mental resources. In particular, rational decisions are rational only if the agent takes all its knowledge into account. For realistic agents with large amounts of knowledge, this comprehensiveness is unworkable. A better approach is to further limit ratiocinative effort (and hence rationality) by directing attention to some areas and ignoring others. In this approach, each episode of reasoning must choose where to begin. This usually means choosing what terms to take as primitive and what facts to take as axioms, leaving all other knowledge aside as irrelevant to the reasoning task or as too much to take into account all at once. Savage [26] calls such limited settings "small worlds." Focusing attention increases efficiency, but at a price, since the path of reasoning may diverge greatly from paths it would have taken had the ignored areas been considered, and as a consequence the agent must occasionally suffer surprises. We follow Leibenstein [15] in calling the result of such measured attention *selective* rationality.

One important way to direct attention is to use the agent's intentions, plans and procedures about reasoning to concentrate effort on one task to the temporary exclusion of others. Plans and procedures may be viewed as expressing patterns of intentions, and in plan-governed reasoning these plans these intentions specify the base, aims, and methods of reasoning during specific episodes. Because intentions and procedures specify steps to take in a manner independent of rational calculation of what is best all things considered, intentional reasoning ignores many possibilities that rational action or search might consider.

One difference between purely rational reasoning and intentional reasoning is that in the latter the agent distinguishes between the intended and unintended changes wrought by steps of reasoning, while the former merely chooses entire states as best all things considered, with all effects of actions treated equally. While some philosophers have proposed theories of action that involve only beliefs and desires, making elaborate constructions attempting to discriminate intentionality of effects purely on the basis of beliefs and desires, our view is that intentionality is indicated by the agent's plans, which

Figure 4: Action divided into steps of volition (choice of intention to act upon) and accommodation (of the effects of acting).

explicitly state which changes are intentional and implicitly indicate that all other changes are unintentional. In our view, the process of acting is divided into two steps (see Figure 4). The first step is that of volition, in which the agent selects (or constructs) an intention upon which to act. The second step is that of accommodation, in which the agent carries out the intended action and adjusts its state with regard to the effects of the action. Volition determines the intended effects of the action (which may in fact not occur), while accommodation determines the unintended effects of the action (if any).

The simplest and most widely studied case of intentional changes of state is that in which reasoning intentions specify explicit incremental sets of changes in the current state. These explicit changes include attitudes to be adopted in the new state and attitudes to be removed from the current state, as in STRIPS's [9] "addlists" and "deletelists" (though in STRIPS these merely represented expected changes due to actions, not necessarily the changes the actions were intended to bring about). These simple changes have been studied as database updates [8] and as changes of belief [10]. The attitudes to be removed from the current state are called *retractions*, and the attitudes to be added to the current state are called *extensions* if they are consistent with the state and *revisions* if they are inconsistent with the current state. While handling extensions of current attitudes need not be problematic, handling retractions and revisions usually involves difficulties, as there are usually several ways of effecting each retraction or revision, and choices must be made among these alternatives.

3 Rationality in reasoning

Making rational reasoning intentional instead of simply rational breaks individual steps of reasoning into distinct steps of first choosing the intended properties of the next state, and then choosing the next state to exhibit these intended properties. The first type of choice we call *progressive* reasoning, as it involves choosing specifications for the new state so as to make progress towards achieving the reasoner's goals. The second type of choice we call *conservative* reasoning, as it involves choosing the new state so as to conserve as much as possible of the current state. Where progressive reasoning involves making intentional modifications in the reasoner's state, conservative reasoning involves making any unintentional modifications entailed by the intentional ones. The reasoner might have foreseen some of these unintentional changes during selection of its intended changes, but the focus of attention during progressive reasoning means that there usually will be unforeseen unintended changes as well. Since the unforeseen changes were not rationally chosen, they represent non-rational or irrational changes which may defeat the agent's purposes. Conservative reasoning seeks to effect the changes specified by progressive reasoning in an efficient manner, maximizing the rationality of the agent by minimizing the irrational component of changes.

3.1 Progressive reasoning

Progressive reasoning covers most of the forms of reasoning studied in artificial intelligence, such as deduction, search, planning, deliberation, assuming, and learning. In it, utilitarian considerations are used to control the adoption and retraction of specific attitudes. Typically, the reasoner possesses numerous rules which indicate possible inferences. At each step of reasoning, the reasoner selects one or more of these rules to apply. Ideally, this selection is a rational choice using the agent's preferences and expectations to guide or control the progress of reasoning. In practice, the selection is sometimes mere blind search, with little or no means for applying relevant knowledge to control application of the rules. On application, the rules specify new attitudes to be added or old attitudes to be removed from the current set of attitudes. Rules that specify changes to the beliefs of the agent are used to make deductions, to make assumptions, or to learn new concepts or propositions, depending on whether the rules are sound (for deduction) or unsound (for assumptions and learning). Rules that specify changes to the intentions of the agent are used in planning, and rules that specify changes to desires and preferences are used in deliberating and introspection.

3.1.1 Rational assumptions

Artificial agents ordinarily possess only finite amounts of knowledge. In consequence, the agent's knowledge of most subjects is usually incomplete. This poses a problem, for the missing information is often needed in deciding how to act. One response to lack of information is caution or skepticism, refusing to make any decisions for which the needed information is lacking. But caution and skepticism are not always reasonable. Sometimes the more appropriate response is to make guesses or assumptions about the missing information. In such cases, we wish to use rationality as a standard for adopting assumptions by saying that an assumption should be adopted if the expected utility of holding it exceeds the expected utility of not holding it.

The classic example showing a case of skepticism to be irrational goes by the name of "Pascal's wager" and concerns religious belief. Pascal [22] framed his problem of belief in God as a wager about the consequences of belief and disbelief in worlds in which God exists or does not exist. If God exists and Pascal believes, he gains eternal salvation, but if he doubts he suffers eternal damnation. If God does not exist, belief may lead Pascal to forgo a few possible pleasures during his life that doubt would permit him to enjoy. We summarize Pascal's evaluations in the decision matrix shown in Figure 5, where ϵ represents the finite amount of pleasure enjoyed or foregone due to belief during his life. He judged his expected utility of belief in God to be (infinitely) higher than his expected utility in disbelief, and so proceeded to inculcate belief.

Much later, William James [14] made the case that skepticism is also irrational in many mundane situations. Today, James's theory of the "will to believe" is one of the pillars of artificial intelligence practice, for knowledge representation and reasoning systems are filled with mechanisms for mak-

	God exists	doesn't
Believe	$+\infty$	$-\epsilon$
Doubt	$-\infty$	$+\epsilon$

Figure 5: Pascal's utility assessments of the possible consequences of his decision about belief in God.

ing assumptions in response to incomplete information. These mechanisms, including taxonomic defaults, threshold probabilities, and nonmonotonic or circumscriptive proof procedures, are ordinarily not presented in terms of rational choice, and their mechanization usually involves no decision theoretic calculations. But when closely examined, they are clearly based on rational responses to computational problems involving incomplete information (see [3] and [27]), as they help minimize or avoid information-gathering and inference-making costs. Each particular case of default reasoning appearing in artificial intelligence represents a judgment that it is easier to make an informed guess and often be right than to remain agnostic and work to gather the information. (See Levi [17] for more on the rationality of decisions to believe.)

One may pursue this view of default reasoning even further and interpret default rules as expressions of preferences about different states of belief. For example, Doyle and Wellman [7] show how a default rule $P : Q/R$ (read "if P is believed and $\neg Q$ is not believed, conclude R") may be viewed as expressing the preferences $\sigma \prec \sigma' \prec \sigma''$, where

$$
\begin{aligned}
\sigma &= LP \wedge \neg L\neg Q \wedge \neg LR, \\
\sigma' &= LP \wedge L\neg Q, \text{ and} \\
\sigma'' &= \neg LP \vee (LP \wedge \neg L\neg Q \wedge LR),
\end{aligned}
$$

and where $x \prec y$ is interpreted to mean that x and y are mutually inconsistent sentences, that each model of y is preferable to each model of x, and that different models of x and y are indifferent (see Figure 6). That is, if P is believed, the default rule $P : Q/R$ prefers believing R to believing $\neg Q$, and

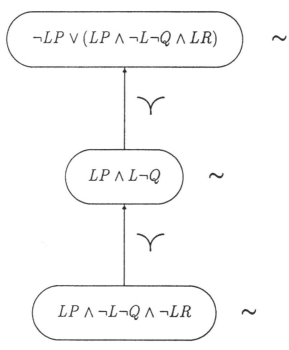

Figure 6: The preference order expressed by the default rule $P : Q/R$.

prefers believing either R or $\neg Q$ to believing none of these. Viewed this way, nonmonotonic logics and theories of default reasoning amount to theories of how to use numerous partial preferences about states of belief to rationally choose preferred sets of conclusions.

3.1.2 Rational learning

Rationality enters learning in the rational selection of what to learn or investigate, what to assume, what to consider, and what conclusions to seek. The first choice is that of subject, of the aim of learning. In many cases outside of motor skills and perhaps infant language learning, one learns (towards specific or abstract ends) because one wants to learn. Once a subject is chosen for learning, the agent must choose how to gain information about or experience with the subject. In some cases, the aim will be to learn something from what the agent already knows or has experienced. In other cases, the agent must select from among the many additional investigations that might be conducted. But once these decisions are made (and they are subject to repeated revision, of course), the biggest problem in learning is that alternative theories or explanations must be compared. For example, in improving one's skills through self-analysis, one must choose among alternative explanations of the flaws in one's skills (a choice called "credit assignment" in artificial intelligence) before one can formulate possible improvements to one's skills. The grounds of these comparisons are naturally viewed as reflecting the preferences of the agent about what explanations are better than others. Special cases of such choices include comparisons of alternative formulations or conceptual organizations on grounds of their costs in memory and time: the memory needed to store the information, and the time needed to use it. Economic comparisons of theories in terms of the time needed to use them are at the heart of what is called heuristic. Heuristics are rules or algorithms for reasoning that trade off accuracy and certainty for speed and cheapness of use. A prime example in learning is Valiant's [30] notion of probably approximately correct concepts. But in Valiant's theory, the rational bargain one makes is well understood, in that the risks of error and inaccuracy can be quantified, indeed, chosen by design. Artificial intelligence makes heavy use of less well understood heuristics, of rules for making cheap guesses which are only hoped, not known, to help. For instance, one employs methods which one subjectively expects to be likely correct or only slightly inaccurate, even when these bounds themselves are mere guesses, not guarantees. In really difficult problems, trying all the heuristics one can think of is all one can do, for to wait for an exact solution is tantamount to giving up.

3.1.3 Rational planning

Rational planning consists of formulation, selection, and revision of intentions and priorities for guiding the agent's activities. These include intentions about what actions should be performed, intentions about how these will be performed, and priorities influencing the temporal order in which these intentions will be carried out. As in assuming and learning, the reasoner's intentions and priorities may be revised through reflection on their consistency and completeness. For example, different levels of abstraction in plans may be considered one at a time to see if the planned actions at each level achieve their aim, to see if ways are known for carrying out intentions at one level with definite methods in another (see, for instance, [19]), and to see if different intentions at different levels are consistent with each other, perhaps abandoning some to restore consistency. Alternatively, some inconsistent intentions can be made consistent by adopting a priority (either in advance or when needed) so that both are not considered for action at the same time. In addition, intentions may be adopted and abandoned through reflection on the reasoner's desires. For example, the reasoner might decide to adopt an intention to satisfy some current desires whose goal is most preferred among all desired ends, and might abandon an intention whose aim opposes the goal of some strongly held desire. This decision closely parallels the case of rationally adopting or abandoning assumptions.

Another way rationality enters planning is in choosing what plan should be used to carry out some intention. There usually are numerous plans which achieve a given end, but most are highly inefficient with respect to the agent's expectations and preferences. A good example is planning for contingencies. One can increase the completeness of a plan by adding subplans for different contingencies that might arise. But while one can plan for some contingencies, one cannot plan for all, since there are infinitely many. Rationality provides a standard for deciding which contingencies deserve their own plans; specifically, that the expected utility of having the plan outweighs the costs of constructing it. Ordinarily, this means the only contingencies worth the effort of advance preparation are those covering common or crucial situations.

3.1.4 Rational deliberation

Reasoning about what to do is called deliberation. Any mechanization of ordinary decision theory conducts deliberation, reasoning from alternatives, expectations, and preferences to a choice. But in ordinary life and in artificial intelligence, one cannot always take preferences to be givens of the decision-making process. Instead, in many cases one must perform some amount of reasoning to determine which of one's preferences apply to a particular decision, or more fundamentally, what one's preferences are regarding some heretofore unconsidered possibility. Filling in incompletenesses in one's preferences and resolving inconsistencies between one's preferences mean that deliberation involves choosing or inventing a set of preferences relevant to a decision problem. Rational deliberation involves many of the same issues as rational assuming and learning, for often the only basis for choosing among preferences is one of convenience, of expected utility. As with beliefs, preferences have consequences, since adopting preferences that are hard to satisfy may mean adopting a way of life filled with disappointment and dissatisfaction.

3.2 Conservative reasoning

The intended conditions placed on the successor state in intentional reasoning may badly underdetermine the new state. For example, if the selected intention is that some belief P should be adopted, then choosing $\text{Th}(P)$ as the new set of beliefs (giving up all beliefs not reasserted) satisfies these restrictions on changes and violates no rule of logic. Computational systems like STRIPS finessed this problem by using a mutable database to store their beliefs. Such systems simply made a few additions to and subtractions from the database to account for the explicit changes, and carried along all other beliefs unchanged. Waldinger [32] called this the "STRIPS assumption," but it is merely a special case of the older philosophical idea of conservatism.

3.2.1 Conservatism as minimizing change

Most theoretical prescriptions in philosophy (see especially Quine and Ullian [23] and Gärdenfors [10]) and actual practice in artificial intelligence restrict the admissible changes of state to ones which keep as much of the previous state as possible. For example, in addition to the STRIPS assumption, each of the backtracking procedures used in artificial intelligence represents some notion of minimal revisions. In "chronological" backtracking, the agent keeps all beliefs except the ones most recently added. "Non-chronological" or "dependency-directed" backtracking is even more conservative, abandoning as small a set of beliefs as possible regardless of the order in which they were adopted. For instance, the DDB procedure [2] for dependency-directed backtracking minimizes the changes by abandoning only "maximal assumptions." For obvious reasons, conservatism figures similarly in studies of updates in databases (see, for example, [8]). But more surprisingly, conservatism also plays a role in some forms of progressive reasoning. For example, analogies and metaphors are often very useful in problem solving and learning. While all forms of learning call for the reasoner to adapt explanations, hypotheses, and theories to new information, in using analogies and metaphors the reasoner deforms one explanation or concept into another and judges the aptness of different deformations according to how mildly or greatly they torture the original (see [1]). Thus finding the mildest deformation is just another version of conservatism in reasoning.

Conservatism supposes the existence at each instant t of a comparison relation $\preceq_t$ between states, a way of comparing the relative sizes of changes from the current state S_t entailed by moves to different states in σ_t, the set of states satisfying the intention guiding the current action. We say that the change from state S_t to the next state S_{t+1} is conservative if the change is not larger than that made by moving to any other permissible successor state in σ_t. That is, the set γ_t of minimal changes or closest successors is given by

$$\gamma_t = \{S \in \sigma_t \mid \forall S' \in \sigma_t \quad S' \preceq_t S \supset S \preceq_t S'\}$$

(A formally similar notion appears in logical treatments of counterfactuals, where the measure of size of change is called a comparative similarity relation (see [18]). This formulation does not restrict the choices of measures of the closeness of states in any substantive way, since the weakest comparison relation in which every state is equally close to every other is one possibility. Under this relation every change is minimal, hence conservative. More practically, the complicated conservatism of DDB, which distinguishes "premises" from auxiliary "assumptions," embodies a measure of changes in terms of the state differences they represent. DDB's intended comparison relation (see [3]) compares sets of differences from the initial state, that is, the sets of added and deleted elements: S is as close to the current state S_t as is S' just in case each element added or deleted by S is also added or deleted by S', or formally,

$$S \preceq_t S' \equiv S_t \triangle S \subset S_t \triangle S'$$

(where $\triangle$ denotes symmetric difference). A related measure, which Harman [12] calls the Simple Measure, compares the cardinality of these sets of differences instead of their contents, judging changes smaller if they add or delete fewer elements, or formally,

$$S \preceq_t S' \equiv |S_t \mathbin{\triangle} S| \le |S_t \mathbin{\triangle} S'|.$$

3.2.2 Rational conservatism

Even though the intended conservatism of DDB exhibits an appealing formal simplicity, it is unsatisfactory for practical use except in simple cases that do not depend much on conservatism for success. The same holds as well for the other "blind" backtracking systems widely used in artificial intelligence. Both of the specific comparison relations defined above treat all beliefs equally, and are as ready to discard eternal truths as they are to discard rumor and raving. They are not unreasonable comparison relations for systems like DDB that manipulate representations of beliefs without regard to the meanings of those beliefs, but the cases of interest in scientific and mundane reasoning (whether human or machine) call for conservatism to respect the differing values of beliefs of differing content, to not consider all consistent sets of beliefs equally acceptable. In meaningful revisions, the comparison measure compares the values of the beliefs adopted and the beliefs abandoned; one state will rank closer than another if it abandons less valuable beliefs or adopts more valuable ones. These values represent preferences about possible revisions.

While one might design reasoners to respect the designer's preferences about possible changes, as in the case of DDB, it is more natural to think of belief revision as guided by the reasoner's preferences, in this case preferences about which beliefs it should hold, preferences about its own nature. In this case, we define the comparison order in terms of the expected utility order, or formally,

$$S \preceq_t S' \equiv \hat{u}_{S_t}(S) \le \hat{u}_{S_t}(S').$$

We call this form of revision *rational* conservatism. For example, in our own (human) reasoning, the preferences guiding belief revision are often our own. Our greater credence in Newton's laws than in our neighbor's gossip is not something inherent in our construction (though there may be innate features of our reasoning). That greater credence reflects the values we have developed or learned. The preferences involved in conservative reasoning need not be different than those involved in progressive reasoning. Even if they are the same in both cases, conservative reasoning is not redundant, since progressive reasoning does not consider all consequences of the changes it proposes, only those relevant to its intentions. That is, both progressive and conservative reasoning involve the same sort of choice, but they involve different alternatives since some previously unforeseen effects may have become apparent through the taking of the action.

4   Rationality in representation

It is a truism that effective reasoning depends on good representations. Indeed, the field of algorithm design is to a great degree the study of which data structures facilitate various tasks, and several efforts in automatic programming have concentrated on the task of choosing data structures for particular problems. The usual criteria for choosing among different representations involve comparisons of time and space consumption, in either the worst case or the average case (given some distribution of usages). These measures do not suffice to choose an appropriate representation by themselves, since each circumstance of application may involve different limits or costs to different amounts of time or space usage (the same algorithm that works well as part of a compiler may be fatally slow as part of an aircraft guidance system). Time and space only serve as factors entering into an application's measure of utility. The true basis for choice of representation, as for action, is comparison of expected utility (see [6]). Note that in general, expected utility is not simply a function of expected time or space: cars designed for average height drivers poorly serve a bimodal population of very tall and very short drivers. Expected utility necessarily averages over utilities, not over factor inputs. Expected utility also depends on how utility varies over time, with utilities measured at each instant including the present value of past and future utilities or disutilities.

It is a bit odd to speak of the expected utility of a representation since representations are not actions, but are properties of states. Properly speaking, one imputes utility directly only to algorithms using a representation, with different algorithms using the same representation possessing different utilities. Thus to assess the value of a representation, one must assess the worth of the whole system using the representation. This involves averaging utility over the set of algorithms making use of the representation.

Accurately assessing all these utilities and expectations is often difficult, but once done allows traditional theories of data structure selection to incorporate rational choices. Rather than pursue this possibility, however, we examine two more fundamental roles for rationality in representation. These involve forms of representation intimately connected with reasoning and the control of reasoning, forms which are more active than many standard types of passive representations that exist independently of the reasoning processes employing them.

4.1 Constitutions

Every representation supplies a bit of structure to be part of mental states. Turning this around, every representation imposes a measure of order on the structure of states, or equivalently, places some restrictions on the permissible states of the reasoner. For example, the reasons or justifications enforced by reason maintenance systems (see, for example, [2,3]) forbid the agent from entering states which embody certain otherwise acceptable sets of attitudes, such as states containing certain consistent beliefs or combinations of beliefs, or states lacking other beliefs. We call the collection of all restrictions placed on the agent's permissible states by the agent itself or by its designer the agent's *constitution*. Viewed abstractly, constitutions import the notion of state space into decision theory and psychology from automata theory. All descriptions of automata begin by describing the space of legal states of the machines, perhaps as legal combinations of more primitive elements. Theories of rational action also view states as composed of more primitive elements (specifically, as sets of beliefs, preferences, intentions, and other attitudes), but decision theory permits rational agents to hold any set of attitudes which satisfies agent-independent consistency and completeness axioms. Constitutions of rational agents simply add the notion that some combinations of attitudes are legal and some are illegal for each agent (see Figure 7).

Mental constitutions may be employed to improve the overall rationality of the agent by steering the agent away from activities expected to be

Decision Theory	AI
Ideal rationality	*Limited rationality*
Complete knowledge	Incomplete beliefs Incomplete preferences
Consistent knowledge	Inconsistent beliefs Inconsistent preferences
Unlimited resources + Unrestricted states (e.g., any beliefs)	Limited resources + Restricted states (forbidden belief sets)

Figure 7: Further differences between assumptions in decision theory and artificial intelligence

useless and toward activities expected to be useful, thus conserving scarce resources. Such improvements often arise when what is rational in the short run differs from what is rational in the long run, since foreseeing the long term consequences of a course of action is often difficult, while foreseeing short term consequences is usually easy. In such cases, the reasoner may be misled into taking the overly limited view of what is best to do. In such situations, constitutional restrictions permit the agent to efficiently improve its long-term rationality by simply avoiding consideration of alternatives whose dangers are too hard to derive, thus avoiding the costs of reconsidering them at every instant. In addition, constitutions may be beneficial when the consequences of steps of reasoning cannot be predicted, whether because they take too long to predict, or because the information needed to predict them is lacking. For example, reason maintenance systems are based on the assumption that using reasons to determine the agent's current set of beliefs is worthwhile. The grounds for making this assumption are that the costs of recording and thoughtlessly reusing inferences is usually less than the costs of rederiving them from scratch. These grounds are strengthened by the way in which reason maintenance systems are supposed to be used, in which the reasoner decides what inferences are worth making in a situation after making them the first time, with demonstrated utility in one situation taken as evidence for utility in others.

Constitutions need not be viewed strictly as designer-imposed restrictions on the rationality of an agent since we may design agents that can specify or modify their own constitutions (for example, to employ reason maintenance systems for controlling their beliefs). In such agents, rational control of reasoning involves the agent rationally emending its constitution to serve its own purposes as well as rational choice of steps of reasoning and rational choice of representation forms. To obtain such controllability, we must go beyond the the *external* (or eternal, or designer's) perspective traditional in automata theory in which a constitution is just an axiomatization of the agent's state space, formulated in a language over sets of attitudes. From this perspective, the agent's states resembles database states, and constitutions are essentially the same as sets of integrity constraints, as the notion appears in database theory (see especially Reiter [24], who views integrity constraints as statements about the database contents). It is instead more interesting to take the *internal* (or temporal, or agent's) perspective, and view a constitution as a set of constraints on states and transitions changeable at will in whole or in part. Where the external perspective defines a single set of legal states constituting all the states legal at any time in some history, the internal perspective views the constitution as a time-varying structure, with different sets of legal states at different times. In the external perspective, the agent's constitution is something external to and unchangeable by the agent. In the internal perspective, the constitution is internal to and changeable by the agent. The external and internal perspectives can be assimilated by representing internal constitutions as distinguished subsets of the agent's attitudes, and having the external constitution set forth the meanings of all possible laws of thought. One example of such an external form of internal constitutions is given by Minsky [21], who studies internal constitutions for complex programming systems under the name of "law-governed systems."

We will not explore fully how to specify controllable constitutions (see [4] for further discussion), but the main ideas may be stated briefly. In short, constitutions can be viewed as having two (possibly vacuous) parts. The first is the fixed part, the most important form of which is called a *constitutive logic*, that is, a logic that specifies the minimal consistency and closure properties of states. The second part is the variable part, called the set of *laws of thought* or *constitutive intentions*, that is, the rules for self-regulation that the agent may adopt or abandon. The *legal* or constitutionally permissible states of the agent are then those states closed and consistent with respect to the constitutive logic and legal according to each of the laws of thought they contain. Formally, we characterize a constitutive logic with an entailment relation $\vdash$ and a consistency relation C over finite sets of attitudes. We say that a set X is closed just in case $x \in X$ whenever $Y \vdash x$ for some finite $Y \subseteq X$, and that a set X is consistent just in case $C(Y)$ for each finite $Y \subseteq X$. We characterize the import of laws of thought by an interpretation function I defined so that $I(x)$ is the set of all sets of attitudes satisfying the constitutive intention x, or the set of all sets of attitudes if x is not a constitutive intention. Then a set X closed and consistent with respect to $\vdash$ and C is legal just in case $X \in I(x)$ for every $x \in X$.

4.2 Constructive representation

One of the most important forms of constitutional structure is that of constructive representation. Many theories of knowledge in artificial intelligence draw a distinction between mental attitudes explicitly and implicitly represented by an agent. The agent's explicitly represented attitudes appear as entries open to view in the agent's memory or database, and the agent's implicitly represented attitudes consist of readily computable conclusions not directly expressed but entailed by or in some way derivable from the explicitly represented attitudes. Let us call these two sorts of attitudes *manifest* and *constructive*, respectively (see [5]). This distinction refines Levesque's [16] notion of *implicit* and *explicit* belief, as both manifest and constructive beliefs are explicit (i.e., they are the beliefs on which the agent acts). In that view, manifest beliefs represent both explicit and implicit beliefs and act as a sort of "really explicit" belief.

The distinction between manifest and constructive attitudes is important because while theories of ideal action (like decision theory) require agents to hold infinitely many opinions and preferences about the world, the first limitation imposed by computational mechanisms in artificial intelligence is that individual states of the agent must be finitely describable. Distinguishing between manifest and constructive attitudes makes it conceivable that finite agents might nevertheless possess infinitely many opinions, since even finite sets of beliefs may represent, via entailment, infinitely many conclusions.

As this motivation suggests, the most common view of constructive representations is a logical one, with, for instance, the derivation of constructive and implicit beliefs from manifest beliefs described by a logic of belief. But when one considers the notion of rational representation, a more appropriate view is that the composition of the agent's constructive beliefs depends on its preferences about its states of belief as well as on its manifest beliefs. The representations explicitly possessed by the agent are not themselves viewed as functioning beliefs, but only as materials or *prima facie* beliefs from which the agent rationally constructs the beliefs on which it bases its actions. The agent's explicit beliefs are identified with its constructive beliefs, rather than with the sum of constructive and manifest beliefs, so that the set of explicit beliefs may be either more or less than the beliefs entailed logically by the manifest ones. That is, we keep the idea that manifest beliefs represent explicit and implicit beliefs, but change the nature of the representation relation from logical closure under derivations to rational choice.

The clearest example of the rational nature of constructive representation involves agents whose attitudes are inconsistent. Conflicting information may reach the agent through many different sensors and informants. In the simplest case, inconsistencies appear because the agent's beliefs are drawn from several experts who disagree about the facts (in which case the inconsistency may be manifest), or who think they agree because the inconsistencies in their views are too subtle to detect (in which case the inconsistency may not be explicit). It is not always possible to decide immediately which information is correct and which is false and accept the true and reject the false. Instead, many conflicts require extended reasoning or investigation to resolve. Meanwhile, the agent must continue to decide what to do in spite of these conflicts.

As noted earlier, logic does not offer much guidance about what to do when the manifest beliefs are inconsistent, since every conclusion is entailed by an inconsistent set of hypotheses. At best, logic says we should confine attention to a consistent set of beliefs and act on that basis. Fortunately, however, there are many similarities between the cases of acting on incomplete information and acting on inconsistent information. With inconsistent beliefs, the agent faces a situation of ambiguity, just as in the case of incomplete beliefs, but now the alternatives are the consistent subsets of beliefs rather than the disjuncts of some disjunction. Moreover, just as in the case of incomplete beliefs, there is often information available about which choice is better, about which subset to prefer. The major difference between the cases of incomplete and inconsistent belief is that while the agent may rationally refuse to make any assumptions in some cases of incomplete belief, an agent possessing conflicting beliefs cannot refuse to choose a basis for action.

A choice of basis for action can be approached rationally in the same way as a choice of assumptions, with the agent applying its preferences about consistent subsets of its manifest beliefs to rationally choose one, and then using this subset to choose a consistent body of constructive beliefs. This approach to constructive representation permits the agent to select different subsets of the manifest beliefs for different actions even if the manifest beliefs remain constant. In such cases, the logical inconsistency of the agent's beliefs is exhibited in the "inconsistency" of the agent's actions in unchanging circumstances. This "inconsistency in action" can be minimized by employing the notion of conservative revisions of constructive beliefs.

In choosing consistent sets of constructive beliefs based on inconsistent manifest beliefs, we may think of the constructed beliefs as "representing" the inconsistent manifest beliefs for the purpose of the action at hand, just as we think of the elected officers of a political organization as representing its membership. This sense of "representation" is different from the one we have been studying so far. In the first sense, the manifest beliefs represent the constructive beliefs: in the second, the constructive beliefs also represent the manifest beliefs. This second sense is not merely a curious coincidence of words. The most common and unavoidable form of inconsistent knowledge employed in artificial intelligence is not inconsistent belief, but conflicting default rules and the conflicting preferences they embody. As shown by Doyle and Wellman [7], reasoning with conflicting.default rules turns out to be formally the same problem as decision-making or self-government by groups of people, thus justifying the second sense of the term "representation." This connection between rational knowledge representation and theories of social or political decision-making makes the lack of a normative theory of limited rationality more understandable, since mental self-government corresponds to social or political government, about which there is no agreement on the proper form. Indeed, as Doyle and Wellman show (drawing on Arrow's theorem from economics), there is probably no universally acceptable method for rationally resolving conflicts in default reasoning.

5 Conclusion

The standard notion of ideal rationality is that at each instant the agent acts as if it had considered all possible actions and evaluated the likelihood and desirability of each of their consequences. The notion of rational self-government applies this standard to the conduct of reasoning, so that at each instant the agent chooses how it would like to change its beliefs, preferences, and plans, or change how it represents and formulates things, or how it does things, taking into account the consequences of holding different beliefs, desires, etc. Often limitations of time or other resources mean that it is not feasible to consider *all* possible actions or all of their consequences, but only some actions, some consequences, and only guesses at their likelihoods and desirabilities. This leads to the notion of bounded or limited rationality. Rational self-government provides an appealing approach to the conduct of reasoning by asking that the resource allocation decisions and other decisions guiding reasoning be made in a manner as rational as possible.

One of the fundamental forms of limitations guiding reasoning is how the agent is constituted, the nature of its legal states. The agent's constitution provides lower bounds on rationality, the approximation to rationality available without expense of time or attention. One of the most common organizations of constitutions divides the explicit attitudes held by the agent into those manifestly represented and those constructed from the manifest ones. Constructive representations are intimately tied up with the notion of reasoning itself, and many techniques for-reasoning with incomplete or inconsistent information by rationally choosing what assumptions to make or to use in taking action are appropriate for use in constructive representation as well.

The theory of rational self-government shows that decision theory and economics have much to contribute to the understanding and automation of thinking. But much work remains to be done. The prior work of artificial intelligence suggests some mechanizable forms of limited rationality, and the prior work of decision theorists and economists should help compare these with each other. It also makes sense to seek new mechanizable forms of rationality in economic theories. The fundamental problems, however, will likely be with us a long while.

References

[1] J. G. Carbonell. Derivational analogy: a theory of reconstructive problem solving and expertise acquisition. In R. S. Michalski, J. G. Carbonell, and T. M. Mitchell, editors, *Machine Learning: An Artificial Intelligence Approach*, volume 2, pages 371–392. Morgan Kaufmann, 1986.

[2] J. Doyle. A truth maintenance system. *Artificial Intelligence*, 12(2):231–272, 1979.

[3] J. Doyle. Some theories of reasoned assumptions: an essay in rational psychology. Technical Report 83-125, Department of Computer Science, Carnegie Mellon University, Pittsburgh, PA, 1983.

[4] J. Doyle. Artificial intelligence and rational self-government. Technical Report CS-88-124, Carnegie-Mellon University Computer Science Department, 1988.

[5] J. Doyle. Constructive belief and rational representation. *Computational Intelligence*, 5(1):1–11, February 1989.

[6] J. Doyle and R. S. Patil. Two dogmas of knowledge representation: language restrictions, taxonomic classifications, and the utility of representation services. TM 387b, Massachusetts Institute of Technology, Laboratory for Computer Science, 545 Technology Square, Cambridge, MA, 02139, September 1989.

[7] J. Doyle and M. P. Wellman. Impediments to universal preference-based default theories. In R. J. Brachman, H. J. Levesque, and R. Reiter, editors, *Proceedings of the First International Conference on Principles of Knowledge Representation and Reasoning*, pages 94–102, San Mateo, CA, May 1989. Morgan Kaufmann.

[8] R. Fagin, J. D. Ullman, and M. Y. Vardi. On the semantics of updates in databases. In *Proceedings of the Second ACM SIGACT-SIGMOD Conference*, pages 352–365, 1983.

[9] R. E. Fikes and N. J. Nilsson. STRIPS: A new approach to the application of theorem proving to problem solving. *Artificial Intelligence*, 2:189–208, 1971.

[10] P. Gärdenfors. *Knowledge in Flux: Modeling the Dynamics of Epistemic States*. MIT Press, Cambridge, MA, 1988.

[11] I. J. Good. Rational decisions. *Journal of the Royal Statistical Society B*, 14:107–114, 1952.

[12] G. Harman. *Change in View: Principles of Reasoning*. MIT Press, Cambridge, MA, 1986.

[13] E. J. Horvitz. Reasoning under varying and uncertain resource constraints. In *Proceedings of the Seventh National Conference on Artificial Intelligence*, pages 111–116, San Mateo, CA, 1988. AAAI, Morgan Kaufmann.

[14] W. James. *The Will to Believe and Other Essays in Popular Philosophy*. Longmans, Green, and Co., New York, 1897.

[15] H. Leibenstein. *Beyond Economic Man: A new foundation for microe-conomics.* Harvard University Press, Cambridge, MA, second edition, 1980.

[16] H. J. Levesque. A logic of implicit and explicit belief. In *Proceedings of the National Conference on Artificial Intelligence*, pages 198–202. American Association for Artificial Intelligence, 1984.

[17] I. Levi. *The Enterprise of Knowledge.* MIT Press, Cambridge, MA, 1980.

[18] D. Lewis. *Counterfactuals.* Blackwell, Oxford, 1973.

[19] D. McDermott. Planning and acting. *Cognitive Science*, 2:71–109, 1978.

[20] D. McDermott. A critique of pure reason. *Computational Intelligence*, 3:151–160, 1987.

[21] N. H. Minsky. Law-governed systems. Technical report, Rutgers University, Computer Science Department, New Brunswick, 1988.

[22] B. Pascal. *Pensées sur la religion et sur quelques autres sujets.* Harvill, London, 1962. Translated by M. Turnell, originally published 1662.

[23] W. V. Quine and J. S. Ullian. *The Web of Belief.* Random House, New York, second edition, 1978.

[24] R. Reiter. On integrity constraints. In M. Y. Vardi, editor, *Proceedings of the Second Conference on Theoretical Aspects of Reasoning About Knowledge*, pages 97–111, Los Altos, 1988. Morgan Kaufmann.

[25] S. Russell and E. Wefald. Principles of metareasoning. In R. J. Brachman, H. J. Levesque, and R. Reiter, editors, *Proceedings of the First International Conference on Principles of Knowledge Representation and Reasoning*, pages 400–411, San Mateo, CA, 1989. Morgan Kaufmann.

[26] L. J. Savage. *The Foundations of Statistics.* Dover Publications, New York, second edition, 1972.

[27] Y. Shoham. *Reasoning about Change: Time and Causation from the Standpoint of Artificial Intelligence*. MIT Press, 1988.

[28] H. A. Simon. From substantive to procedural rationality. In S. J. Latsis, editor, *Method and Appraisal in Economics*, pages 129–148. Cambridge University Press, 1976.

[29] D. E. Smith and M. R. Genesereth. Ordering conjunctive queries. *Artificial Intelligence*, 26:171–215, 1985.

[30] L. G. Valiant. A theory of the learnable. *Communications of the ACM*, 18(11):1134–1142, 1984.

[31] J. von Neumann and O. Morgenstern. *Theory of Games and Economic Behavior*. Princeton University Press, Princeton, third edition, 1953.

[32] R. Waldinger. Achieving several goals simultaneously. In E. Elcock and D. Michie, editors, *Machine Intelligence 8*, pages 94–136. Edinburgh University Press, 1977.

Models of
Theory Change

COMPUTATIONAL ISSUES IN BELIEF REVISION

João P. Martins
Instituto Superior Técnico
Av. Rovisco Pais
1000 Lisboa, Portugal
(ist_1416@ptifm.bitnet)

Abstract

Belief revision systems are computer programs that deal with contradictions. They reason from the propositions in a knowledge base, "filtering" those propositions so that only part of the knowledge base is perceived, namely, the propositions that are under consideration, called the believed propositions. When the belief revision system considers another one of these sets, we say that it changes its beliefs.

In this paper we discuss problems that researchers in belief revision have to address: *inference*, which studies how do new beliefs follow from old ones; *non-monotonicity*, which studies the methods of recording that one belief depends on the absence of another; *dependency-recording*, which concerns the study of the methods for recording that one belief depends on another one; *disbelief propagation*, which worries about how one fails to believe all the consequences of a proposition that is disbelieved; and, *revision of beliefs*, which studies how to change beliefs in order to get rid of a contradiction. These problems are illustrated under the perspective of a belief revision system called SNeBR.

1   Introduction

Most computer programs constructed by researchers in Artificial Intelligence
(AI) maintain a model of their environment (external and/or internal), which
is updated to reflect the perceived changes in the environment. This model is
typically stored in a knowledge base, and the program draws inferences from
the information in the knowledge base. All the inferences drawn are added
to the knowledge base. One reason for model updating (and thus knowledge-
base updating) is the detection of *contradictory information*. In this case,
the updating should be preceded by a decision about what proposition is the
culprit for the contradiction, its removal from the knowledge base,[1] and the
subsequent removal of every proposition that depends on the selected culprit.

   Belief revision systems [Doyle and London 80; Martins 87] are AI programs that deal with contradictions (these systems are also called *truth maintenance systems* and *reason maintenance systems*). They reason from the
propositions in a knowledge base, "filtering" those propositions so that only
part of the knowledge base is perceived, namely, the propositions that are
under consideration, called *believed propositions*. In this context, *beliefs* are a
subset of the propositions in the knowledge base. We take the word "belief"
to denote *justified belief*: a proposition is believed either because the belief
revision system was told so or because it depends on believed propositions.
When the belief revision system considers another one of these sets, we say
that it *changes its beliefs*. Typically, a belief revision system explores alternatives, makes choices, explores the consequences of its choices, and compares
results obtained when using different choices. If, during this process, a contradiction is detected, the belief revision system will revise the knowledge
base, changing its beliefs in order to get rid of the contradiction.

   There are several problems that researchers in belief revision have to
address: *inference*, which studies how do new beliefs follow from old ones;
non-monotonicity, which studies the methods of recording that one belief
depends on the absence of another; *dependency-recording*, which concerns
the study of the methods for recording that one belief depends on another
one; *disbelief propagation*, which worries about how one fails to believe all

---

[1] Or making it inaccessible to the program.

the consequences of a proposition that is disbelieved; and, *revision of beliefs*, which studies how to change beliefs in order to get rid of a contradiction.

No single system or researcher has addressed all these problems. In this paper we take a look at these issues and discuss how they were addressed by a particular belief revision system, SNeBR [Martins and Shapiro 88].

2 Inference

Belief revision systems have to keep a record of where each proposition in the knowledge base came from—the *support* of the proposition. The support is used both during the identification of the possible culprits for a contradiction and in the process of changing the system's beliefs.

The issue discussed here concerns the computation of the supports of derived propositions. This is a problem area that has been mostly ignored by researchers: in most belief revision systems inferences are made outside the system, which just passively records them. It would be desirable to put the responsibility of computing these dependencies on the system itself, so that as new beliefs are generated their dependency on old beliefs will be *automatically* computed.

In this section we discuss a logic, SWM*,[2] that was developed to support belief revision systems. The interesting aspect of supporting a belief revision system in SWM* is that the dependencies among propositions can be computed by the system itself rather than having to force the user (or an outside system) to do this, as in many existing systems.

SWM* is loosely based on the FR system of relevance logic [Anderson and Belnap 75, pp.346-348]. The main features of relevance logic used in SWM* are the association of each wff with a set containing all hypotheses[3] that were *really* used in its derivation (we call this set the origin set) and the statement of the rules of inference taking origin sets into account, specifying what should be the origin set of the resulting wff.

---

[2] After *S*hapiro, *W*and, and *M*artins. The SWM* system is a successor of the SWM system [Martins and Shapiro 88], which, in turn, is a successor of the system of [Shapiro and Wand 76].

[3] Non-derived propositions.

2.1 Knowledge states

The use of origin sets takes care of one of the important issues in belief revision: how to keep track of and propagate propositional dependencies. Another important issue in belief revision systems consists in the recording of the conditions under which contradictions may occur. This is important, because once we discover that a given set is inconsistent, we may not want to consider it again, and even if we do want to consider it, we want to keep in mind that we are dealing with an inconsistent set.

SWM* deals with objects called knowledge states. Informally, a knowledge state is a pair containing a knowledge base and a set of sets known to be inconsistent. The knowledge base contains propositions (written as wffs) associated with a support, i.e., an indication of dependencies between a particular wff and other wffs in the knowledge base. The set of known inconsistent sets records all sets in the knowledge base that were discovered to be inconsistent.

The *knowledge base* is a set of supported wffs. A *supported wff* consists of a wff and an associated pair, its support, containing an origin tag and an origin set. For a particular supported wff, the origin tag indicates how the supported wff was placed in the knowledge base (i.e., whether it was supplied by an outside system or it was generated during deduction) and the origin set indicates the dependencies of this supported wff on other wffs (hypotheses) in the knowledge base. There are standard formation rules for wffs, and the language that they define is represented by $\mathcal{L}$.

Supported wffs are objects of the form $<A, \tau, \alpha>$, where A is a wff with origin tag τ and origin set α. We define the functions $wff(<A, \tau, \alpha>) = A$, $ot(<A, \tau, \alpha>) = \tau$, and $os(<A, \tau, \alpha>) = \alpha$. The pair (τ, α) is called the *support* of the supported wff $<A, \tau, \alpha>$. The support of a wff is not part of the wff itself but rather associated with a *particular occurrence of the wff.*

The *origin tag* is an element of the set $\{hyp, der, ext\}$: *hyp* identifies hypotheses, *der* identifies normally derived wffs within SWM*, and *ext* identifies special wffs whose origin set was extended.[4]

The *origin set* is a set of hypotheses. The origin set of a supported wff

---

[4]A supported wff with *ext* origin tag has to be treated specially in order to avoid the introduction of irrelevancies. For a discussion on this issue see [Martins and Shapiro 88].

contains those hypotheses that were *actually used* in the derivation of that wff. The rules of inference of SWM* guarantee that: (1) The origin set of a supported wff contains *every* hypothesis that was used in its derivation. (2) The origin set of a supported wff contains *only* the hypotheses that were used in its derivation.

In summary, supported wffs are objects of the form $<A, \tau, \alpha>$, where $A \in \mathcal{L}$, $\tau \in \{hyp,\ der,\ ext\}$, and $\alpha \subset \mathcal{L}$.

A *knowledge state*, written $[[KB, KIS]]$, is a pair containing a knowledge base (KB) and a set of known inconsistent sets (KIS). The *knowledge base* is a set of supported wffs; the *set of known inconsistent sets* is a set containing all sets in the KB known to be inconsistent.[5]

2.2 Some inference rules

In this section we present some of the rules of inference of SWM*. These rules are grouped into two sets, pure logic rules and computational rules. *Pure logic rules* are like traditional rules of inference, they allow the introduction of new supported wffs into the knowledge base. Pure logic rules rules transform $[[KB, KIS]]$ into $[[KB\prime, KIS]]$. *Computational rules* are rules that update the information about sets known to be inconsistent. Computational rules transform $[[KB, KIS]]$ into $[[KB, KIS\prime]]$.

The rules of inference make use of a function (Λ) to compute the origin tag of a supported wff resulting from the application of the rules of inference. This function is defined as:

$$\Lambda(\tau_1, \tau_2) = \begin{cases} ext & \text{if } \tau_1 = ext \text{ or } \tau_2 = ext \\ der & \text{otherwise} \end{cases}$$

$$\Lambda(\tau_1, \tau_2, \ldots, \tau_n) = \Lambda(\tau_1, \Lambda(\tau_2, \ldots, \tau_n))$$

---

[5]It is important to distinguish between a set *being* inconsistent and a set *being known to be* inconsistent. An inconsistent set is one from which a contradiction *can be* derived; a set known to be inconsistent is an inconsistent set from which a contradiction *has been* derived.

2.2.1 Pure logic rules

Hypothesis (Hyp). This rule enables the introduction of hypotheses. Given the knowledge state $[[KB, KIS]]$ and any wff A, such that $< A, hyp, \{A\} > \notin KB$, we may infer $[[KB \cup \{< A, hyp, \{A\} >\}, KIS]]$. The wff A in $<A, hyp, \{A\} >$ is called a *hypothesis*.

Implication Introduction ($\rightarrow$I). From the knowledge state $[[KB, KIS]]$, in which $<B, der, \alpha> \in KB$ and any $H \in \alpha$, we may infer $[[KB \cup \{< H \rightarrow B, der, \alpha - \{H\} >\}, KIS]]$. Any hypothesis in the origin set of B *was used* in its derivation, and thus it implies B under the assumption of the remaining hypotheses.

Modus Ponens – Implication Elimination (MP): From the knowledge state $[[KB, KIS]]$, in which $<A, \tau_1, \alpha_1> \in KB$ and $<A \rightarrow B, \tau_2, \alpha_2> \in KB$, we may infer $[[KB \cup \{<B, \Lambda(\tau_1, \tau_2), \alpha_1 \cup \alpha_2>\}, KIS]]$.

Negation Introduction ($\neg$I). This rule states that from the hypotheses underlying a contradiction we can conclude that the conjunction of any number of them must be false under the assumption of the others. From the knowledge state $[[KB, KIS]]$, in which $<A \wedge \neg A, \tau, \alpha> \in KB$ and any set $\{H_1, \ldots, H_n\} \subset \alpha$, we may infer $[[KB \cup \{<\neg(H_1 \wedge \ldots \wedge H_n), \Lambda(\tau, \tau), \alpha - \{H_1, \ldots, H_n\}>\}, KIS]]$.

And Introduction ($\wedge$I). This enables the introduction of conjunction, either with *der* origin tag or with *ext* origin tag. From the knowledge state $[[KB, KIS]]$ in which $<A, \tau_1, \alpha> \in KB$ and $<B, \tau_2, \alpha> \in KB$, we may infer $[[KB \cup \{<A \wedge B, \Lambda(\tau_1, \tau_2), \alpha>\}, KIS]]$.
From the knowledge state $[[KB, KIS]]$ in which $<A, \tau_1, \alpha_1> \in KB$, $<B, \tau_2, \alpha_2> \in KB$, and $\alpha_1 \neq \alpha_2$ we may infer $[[KB \cup \{<A \wedge B, ext, \alpha_1 \cup \alpha_2>\}, KIS]]$.

And Elimination ($\wedge$E). The rule is only applicable if the origin tag is not extended. This avoids the "smuggling" of hypotheses into the origin sets. From the knowledge state $[[KB, KIS]]$ in which $<A \wedge B, \tau, \alpha> \in KB$, and $\tau \neq ext$, we may infer either $[[KB \cup \{<A, der, \alpha>\}, KIS]]$ or $[[KB \cup \{<B, der, \alpha>\}, KIS]]$.

Universal Introduction ($\forall$I). From the knowledge state $[[KB, KIS]]$ in which $<B(t), der, \alpha \cup \{A(t)\}> \in KB$, and the term t does not appear in any wff in α, we may infer $[[KB \cup \{<\forall x A(x) \rightarrow B(x), der, \alpha>\}, KIS]]$.

Universal Elimination ($\forall$E). From the knowledge state $[[KB, KIS]]$ in which $<\forall x F(x), \tau, \alpha> \in KB$ and any individual constant "c", we may infer $[[KB \cup \{<F(c), \Lambda(\tau, \tau), \alpha>\}, KIS]]$.

Existential Introduction ($\exists$I). From the knowledge state $[[KB, KIS]]$ in which $<F(c), \tau, \alpha> \in KB$ where "c" is an individual constant, we may infer $[[KB \cup \{<\exists x F(x), \Lambda(\tau, \tau), \alpha>\}, KIS]]$.

Existential Elimination ($\exists$E). From the knowledge state $[[KB, KIS]]$ in which $<\exists x F(x), \tau, \alpha> \in KB$ and any individual constant "c" that is not used in any supported wff in KB, we may infer $[[KB \cup \{<F(c), \Lambda(\tau, \tau), \alpha>\}, KIS]]$.

2.2.2 Computational rules

These rules transform $[[KB, KIS]]$ into $[[KB, KIS\prime]]$. They are obligatorily applied.

Updating of Inconsistent Sets (UIS). This rule is obligatorily applied whenever a contradiction is detected. Its effect is to update the information about the sets known to be inconsistent. From the knowledge state $[[KB, KIS]]$ in which $<A, \tau_1, \alpha_1> \in KB$, $<\neg A, \tau_2, \alpha_2> \in KB$, and $\forall s \in KIS (\alpha_1 \cup \alpha_2) \neq s$[6] we *must* generate the knowledge state $[[KB, KIS \cup \{\alpha_1 \cup \alpha_2\}]]$.

Derived Hypothesis (DH). This rule is obligatorily applied when a supported wff is derived such that there is already a hypothesis in the KB with the same wff and that hypothesis belongs to a known inconsistent set. The effect of this rule is to record that the hypotheses underlying the derivation of this new wff together with the remaining hypotheses in that known inconsistent set are a set known

---

[6]The fact that $\forall s \in KIS (\alpha_1 \cup \alpha_2) \neq s$ means that this contradiction was not detected yet.

to be inconsistent. Given the knowledge state $[[KB, KIS]]$ in which $<H, hyp, \{H\}> \in KB$, $<H, \tau, \alpha> \in KB$, $\tau \neq hyp$, and $\exists s \in KIS \ni (H \in s) \ and \ (s - \{H\}) \cup \alpha \notin KIS^7$ then we *must* generate the knowledge state $[[KB, KIS \cup \{\sigma : \exists s \in KIS \ni (H \in s \ and \ \sigma = (s - \{H\}) \cup \alpha]]$.

2.3 Summary

SWM* works with knowledge states, which are objects of the form $[[KB, KIS]]$ in which:

1. $KB \subset \mathcal{L} \times \{hyp, der, ext\} \times 2^{\mathcal{L}}$;

2. $KIS \subset 2^{\mathcal{L}}$.

The rules of inference of SWM* impose the following syntactic restrictions on the formation of knowledge states:

1. $\forall <F, \tau, \alpha> \in KB \ (\forall H \in \alpha \ \exists \mathcal{H} \in KB \ (wff(\mathcal{H}) = H \ and \ ot(\mathcal{H}) = hyp))$. That is, the origin set of every supported wff in the KB contains wffs that correspond to hypotheses existing in the KB.

2. $\forall s \in KIS \ (\forall \sigma \in s \ (\forall H \in \sigma \ \exists \mathcal{H} \in KB(wff(\mathcal{H}) = H \ and \ ot(\mathcal{H}) = hyp))$. That is, for every wff appearing in a known inconsistent set there is a corresponding hypothesis in the KB.

Defining the derivability relation within SWM* ($\vdash_{SWM*}$) as follows, given $\Delta \subset \mathcal{L} \times \{hyp, der, ext\} \times 2^{\mathcal{L}}$ and $\mathcal{F} \in \mathcal{L} \times \{hyp, der, ext\} \times 2^{\mathcal{L}}$, we write $\Delta \vdash_{SWM*} \mathcal{F}$ if and oly if $[[\Delta, \{\}]] \vdash [[\Delta\prime \cup \{\mathcal{F}\}, KIS]]$ where $\Delta \subset \Delta\prime$. The rules of inference of SWM* guarantee the following results involving the derivability relation:

1. $\forall \mathcal{F} \in KB \ \exists \Delta \subset KB \ni \Delta \vdash_{SWM*} \mathcal{F}$.

2. $\forall s \in KIS \ \exists \Delta \subset KB \ (\forall \mathcal{F} \in \Delta \ (wff(\mathcal{F}) \in s \ and \ ot(\mathcal{F}) = hyp) \ and \ \Delta \vdash_{SWM*} \perp)$.[8]

---

[7] The fact that $\exists s \in KIS \ni (H \in s) \ and \ (s - \{H\}) \cup \alpha \notin KIS$ means that this contradiction was not detected yet.

[8] The symbol $\perp$ denotes a contradiction.

3 Non-monotonicity

In systems where we have to make decisions based on incomplete information, it is useful to be able to tell that one belief depends on the absence of another. If this latter becomes believed, then the former is disbelieved. This kind of behavior is called *non-monotonic*.

Non-monotonicity in belief revision systems was addressed by [Doyle 79], [McDermott 83], [Dressler 88] and [Junker 89] among others. The basic idea underlying their approaches is to record, along with each proposition in the knowledge base, both the set of propositions that have to be believed and the set of propositions that have to be disbelieved in order for the proposition to be believed.

SWM* does not address the non-monotonicity problem but work is under way (see [Cravo and Martins 90]).

4 Dependency-Recording

There are two ways of recording the support of propositions, corresponding to justification-based and to assumption-based systems.

In *justification-based* systems, the support of each proposition contains the propositions that *directly* produced it. This approach was taken by [Doyle 79], [McAllester 80], and [McDermott 83].

In *assumption-based* systems, the support of each proposition contains the *hypotheses* (*non*-derived propositions) that produced it. This approach was taken by us, [de Kleer 86], [Dressler 88], and [Junker 89]. In fact, in SWM* each supported wff is associated with all hypotheses underlying its derivation.

5 Disbelief propagation

One important aspect of belief revision systems is the updating of the knowledge base when some proposition is disbelieved. This process should only be initiated by the disbelief of a hypothesis (a proposition that has no other justification than being told to the system) rather than the disbelief of a derived proposition (which, without changing the underlying hypotheses, could be re-derived).

The result of this disbelieving process should be the set of propositions that would have been generated if the system had started without the disbelieved proposition. There are two approaches to disbelief propagation, corresponding to label-based systems and context-based systems.

In a *label-based system*, this is done by labeling the propositions that should be considered (marking propositions rather than erasing them permits some savings when a proposition once believed but later disbelieved is believed once more). These labels are typically IN for believed propositions and OUT for disbelieved propositions. When a proposition is disbelieved, the belief revision system has to go through the knowledge base deciding what the consequences of the removal are and re-labeling propositions. A similar procedure has to take place if we decide to believe in some proposition that is labeled as disbelieved. This approach was followed by [Doyle 79] and [McAllester 80].

In *context-based systems*, the knowledge-base retrieval function has to know which hypotheses are under consideration, whenever it performs a knowledge-base retrieval operation. In context-based systems, there is no labeling of the propositions in the knowledge base, but rather an association of each proposition with the hypotheses underlying its derivation; it is the knowledge-base retrieval function that decides dynamically (every time it performs a knowledge base retrieval) which propositions should be considered. This approach was followed by us, [de Kleer 86], [Dressler 88], and [Junker 89].

5.1   Contexts and belief spaces

We now discuss how SWM*'s features can be used in applications of belief revision: we define the behavior of an abstract context-based belief revision system (i.e., not tied to any particular implementation). SNeBR, the system that we have implemented, corresponds to a particular instance of this abstract system using the SNePS network [Shapiro 79], [Shapiro and Rapaport 87].

We define a *context* to be a set of hypotheses. A context determines a *belief space*, which is the set of all hypotheses defining the context and all the wffs that were derived exclusively from them. Formally, a belief space is represented by $\ll [[KB, KIS]], C \gg$ where $C \subset \mathcal{L}$ and

$$\forall H \in C \; (\exists \mathcal{H} \in KB \ni (os(\mathcal{H}) = \{H\} \; and \; ot(\mathcal{H}) = hyp)).$$

Within the SWM* formalism, the wffs in a belief space are characterized by the existence of a corresponding supported wff in the KB with an origin set that is contained in the context, i.e.,

$$\ll [[KB, KIS]], C \gg = \{F \; : \; \exists \mathcal{F} \in KB \ni (wff(\mathcal{F}) = F \; and \; os(\mathcal{F}) \subset C)\}.$$

Given $\Delta \subset \mathcal{L}$, let

$$hyps(\Delta) = \{< \phi, hyp, \{\phi\} > \; : \; \phi \in \Delta\}$$

and given $\Sigma \subset \mathcal{L} \times \{hyp, der, ext\} \times 2^{\mathcal{L}}$, let

$$wffs(\Sigma) = \{\phi \; : \; < \phi, \tau, \alpha > \in \Sigma\}.$$

Then

$$\ll [[KB, KIS]], C \gg \subset \{F \; : \; F \in wffs(\{\mathcal{F} \; : \; hyps(C) \vdash_{SWM*} \mathcal{F}\})\}.$$

In other words, a belief space determined by a context is a subset of all the wffs existing in the supported wffs derivable (according to the rules of inference of SWM*) from the supported wffs corresponding to the hypotheses in the context. It contains those wffs that *have been derived* in the KB amongst all possible *derivable* wffs.

SNeBR works with contexts and belief spaces. Any operation performed by SNeBR (query, addition, etc.) is associated with a context. We refer to the context under consideration, i.e., the context associated with the operation currently being performed, as the *current context*. While the operation is being carried out, the only propositions that will be considered are the propositions in the belief space defined by the current context. This belief space will be called the *current belief space*. A proposition is said to be *believed* if it belongs to the current belief space.

A common goal of belief revision systems is to stay away from contradictions, i.e., to avoid the simultaneous belief of a proposition and its negation. Taking this into account, it would seem natural to constrain contexts to be consistent sets of hypotheses, not just any sets of hypotheses. Let us note, however, that determining whether a contradiction is derivable from a set of hypotheses is a difficult problem in logic, and thus the condition that contexts are not inconsistent may be very difficult to enforce. For that reason, we may settle for the weaker condition that contexts are not *known* to be inconsistent. Given the knowledge state $[[KB, KIS]]$ and a context C, the condition $\forall (s \in KIS)(s \not\subseteq C)$ guarantees that the context C is *not known* to be inconsistent.

However, it may be the case that someone desires to perform reasoning within the belief space defined by an inconsistent context (a kind of counterfactual reasoning). In SWM*, the existence of contradictions is not as damaging as in classical logic, in which anything can be derived from a contradiction. Besides the dependency-propagation mechanism of relevance logic used in SWM*, this is another advantage in using relevance logic to support belief revision systems. In classical logic, a contradiction implies anything; thus, in a belief revision system based on classical logic, whenever a contradiction is derived, it should be discarded immediately. In a relevance-logic-based belief revision system, we may allow the existence of a contradiction in the knowledge base without the danger of filling the knowledge base with unwanted deductions: all a contradiction indicates is that any inference depending on *all the* hypotheses underlying the contradiction is of no value.

Thus, in SNeBR one may not want to bother discarding hypotheses after a contradiction is detected, since the contradiction will not affect the entire system. For these reasons, the condition that a context is not known to be inconsistent will not be compulsory but rather advisable if one doesn't explicitly want to perform reasoning in a belief space that is known to be inconsistent.

5.2 Detection of contradictions

Let us now consider how SNeBR acts when a contradiction is detected. We discuss two kinds of contradiction detection: contradictions within the current belief space and contradictions within a belief space strictly containing the current belief space. The main difference between them is that the former may require changes in the current context and allows the deduction of new supported wffs, while the latter leaves this context unchanged and does not allow the addition of new wffs to the knowledge base.

Suppose that we are working in the belief space $\ll [[KB, KIS]], C \gg$ and that KB contains the supported wffs $< A, \tau_1, \alpha_1 >$ and $< \neg A, \tau_2, \alpha_2 >$. Suppose, furthermore that $\forall s \in KIS(\alpha_1 \cup \alpha_2) \neq s$. In this case, one of two things will happen:

1. *Only one of the contradictory wffs belongs to the current belief space.*[9] This means that $(\alpha_1 \cup \alpha_2) \not\subset C$. In this case, the contradiction is recorded (through the application of UIS), but nothing more happens. The effect of doing so is to record that some set of hypotheses is now known to be inconsistent.

2. *Both contradictory wffs belong to the current belief space.* This means that $(\alpha_1 \cup \alpha_2) \subset C$. In this case, UIS is applied, resulting in the updating of the sets known to be inconsistent. The rule of negation introduction can be applied (generating new supported wffs in the knowledge base) and a revision of beliefs should be performed if we want to work within a consistent belief space.

5.3 Summary

Disbelief propagation is accomplished by decreasing the current context. Since SNeBR only considers wffs in the current belief space, a decrease in the current context entails the removal of wffs from the current belief space.

---

[9]At least one of the contradictory wffs belongs to the current belief space, since a contradiction is detected whenever some newly derived wff contradicts some existing one, and newly derived wffs always belong to the current belief space.

The resolution of a contradiction in the current belief space entails a *contraction* in Gärdenfors and Makinson' sense [Gärdenfors and Makinson 88]. This contraction is performed through a function R^-:

$$R^-(\ll [[KB, KIS]], C \gg) = \ll [[KB, KIS]], C^- \gg$$

where $C^- \subset C$ and $C^- \neq C$. From SWM*'s standpoint, after the discovery of the inconsistent set α ($\alpha \subset C$), the removal of *any one* of the hypotheses in α is *guaranteed* to remove this contradiction from the current belief space and restore consistency to the current context if it was not known to be inconsistent before discovery of this contradiction.

6 The Revision of beliefs

The revision of beliefs is the ultimate task for which a belief revision system is designed. It uses all the previously discussed features in deciding about the possible culprits for a contradiction, in "removing" one of them from the knowledge base, and in changing its beliefs accordingly. The revision of beliefs is carried through a function R^* from belief spaces into belief spaces.

$$R^*(\ll [[KB, KIS]], C \gg) = \ll [[KB, KIS]], C\prime \gg .$$

The effect of this function will be to remove one or more hypotheses from the context C (the culprits for the contradiction) and possibly to add some new hypotheses to the context C, generating another context, $C\prime$, that is not known to be inconsistent.

No system has addressed the problem of selecting *the* culprit from the set of possible culprits for a contradiction, although some proposals have been made [Doyle 79], [McAllester 80], [Martins 83], [Campbell and Shapiro 86]. The problems addressed here concern the recording of the occurrence of the contradiction and the justification for disbelieving or for believing some propositions from its occurrence. In the actual version of SNeBR, the revision of beliefs is done by an outside system (a human) that picks the culprit(s) for the contradiction and generates the new context.

In this section we propose an architecture whose goal is to select *the* culprit for a contradiction detected during reasoning. This task will be handled by a component that we call the *belief reviser*. We envisage the task of the belief reviser as being carried out by an organized set of communicating agents or *critics*. Each one of them has expertise on a specific class of problems and supplies a tentative solution based on its own knowledge (i.e., blames the fault on a particular hypothesis). The possible set of solutions is then given to a referee that can take one of the following actions:

1. Select one of the hypotheses as the culprit, based on the suggestions received and the possible hierarchy among the critics who supplied them;

2. Ask a critic the reason why some hypothesis is being selected as the culprit. This action may be used to inform the user of the system about the reason why a particular hypothesis was deleted;

3. Report failure to the user of the system and ask for help in the task of culprit selection.

We envisage each of the critics as being held responsible for its recommendations. If a decision is made, by suggestion of some critic, to drop an hypothesis that is later on recognized to have not been responsible for the contradiction, then this critic is penalized and its future suggestions will be less important; likewise, a critic whose suggestion turns out to be profitable is rewarded and its suggestions become more important.

Details of this proposal can be found in [Martins and Cravo 89].

7 Examples

7.1 Example 1: flying horses

Suppose that we begin with the knowledge state $[[\{\}, \{\}]]$, and that we add the following supported wffs using the rule of hypothesis.[10]

$swff1 : \; < White(Pegasus), hyp, \{wff1\} >$

---

[10]We use the notation $swff1 : \; < White(Pegasus), hyp, \{wff1\} >$ to denote that $< White(Pegasus), hyp, \{White(Pegasus)\} >$ is a supported wff called $swff1$ and that the wff $White(Pegasus)$ is represented by $wff1$.

$swff2:$ $< Horse(Tornado), hyp, \{wff2\} >$
$swff3:$ $< \forall x(Horse(x) \rightarrow \neg Flies(x)), hyp, \{wff3\} >$
$swff4:$ $< \forall x(WingedHorse(x) \rightarrow Flies(x)), hyp, \{wff4\} >$
$swff5:$ $< \forall x(WingedHorse(x) \rightarrow Horse(x)), hyp, \{wff5\} >$
$swff6:$ $< \forall x(WingedHorse(x) \rightarrow HasWings(x)), hyp, \{wff6\} >$
$swff7:$ $< WingedHorse(Pegasus), hyp, \{wff7\} >$

At this point our knowledge state is:

$$[[\{swff1, swff2, swff3, swff4, swff5, swff6, swff7\}, \{\}]].$$

Suppose that we are performing reasoning in the belief space:

$$\ll [[\{swff1, swff2, swff3, swff4, swff5, swff6, swff7\}, \{\}]],$$
$$\{wff1, wff2, wff3, wff4, wff5, wff6, wff7\} \gg.$$

In this belief space we can derive $swff8$ and $swff9$:

$swff8:$ $< \neg Flies(Pegasus), der, \{wff3, wff5, wff7\} >$
$swff9:$ $< Flies(Pegasus), der, \{wff4, wff7\} >$

And thus discover that the set of hypotheses $\{wff3, wff4, wff5, wff7\}$ is inconsistent. When this happens the rule of UIS is applied resulting in the following updated knowledge state:

$$[[\{swff1, swff2, swff3, swff4, swff5, swff6, swff7, swff8, swff9\},$$
$$\{\{wff3, wff4, wff5, wff7\}\}]].$$

If further reasoning is to be performed, we are advised to revise the system's beliefs by removing from the current context at least one hypothesis from the set $\{wff3, wff4, wff5, wff7\}$. The most natural decision would be to drop the hypothesis that $\forall x(WingedHorse(x) \rightarrow Horse(x))$, and to consider the belief space:

$$\ll [[\{swff1, swff2, swff3, swff4, swff5, swff6, swff7, swff8, swff9\},$$
$$\{\{wff3, wff4, wff5, wff7\}\}]],$$
$$\{wff1, wff2, wff3, wff4, wff6, wff7\} \gg.$$

7.2 Example 2: the Russell set

Suppose we have the knowledge state:

$$[[\{< \exists s \forall x((x \in x) \rightarrow x \in s) \land (x \in s \rightarrow \neg(x \in x))), hyp, \{wff1\}\} >, \{\}]].$$

In the belief space defined by the context $\{wff1\}$ we can derive $swff2$ (using the rule of existential elimination) and $swff3$ (using the rule of universal elimination): "S" is *the* set containing precisely those sets that do not contain themselves.

$swff2$: $< \forall x((\neg(x \in x) \rightarrow x \in S) \land (x \in S \rightarrow \neg(x \in x))), der, \{wff1\} >$
$swff3$: $< (\neg(S \in S) \rightarrow S \in S) \land (S \in S \rightarrow \neg(S \in S)), der, \{wff1\} >$

If we know add to the knowledge base the proposition that states that "S" is contained in itself ($swff4$) and perform reasoning in the belief space defined by the context $\{wff1, wff4\}$ we can obtain $swff5$ and $swff6$:

$swff4$: $< S \in S, hyp, \{wff4\} >$
$swff5$: $< S \in S, \rightarrow \neg(S \in S), der, \{wff1\} >$
$swff6$: $< \neg(S \in S), der, \{wff1, wff4\} >$

At this point a contradiction is detected between $swff4$ and $swff6$, triggering the application of UIS, which originates the knowledge state:

$$[[\{swff1, swff2, swff3, swff4, swff5, swff6\}, \{\{wff1, wff4\}\}]]$$

We can apply the rule of $\wedge I$ between $swff4$ and $swff6$ and subsequently $\neg I$, to originate $swff7$:

$$swff7: \; < \neg(S \in S), ext, \{wff1\} >$$

We now revise the system's beliefs by applying the following contraction:

$$R^-(\ll [[\{swff1, swff2, swff3, swff4, swff5, swff6, swff7\},$$
$$\{\{wff1, wff4\}\}]],$$
$$\{wff1, wff4\} \gg) =$$
$$\ll [[\{swff1, swff2, swff3, swff4, swff5, swff6, swff7\},$$
$$\{\{wff1, wff4\}\}]],$$
$$\{wff1\} \gg$$

We can perform further reasoning, generating by $swff8$ by $\wedge E$ applied to $swff3$ and $swff9$ by MP applied between $swff7$ and $swff8$:

$$swff8: \; < \neg(S \in S) \rightarrow S \in S, der, \{wff1\} >$$
$$swff9: \; < S \in S, ext, \{wff1\} >$$

Again, UIS is applied between $swff7$ and $swff9$ resulting in the knowledge state:

$$[[\{swff1, swff2, swff3, swff4, swff5, swff6, swff7, swff8, swff9\},$$
$$\{\{wff1, wff4\}, \{wff1\}\}]].$$

If further reasoning is to be performed in a consistent belief space then $wff1$ (which is itself inconsistent) must be removed from the current context.

8 Summary

We presented a belief revision system based on a logic specifically conceived to support belief revision systems, discussed the properties of the system independently of its implementation (the abstract system), and presented a particular implementation of our abstract model (SNeBR) using the SNePS Semantic Network Processing System.

A version of SNeBR [Martins 83], [Pinto-Ferreira, Mamede, and Martins 89] is actually part of the SNePS system [Shapiro 79], [Shapiro and Rapaport 87], written in COMMON LISP and running on Explorer and Symbolics LISP Machines, Sun Stations, and VAX systems at the Department of Computer Science, State University of New York at Buffalo, and at the Instituto Superior Técnico (School of Engineering of the Technical University of Lisbon, Portugal).

9 Acknowledgements

Stuart C. Shapiro helped in the development of SNeBR and contributed with the Russell Set example. Maria R. Cravo contributed for the architecture discussed in Section 6 and with the Flying Horses example. Many thanks also go to John Corcoran, Ernesto Morgado, Nuno J. Mamede, J. Terry Nutter, Carlos Pinto-Ferreira, William J. Rapaport, and members of the SNePS Research Group for their criticisms and suggestions.

This work was partially supported by Junta Nacional de Investigação Científica e Tecnológica (JNICT), under Grant 87-107 and by the Instituto Nacional de Investigação Científica.

Martins J., "Belief Revision", in *Encyclopedia of Artificial Intelligence*, Shapiro (ed.), New York, N.Y.: John Wiley and Sons, pp.58-62, 1987.

Martins J.P. and Cravo M.R., "Revising Beliefs Through Communicating Critics", Technical Report GIA 89/08, Lisbon, Portugal: Instituto Superior Tecnico, Technical University of Lisbon, 1989.

Martins J. and Shapiro S., "A Model for Belief Revision", *Artificial Intelligence 35*, No.1, pp.25-79, 1988.

McAllester D., "An Outlook on Truth Maintenance", AI Memo 551, Cambridge, MA: Massachusetts Institute of Technology, AI Lab., 1980.

McDermott D., "Contexts and Data Dependencies: A Synthesis", *IEEE Transactions on Pattern Analysis and Machine Intelligence PAMI-5*, No.3, pp.237-246, 1983.

Pinto-Ferreira C., Mamede N.J., and Martins J.P., "SNIP 2.1 – The SNePS Inference Package", Technical Report GIA 89/05, Lisbon, Portugal: Instituto Superior Tecnico, Technical University of Lisbon, 1989.

Shapiro S., "The SNePS Semantic Network Processing System", in *Associative Networks: Representation and Use of Knowledge by Computers*, Findler (ed.), New York, N.Y.: Academic Press, pp.179–203, 1979.

Shapiro S. and Rapaport W., "SNePS Considered as a Fully Intensional Propositional Semantic Network", in *The Knowledge Frontier: Essays in the Representation of Knowledge*, McCalla and Cercone (eds.), New York, N.Y.: Springer-Verlag, pp.262–315, 1987.

Shapiro S. and Wand M., "The Relevance of Relevance", Technical Report No.46, Bloomington, IN: Computer Science Department, Indiana University, 1976.

Martins J., "Belief Revision", in *Encyclopedia of Artificial Intelligence*, Shapiro (ed.), New York, N.Y.: John Wiley and Sons, pp.58-62, 1987.

Martins J.P. and Cravo M.R., "Revising Beliefs Through Communicating Critics", Technical Report GIA 89/08, Lisbon, Portugal: Instituto Superior Tecnico, Technical University of Lisbon, 1989.

Martins J. and Shapiro S., "A Model for Belief Revision", *Artificial Intelligence 35*, No.1, pp.25-79, 1988.

McAllester D., "An Outlook on Truth Maintenance", AI Memo 551, Cambridge, MA: Massachusetts Institute of Technology, AI Lab., 1980.

McDermott D., "Contexts and Data Dependencies: A Synthesis", *IEEE Transactions on Pattern Analysis and Machine Intelligence PAMI-5*, No.3, pp.237-246, 1983.

Pinto-Ferreira C., Mamede N.J., and Martins J.P., "SNIP 2.1 – The SNePS Inference Package", Technical Report GIA 89/05, Lisbon, Portugal: Instituto Superior Tecnico, Technical University of Lisbon, 1989.

Shapiro S., "The SNePS Semantic Network Processing System", in *Associative Networks: Representation and Use of Knowledge by Computers*, Findler (ed.), New York, N.Y.: Academic Press, pp.179–203, 1979.

Shapiro S. and Rapaport W., "SNePS Considered as a Fully Intensional Propositional Semantic Network", in *The Knowledge Frontier: Essays in the Representation of Knowledge*, McCalla and Cercone (eds.), New York, N.Y.: Springer-Verlag, pp.262–315, 1987.

Shapiro S. and Wand M., "The Relevance of Relevance", Technical Report No.46, Bloomington, IN: Computer Science Department, Indiana University, 1976.

Some Results on Theory Revision

Karl Schlechta

IBM Germany, IWBS W&S3

POBox 80 08 80

D-7000 Stuttgart 80

West Germany

and University of Hamburg

Abstract

The problem of Theory Revision is to "add" a formula to a theory, while preserving consistency and making only minimal changes to the original theory. A natural way to uniquely determine the process is by imposing an order of "epistemic entrenchment" on the formulae, as done by Gärdenfors and Makinson. We improve their results as follows: We define orders which generate unique revision processes too, but in addition, 1) have nice logical properties, 2) are independent of the theory considered, and thus well suited for iterated revision and computational purposes, 3) have a natural probabilistic construction. Next, we show that the completeness problems of Theory Revision carry over to a certain extent to an approach based on revising axiom systems. In the last section, we consider a more general situation: First, we will have only a partial order (on axioms) at our disposal. Second, the underlying logic will be non-monotonic. Ideas taken from defeasible inheritance will help us solve the problem.

1   Introduction

Recent years have seen an increasing interest in theory revision, which has partly centered around the work of Gärdenfors and his co-authors ([AGM], [AM], [G], [GM], [M]). In [G] and [GM], the problem of choice in theory revision (more precisely: maxichoice contraction/revision) finds a natural solution in the concept of epistemic entrenchment: An order on the formulae tells us which to choose. The orders of [G] and [GM] have, however, theoretical as well as computational drawbacks: 1) They are tailored to fit the requirements of theory revision and will not respect other natural demands like $\phi \leq \psi$ iff $\neg\psi \leq \neg\phi$ (if I tend to believe more in ψ than in ϕ, then I might tend to believe more in $\neg\phi$ than in $\neg\psi$) . 2) For each revision of a new theory (in a fixed language) we have to find a new order, so iterated revision means iterated effort in ordering. Note that "theory" is used here in a technical sense: a deductively closed set of formulae (the deductive closure of a database). Thus two theories might be closely related, and are not necessarily as different, as say a physical and a medical theory. So iterated theory revision in this sense is a very common phenomenon for cognitive systems. The main aim of this paper is to show how to overcome these drawbacks: 1) To prove that one order of a very simple kind will do for all theories of a given language and thus for all revisions (Proposition 2.1). 2) To show how to construct such an order with particularly nice and natural properties for countable propositional languages (Propositions 2.3 and 2.4). For a different treatment of iterated revision, see Spohn's work, e.g. [Sp].

The last two chapters are independent of the first part. In Section 1 and 2, we consider what Gärdenfors and his co-authors call maxichoice contraction - choosing a maximal subset K' of K, such that $K' \nvdash A$. As pointed out in [AGM], [G] and [M], maxichoice contraction suffers from a completeness problem. Our point in Section 3 is, that Theory Revision with underlying axiom sets is plagued by essentially the same problems (and some more). We consider systems $< K, A >$, where K is a deductively closed set of formulae, and A is a set of axioms for K. Theory Revision for $< K, A >$ will essentially amount to the choice of a suitable subset of A. Proposition 3.1 shows that there is a continuum between too coarse axiom sets (and too coarse revision) and too fine-grained axiom sets (resulting in full completeness at revision).

In Section 4, we will treat a (partially) order sorted language of predicate calculus, augmented by defeasible (default) information. The "soft" information will be "appended" to sorts in the sense that "normally fly" is appended to the sort "birds". More specific information (ordered by sort inclusion) is supposed to be the more reliable one in case of conflict. Incomparable (recall that the order is only partial) information is to be treated fairly (sceptically in the sense of defeasible inheritance). We shall discuss several methods of choosing a reasonable consistent subset of a partially ordered set of conflicting "hard" and default information.

Remark   The material covered in Section 1 - 3 will appear in the Notre Dame Journal of Formal Logic.

For the convenience of the reader, we now repeat the - for our purposes - main definitions and results of Gärdenfors and Makinson. But before that, let's give an example to point out the basic problem of underdeterminacy.

A Problem of Theory Revision: Let T be a theory, i.e. a deductively closed set of formulae. Suppose $\{A, B\} \subseteq T$, thus $A \wedge B \epsilon T$, and we would like to revise T to a maximal theory $T' \subseteq T$ such that $A \wedge B \notin T'$. So $\{A, B\} \subseteq T$ is impossible, and we have to withdraw A, B, or both. (Leaving aside extreme cases like $\vdash A \leftrightarrow B$) "both" is unsatisfactory, as T' should be maximal. So we can and have to chose which of A or B, but logic won't tell us which. If we have an order $A < B$ telling us that we like A less than B, we are finished. This is the idea of

Gärdenfors's and Makinson's Solution: In the following, we adopt Gärdenfors' and Makinson's terminology to make this article more readable for those familiar with their work. They denote by "theory contraction" the process of removing a formula from a theory, and by "theory revision" adding a formula A to a theory T so that the resulting theory T' is consistent (if A is) and $A \epsilon T'$. This is made precise in the following

Definition 1.1 *Given a language $\mathcal{L}$, an inference rule $\vdash$ (we will not be more specific here, and the interested reader is referred e.g. to [G]), and a "knowledge set" K, i.e. a set of formulae of $\mathcal{L}$ closed under $\vdash$, then a function $K- :$ Formulae of $\mathcal{L} \to$ Sets of Formulae of $\mathcal{L}$ is called a contraction function for K, iff it satisfies the postulates (K-1) to (K-8) below, and a function $K* :$ Formulae of $\mathcal{L} \to$ Sets of Formulae of $\mathcal{L}$ is called a revision function for K, iff it satisfies the postulates (K*1) to (K*8) below.*

Proposition 1.1 *Both notions are interdefinable by the following equations: $K * A := (K - \neg A) + A$ (where $L+B$ is the deductive closure of $L \cup \{B\}$) i.e., if $K-$ is a contraction function, then $K*$ so defined is a revision function, and $K - A := K \cap (K * \neg A)$ i.e. if $K*$ is a revision function, then $K-$ so defined will be a contraction function.*

The proofs are straightforward. $\square$

We now state the axioms for $K-$ and $K*$, some very short comments are given in parentheses, the reader will find more motivation e.g. in [G]:

Definition 1.2 :

(K-1) $K - A$ is a knowledge set (i.e. deductively closed under $\vdash$)

(K-2) $K - A \subseteq K$

(K-3) If $A \notin K$, then $K - A = K$ (the desired result already applies to K)

(K-4) If $\not\vdash A$, then $A \notin K - A$ (success, if possible)

(K-5) $K \subseteq (K - A) + A$ (where $L+B$ is the deductive closure of $L \cup \{B\}$, the "postulate of recovery")

(K-6) If $\vdash A \leftrightarrow B$, then $K - A = K - B$

(K-7) $(K - A) \cap (K - B) \subseteq K - (A \wedge B)$ (a condition of minimality)

(K-8) If $A \notin K - (A \wedge B)$, then $K - (A \wedge B) \subseteq K - A$ (In general, the more specific a formula is, the less the change necessary for revision. If $A \notin K - (A \wedge B)$, however, then contraction by $A \wedge B$ will do already.)

   and

(K*1) $K * A$ is a knowledge set

(K*2) $A \epsilon K * A$ (success)

(K*3) $K * A \subseteq K + A$ (the purpose of $K*A$ is to "add" A to K, if consistently possible)

(K*4) If $\neg A \notin K$, then $K + A \subseteq K * A$, see (K*3)

(K*5) $K * A = K_\perp$ ($K_\perp$ the inconsistent theory) only if $\vdash \neg A$ (preserve consistency, if possible)

(K*6) If $\vdash A \leftrightarrow B$, then $K * A = K * B$

(K*7) $K * (A \wedge B) \subseteq (K * A) + B$ (consider (K*2) and minimality for motivation)

(K*8) If $\neg B \notin K * A$, then $(K * A) + B \subseteq K * (A \wedge B)$ (see (K*4) !)

By the above interdefinability result, it suffices for our purposes to consider contraction only in the following. As already pointed out, a suitable order on the formulae of $\mathcal{L}$ will give rise to a unique contraction function for maxichoice contraction. Gärdenfors and Makinson consider relations of "epistemic entrenchment", where $A \leq B$ means that B is more deeply entrenched, and we are more willing to give up A than to give up B, if need be, and provided we have a choice. This is made precise in

Definition 1.3 *Let $\leq = \leq_K$ be a relation relative to a knowledge set K on the formulae of $\mathcal{L}$ such that*

(EE1) If $A \leq B$ and $B \leq C$, then $A \leq C$ (transitivity)

(EE2) If $A \vdash B$, then $A \leq B$ (If $A \vdash B$, then we believe at least as much in B as in A.)

(EE3) For any A and B, $A \leq A \wedge B$ or $B \leq A \wedge B$ (Essentially this property makes $\leq$ a total order, and gives the necessary decision for contraction.)

(EE4) When $K \neq K_\perp$ (the set of all formulae of $\mathcal{L}$), then $A \notin K$ iff $A \leq B$ for all B (It is here that K matters !)

(EE5) If $B \leq A$ for all B, then $\vdash A$. (Only Truth is maximally entrenched). We then call $\leq$ a relation of epistemic entrenchment for K.

We may read $\leq$ as strength of belief, where everything outside K is not believed at all.

Again, we have an interdefinability result:

Proposition 1.2 *The function $K-$ and the ordering $\leq_K$ are interdefinable in the following sense:*
Define $K - A$ by $B\epsilon K - A :\leftrightarrow B\epsilon K$ and $(A < A \vee B$ or $\vdash A)$ $(A < B$ means: $A \leq B$, and not $B \leq A$). If $\leq$ satisfies (EE1)-(EE5), then $K-$ so defined will satisfy (K-1)-(K-8).
Define $A \leq B$ (on the formulae of $\mathcal{L}$) by $A \leq B :\leftrightarrow A \notin K - (A \wedge B)$ or $\vdash A \wedge B$. If $K-$ satisfies (K-1)-(K-8), then $\leq$ so defined will satisfy (EE1)-(EE5).

Outline of the results presented here: As emphasized, any $\leq$ satisfying (EE1)-(EE5) will depend essentially on K. Thus, for iterated revision, as K changes, we need a new order $\leq_K$ for every step. Our Proposition 2.1 will show that, given a preference relation $\leq$ for $\mathcal{L}$, i.e. a total ordering of the formulae of $\mathcal{L}$ which satisfies some very natural requirements (and which correspond well with the order of the Lindenbaum-Tarski algebra), we can construct from that $\leq$ for all K an order $\leq_K$ satisfying (EE1)-(EE5). Proposition 2.2 will show the inverse: Given an epistemic entrenchment relation, we have a preference relation too, such that the construction of Definition 2.1 will recover the epistemic entrenchment relation again. Proposition 2.3 and 2.4 will show how to naturally define an order satisfying the prerequisites of Proposition 2.1.

2 Preference Relations

Definition 2.1 *a. Call a relation $\leq$ on the formulae of $\mathcal{L}$ a preference relation for $\mathcal{L}$ iff $\leq$ is a binary relation such that (1.) $A \vdash B \rightarrow A \leq B$, (2.) $\leq$ is transitive, (3.) $\leq$ is total, (4.) $\forall B.B \leq A \rightarrow \vdash A$*
b. Let K be closed under $\vdash$, and a preference relation $\leq$ for $\mathcal{L}$ be fixed. Define $A \trianglelefteq B$ iff (D1.) $A \vdash B$ or (D2.) $A \notin K$ or (D3.) $B = A \wedge C$ and $A \leq C$ and $A \wedge C = B \epsilon K$. Furthermore, define $\preceq$ as the transitive closure of $\trianglelefteq$.

Fact 2.1 *There is a standard way of establishing $A \preceq B$: Let $A, C\epsilon K$, then there is B such that $A \trianglelefteq A \wedge B$ by D3, and $A \wedge B \trianglelefteq C$ by D1 iff $A \leq A \rightarrow C$.*

Proof: "$\leftarrow$": As $A, C\epsilon K$, $A \wedge (A \rightarrow C)\epsilon K$, so $A \trianglelefteq_{D3} A \wedge (A \rightarrow C) \trianglelefteq_{D1} C$.
"$\rightarrow$": As $\vdash A \wedge B \rightarrow C$, $\vdash B \rightarrow (A \rightarrow C)$, and by Conditions 1 and 2 above $A \leq B \leq A \rightarrow C$. □

Proposition 2.1 *If $\leq$ is a preference relation for $\mathcal{L}$, and $\preceq$ defined as in Definition 2.1, then $\preceq$ satisfies (EE1)-(EE5).*

Thus, given one global preference relation for $\mathcal{L}$, we can easily obtain epistemic entrenchment relations for all knowledge sets K of $\mathcal{L}$.

Proof: We first show two claims, the proof will then be trivial.
Claim 1: For no $A \epsilon K$, $B \notin K$ we have $A \preceq B$. Proof: Suppose the contrary. Let $A = A_1 \trianglelefteq A_2 \trianglelefteq \ldots \trianglelefteq A_n = B$. We have to "cross the border between K and $\mathcal{L} - K$" somewhere: There is $A_i \trianglelefteq A_{i+1}$ such that $A_i \epsilon K$, $A_{i+1} \notin K$. Examine the cases of $\trianglelefteq$. D1 can't be, as $A_i \epsilon K$, $A_i \vdash A_{i+1}$ implies $A_{i+1} \epsilon K$. D2 can't be, as $A_i \epsilon K$. D3 can't be, as $A_{i+1} \notin K$. Contradiction. $\square$ (Claim 1)
Claim 2: $\forall B . B \preceq A$ implies $\vdash A$. Proof: (Induction on the length of the $\trianglelefteq$ - chain.) By Condition 1., it suffices to consider B:=True. True $\trianglelefteq_{D1} A$ implies $\vdash A$. True $\trianglelefteq_{D2} A$ can't be, as True ϵ K. True $\trianglelefteq_{D3} A = True \wedge C$ implies $True \leq C$ implies $\vdash C$ by maximality of True and 4. of $\leq$. $\square$ (Claim 2)
We prove the proposition: (EE1) is trivial by definition. (EE2) by D1. (EE3) We have to prove $A \preceq A \wedge B$ or $B \preceq A \wedge B$. By 3. of $\leq$, $A \leq B$ or $B \leq A$. Case 1: $A \wedge B \epsilon K$. If $A \leq B$, then $A \trianglelefteq A \wedge B$ by D3. $B \leq A$ analogously. Case 2: $A \wedge B \notin K$. Then $A \notin K$ or $B \notin K$, continue with D2. (EE4) " $\rightarrow$ " $A \notin K$ implies $A \trianglelefteq B$ by D2 for all B. " $\leftarrow$ " : Let $K \neq K_\perp$, $A \preceq B$ for all B. Suppose $A \epsilon K$. By $K \neq K_\perp$, there is $B \notin K$, and by prerequisite $A \preceq B$, contradicting Claim 1. (EE5) Claim 2. $\square$ (Proposition 2.1)

Gärdenfors (in personal communication) has raised the question whether we can, given a relation of epistemic entrenchment, define from this relation a preference relation and recover the epistemic entrenchment relation again as in Definition 2.1. The answer is "yes" (in a simplified version due to David Makinson):

Proposition 2.2 *Let $\leq_K$ be an epistemic entrenchment relation for a knowledge set K. Then, by definition, $\leq_K$ is a preference relation and $\preceq$ defined for this $\leq_K$ and K as in Definition 2.1.b is equal to $\leq_K$.*

Proof: " $\preceq \subseteq \leq_K$ ": It suffices to prove $\trianglelefteq \subseteq \leq_K$. D1 and D2 are trivial. D3: Let $A \trianglelefteq A \wedge B$ by $A \leq_K B$. If $B \leq_K A \wedge B$, then $A \leq_K B \leq_K A \wedge B$, and we are finished by (EE3). " $\leq_K \subseteq \preceq$ " : Let $A \leq_K B$. If $A \notin K$, then $A \trianglelefteq B$ by D2. If $A \epsilon K$, then $B \epsilon K$ by (EE4), so $A \wedge B \epsilon K$, thus $A \trianglelefteq_{A \leq_K B} A \wedge B \trianglelefteq_{\vdash} B$. $\square$

We now turn to the task of defining such a total order on the formulae of $\mathcal{L}$ in a natural way.

Let, in the following, $\mathcal{D}$ be the Lindenbaum-Tarski algebra for the language $\mathcal{L}$ and the empty theory. (Thus, elements of $\mathcal{D}$ have the form $[\phi]$, where ϕ is a formula of $\mathcal{L}$, and $[\phi] = [\psi]$ iff $\vdash \phi \leftrightarrow \psi$. Moreover, $[\phi] \wedge [\psi] := [\phi \wedge \psi]$, $-[\phi] := [\neg\phi]$, and $[\phi] \leq [\psi] :\leftrightarrow [\phi] \wedge [\psi] = [\phi]$.)

We have a first constructive result:

Lemma 2.1 *Extending the natural ordering on the formulae of $\mathcal{L}$ given by $\mathcal{D}$ to a total order, preserving [True] as the only maximal element, will give a preference relation for $\mathcal{L}$, and thus, by Proposition 2.1, epistemic entrenchment relations $\leq_K$ for all knowledge sets K of $\mathcal{L}$.* $\square$

Next, we assign probability values to formulae of $\mathcal{L}$, i.e. each $\phi \epsilon \mathcal{L}$ will have a real value $\nu(\phi)$, and the natural order of the real numbers will order the formulae too. Of course, logically equivalent formulae should be given the same probability. We proceed indirectly, assigning first probabilities to models, and defining the probability of a formula as the sum of the probabilities of its models. The above equivalence condition will then be trivially true. It is easily seen (Proposition 2.3), that our construction will give a preference relation $\leq$ for $\mathcal{L}$ as needed to define the epistemic entrenchment relations $\leq_K$. We can improve our result and the equivalence condition to obtain ($\phi \leq \psi$ and $\psi \leq \phi$) iff $\vdash \phi \leftrightarrow \psi$ (Proposition 2.4). For this end, we use algebraic closure properties of the reals (Fact 2.4). We can thus construct in a natural way a total (and natural) extension of the natural order of the Lindenbaum-Tarski algebra $\mathcal{D}$, such that ($[\phi] \leq [\psi]$ and $[\psi] \leq [\phi]$) is equivalent to $[\phi] = [\psi]$. In conclusion, we remark that the whole process can be easily relativized to a fixed theory, by considering only models of that theory (see Definition 2.5).

But first, we need some constructions:

Let $\mathcal{A}$ be the $\sigma - Algebra$ (i.e. the $\aleph_1 - complete$ Boolean algebra) of Lebesgue-measurable sets restricted to subsets of the unit interval $[0,1)$. Let μ be the usual Lebesgue measure. (The reader unfamiliar with these notions will find definitions and properties in any book on measure and integration theory.)

Definition 2.2 *Let $< x_i : i \epsilon \omega >$ be a sequence of reals in the open interval $(0,1)$. Define by induction: $a_0 := [0, x_0)$, $b_0 := \{0, x_0, 1\}$. Let a_n, b_n be defined ($n \epsilon \omega$). b_n will be a set of $2^{n+1} + 1$ elements, a_n a disjoint union of 2^n non-empty intervals. Let $b_n = \{y_j : j < 2^{n+1} + 2\}$, the y_j in increasing order. Define $a_{n+1} := \bigcup \{ [y_j, y_j + (y_{j+1} - y_j) * x_{n+1}) : j < 2^{n+1} + 1 \}$*

and $b_{n+1} := b_n \cup \{y_j + (y_{j+1} - y_j) * x_{n+1} : j < 2^{n+1} + 1\}$. *Finally, set* $\overline{a_n} :=$ $[0,1) - a_n$. *(See Diagram 2.1 below.)*

Let $\mathcal{B}$ be the $\aleph_1$ − *complete subalgebra of* $\mathcal{A}$ *generated by* $\{a_i : i\epsilon\omega\}$

Fact 2.2 *For the* a_i *thus defined we have: (1)* $\mu(a_n) = x_n$, *(2)* $\mu(\overline{a_n}) =$ $1 - \mu(a_n)$ *(trivial), (3)* $\mu(\cap\{c_n : n\epsilon X\}) = \Pi\{\mu(c_n) : n\epsilon X\}$ *where* c_n *is either* a_n *or* $\overline{a_n}$ *for* $X \subseteq \omega$ *finite, by the "independence" of the construction. This property is essential to all that follows.* □

Let, in the rest of the paper, $\mathcal{L} = \{p_i : i\epsilon\omega\}$ be a countable language of propositional calculus.

Definition 2.3 *a) Define* $f : \mathcal{L} \to \{a_i : i\epsilon\omega\}$ *by* $f(p_i) := a_i$, *i.e.* $\mu(f(p_i)) =$ x_i. *b) Let* M *be the set of assignments of truth values to finite subsets of* $\mathcal{L}$, $t\epsilon M$, *t defined on* $\mathcal{L}' \subseteq \mathcal{L}$. *(It suffices to consider finite subsets, as standard propositional calculus admits only finite formulae.) Define* $g(t) := \cap\{a_i :$ $p_i\epsilon\mathcal{L}', t(p_i) = true\} \cap \cap\{\overline{a_n} : p_i\epsilon\mathcal{L}', t(p_i) = false\}$.

Thus, $\mu(g(t)) = \mu(\cap\{a_i : p_i\epsilon\mathcal{L}', t(p_i) = true\} \cap \cap\{\overline{a_n} : p_i\epsilon\mathcal{L}', t(p_i) =$ $false\}) = \Pi\{x_i : p_i\epsilon\mathcal{L}', t(p_i) = true\} * \Pi\{1 - x_i : p_i\epsilon\mathcal{L}', t(p_i) = false\}$, and we have defined for every assignment $t\epsilon M$ a real value $\mu(g(t))$. There is a natural way to extend this function to formulae:

Definition 2.4 *Let* ϕ *be a formula with propositional variables* $p_i\epsilon\mathcal{L}_\phi \subseteq \mathcal{L}$ *finite.*
a) Let $Val(\phi) := \{t\epsilon M : dom(t) = \mathcal{L}_\phi, t(\phi) = true$, *i.e.* ϕ *is true under* $t\}$.
b) So we can define $\nu(\phi) := \Sigma \{\mu(g(t)) : t\epsilon Val(\phi)\}$. *(See Diagram 2.1.)*

Diagram 2.1: Let $\mathcal{L} = \{p,q\}$, t(p)=true, t(q)=false, t'(p)=false, t'(q)=true, $\phi = p \leftrightarrow \neg q$

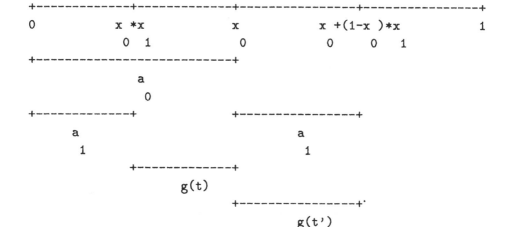

Thus, $\mu(a_0) = x_0$, $\mu(a_1) = x_1$, $\nu(\phi) = \mu(g(t)) + \mu(g(t')) = x_0 * (1 - x_1)$
$+ (1 - x_0) * x_1$.

Our construction has the following properties:

Lemma 2.2 :
1) $\nu(\phi)$ is independent of dom(t) in the following sense: Let $\mathcal{L}_\phi \subseteq \mathcal{L}' \subseteq \mathcal{L}$ finite. Then $\nu(\phi) := \Sigma \{\mu(g(t)) : t\epsilon Val(\phi)\} = \Sigma \{\mu(g(t)) : t\epsilon M, dom(t) = \mathcal{L}', t(\phi) = true\}$.
2) By definition of Val and ν, logically equivalent formulae will have the same real value $\nu(\phi)$.
3) $\vdash \phi \to \psi$ implies $\nu(\phi) \leq \nu(\psi)$. (To see this, consider $\mathcal{L}' = \mathcal{L}_\phi \cup \mathcal{L}_\psi$, use 1) and the fact, that every assignment which makes ϕ true, will make ψ true too.)
4) $\nu(\neg\phi) = 1 - \nu(\phi)$. (Use $\nu(true) = \Sigma \{\mu(g(t)) : t\epsilon M, dom(t) = \mathcal{L}' finite\} = 1$, $t(\phi) = true \leftrightarrow t(\neg\phi) = false$, and for $t, t'\epsilon M$ with the same domain $t \neq t' \to g(t) \cap g(t') = \emptyset$.)
5) Exactly the valid formulae will have real value $\nu(\phi) = 1$. ($g : \mathcal{D} \to \mathcal{B}$ (extended suitably to formulae) is an injective homomorphism of Boolean algebras, and use the above arguments.)
6) $\nu(\phi) \leq \nu(\psi) \leftrightarrow \nu(\neg\psi) \leq \nu(\neg\phi)$ (by 4).
7) $\nu(\phi \vee \psi) \leq \nu(\phi) \leftrightarrow \vdash \psi \to \phi$. " $\leftarrow$ " by 3). " $\to$ " : Suppose $\nvdash \psi \to \phi$. Thus $M' := \{t : t \models \phi\} \subset M := \{t : t \models \phi \vee \psi\}$, let $t\epsilon M - M'$. As $x_i\epsilon(0,1)$, $\mu g(t) \neq 0$, thus $\nu(\phi) := \Sigma\{\mu g(t) : t\epsilon M'\} < \Sigma\{\mu g(t) : t\epsilon M\} =: \nu(\phi \vee \psi)$.
8) We can't expect $\nu(\phi \wedge \psi) = \nu(\phi) * \nu(\psi)$ or $\nu(\phi \vee \psi) = \nu(\phi) + \nu(\psi)$, just think of $\phi = \psi$. These equations can only be valid if ϕ and ψ are independent. For this reason, we gave first a value to models, which are independent, and then to formulae. $\square$

We have thus proved our main constructive result:

Proposition 2.3 Let $p_i : i\epsilon\omega$ be given a probability $x_i\epsilon(0,1)$, then this gives rise naturally to probabilities $\nu(\phi)$ for any formula in $\mathcal{L}$, such that 1) - 6) of Lemma 2.2 are valid, and thus to a preference relation $\leq$ for $\mathcal{L}$, i.e. satisfying 1. - 4. of $\leq$ in Definition 2.1, and thus the prerequisites of Proposition 2.1. $\square$

Fact 2.3 Let $0 \leq a \leq b < 1$. Augment the natural order of the reals by setting $x \leq^+ y$ for all $a \leq x, y \leq b$, i.e. "identify" all elements of the interval $[a, b]$. Let ν be defined as in the construction leading to Proposition 2.3 and set $\phi \leq \psi$ iff $\nu(\phi) \leq \nu(\psi)$ or $\nu(\psi) \leq^+ \nu(\phi)$. Then $\leq$ is still a preference relation on $\mathcal{L}$.

Proof: In Definition 2.1, 1. and 3. are trivial, 4. holds by $b < 1$. But 2 is simple too: consider e.g. $x \leq y \leq^+ z$. If $x > z$, then $a \leq z \leq x \leq y \leq b$, and $x \leq^+ z$. $\square$

Example 2.1 *Consider now $\mathcal{L} := \{A, B, C\}$, and set $\mu f(A) := 1/2$, $\mu f(B) := 1/3$, $\mu f(C) := 1/5$, $a := 5/30$, $b := 10/30$, and identify in the interval $[a,b]$ as described in the above Fact. Then $\nu(A) = 15/30$, $\nu(B) = 10/30$, $\nu(A \wedge B) = 5/30$, $\nu(A \vee C) = 18/30$, $\nu(B \vee C) = 14/30$, $\nu((A \wedge B) \vee C) = 10/30$. By identification, $(A \wedge B) \vee C \leq A \wedge B$, but neither $A \vee C \leq A$ nor $B \vee C \leq B$.* $\square$

So far, it is quite possible that $\nu(\phi) = \nu(\psi)$, but $\nvdash \phi \leftrightarrow \psi$. We now make ν injective (modulo $\leftrightarrow$). Thus, we improve our result such that ($\phi \leq \psi$ and $\psi \leq \phi$) iff $\vdash \phi \leftrightarrow \psi$. Choosing the x_i of Definition 2.2 above according to the following fact on the reals will do the trick:

Fact 2.4 *Let $X := \{x_i : i\epsilon\omega\} \subset I \subseteq \mathcal{R}$ (the reals), I uncountable be given. Then there is $x'\epsilon I$ such that x' is not equal to any real that can be obtained by finite addition, subtraction, multiplication, division from elements of $\mathcal{Q} \cup X$ ($\mathcal{Q}$ the rationals). ($Card(I) > card(\mathcal{Q} \cup X) = \aleph_0$ suffices for the proof.)* $\square$

We choose the x_i for the above construction of the a_i in Definition 2.2 according to this fact. Suppose that ϕ, ψ are not equivalent, but $\nu(\phi) = \nu(\psi)$. Thus, there is an assignment t such that $t(\phi) \neq t(\psi)$. So $\bigcup\{g(t) : t\epsilon Val(\phi)\} \neq \bigcup\{g(t) : t\epsilon Val(\psi)\}$ (w.l.o.g. all t with the same domain $p_0 \ldots p_n$, and n chosen least such that the assumption is valid), but $\nu(\phi) = \nu(\psi)$. Thus, $\nu(\phi) = \Sigma_{i=0,m} \Pi_{j=0,n} y_{i,j}$, $\nu(\psi) = \Sigma_{i=0,m'} \Pi_{j=0,n} y'_{i,j}$, where the $y_{i,j}$, $y'_{i,j}$ are either x_j or $1 - x_j$. After multiplication, the equation looks like this: $s_1 + \ldots + s_k = t_1 + \ldots + t_l$, the s_u and t_u are of the form: 1 or $\pm x_{r_1} * \ldots * x_{r_h}$, and each x_j occurs at most once in each summand. After cancelling summands of the same form that occurr on both sides of the equation, x_n will still occurr in at least one of the summands, as n was chosen least. So, we can solve the equation (linear in x_n) for x_n and have $x_n = f(x_0 \ldots x_{n-1})$, where f is composed of addition, subtraction, multiplication, division - contradicting Fact 2.4. As the x_i can be chosen within any distance > 0 from a desired value, choosing x_i according to this fact is no real restriction. We have thus obtained our injectivity result and shown

Proposition 2.4 *Let $p_i : i\epsilon\omega$ be given a probability $x_i\epsilon(0,1)$, chosen according to Fact 2.4, then this gives rise naturally to probabilities $\nu(\phi)$ for any formula in $\mathcal{L}$, such that 1) - 6) of Lemma 2.2 are valid, and ($\phi \leq \psi$ and $\psi \leq \phi$) iff $\vdash \phi \leftrightarrow \psi$. In other words, this defines a total (and natural) extension of the natural order of the Lindenbaum-Tarski algebra $\mathcal{D}$, and, in addition, ($[\phi] \leq [\psi]$ and $[\psi] \leq [\phi]$) iff $[\phi] = [\psi]$.* $\square$

Remark 2.1 *So far, we have worked over the empty theory and its Linden-baum Tarski algebra. It is easy to extend our results to non-empty theories, by considering only models of that theory in our Definition 2.4.*

Thus, we can define e.g.

Definition 2.5 *Let T be a theory in $\mathcal{L}_T \subseteq \mathcal{L}$ finite, and $\mathcal{L}' := \mathcal{L}_T \cup \mathcal{L}_\phi$. Set*

$$\nu_T(\phi) := \frac{\sum\{\mu(g(t)) : dom(t) = \mathcal{L}', t(\phi) = true, t(\psi) = true \text{ for all } \psi \epsilon T\}}{\sum\{\mu(g(t)) : dom(t) = \mathcal{L}', t(\psi) = true \text{ for all } \psi \epsilon T\}}$$

So $\nu_T(\phi)$ and $\nu_T(\phi')$ will be equal, iff the models that make T true treat ϕ and ϕ' in the same way.

Remark 2.2 *We can work backwards in the following sense too: Suppose we are given a set of formulae $\{\phi_i : i \epsilon I\}$ and preferences (probabilities) $\pi(\phi_i)$ for all $i \epsilon I$. Can we find a sequence $x_i : i \epsilon \omega$ such that, constructing as above, $\pi(\phi_i) = \nu(\phi_i) := \sum\{\mu(g(t)) : dom(t) = \mathcal{L}_{\phi_i}, t \models \phi_i\}$? The answer is trivial and canonical. We have a number of equations $\pi(\phi_i) = \sum \{ \Pi\{x_j : t(p_j) = true\} * \Pi\{(1 - x_j) : t(p_j) = false\} : t \epsilon Val(\phi_i) \}$ and any solution $\{x_j : j \epsilon \omega, x_j \epsilon (0,1)\}$ (if there is one) of this system of equations, and $\{a_j : j \epsilon \omega\}$ chosen as above will do what we need.*

3 Measuring Theories, and an Outlook for a Different Treatment of Theory Revision

In this section, we discuss three somewhat different approaches to Theory Contraction. In the first two, we extend our measure from formulae to theories, and use it to do contraction. The first attempt is very naive, and mentioned only for illustration. The second approach is again (i.e. as in Section 2) "maxichoice contraction" in the sense of [AGM], [G], [M], and as such plagued by the well-known completeness result: $K - A \cup \{\neg A\}$ is a complete theory (see below for a proof).

In the third case, we take a totally different approach and consider pairs $< K, X >$, where K is a theory, and X an axiom set for K. This approach suffers from another defect: it is highly dependent on the syntactic structure of the axiom set: The "coarser" the axiom set is (in the one extreme the conjunction of K), the more drastic and coarse a contraction will be; the more fine-grained it is (in the other extreme K itself), the more we approach the above completeness result. This is made precise in Proposition 3.1, which, basically, shows that splitting an axiom ψ into $\{\psi \vee \phi, \psi \vee \neg\phi\}$ will decide ϕ, i.e. give completeness with respect to ϕ.

Consider now theories T, T' .... in some finite $\mathcal{L}' \subseteq \mathcal{L}$. It is natural to define $\nu(T) := \Sigma \ \{\mu(g(t)) : dom(t) = \mathcal{L}', t \models T\}$. ($t \models T$ means, of course, $t(\phi) = true$ for all $\phi \epsilon T$, see Remark 2.1.) In other words, $\nu(T)$ is the sum of the probabilities of all $\mathcal{L}'$—models t that make all $\phi \epsilon T$ true. The more specific a theory is, the less likely it is, too: $T \subseteq T'$ implies $\nu(T') \leq \nu(T)$, and the empty theory has probability 1. On the other hand, we are interested in "good choices", i.e. we prefer ϕ to $\neg\phi$ if $\nu(\phi) > \nu(\neg\phi)$. So ν will be a good measure only for theories of the same level of specificity. In other words, $K - A$ (here, $K - A$ means some contraction of K w.r.t. A) cannot sensibly be the ν—maximal $K' \subseteq K$ such that $K' \not\vdash A$, as this is always the empty theory.

A better choice might be a ν—maximal one (if it exists) among $K_A :=$ $\{K' \subseteq K$ maximal : $K' \not\vdash A$, K' is $\vdash$ —closed$\}$, this is again "maxichoice contraction".

But there is a problem to maxichoice contraction, pointed out in [AM]: For any $K' \epsilon K_A$, $A \epsilon K$, $Th(K' \cup \{\neg A\})$ will be a complete theory. (The proof is very simple: Let B be given. As $A \epsilon K$, $A \vee B$ and $A \vee \neg B$ are in K. Suppose $A \vee B \notin K'$, $A \vee \neg B \notin K'$. As $A \vee B \notin K'$, by maximality there is $C_0 \epsilon K'$ such that $C_0 \wedge (A \vee B) \vdash A$, and as $A \vee \neg B \notin K'$, there is $C_1 \epsilon K'$ with $C_1 \wedge (A \vee \neg B) \vdash A$. Thus, for $C := C_0 \wedge C_1 \epsilon K'$, $C \wedge (A \vee B) \vdash A$, $C \wedge (A \vee \neg B) \vdash A$, consequently $C \wedge B \vdash A$, $C \wedge \neg B \vdash A$, and $C \vdash A$, contradicting $C \epsilon K' \epsilon K_A$. Thus, $A \vee B \epsilon K'$ or $A \vee \neg B \epsilon K'$, and $K' \cup \{\neg A\} \vdash B$, or $K' \cup \{\neg A\} \vdash \neg B$.)

We now show that this problem essentially carries over to Theory Revision based on axiom sets too.

So far, we have examined theories without any specified axiom system generating the theory. In the following, we consider pairs $< K, X >$, where X is an axiom set for K. Define $\overline{K}_{A,X} := \{< K', X' > : X' \subseteq X$ maximal, $X' \not\vdash A$, K'=Th(X')$\}$ and choose $K - A$ as a ν—maximal $< K', X' >$ from $\overline{K}_{A,X}$ (if possible). Consider now $< K, X_1 >, < K, X_2 >$, where $X_1 :=$ $\{\phi, \phi \to \psi, \psi\}$, and $X_2 := \{\phi, \phi \to \psi\}$. In both cases, we can infer ψ, and the resulting theories are the same. Suppose we now retract $\phi \to \psi$. In case 1, it is very sensible to uphold ψ, whereas in case 2, it will not be a good choice. (This example can be found analogously in [GM] and [FUV].) So we are highly dependant on the syntactic form of the axioms, and this is certainly not very desirable. As another example, consider revising a theory which is given by the axiom sets $\{a_1, a_2\}$ or $\{a_1 \wedge a_2\}$. So revision may give different results ($\{a_1\}$ or $\{a_2\}$ vs. the empty theory), which is a doubtful outcome. To avoid this influence of the syntactic form, we might split the axioms as far as possible to obtain optimal results. This procedure, however, approaches completeness, as the following proposition will show:

Let $Y := \{y_1 \ldots y_m\}$ be minimal with $Y \vdash A$. Let $Y' := \{y_2 \ldots y_m\}$. Split y_1 into $\{y_1 \vee \phi, y_1 \vee \neg\phi\}$. Both $Y' \cup \{y_1 \vee \phi\} \vdash A$ and $Y' \cup \{y_1 \vee \neg\phi\} \vdash A$ can't be, since otherwise $Y' \vdash A$, contradicting minimality of Y. So $Y_0 := Y' \cup \{y_1 \vee \phi\}$ or $Y_1 := Y' \cup \{y_1 \vee \neg \phi\}$ is a good candidate for $Y - A$, i.e. for contracting Y w.r.t. A. So, let $Y - A$ be Y_0 if $Y_0 \not\vdash A$, and Y_1 otherwise.

Proposition 3.1 *If $Y - A$ is as just defined, then $\overline{Y} := Y - A \cup \{\neg A\}$ decides ϕ.*

Proof: We have $y_1 \wedge \ldots \wedge y_m \vdash A$, thus $\neg A \wedge y_2 \wedge \ldots \wedge y_m \vdash \neg y_1$. Consequently, $\overline{Y} \vdash \neg y_1$. If $Y - A$ is Y_0, then (by $y_1 \vee \phi \epsilon \overline{Y}$) $\overline{Y} \vdash \phi$, if $Y - A$ is Y_1, then $\overline{Y} \vdash \neg \phi$ $\square$

This is further illustrated by the following point of view: We may consider "maxichoice contraction" as theory revision with axioms - taking the full theory as axiom set, and choosing a maximal subset from which A does not follow - resulting in full completeness.

4 Sceptical Revision of Partially Ordered Defaults

4.1 Introduction

We will treat here a special case of theory revision based on axiom systems. Consider a situation of a (possibly inconsistent) partially ordered set of defaults. Our task will be to choose a consistent subset of those defaults, using the given partial order, but being fair otherwise. Consequently, we will proceed sceptically, i.e. not necessarily choose a maximal consistent subset, as two contradictory defaults of the same or incomparable quality should both be excluded - as fairness dictates. We shall refrain ourselves to (open) normal defaults, and give a semantics and proof theory in Section 2, so the above notion of "consistency" of defaults will have a precise meaning. Until then, the reader may as well assume that all formulae considered are classical ones, and the notion of consistency is the usual one. As a matter of fact, logic will play only a marginal role, being restricted to the notion of consistency. First, we will introduce some basic definitions, and subsequently discuss several approaches to making a good and fair choice. Readers familiar with non-monotonic inheritance theories will find many ideas from this area applied to and generalized in the following (see e.g. [HTT]).

4.2 Basic Definitions and Approaches

Let Σ be a set of sorts S, partially ordered by $\leq$, and Δ a set of defaults, where each $\delta\epsilon\Delta$ belongs to some sort s, written $s \models \delta$, thus Δ inherits the order $\leq$ from the sorts. To avoid inessential complications, we assume Σ and Δ to be finite. "$s \models \delta$" is supposed to read something like "normally, all elements of the sort s, have the property $\delta(x)$". (In addition, at sort s we might have classical information, but we shall always assume that the total classical information is consistent, and also that the defeasible information written directly to some s is always consistent too (even when taking the classical information into account). This will simplify matters, but is not essential.) Thus, for some $x\epsilon s$, $s < t < u$, $t \models \phi$, $u \models \psi$, it is natural to consider $\phi(x)$ to be the stronger information than $\psi(x)$, because it is the more specific information. Thus, in case of conflict, ϕ should win over ψ. (Quality decreases with increase by $\leq$!) If, however, t and u are incomparable, fairness dictates that a conflict between ϕ and ψ should result in disbelief of both ϕ and ψ. We thus consider $f := \mathcal{P}(\Delta) - \{\emptyset\} \rightarrow \mathcal{P}(\Delta)$ ($\mathcal{P}$ the power set operator) with $f(\alpha) \subset \alpha$, where f is supposed to choose the "best" elements of α - if there are none, $f(\alpha)$ will be empty. Let further $\overline{f}(\alpha) := \alpha - f(\alpha)$. Any such f gives rise naturally to a notion of quality of the choice: Suppose $card(\alpha) > 1$. If $card(\overline{f}(\alpha)) = 1$, then $\overline{f}(\alpha)$ is a very definite choice, if $f(\alpha) = \emptyset$, i.e. $card(\overline{f}(\alpha)) = card(\alpha)$, $\overline{f}(\alpha)$ is very indefinite. We can thus define the definiteness of the choice $f(\alpha)$ by

$$d(f(\alpha)) := \begin{cases} 1 & \text{iff } card(\alpha) = 1 \\ \frac{card(f(\alpha))}{card(\alpha)-1} & \text{otherwise} \end{cases}$$

(Thus, in the first case, $d(f(\alpha)) = 1$, in the second one $d(f(\alpha)) = 0$.) Speaking in terms of defeasible inheritance, $d(f(\alpha)) = 1$ corresponds to preclusion, $d(f(\alpha)) = 0$ to contradiction. We shall not use the notion of definiteness until the third approach, when we need a relation $\lhd$ on minimal inconsistent subsets.

Examples:

Let $g(\alpha)$ be the greatest element of α - i.e. for all $x\epsilon\alpha$, $x \neq g(\alpha)$, $x < g(\alpha)$ - if it exists.

$$f_1(\alpha) := \begin{cases} \alpha - \{g(\alpha)\} & \text{iff } g(\alpha) \text{ is defined} \\ \emptyset & \text{otherwise} \end{cases}$$

$$f_2(\alpha) := \begin{cases} \{x\epsilon\alpha : \text{x is no non-trivial} \\ \quad \text{maximum, i.e.} \\ \exists y\epsilon\alpha(x < y)\text{or}\neg\exists y\epsilon\alpha(y < x)\} & \text{iff there are } x,y\epsilon\alpha \text{ such that } x < y \\ \emptyset & \text{otherwise} \end{cases}$$

$f_3(\alpha) := \{ \; x\epsilon\alpha : \text{x is a non-maximal element, i.e. } \exists y\epsilon\alpha(x < y) \; \}$

By $f(\alpha) \subset \alpha$, $f(\alpha)$ will be consistent, if α is minimal inconsistent. This suggests the probably simplest

Approach 1:   Iterate some fixed f, starting on Δ, until consistency is reached. By finiteness of Δ and antitony of f, this will always work. This approach has some effects which may not always be desirable: Let $s < t < u$, $s \models \phi$, $t \models \neg\phi$, $u \models \psi$, where $\vdash \psi \rightarrow \phi$. ψ being the weakest information, it should always be eliminated first by f. On the other hand, one might argue that $\{\phi, \psi\}$ is a good choice, as ϕ should be accepted by being the best information, thus $\neg\phi$ should be out, leaving the way open to ψ.

Approach 2:   We shall leave momentarily the above introduced function f, and even the order $\leq$ on sorts and defaults, and discuss a quite different way. We now consider arguments, which we identify with subsets of Δ, choosing the best ones, and hoping that the union of the best arguments is consistent. This meets with some problems. An order $\prec$ on arguments should respect the following properties: Let α, β etc be subsets of Δ. (Again, strength will decrease with increasing $\prec$.)
1. $\prec$ should be transitive, i.e. $\alpha \prec \beta \prec \gamma \rightarrow \alpha \prec \gamma$
2. $\alpha \prec \beta \subseteq \gamma \rightarrow \alpha \prec \gamma$. Reason: simply adding some information to an argument should not make it stronger. Adding the truth 2+2=4 to an argument should not give it more power. It is rather that the weakest part should determine its force.
3. $\forall i\epsilon I(\alpha_i \prec \beta) \rightarrow \bigcup\{\alpha_i; i\epsilon I\} \prec \beta$: just putting arguments together should not violate a common upper bound. This seems to be well in accord with many natural definitions based purely on an order $\leq$ as given above - though not on all. (Consider e.g. $\alpha \prec \beta :\leftrightarrow \exists x\epsilon\beta\forall y\epsilon\alpha(y < x)$.)
4. The inverse seems to be very doubtful: $\beta \prec \bigcup\{\alpha_i : i\epsilon I\} \rightarrow \exists i\epsilon I(\beta \prec \alpha_i)$. This is already violated by $\alpha \prec \beta :\leftrightarrow \forall x\epsilon\alpha\exists y\epsilon\beta(x < y)$. Yet rule 4 seems to suggest itself in our present approach, when trying to prove consistency: Let α, β, γ be pairwise consistent, but $\neg Con(\alpha \cup \beta \cup \gamma)$. If $\alpha \prec \beta$ and $\beta \prec \gamma$, then by 3., $\alpha \cup \gamma \prec \gamma$, and γ will be omitted in the inductive procedure, resulting in a consistent choice. If, however, $\alpha\perp\gamma$ (incomparable), and $\beta\perp\gamma$, then maybe $\gamma \prec \alpha \cup \beta$ (unless 4. holds), so $\alpha \cup \beta$ will not be chosen, but maybe each of α, β, γ, resulting in an inconsistent theory.

Approach 3:   We now work more closely again with the introduced functions f. First, a combinatorial result.

Definition 4.1 *Let D be a finite set, $M' \subseteq \mathcal{P}(D)$, $\lhd$ an acyclic binary relation on M', for $A \epsilon M'$ let $\emptyset \neq X_A \subseteq A$ be defined. Define inductively for $i \epsilon \omega$:*

$M'_i := \{\, A \epsilon M' : A \lhd - minimal\ in\ M' - \bigcup_{j<i} M'_j \,\}$,
$M_i := \{\, A \epsilon M'_i : \forall j < i \forall B \epsilon M_j (B \lhd A \rightarrow A \cap X_B = \emptyset) \,\}$,
$X_i := \bigcup \{X_A : A \epsilon M_i\}$ *and*
$M := \bigcup \{M_i : i \epsilon \omega\}$, $X := \bigcup \{X_i : i \epsilon \omega\}$, $D' := D\text{-}X$.

Let, in the sequel, the situation of the definition be given.

Lemma 4.1 *For all $A \epsilon M'$, $A \cap X \neq \emptyset$.*

Proof: Let $A \epsilon M'_i$, $i < \omega$. If $A \epsilon M_i$, $X_A \subseteq X_i \subseteq X$, so $A \cap X \neq \emptyset$. If $A \epsilon M'_i - M_i$, then there is $j < i$, $B \epsilon M_j$, $B \lhd A$ such that $A \cap X_B \neq \emptyset$. By $X_B \subseteq X_j \subseteq X$, $A \cap X \neq \emptyset$. $\square$

Remark 4.1 :
1) It suffices to choose $\lhd$ well-founded in the above definition, D and M' can then be infinite, too. We do not need the more general result, however.
2) Evidently, $\lhd$ may be chosen as the empty relation.
3) Let $A \epsilon M'$. Then $A \epsilon M \leftrightarrow \forall B \lhd A (B \epsilon M \rightarrow A \cap X_B = \emptyset)$.

Proof: *(By induction.) Let $A \epsilon M'_i$ be minimal such that the result fails.* " $\rightarrow$ " : *If $A \epsilon M_i$ and $\exists B \lhd A (B \epsilon M, A \cap X_B \neq \emptyset)$, then $B \epsilon M_j$ for some $j < i$, and $A \notin M_i$ by construction.* " $\leftarrow$ " : *Let $A \epsilon M'_i - M_i$ such that $\forall B \lhd A (B \epsilon M \rightarrow A \cap X_B = \emptyset)$. Thus, for all $j < i$, $B \epsilon M_j$, $B \lhd A$ $A \cap X_B = \emptyset$, and $A \epsilon M_i$ by construction again.* $\square$

Corollary 4.1 *Let D be a finite set of formulae, $M' \subseteq \mathcal{P}(D)$ the set of minimal inconsistent sets of formulae from D. If X is defined as above, D' will be consistent.*

Proof: *Suppose not, so D' contains some $A \epsilon M'$, so $A \cap X = \emptyset$, contradiction.* $\square$

Thus, letting f be as above, defining $X_A := A - f(A)$, any acyclic $\lhd$ on minimal inconsistent subsets of Δ will give a consistent subset $\Delta' \subseteq \Delta$. Choosing $\lhd$ non-empty will lead to some inconsistencies "being invisible", since some elements responsible are eliminated already. The effect can be seen easily when looking back at the example discussed in the first approach: Letting $\{\phi, \neg\phi\} \lhd \{\neg\phi, \psi\}$, $\neg\phi$ might be eliminated (by suitable f and X) as $\{\phi, \neg\phi\}$ is $\lhd - minimal$, leaving $\{\neg\phi, \psi\}$ out of consideration. The discussion of $\lhd$ will be resumed in a moment. Next, we look at the compatibility of

this approach with an order on arguments (subsets of Δ). It is natural to define for $\alpha, \beta \subseteq \Delta$: $\alpha \prec \beta :\leftrightarrow \alpha \subseteq f(\alpha \cup \beta)$ - leaving all logic aside for the moment. We have discussed the postulates 1.-3. for orders on arguments above, and examine now which of the above introduced f_i satisfy some or all of these postulates. f_1 will violate 2., as the addition of any element, such that the largest element does not exist any more, will show. Consider f_2, and let $\alpha := \{x\}$, $\beta := \{y, z\}$, ordered by $y < z$ (as defaults) only. Then $f(\alpha \cup \beta) = \{x, y\}$, thus $\alpha \prec \beta$ (as arguments), which seems very unnatural. Looking at f_3, which preserves all non-maximal elements, we see that the order on arguments generated by f satisfies indeed 1.-3. This is immediate by $\alpha \prec \beta \leftrightarrow \alpha \subseteq f_3(\alpha \cup \beta) \leftrightarrow \forall x \epsilon \alpha \exists y \epsilon \alpha \cup \beta (x < y) \leftrightarrow \forall x \epsilon \alpha \exists y \epsilon \beta (x < y)$, the last equivalence by transitivity of the partial order on Σ. We have now for $\delta \epsilon \Delta$ ($\lhd = \emptyset$ again, M' being the minimal inconsistent subsets of Δ, thus by $\lhd = \emptyset$ M=M') : $\delta \epsilon \Delta' \leftrightarrow \forall A \epsilon M'(\delta \notin X_A) \leftrightarrow \forall A \epsilon M'(\delta \epsilon A \rightarrow \delta \epsilon f(A))$ $\leftrightarrow \forall A \epsilon M'(\delta \epsilon A \rightarrow \{\delta\} \prec A - \{\delta\}) \leftrightarrow \forall \beta \subseteq \Delta(\neg Con(\delta, \beta) \rightarrow \{\delta\} \prec \beta)$. In the last equivalence, we use property 2.: " $\leftarrow$ " is trivial. " $\rightarrow$ ": Suppose there is β, $\neg Con(\delta, \beta)$, $\neg\{\delta\} \prec \beta$. Take $\beta' \subseteq \beta$ such that $\{\delta\} \cup \beta'$ is minimal inconsistent, by $\delta \epsilon \Delta'$ and definition of $\prec$ on arguments $\{\delta\} \prec \beta'$, and by property 2. $\{\delta\} \prec \beta$. Moreover, for $\alpha \subseteq \Delta'$, we have $\neg Con(\alpha \cup \beta) \rightarrow \alpha \prec \beta$: Let $\alpha \subseteq \Delta'$ and $\beta' \subseteq \beta$ such that $\alpha \cup \beta'$ is minimal inconsistent. As $\alpha \subseteq \Delta'$, $X_{\alpha \cup \beta'} \cap \alpha = \emptyset$, thus $\alpha \subseteq f(\alpha \cup \beta')$ and $\alpha \prec \beta'$, by 2. $\alpha \prec \beta$. Let us resume the discussion of $\lhd$. What are the meaning and properties of the $\lhd-$ relation ? Let $A \lhd B$. Thus, the elimination of the inconsistency A by eliminating the elements of X_A is estimated so strong that the inconsistency B need not be considered any more. In other words, the argument $B - X_B$ against X_B looses its importance. Now, we have by f a relation $\prec$ on arguments. Moreover, we have a notion of definiteness, resulting from f as well, as introduced at the beginning of the section.
A natural definition of $\lhd$ will be e.g.: $A \lhd B :\leftrightarrow$ 1.) $\overline{f}(A) \subseteq B$, 2.) $A - B \prec B$, 3.) $d(f(A))=1$, $d(f(B)) \neq 1$. By 3., any such $\lhd$ will be acyclic. Transitivity cannot be expected (by 1.). To conclude $A \lhd B \subseteq C \rightarrow A \lhd C$ for C such that $d(f(C)) \neq 1$, we need $A - C \prec C$, which will not always hold. (It will hold for $\prec$ defined by f_3.)

Approach 4: As a last alternative, we shall discuss a more "procedural approach", which tries to directly find a suitable subset $\Delta' \subseteq \Delta$. Again we suppose some subset function f to be given. Let $\phi_1 < \phi_2 < \phi_3$, $\phi_1 < \psi < \rho < \phi_4$ be defaults ordered by their sorts. The ψ, ρ are (logically) unimportant here and might be tautologies. Suppose further $\{\phi_1, \phi_2, \phi_4\}$ and $\{\phi_2, \phi_3\}$ are the minimal inconsistent subsets. Suppose further $f(\{\phi_1, \phi_2, \phi_4\}) = \{\phi_1\}$, $f(\{\phi_2, \phi_3\}) = \{\phi_2\}$, which seems a natural choice. Proceeding now by the rank of the ϕ_i in the $< -order$, at rank 2 ϕ_3 will be eliminated, as the elimination of ϕ_2 and ϕ_4 will be discovered only at rank 3. In other words, we have here a result similar to the one discussed in the first approach. (It corresponds again to choosing the empty order $\lhd$ on minimal inconsistent subsets.)

4.3 Model and Proof Theory of Normal Open Defaults

We now give the promised notion of consistency, essentially repeating the definitions and results of [S].

Definition 4.2 Call $\mathcal{N}(M) \subseteq \mathcal{P}(M)$ $(=$ the powerset of $M)$ a $\mathcal{N}-$system over M iff
a. $M \in \mathcal{N}(M)$
b. $A \in \mathcal{N}(M),\ A \subseteq B \subseteq M \rightarrow B \in \mathcal{N}(M)$
c. $A, B \in \mathcal{N}(M) \rightarrow A \cap B \neq \emptyset$ if $M \neq \emptyset$ (thus, $\emptyset \notin \mathcal{N}(M)$, if $M \neq \emptyset$)

Definition 4.3 Call any formula of $\mathcal{L}$, possibly containing ∇ a $\nabla-\mathcal{L}-$ formula.

Definition 4.4 Let $\mathcal{L}$ be a first order language, and M be a $\mathcal{L}-$structure. Let $\mathcal{N}(M)$ be a $\mathcal{N}-$system over M. Define $< M, \mathcal{N}(M) > \models \phi$ for any $\nabla - \mathcal{L} - $formula inductively as usual, with the additional induction step:
$< M, \mathcal{N}(M) > \models \nabla x\phi(x)$ iff there is $A \in \mathcal{N}(M)$ such that
$\forall a \in A\ (< M, \mathcal{N}(M) > \models \phi[a])$.

Definition 4.5 Let any axiomatization of predicate calculus be given. Augment this with the axiom schemata
1. $\nabla x\phi(x) \wedge \forall x(\phi(x) \rightarrow \psi(x)) \rightarrow \nabla x\psi(x)$
2. $\nabla x\phi(x) \rightarrow \neg\nabla x\neg\phi(x)$
3. $\forall x\phi(x) \rightarrow \nabla x\phi(x) \rightarrow \exists x\phi(x)$
(for all ϕ, ψ).

Lemma 4.2 The following formulae are derivable:
a. $\nabla x\phi(x) \wedge \nabla x\psi(x) \rightarrow \exists x(\phi \wedge \psi)(x)$
b. $\nabla x\phi(x) \wedge \neg\nabla x\psi(x) \rightarrow \exists x(\phi \wedge \neg\psi)(x)$
c. $\neg\nabla x\neg\phi(x) \rightarrow \exists x\phi(x)$ $\square$

Lemma 4.3 Let T be a $\nabla - \mathcal{L} - $theory. Then T is consistent under the axioms of Definition 4.5 iff T has a model as defined in Definition 4.4.

Theorem 4.1 The axioms given in Definition 4.5 are sound and complete for the semantics of Definition 4.4, "they capture the $\mathcal{N}-$semantics of ∇".

Definition 4.6 *We call the following axiom schema Iterability for defaults without prerequisites:* $\nabla x \phi(x) \wedge \nabla x \psi(x) \rightarrow \nabla x (\phi \wedge \psi)(x)$

Lemma 4.4 *Let D be a finite set of defaults of the form $\nabla x \phi_i(x)$, $i < n$, where ϕ_i is a classical formula, and let T' be a set of classical formulae, and suppose that D is closed under iterability. Then $D \cup T'$ is consistent iff $T' \cup \{ \exists x (\phi_1 \wedge \ldots \wedge \phi_{n-1})(x) \}$ is consistent.*

Definition 4.7 *Call $\mathcal{N}^+(M) = < \mathcal{N}(N) : N \subseteq M >$ a $\mathcal{N}^+ - $ system over M iff for each $N \subseteq M$ $\mathcal{N}(N)$ is a $\mathcal{N} - $ system over N. Call $\mathcal{N}^+(M)$ a smooth $\mathcal{N}^+ - $ system over M, iff it is a $\mathcal{N}^+ - $ system over M, and for each $N, N' \subseteq M$, $N \subseteq N'$, $A \epsilon \mathcal{N}(N')$, $A \subseteq N$ implies $A \epsilon \mathcal{N}(N)$. (It suffices to consider the definable subsets of M.)*

Definition 4.8 *Extend the language of first order predicate calculus inductively by (the ordinary and bounded new quantifiers)*
$\nabla x \phi(x)$ and $\nabla x \phi(x) : \psi(x)$ for all ϕ, ψ
and add the axiom schemata
1.) a.) $\nabla x \phi(x) \leftrightarrow \nabla x (x = x) : \phi(x)$
b.) $\forall x (\sigma(x) \leftrightarrow \tau(x)) \wedge \nabla x \sigma(x) : \phi(x) \rightarrow \nabla x \tau(x) : \phi(x)$
2.) $\nabla x \phi(x) : \psi(x) \wedge \forall x (\phi(x) \wedge \psi(x) \rightarrow \vartheta(x)) \rightarrow \nabla x \phi(x) : \vartheta(x)$
3.) $\exists x \phi(x) \wedge \nabla x \phi(x) : \psi(x) \rightarrow \neg \nabla x \phi(x) : \neg \psi(x)$
4.) $\forall x (\phi(x) \rightarrow \psi(x)) \rightarrow \nabla x \phi(x) : \psi(x) \rightarrow [\exists x \phi(x) \rightarrow \exists x (\phi(x) \wedge \psi(x))]$
and for smoothness
5.) $\nabla x \phi(x) : \psi(x) \wedge \forall x (\sigma(x) \rightarrow \phi(x)) \wedge \forall x (\phi(x) \wedge \psi(x) \rightarrow \sigma(x)) \rightarrow \nabla x \sigma(x) : \psi(x)$
(for all $\phi, \psi, \vartheta, \sigma, \tau$).

Definition 4.9 *Let $\mathcal{L}$ be a first order language, and M a $\mathcal{L} - $ structure. Let $\mathcal{N}^+(M)$ be a $\mathcal{N}^+ - $ system over M. Define $< M, \mathcal{N}^+(M) > \models \phi$ for any formula inductively as usual, with the additional induction steps:*
1. $< M, \mathcal{N}(M) > \models \nabla x \phi(x)$ iff there is $A \epsilon \mathcal{N}(M)$ such that $\forall a \epsilon A \ (< M, \mathcal{N}(M) > \models \phi[a])$.
2. $< M, \mathcal{N}^+(M) > \models \nabla x \phi(x) : \psi(x)$ iff there is $A \epsilon \mathcal{N}(\{x : M \models \phi(x)\})$ such that $\forall a \epsilon A \ (< M, \mathcal{N}^+(M) > \models \psi[a])$.

Theorem 4.2 *Axioms 1-4 of Definition 4.8 capture $\mathcal{N}^+ - $ semantics of ∇, and axioms 1-5 of Def. 4.8 capture smooth $\mathcal{N}^+ - $ semantics of ∇.*

Definition 4.10 *We call the following axiom schemata Iterability for de faults with prerequisites:*
$\nabla x \phi(x) \wedge \nabla x \sigma(x) : \psi(x) \rightarrow \nabla x \sigma(x) : (\phi \wedge \psi)(x)$
$\nabla x \sigma(x) : \psi(x) \wedge \nabla x \sigma'(x) : \psi'(x) \rightarrow \nabla x (\sigma \wedge \sigma')(x) : (\psi \wedge \psi')(x)$

Definition 4.11 *We call the following axiom schemata Chaining:*

$$\nabla x \phi(x) \wedge \nabla x \phi(x) : \psi(x) \rightarrow \nabla x \psi(x)$$
$$\nabla x \sigma(x) : \psi(x) \wedge \nabla x \psi(x) : \psi'(x) \rightarrow \nabla x \sigma(x) : \psi'(x)$$

Lemma 4.5 *Let D be a finite set of defaults of the form $\nabla x \phi_i(x)$, $i < n$, let P be a finite set of defaults of the form $\nabla x \sigma_i(x) : \psi_i(x)$, $i < m$, where all ϕ_i, σ_i, ψ_i are classical formulae, and let T' be a set of classical formulae, and suppose that D and P are closed under iterability. Then $D \cup P \cup T'$ is consistent iff the following set of (classical) formulae is consistent: $C := T'$ $\cup \{\exists x (\bigwedge_{i<n} \phi_i)(x)\} \cup \{ \exists x (\bigwedge_{i \in p} \sigma_i)(x) \rightarrow \exists x (\bigwedge_{i \in p} \sigma_i \wedge \bigwedge_{i \in p} \psi_i \wedge \bigwedge_{i<n} \phi_i)(x) : p \subseteq m \}$*

A Simplification - and its Consequences   In an implementation currently being made within IBM's LILOG-project at Stuttgart, the following simplification is made for practical purposes: Consistency of defaults is checked by elements, not as a whole. This may lead to discrepancies, as the following example shows: Let $\neg \phi(a)$ be given classically, $\nabla x \phi(x) < \nabla x \psi(x)$ (by the order on sorts), and $\nabla x \psi(x) \rightarrow \neg \nabla x \phi(x)$. Any reasonable choice of defaults will make $\nabla x \phi(x)$ valid (with an exception), and $\nabla x \psi(x)$ not valid. Proceeding by considering just single elements, will however make $\phi(a)$ invalid, because we have the (still better) classical information $\neg \phi(a)$, and may thus make $\psi(a)$ valid. So, in the "general" approach, we will have just $\neg \phi(a)$, in the one by single elements, $\neg \phi(a) \wedge \psi(a)$. With more complicated $\triangleleft - relations$, similar examples may work.

Acknowledgements: I would like to thank S. Koppelberg for correcting a proof, and S. Pribbenow for discussions, P. Gärdenfors for his suggestions, and D. Makinson for suggestions and discussions and the simplified version of Proposition 2.2. Concerning the last Section, I would like to thank Gerd Brewka for inciting me to think about the problems in terms of Theory Revision, and Sven Lorenz for implementing the ideas as part of IBM's Stuttgart LILOG project.

References

[AGM]   C. Alchourron, P. Gärdenfors, D. Makinson: On the Logic of Theory Change, Journal of Symbolic Logic 50, 1985, p. 510-530

[AM]   C. Alchourron, D. Makinson: On the Logic of Theory Change: Contraction functions and their associated revision functions; Theoria 48 (1982) p.14-37

[FUV]   R. Fagin, J.D. Ullmann, M.Y. Vardi: On the Semantics of Updates in Databases, Proc. Second ACM SIGACT-SIGMOD, 1983, p. 352-365

[G]   P. Gärdenfors: Knowledge in Flux, MIT Press 1988

[GM]   P. Gärdenfors, D. Makinson: Revisions of Knowledge Systems Using Epistemic Entrenchment; in: Theoretical Aspects of Reasoning about Knowledge, M.Y.Vardi ed., Morgan Kaufmann, Los Altos, Cal., 1988, p.83-95

[HTT]   J.Horty, R.Thomason, D.Touretzky: A Skeptical Theory of Inheritance in Nonmonotonic Semantic Networks, CMU Report CMU-CS-87-175

[M]   D. Makinson: How to give it up: A Survey of Some Formal Aspects of the Logic of Theory Change; Synthese 62 (1985), 347-363

[S]   K.Schlechta: Reasoning with and about defaults (Unpublished)

[Sp]   W. Spohn: "Ordinal conditional functions: A dynamic theory of epistemic states" in Causation in Decision, Belief Change, and Statistics, W.L.Harper and B.Skyrms, eds. Dordrecht 1988, Reidel, vol. 2, 105-134

EPISTEMIC ENTRENCHMENT WITH INCOMPARA-BILITIES AND RELATIONAL BELIEF REVISION [1]

Sten Lindström and Wlodzimierz Rabinowicz

Department of Philosophy, University of Uppsala, Villavägen 5, S-752 36 Uppsala, Sweden.

1. Introduction

In an earlier paper (Lindström & Rabinowicz, 1989), we proposed a generalization of the approach to belief revision due to Alchourrón-Gärdenfors-Makinson. Our proposal was to view belief revision as a relation rather than as a function on theories (or belief sets). The idea was to allow for there being several equally reasonable revisions of a theory with a given proposition. The same approach was used — and developed further — in our study (1990) of belief revision and epistemic conditionals.

In the present paper, we want to show that the relational approach is the natural result of generalizing in a certain way an approach to belief revision which is due to Adam Grove. In his (1988) paper, Grove presents two closely related modelings of functional belief revision, one in terms of a family of "spheres" around the agent's theory G and the other in terms of an epistemic entrenchment ordering of propositions.[2] Intuitively, a proposition A is at least as entrenched in the agent's belief set as another proposition B if and only if the following holds: provided the agent would have to revise his beliefs so as to falsify the conjunction A ∧ B, he should do it in such a way as to allow for the falsity of B.

The "sphere"-terminology is natural when one looks upon theories and propositions as being represented by sets of possible worlds. Grove's spheres may be thought of as possible "fallback" theories relative to the agent's original theory: theories that he may reach by deleting propositions that are not "sufficiently" entrenched (according to standards of sufficient entrenchment of varying stringency). To put it differently, fallbacks are theories that are closed upwards under entrenchment: if T is a fallback, A belongs to T and B is at least as entrenched as A, then B also belongs to T. The entrenchment ordering can be recovered from the family of fallbacks by the definition: A is at least as entrenched as B iff A belongs to every fallback to which B belongs.

Representing theories and propositions as sets of possible worlds, the following picture illustrates Grove's family of spheres around a given theory G and his definition of revision.

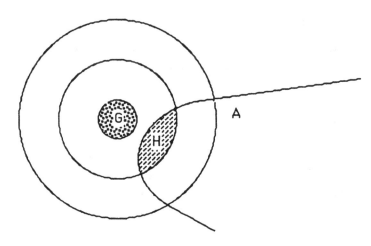

Figure 1.

Notice that the spheres around a theory are "nested", i.e., simply ordered. For any two spheres, one is included in the other. Grove's family of spheres closely resembles Lewis' sphere semantics for counterfactuals, the main difference being that Lewis' spheres are "centered" around a single world instead of a theory (a set of worlds).

The shaded area H in Figure 1 represents the revision of G with a proposition A. The revision of G with A is defined as the strongest A-permitting fallback theory of G expanded with A. In the possible worlds representation, this is the intersection of A with the smallest sphere around G that is compatible with A. (Any revision has to contain the proposition we revise with. Therefore, if A is logically inconsistent, the revision with A is taken to be the inconsistent theory.)

The relational notion of belief revision that we are interested in, results from weakening epistemic entrenchment by not assuming it to be *connected*. In other words, we want to allow that some propositions may be incomparable with respect to epistemic entrenchment. As a result, the family of fallbacks around a given theory will no longer have to be nested. It will no longer be a family of spheres but rather a family of "ellipses". This change opens up the possibility for several different ways of revising a theory with a given proposition.

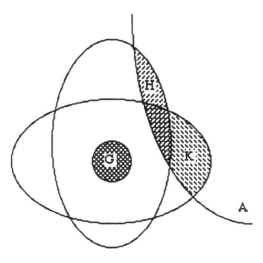

Figure 2.

In this figure, the two ellipses represent two different fallback theories for G, each of which is a strongest A-permitting fallback. Consequently, there are two possible revisions of G with A: each one of H and K is the intersection of A with a strongest A-permitting fallback.

Given connectedness for epistemic entrenchment, there is a way of defining revision directly from entrenchment, without going via fallbacks. The revision of G with A (in symbols, G_A^*) may then be defined thus (for the interesting case in which A is logically consistent):

$B \in G_A^*$ iff $A \to B$ is more entrenched than $A \to \neg B$ (relative to G).

G_A^* defined in this way will coincide with the intersection of A with the maximal A-permitting fallback. However, when we give up connectedness there may not be a *unique* fallback of this kind. Therefore, this direct way of defining revision from entrenchment is no longer available.

Why is it that a non-nested family of fallbacks allows for incomparabilities with respect to epistemic entrenchment? Figure 3 below provides an explanation. In this picture, there is one fallback theory, H, in which A is true but B is not, and another, K, in which B is true but A is not. Hence, neither B is at least as entrenched as A nor vice versa. A and B are incomparable.

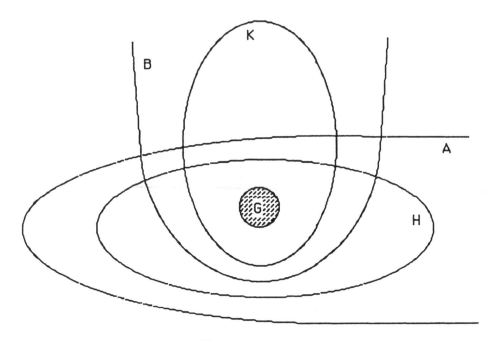

Figure 3.

The next section provides the logical background for our discussion. In Section 3, we introduce an axiom system for epistemic entrenchment without connectedness. We also provide an axiomatic characterization of fallback families. We prove that the two notions are interdefinable and that, in fact, there is a one-to-one correspondence between entrenchment orderings and fallback families.

In Section 3, we also show that non-connected epistemic entrenchment orderings can be viewed as intersections of families of connected entrenchment orderings. There is an analogy here with probabilistic representations of epistemic states. Working with a non-connected entrenchment ordering is analogous to a representation of the agent's epistemic state by an "interval-valued" probability assignment. On the other hand, the representation in terms of a family of connected entrenchment orderings is like the approach in which an epistemic state is viewed as a class of real-valued probability assignments. Gärdenfors' functional approach in terms of a unique connected entrenchment ordering corresponds to the classical Bayesian approach in which the epistemic state is identified with a unique real-valued probability assignment. Of course, this is only an analogy; entrenchment orderings and probability functions do not obey the same axioms.

In Section 4, we define relational belief revision from (non-connected) epistemic entrenchment, via the intermediate notion of a fallback family. We also show that the original entrenchment ordering can be recovered from the resulting belief revision relation by means of the following definition:

(D≤)   A is at least as entrenched in G as B iff either (i) A is logically true or (ii) for every theory H, if H is a possible revision of G with ¬(A∧B), then B does not belong to H.[3]

In the same section, we also provide an axiom system for relational belief revision, which, given the definition (D≤), is sufficient for the derivation of our postulates for epistemic entrenchment. We also prove that our axiom system for belief revision is not sufficiently strong to guarantee that all belief revision systems that satisfy our axioms are *representable,* that is, that they are definable in the appropriate way from an epistemic entrenchment relation. In the special case, when we consider functional belief revision only, our axioms are sufficient to guarantee representability. This result is essentially equivalent to Grove's representation theorem for Gärdenfors-type belief revision in terms of families of spheres. However, the problem of giving a nice axiomatic characterization of just those relational belief revision systems that are representable still remains to be solved.

Finally, in Section 5, we discuss the relationship between belief revision and belief *contraction.* According to Levi (1980), belief revision can be seen as a two-step process: a contraction followed by an expansion. In order to revise our theory G with A, we first contract G with ¬A — move to a weaker theory K in which ¬A is no longer present — and then we expand K with A (i.e., we add A to K and close under logical consequence). In our approach, revision is also viewed as a two-step process, but the first step is different. Instead of contracting G with A, we move to a maximal A-permitting fallback of G. In Section 5, we argue that contractions and maximal fallbacks are different concepts. Nor is it possible to construct contraction from fall-backs, or what amounts to the same, from epistemic entrenchment. Such a construction would yield the so-called postulate of Recovery for contraction, which we reject. According to this postulate, if A ∈ G and K is a contraction of G with A, one can recover the original theory G from K by expanding the latter with A.

On the other hand, it is possible to impose reasonable constraints on contraction in the presence of which Levi's definition of revision in terms of contraction will follow from our definition in terms of fallbacks. In this way, the two approaches may, after all, be complementary.

2. Logics

We consider a fixed sentential language L with the following symbols: (i) atomic sentences: $p_1, p_2,...$; (ii) classical connectives: $\bot$ (falsity), $\rightarrow$ (the material conditional); (iii) possibly some non-classical connectives; (iv) parentheses. The set Φ of *sentences* is the smallest set such that: (i) all atomic sentences are in Φ; (ii) $\bot \in \Phi$; (iii) if A, B $\in \Phi$, then (A $\rightarrow$ B) is in Φ; (iv) if $\square$ is an n-ary non-classical connective in L and $A_1,..., A_n$ are in Φ, then $\square(A_1,..., A_n) \in \Phi$. The connectives $\neg$ (negation), $\wedge$ (conjunction), $\vee$ (disjunction) and $\leftrightarrow$ (the material biconditional) are introduced as abbreviations in the metalanguage in the usual way. For instance, $\neg A = A \rightarrow \bot$.

A *logic* L is a set of sentences such that: (i) all truth-functional tautologies are in L; (ii) L is closed under *modus ponens*. For every logic L and set Γ of sentences, we define $Cn_L(\Gamma)$ to be the smallest set of sentences that includes $\Gamma \cup L$ and is closed under modus ponens. We say that A is an *L-consequence* of Γ (also written as $\Gamma \vdash_L A$) if $A \in Cn_L(\Gamma)$. Note that every logic L satisfies *compactness* and the *deduction theorem*:

$\quad$ (i) $\quad$ if $\Gamma \vdash_L A$, then for some finite $\Delta \subseteq \Gamma, \Delta \vdash_L A$;

$\quad$ (ii) $\quad$ if $\Gamma \cup \{A\} \vdash_L B$, then $\Gamma \vdash_L A \rightarrow B$.

Let L be a logic. L is (absolutely) *consistent* if and only if $L \neq \Phi$. A set $\Gamma \subseteq \Phi$ is said to be *L-consistent* if $Cn_L(\Gamma) \neq \Phi$. A is said to be L-consistent if $\{A\}$ is L-consistent. Γ is an *L-theory* if and only if $L \subseteq \Gamma$ and Γ is closed under modus ponens. In other words, Γ is an L-theory just in case $\Gamma = Cn_L(\Gamma)$. Note that every L-theory is a logic in its own right. A set Γ is *L-maximal* if and only if Γ is L-consistent and for every Δ, if $\Gamma \subseteq \Delta$ and Δ is L-consistent, then $\Gamma = \Delta$. Every L-maximal set is an L-theory.

G, H, K, T, T',... are variables ranging over L-theories. The set of such theories is denoted by $\mathcal{T}_L$.

3. Epistemic Entrenchment

In the following, we let L be a consistent logic.

DEFINITION 3.1. Let G be any L-theory. An *epistemic entrenchment ordering for* G is a binary relation $\leq$ of the sentences in L satisfying the following postulates:

(≤1)	If A ≤ B and B ≤ C, then A ≤ C.	*(Transitivity)*
(≤2)	If A ⊢$_L$ B, then A ≤ B.	*(Dominance)*
(≤3)	If A ≤ B and A ≤ C, then A ≤ B ∧ C.	*(Conjunctive Closure)*
(≤4)	If ⊥ ∉ G, then A ∉ G iff A ≤ ⊥.	*(Bottom)*
(≤5)	If T ≤ A, then ⊢$_L$ A.	*(Top)*

Here, T =$_{df}$ ¬⊥.

If A ≤ B, we say that B *is at least as (epistemically) entrenched in G as* A. (If we want to make the reference to G explicit, we write A ≤$_G$ B rather than A ≤ B. Sometimes, we might also write B ≥ A or B ≥$_G$ A instead of A ≤ B.) The corresponding strict ordering < is defined by: A < B iff A ≤ B and not B ≤ A. A < B is to be read as "B *is (epistemologically) more entrenched in G than* A". We also define the corresponding equality relation, A *and* B *are (epistemologically) equally entrenched in* G (in symbols, A ≈ B or A ≈$_G$ B), as: A ≤ B and B ≤ A.

Let us now look at the intuitive motivation for the above axioms. The theory G consists of all those sentences (in *L*) that are accepted (or believed) by the agent. Although the agent has full belief in all the sentences in G, some of his beliefs are held more firmly than others: the more firm — or epistemically entrenched — a belief is, the less willing the agent is to give it up when faced with new information. In other words, A ≤ B holds just in case the agent's determination to keep B in the face of new information is at least as strong as his determination to keep A. The axioms (≤1) - (≤5) should be viewed as rationality requirements on such a relation for logically omniscient agents.

Clearly, the relation ≤ should be transitive, that is, we have (≤1). Furthermore, if A ⊢$_L$ B, then the agent being logically omniscient knows that he cannot keep A without keeping B and he also knows that he cannot give up B without giving up A. Being rational he realizes that he cannot fight what is unavoidable. Thus, he should be at least as willing to give up A as to give up B (alternatively, he should be at least as determined to keep B as to keep A). This line of reasoning yields Axiom (≤2).

Axiom (≤3) says that if the agent's determination to keep B is at least as strong as his determination to keep A and his determination to keep C is also at least as strong as his determination to keep A, then the agent's determination to keep the conjunction B ∧ C is at least as strong as his determination to keep A. For, clearly, if he were to give up B ∧ C, he would give up either B or C (or both), but his preparedness to give up A is at least as strong.

Intuitively, the relation of epistemic entrenchment is only defined for sentences that are accepted, i.e., that belong to G. It is, however, convenient to extend it to sentences that are not in G by stipulating that those sentences are less entrenched than all the sentences in G. This convention is expressed in Axiom ($\leq$4). In the presence of ($\leq$1) and ($\leq$2), Axiom ($\leq$4) is equivalent to the conjunction of the following two conditions:

($\leq$4.1)   If $A \notin G$ and $B \in G$, then $A < B$.
($\leq$4.2)   If $A \notin G$ and $B \notin G$, then $A \approx B$.

It follows from ($\leq$2) that if $\vdash_L A$, then $B \leq A$, for all B. In particular, we have $T \leq A$ in this case. Axiom ($\leq$5) says that the logical truths are the only sentences A such that $T \leq A$. In other words, the logical truths are precisely those sentences that are maximally entrenched. Intuitively, those are only the sentences that the agent is determined to keep under any circumstances.

Observe that we differ from Gärdenfors (1988) in not assuming epistemic entrenchment relations to be connected. If we were to add:

$$A \leq B \text{ or } B \leq A \qquad\qquad (Connectedness)$$

our axioms would be equivalent to Gärdenfors' postulates (EE1) - (EE5). In particular, connectedness together with ($\leq$1) and ($\leq$3) would imply Gärdenfors' postulate:

(EE3) $A \leq A \wedge B \text{ or } B \leq A \wedge B$ (Conjunctiveness)

Proof: By connectedness, we have: $A \leq B$ or $B \leq A$. Suppose now that $A \leq B$ (the other case is similar). Connectedness also yields $A \leq A$. Hence, by ($\leq$3), $A \leq A \wedge B$.   □

Conversely, (EE3) together with Transitivity and Dominance, which are among Gärdenfors' postulates, imply Connectedness.

(EE3) and Dominance yield:

$$A \approx A \wedge B \text{ or } B \approx A \wedge B,$$

that is, $A \wedge B$ is equally entrenched as A or equally entrenched as B. In fact, on Gärdenfors' approach, $A \wedge B$ is equally entrenched as the least entrenched sentences among A and B. On our approach, however, A and B may be incomparable with respect to epistemic entrenchment, in which case $A \wedge B$ is strictly less entrenched than both A and B. Instead of Gärdenfors' (EE3), we have:

$$\text{if } A \leq B, \text{ then } A \leq A \wedge B.$$

In fact, we have the following "definition" of $\leq$ in terms of $\approx$:

$$A \leq B \text{ iff } A \approx A \wedge B.$$

In the following, we let G be any fixed L-theory and $\leq$ an epistemic entrenchment ordering for G.

DEFINITION 3.2.

(a) A set Γ of sentences is a *filter* (relative to $\leq$) if it satisfies the following conditions:

(i) $\Gamma \neq \emptyset$;
(ii)   If $A \in \Gamma$ and $A \leq B$, then $B \in \Gamma$;
(iii) If $A, B \in \Gamma$, then $A \wedge B \in \Gamma$.

Alternatively, we can characterize a filter as a non-empty set Γ of sentences which satisfies the following two conditions:

(iv) $A, B \in \Gamma$ iff $A \wedge B \in \Gamma$;
(v)   If $A \approx B$, then $A \in \Gamma$ iff $B \in \Gamma$.

It is easily seen that these characterizations are equivalent. We say that a filter Γ is *proper* if $\perp \notin \Gamma$.

(b) We let $F(\leq)$ be the set of all filters. We also refer to the elements of $F(\leq)$ as *fallbacks* (with respect to $\leq$). Proper filters are also called *proper* fallbacks.

(c) A family of sets X is said to be *directed* (with respect to $\subseteq$) if for any Γ and Δ in X, there is a Σ in X such that $\Gamma \subseteq \Sigma$ and $\Delta \subseteq \Sigma$. In other words, X is directed if every finite subset of X has an upper bound in X.

Intuitively, a proper fallback (w. r. t. an entrenchment ordering $\leq$ for G) is a weakening of G — a subtheory of G — which we obtain by removing from G all sentences that are not "sufficiently entrenched". We choose as our entrenchment standard some non-empty subset Γ of G which is closed under conjunctions and whose elements are all sufficiently entrenched for our purposes and we keep only those sentences that are at least as entrenched as some sentences in Γ.

LEMMA 3.3. The set $F(\leq)$ of all filters (or fallbacks) with respect to $\leq$ has the following properties:

(F1)   Every element of $F(\leq)$ is an L-theory.
(F2)   If X is a subset of $F(\leq)$, then $\cap X \in F(\leq)$.
(F3)   If X is a non-empty directed set of elements in $F(\leq)$, then $\cup X \in F(\leq)$.
(F4)   If $H \in F(\leq)$ and $\perp \notin H$, then $H \subseteq G$.
(F5) $L \in F(\leq)$.
(F6) $G \in F(\leq)$.

For the proof of this lemma and the proofs of the main lemmas and theorems to follow, see the Appendix.

(F2) says that $F(\leq)$ is a *closure system*.[4] A closure system satisfying condition (F3) is called *algebraic*. $F(\leq)$ is a complete lattice (with respect to the ordering under inclusion), where for each $X \subseteq F(\leq)$, $\inf(X) = \cap X$ and $\sup(X) = \cap\{H \in F(\leq): \cup X \subseteq H\}$. The *bottom* (or least element) of $F(\leq)$ is L and its *top* (or greatest element) is the inconsistent L-theory $K_\perp$ $(= \cap \varnothing)$. If G is consistent, then the proper or consistent elements of $F(\leq)$ are exactly those that are included in G. In this case, the set of all proper filters is directed and G is its union. It should also be noted that if X is a non-empty directed set of *proper* filters, then $\cup X$ is a proper filter.

For any set of sentences Γ, there exists a smallest member of $F(\leq)$ which includes Γ, namely

$$\uparrow(\Gamma) = \cap\{H \in F(\leq): \Gamma \subseteq H\}.$$

We refer to $\uparrow(\Gamma)$ as *the filter generated by* Γ.

LEMMA 3.4. If $\Gamma \neq \varnothing$, then

$$\uparrow(\Gamma) = \{A: \exists\, B_1,..., B_n \in \Gamma \ (n \geq 1),\ B_1 \wedge ... \wedge B_n \leq A\}.$$

LEMMA 3.5. The operation $\uparrow: P(\Phi) \to P(\Phi)$ satisfies the following conditions:

($\uparrow 1$) $\Gamma \subseteq \uparrow(\Gamma)$.
($\uparrow 2$) $\uparrow(\Gamma) = \uparrow(\uparrow(\Gamma))$.
($\uparrow 3$) If $\Gamma \subseteq \Delta$, then $\uparrow(\Gamma) \subseteq \uparrow(\Delta)$.
($\uparrow 4$) $Cn_L(\Gamma) \subseteq \uparrow(\Gamma)$.
($\uparrow 5$) If $\perp \notin G$, then $\perp \notin \uparrow(\Gamma)$ iff $\Gamma \subseteq G$.
($\uparrow 6$) $\uparrow(G) = G$.
($\uparrow 7$) $\uparrow(\varnothing) = L$.
($\uparrow 8$) $\uparrow(\{A \wedge B\}) = \uparrow(\{A, B\})$.
($\uparrow 9$) If $\Gamma \neq \varnothing$, then $\uparrow(\Gamma) = \cup\{\uparrow(\Delta): \Delta \subseteq \Gamma$ and Δ is finite$\}$.

Moreover, $F(\leq) = \{\Gamma \subseteq \Phi: \uparrow(\Gamma) = \Gamma\}$.

The proof of Lemma 3.5 is omitted here. (The proofs of ($\uparrow 8$) and ($\uparrow 9$) use Lemma 3.4.)

LEMMA 3.6. $A \leq B$ iff for every $H \in F(\leq)$, if $A \in H$, then $B \in H$.

Proof: The left-to-right direction is trivial. To prove the other direction, assume that not($A \leq B$). Consider $F = \{C: A \leq C\}$. We want to show that F is a filter such that $A \in F$ and $B \notin F$. $A \in F$ by (≤ 2), and $B \notin F$ by the assumption. From (≤1) follows that F is closed upwards under ≤. Let C, D ∈ F. Then A ≤ C and A ≤ D. So by axiom (≤3), A ≤ C ∧ D, which means that C ∧ D ∈ F. Hence, F is a filter □

COROLLARY 3.7. A ≤ B iff ↑({B}) ⊆ ↑({A}).

DEFINITION 3.8. Let G be an L-theory. A *fallback family* for G is a family F of sets of sentences satisfying the conditions (F1) - (F6) of Lemma 3.3.

Let G be a given L-theory. For any epistemic entrenchment ordering ≤ for G, we call **F**(≤) *the fallback family for G determined by* ≤, where **F**(≤) is the family of all filters with respect to ≤. As we have seen above, Lemma 3.3, **F**(≤) is indeed a fallback family. We also saw (Lemma 3.6) that the relation ≤ is definable in terms of **F**(≤). Thus, every epistemic entrenchment ordering ≤ for G can be thought of as being defined from a fallback family, namely from the family **F**(≤). Suppose now that ≤ and ≤' are epistemic entrenchment relations such that **F**(≤) = **F**(≤'). Via Lemma 3.6 we then get that ≤ = ≤'. That is, the relation of determination between entrenchment relations and fallback families is one-to-one.

Next, we want to show that for *any* fallback family F, the relation ≤ defined by:

(D)   A ≤ B iff for all H ∈ F if A ∈ H, then B ∈ H.

is an epistemic entrenchment relation and that, furthermore, **F** = **F**(≤). That is, there is a one-to-one correspondence between epistemic entrenchment relations and fallback families (for a given G).such that for any entrenchment relation the corresponding fallback family is set-theoretically definable from it and vice versa.

LEMMA 3.9. Let F be any fallback family for G and ≤ the corresponding ordering of the sentences in L defined by condition (D). Then ≤ is an epistemic entrenchment ordering for G.

Proof: We prove that ≤ satisfies the postulates (≤1) - (≤5) for entrenchment orderings. The easy verifications of (≤1) - (≤3) using (F1) and (D) are omitted.

(≤4) Suppose ⊥ ∉ G. Assume also that A ∉ G. Consider any H ∈ F such that A ∈ H. Then not(H ⊆ G), so by (F4), ⊥ ∈ H. Hence, by (D), A ≤ ⊥. For the other direction, assume that A ≤ ⊥. If A ∈ G, then by (F6) and (D), ⊥ ∈ G. Hence, A ∉ G.

(≤5) Suppose T ≤ A. (F5) and (D) then yield A ∈ L. □

In view of the previous Lemma, for any fallback family F for G, we may speak of the ordering $\leq$ which is defined from F via (D) as *the epistemic entrenchment ordering corresponding to* F.

LEMMA 3.10. Let F be a fallback family for G and let $\leq$ be the corresponding entrenchment ordering. Then $F = F(\leq)$. That is, the elements of F are precisely the filters with respect to the corresponding entrenchment ordering.

Proof: We first prove that $F \subseteq F(\leq)$. Let $H \in F$. Using (F1) and (D), it is easy to verify that H is a filter with respect to $\leq$. That is, $H \in F(\leq)$.

For the other direction, let $H \in F(\leq)$. Then using Lemma 3.5, we get

$$H = \cup\{\uparrow(\Delta): \Delta \subseteq H \text{ and } \Delta \text{ is finite}\} = \cup\{\uparrow(\{A\}): A \in H\}$$

However, for any A, $\uparrow(\{A\}) = \{B: A \leq B\}$, by Lemma 3.4. Hence, by (D), for any B, $B \in \uparrow(\{A\})$ iff for all $K \in F$, if $A \in K$, then $B \in K$. That is, $\uparrow(\{A\}) = \cap\{K \in F: A \in K\}$. (F2) then yields that $\uparrow(\{A\}) \in F$, for any A. Now, $\{\uparrow(\{A\}): A \in H\}$ is a non-empty directed set. For let $A_1, A_2 \in H$. Then $\uparrow(\{A_1\}), \uparrow(\{A_2\}) \subseteq \uparrow(\{A_1 \wedge A_2\})$. Hence, by (F3), $\cup\{\uparrow(\{A\}): A \in H\} \in F$. That is, $H \in F$. $\square$

LEMMA 3.11. An epistemic entrenchment ordering $\leq$ is connected iff the corresponding fallback family $F(\leq)$ is a chain (i.e., is linearly ordered by inclusion).

Proof: Suppose the entrenchment ordering $\leq$ for G is connected, i.e., for all sentences A, B

(*) $A \leq B$ or $B \leq A$.

We want to show that for all H, $K \in F(\leq)$, $H \subseteq K$ or $K \subseteq H$. Suppose that neither $H \subseteq K$ nor $K \subseteq H$. Then there are A, B such that $A \in H$, $A \notin K$, $B \in K$ and $B \notin H$. But then by the definition of a filter, neither $A \leq B$ nor $B \leq A$, contrary to (*).

For the other direction, assume that $F(\leq)$ is linearly ordered by inclusion. Consider any sentences A, B. Then $\uparrow(\{B\}) \subseteq \uparrow(\{A\})$ or $\uparrow(\{A\}) \subseteq \uparrow(\{B\})$. This implies, by Corollary 3.7, that $A \leq B$ or $B \leq A$. $\square$

Notice that if $F(\leq)$ is a chain, then every non-empty subset of $F(\leq)$ is directed. It follows that $F(\leq)$ in this case is closed under the formation of arbitrary unions of non-empty subsets.

DEFINITION 3.12. Let $\leq$ be an epistemic entrenchment ordering for G. A fallback H in $F(\leq)$ is said to be *A-permitting* if $\neg A \notin H$. $H \in F(\leq)$ is a *maximal A-permitting fallback (for G)* if:

(i)   ¬A ∉ H; and
(ii)   for any K ∈ F(≤), if H ⊂ K, then ¬A ∈ K.

LEMMA 3.13. Let ≤ be an epistemic entrenchment ordering for G. Every A-permitting fallback in F(≤) is included in a maximal A-permitting fallback.
Proof: Let H ∈ F(≤) such that ¬A ∉ H. We let

$$\mathcal{K} = \{K \in F(\leq): H \subseteq K \text{ and } \neg A \notin K\}.$$

$\mathcal{K} \neq \emptyset$, since H ∈ $\mathcal{K}$. Let $\emptyset \neq C \subseteq \mathcal{K}$ be a chain in $\mathcal{K}$. Then C is a directed set, so by (F3), $\cup C \in F(\leq)$. Clearly, $H \subseteq \cup C$. Moreover, $\neg A \notin \cup C$, for otherwise, for some $K \in C, \neg A \in K$, which is impossible. Hence, $\cup C \in \mathcal{K}$. We have shown that every non-empty chain in $\mathcal{K}$ has an upper bound in $\mathcal{K}$. Zorn's lemma then yields that $\mathcal{K}$ has a maximal element.   □

We shall end this section by showing that entrenchment orderings that do not satisfy connectedness can be represented by *families* of connected entrenchment orderings. The basic idea, due to Hans Rott (personal communication), is the following: Consider any non-empty set X_G of entrenchment orderings for G. Then, as is easily seen, $\cap X_G$ is an entrenchment ordering for G. That is, $\cap X_G$ satisfies the postulates (≤1) - (≤5). Now, if X_G is a non-empty family of *connected* entrenchment orderings for G, then, of course, $\cap X_G$ is an entrenchment ordering for G. However, $\cap X_G$ need not be connected!

This idea gives rise to a question: Can any epistemic entrenchment ordering ≤ for G be represented as $\cap X_G$ for some non-empty family X_G of *connected* entrenchment orderings for G? Below, we show that the answer to this question is affirmative.

Consider any entrenchment ordering ≤ for G. We say that ≤' is a *connected extension* of ≤ (relative to G) if ≤' satisfies the following conditions:

(i)   ≤ ⊆ ≤';
(ii)   ≤' is a connected entrenchment ordering for G.

≤' is a *minimal connected extension* of ≤, if it in addition to (i) and (ii) satisfies:

(iii)   for any ≤", if ≤" satisfies (i) and (ii), then ≤" ⊄ ≤'.

We let E(≤) and ME(≤) be the set of all connected extensions and the set of all minimal connected extensions of ≤, respectively.

The next theorem says that an entrenchment ordering ≤ for G that is not connected can be represented by any set X of connected extensions of ≤ that contains all the minimal connected extensions.

THEOREM 3.14. If ≤ be an entrenchment ordering for G and let X be any set of connected entrenchment orderings such that ME(≤) ⊆ X ⊆ E(≤). Then ≤ = ∩X.

According to the above theorem, there are in general many different sets of connected entrenchment orderings for G that have the same non-connected ordering as their intersections. Therefore, the representation of epistemic entrenchment in terms of sets of connected relations is more *finegrained* or *discriminating* than the representation in terms of non-connected relations. But perhaps such a representation would be *too* discriminating. From the intuitive point of view, it is easy to understand what it means to say that the agent's entrenchment ordering is incomplete (non-connected): from his point of view, there are propositions that are *incomparable* with respect to entrenchment; perhaps because these propositions are so different from each other, or perhaps because they are totally unrelated. But what is the meaning of the claim that the agent's state consists of a *class* of entrenchment orderings? Is the idea that the agent vacillates between different entrenchment orderings? That he sometimes changes his beliefs according to one ordering and sometimes according to another? Or is it rather that his epistemic state is *indeterminate*? But then why not simply say that his entrenchment ordering is incomplete?

There is an analogy here with the probabilistic representation of an agent's epistemic state. The agent's belief state can be represented as (i) a definite real-valued probability function over propositions (the classical Bayesian approach), or (ii) a probability function that takes intervals as values, or as (iii) a class of real-valued probability functions. A class Π of ordinary probability functions, if it satisfies certain conditions, determines an interval-valued probability function. We assign to a proposition A the interval [inf(P(A)), sup(P(A))], where P varies over the members of Π. It is clear, of course, that different classes may induce the same probability intervals. One could say that Gärdenfors' approach in terms of a single connected entrenchment ordering corresponds to alternative (i) above; our approach using an incomplete entrenchment ordering is like the alternative (ii); while working with a class of connected entrenchment orderings is similar to alternative (iii). But entrenchment relations are not like probability orderings: the axiom (≤3) — Conjunctive Closure — would be absurd if ≤ were interpreted as 'at most as probable as'. Therefore, the analogy should not be taken too far.

4. Relational Revision

The Alchourrón-Gärdenfors-Makinson approach treats belief revision as a function on theories: for any theory G and any sentence A, there is a unique revision of G with A. If we think of revision as being defined out of an epistemic entrenchment ordering $\leq$ of sentences, then the functional approach is a natural consequence of the assumption that epistemic entrenchment is connected. Intuitively, when the agent in belief state G receives a new piece of information A, he selects a maximal A-permitting fallback for G and adds A to it. That is, we have the following definition of revision in terms of epistemic entrenchment.

DEFINITION 4.1. Let $\leq$ be an epistemic entrenchment ordering for G. We say that H is a *revision* of G with A relative to $\leq$ if either $\neg A \in L$ and $H = \Phi$ or there exists some maximal A-permitting fallback K in $\mathbf{F}(\leq)$ such that $H = K + A$. (Here, K + A, the *expansion* of K with A, is $Cn_L(K \cup \{A\})$.)

If $\leq$ is connected, then the family $\mathbf{F}(\leq)$ of all fallbacks for G is a chain, so there is a *unique* maximal A-permitting fallback for G. In fact, this fallback is the set of all B such that $B \not\leq \neg A$. Accordingly, in this case there is a unique revision of G with A. If, however, we give up the requirement of connectedness, that is, if we allow sentences to be *incomparable* with respect to epistemic entrenchment, then there may be several maximal A-permitting fallbacks and hence also several revisions of G with A. Revision becomes relational rather than functional.

In the next definition, we formulate a system of axioms for relational belief revision.

DEFINITION 4.2. A *(relational) belief revision system (b.r.s.)* is an ordered pair <L, R> such that L is a consistent logic, $\mathbf{R} \subseteq \mathcal{T}_L \times \Phi \times \mathcal{T}_L$ and the following requirements are satisfied for all L-theories G, H and all sentences A, B:

(R1)	$(\exists H \in \mathcal{T}_L)(GR_A H)$.	*(Seriality)*
(R2)	If $GR_A H$, then $A \in H$.	*(Success)*
(R3)	If $\neg A \notin G$ and $GR_A H$, then $H = G + A$.	*(Expansion)*
(R4)	If $\neg A \notin L$ and $GR_A H$, then $\perp \notin H$.	*(Strong Consistency)*
(R5)	If $\vdash_L A \leftrightarrow B$, then $GR_A H$ iff $GR_B H$.	*(Substitutivity)*
(R6)	If $GR_A H$ and $\neg B \notin H$, then $GR_{A \wedge B}(H + B)$	
		(Revision by Conjunction)

(R7)   If GR_AH and $\forall K(GR_{A\lor B}K \to \neg A \notin K)$,
        then $\exists K(GR_{A\lor B}K$ and $H = K + A)$.

We read GR_AH as "H is a (possible) revision of G with A".

In the presence of *functionality:*

        If GR_AH and GR_AK, then $K = H$,

the axioms (R1) - (R7) are equivalent to Gärdenfors' (1988) axioms (K*1) - (K*8) for belief revision.

LEMMA 4.3. If <L, R> is a belief revision system, then it satisfies the following principles:

(R8)   If $GR_{A\land B}H$ and $\forall K(GR_AK \to \neg B \notin K)$, then $\exists K(GR_AK$ and $H = K + B)$

(R9)   If (i) $GR_{A\lor B}H$ and $\neg B \in H$; and (ii) $\forall K(GR_{B\lor C}K \to \neg B \notin K)$,
        then $GR_{A\lor C}H$ and $\neg C \in H$.   *(Transitivity)*

Moreover, in the presence of the other axioms (in fact, only (R2) and (R5) are needed), (R7) and (R8) are equivalent principles.

As we shall see next, if belief revision is defined from a system of entrenchment orderings — one for each theory G — then it satisfies the axioms (R1) - (R7). Moreover, the original system of entrenchment orderings will be seen to be definable from the corresponding belief revision system. First, however, we introduce the notion of an entrenchment system and the equivalent notion of a fallback system.

DEFINITION 4.4.

(a) An *(epistemic) entrenchment system (e.e.s.)* is an ordered pair <L, ≤ > such that L is a consistent logic and ≤ is a function which assigns to every L-theory G an epistemic entrenchment relation $\leq_G$ for G.

(b) A *fallback system* is an ordered pair <L, F> such that L is a consistent logic and F is a function which assigns to every L-theory G a fallback family F_G for G.

In view of the results in the previous section, there is a natural one-to-one correspondence between entrenchment systems and fallback systems. The next theorem states that every entrenchment system (or equivalently, every fallback system) determines a belief revision system.

THEOREM 4.5. Let <L, ≤ > be an entrenchment system. Define <L, R> as follows: for all L-theories G, H and all sentences A,

(D_R) GR_AH iff H is a revision of G with A relative to $\leq_G$.

Then <L, **R**> is a belief revision system, that is, it satisfies the axioms (R1) - (R7). In addition, the following equivalence holds for all A, B and G:

(D$\leq$)   A $\leq_G$ B iff either B $\in$ L or $\forall$H(if GR$_{\neg(A\wedge B)}$H, then A $\notin$ H).

That is, if the belief revision system <L, **R**> is defined from an entrenchment system <L, $\leq$ > by means of (D$_R$), then <L, $\leq$ > can be recovered from <L, **R**> via (D$\leq$).

THEOREM 4.6. Let <L, **R**> be a belief revision system and define for every L-theory G and all A, B:

(D$\leq$)   A $\leq_G$ B iff either B $\in$ L or $\forall$H(if GR$_{\neg(A\wedge B)}$H, then A $\notin$ H).

The so constructed system <L, $\leq$ > is an epistemic entrenchment system.

Suppose that we consider a belief revision system <L, **R**>. Are our axioms on belief revision (cf. Definition 4.2) sufficient to guarantee that <L, **R**> is *representable*, that is, that there is some epistemic entrenchment system <L, $\leq$> such that for all L-theories G, H and all sentences A,

(D$_R$)   GR$_A$H iff H is a revision of G with A relative to $\leq_G$.

By Theorem 4.6, we know that in terms of <L **R**> we can define an entrenchment system <L, $\leq^R$>. Suppose now that we define a belief revision system <L, S> from <L, $\leq^R$>, where GS$_A$H holds just in case H is a revision of G with A relative to $\leq^R_A$. In view of Theorem 4.5, we know that R is representable if and only if **R** = S.

It can be shown that this representability problem has a negative answer. Not all belief revision systems are representable. The reason for this is that our set of axioms for **R** is not sufficiently strong to exclude an unintended interpretation of belief revision — an interpretation in which belief revisions are not required to be "minimal".

Thus, suppose that we have an entrenchment ordering $\leq$ for G and define the corresponding family F($\leq$) of fallbacks. Now, suppose that we define belief revision in terms of F($\leq$), not as we have done before (cf. Definition (D$_R$) in Theorem 4.5), but as follows:

(D$'_A$)   GR$'_A$H iff either

       (i) $\neg$A $\in$ L and $\perp \in$ H; or

       (ii) $\neg$A $\notin$ G and H = G + A; or

       (iii) $\neg$A $\in$ G and there is a (not necessarily maximal) A-permitting fallback K in F($\leq$) such that H = K + A.

It is easy to check that all the belief revision axioms (R1) - (R7) hold for **R'** given this interpretation. At the same time, the *intended* relation **R** is included in the non-intended **R'**.

In general, **R** will be *properly* included in **R'**. This can be seen if one starts from a connected entrenchment ordering ≤. Then **R** but *not* **R'** will be functional.

Now, we are going to show that **R'** will not in general be representable. Suppose that **R** ⊂ **R'** and that **R'** is representable. Then there exists an entrenchment ordering ≤' such that **R'** is definable from ≤' via definition (D$_R$). But then by Theorem 4.5, ≤' is definable from **R'** by means of (D$_≤$). We are now going to show that ≤ = ≤'. This will entail a contradiction, because the revision relation **R** obtainable from ≤ via (D$_R$) differs from the revision relation **R'** obtainable from ≤' via the same definition.

Proof that if **R'** is representable, then ≤ = ≤'.

By (D$_≤$) and the fact that **R** ⊆ **R'**, it follows immediately that ≤' ⊆ ≤. For the other direction, suppose that A ≤ B. In the limiting case when B ∈ L, it is immediate that A ≤' B. Thus, in order to prove A ≤' B, for the principal case when B ∉ L, suppose that GR'$_{¬A∨¬B}$H. We have to show that A ∉ H. Suppose that A ∈ H. Then there must exist a (¬A ∨ ¬B)-permitting fallback K in F(≤) such that H = K + (¬A ∨ ¬B). But then by lemma 3.13, there exists a maximal (¬A ∨ ¬B)-permitting fallback T such that K ⊆ T. Since, A ∈ H, (i) A ∈ T + (¬A ∨ ¬B). But, by the definition of **R**, we have that (ii) GR$_{¬A∨¬B}$(T + (¬A ∨ ¬B)). But, (i) and (ii) contradict the assumption that A ≤ B. □

We have seen that in general belief revision systems are not representable. This negative result naturally gives rise to the question: how can our system of axioms for relational belief revision be strengthened (in a nice way) so as to guarantee representability?

The situation is different, however, if we want to add functionality: functional belief revision systems are always representable. The theorem below is essentially equivalent to Grove's (1988) representation theorem for functional belief revision in terms of families of spheres. Our proof, however, is different from his. (See the Appendix.)

THEOREM 4.7. Let <L, **R**> be a functional belief revision system. Define the corresponding entrenchment system <L, ≤ > by means of (D$_≤$) and let <L, S> be the belief revision system obtained from <L, ≤ > via (D$_R$). Then **R** = S.

At the end of the previous section, we have discussed the possibility of representing the agent's belief state as a set X_G of connected entrenchment orderings for a given belief set G. If one were to choose this approach, one would have two alternative ways of defining relational belief revision.

Alternative 1. Go to the intersection $\cap X_G$. As we already know, $\cap X_G$ is an entrenchment ordering. Then define **R** in the standard way from $\cap X_G$ via $F(\cap X_G)$.

Alternative 2. For any $\leq'$ in X_G, define the corresponding revision relation $R^{\leq'}$ via $F(\leq')$. Since each such $\leq'$ is connected, $R^{\leq'}$ will of course be a function. Then, we define:

$$GS_AH \text{ iff for some } \leq' \text{ in } X_G, GR_A^{\leq'}H.$$

It is easy to check that S satisfies all our axioms for relational belief revision.

Alternative 2 is more liberal than alternative 1. We get more possible revisions that way. In order to see this, the reader should note that every fallback in $F(\cap X_G)$ is a fallback in $F(\leq')$, for some $\leq'$ in X_G. Therefore, every maximal A-permitting fallback in $F(\cap X_G)$ is a maximal A-permitting fallback in $F(\leq')$, for some $\leq'$ in X_G. But the converse need not hold: a maximal A-permitting fallback in $F(\leq')$ may not be a *maximal* A-permitting fallback in $F(\cap X_G)$.

In what follows, we keep to our preferred interpretation of relational belief revision in terms of a single epistemic entrenchment ordering.

5. Fallbacks and Contractions

According to Isaac Levi (1980, sect. 3.5), belief revision should be seen as a two-step process. In order to revise G with A, we first *contract* G with $\neg A$ and then expand the resulting belief set with A. On our approach, belief revision is also a two-step process. A possible revision of G with A is obtained by first moving to a maximal A-permitting fallback of G and then expanding this fallback with A. This similarity between the two descriptions of belief revision might suggest the identification of contractions with maximal fallbacks: one might think that H is a possible contraction of G with A just in case H is a maximal $\neg A$-permitting fallback of G. (If A is a logically true, we let G itself be the only contraction of G with A.) This tentative suggestion appears in Rott (1989).[5]

If we look at theories as sets of possible worlds (where the latter might be identified with L-maximal theories), then the following figure illustrates the present proposal:

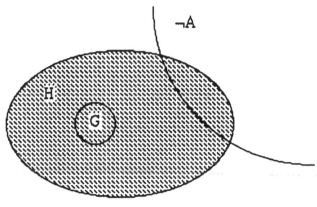

Figure 4.

This way of defining contractions might invite an objection: According to the Alchourrón-Gärdenfors-Makinson approach, contraction is assumed to satisfy the postulate of *recovery*. In terms of our relational approach, this postulate amounts to the following claim:

(Recovery) If A ∈ G and GR̄$_A$H, then H + A = G,

where GR̄$_A$H should be read as: "H is a possible contraction of G with A".

According to Recovery, if one contracts a theory with A and then expands the contraction with A, one recovers the theory one has started with.

Now, it is easy to see that if one moves from a theory G containing A to a maximal ¬A-permitting fallback H and then expands H with A, one will not normally recover G.[6] In order to see this, let A and B be two equally entrenched sentences in G such that their disjunction is logically true, but they are not contradictories (For instance, let A and B be "X is good or neutral" and "X is neutral or bad", respectively.) Since A and B are equally entrenched, it follows from the definition of fallbacks in terms of entrenchment that any ¬A-permitting fallback H must be ¬B-permitting as well. Now, consider H + A. It is easy to see that B ∉ H + A. Otherwise, we would have that A → B ∈ H, which in view of the fact that A ∨ B ∈ L and that B ∉ H, is impossible. But since B ∈ G, it follows that G ≠ H + A. To illustrate:

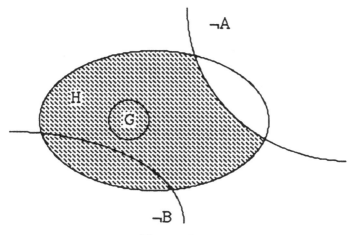

Figure 5.

It is obvious that in this example, H + A differs from G.

Thus, if belief contraction should satisfy Recovery, contractions cannot be identified with maximal fallbacks.

However, the strength of this objection may well be doubted. Recovery is not a particularly convincing condition on contraction. As is easily seen, it has the following consequence:

If $B \in G$ and $B \vdash_L A$, then $GR_A^- H$ implies that $B \in H + A$.

This principle is quite surprising. According to it, if we believe that Jesus was God's son and then retract our belief in Jesus' historical existence, then we are going to recover our belief Jesus' divine origin upon learning that Jesus actually existed. It is difficult to see why this should be the case. For a sustained criticism of Recovery from this point of view, see Niederée (1990). It should also be noted that Isaac Levi has never accepted the Recovery Postulate for contraction.

However, there is another objection against identifying contractions with maximal fallbacks that we find much more convincing. As we know, fallbacks have the following property: if a fallback H is ¬A-permitting and B is at most as entrenched as A, then H is ¬B-permitting as well (This is an easy consequence of the fact that fallbacks are closed upwards under entrenchment.) Therefore, if we were to identify contractions with maximal fallbacks, we would have to accept the following principle:

If $GR_A^- H$ and $B \leq_G A$, then $B \notin H$.

That is, when contracting with A, we would have to give up all the beliefs that are at most as entrenched as A, even those that are quite unrelated to our original belief in A. For example if we were called upon to give up some very entrenched belief of ours, for instance that the Earth rotates around the Sun, we would have to give up all beliefs that are less entrenched, even though they might be quite independent of the belief that is being contracted. For example, we would no longer be able to believe that Salman Rushdie has written "Satanic Verses".

This is not how we do our contractions. Thus, the identification of contractions with maximal fallbacks does not seem to work. There is an alternative, however, which we should consider and which goes back to Grove (1988). We have used maximal fallbacks to define revisions. We might now also use them to define contractions in the following way:

(Grove)   GR$\bar{\text{A}}$H iff A $\in$ L and G = H, or there is a maximal $\neg$A-permitting fallback K in F($\leq_G$) such that H = G $\cap$ (K + $\neg$A).

In the figure below, the shaded area represents Grove's contraction. The theory G $\cap$ (K + $\neg$A) is represented by the union of the sets of worlds corresponding to G and K + $\neg$A.

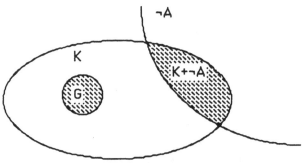

Figure 6.

Given our interpretation of revision in terms of fallbacks, (Grove) amounts to the following definition of contraction in terms of revision:

(Harper)   GR$\bar{\text{A}}$H iff there is some K such that GR$_{\neg A}$K and H = G $\cap$ K.

(Harper) is the relational version of the so-called Harper Identity: G$\bar{_A}$ = G $\cap$ G$^*_{\neg A}$. (Cf. Gärdenfors, 1988, sect. 3.6; G$\bar{_A}$ and G$^*_A$ here stand for functional contraction and functional revision of G with A, respectively.)

(Grove) also yields Levi's reduction of revision to contraction, namely

(Levi)   GR$_A$H iff for some K, GR$\bar{_{\neg A}}$K and H = K + A.

Unfortunately, Grove's proposal implies Recovery for contraction. In fact, Recovery follows from *Harper* (given Success), and as we have seen, *Harper* follows from *Grove*. It seems, therefore, that Grove's contractions are too strong from the intuitive point of view.

On the other hand, we have seen that our original proposal (contractions = maximal fallbacks) gives us contractions that are too weak: we loose all the propositions that are at most as entrenched as the proposition we contract with. One would like to say that the truth lies somewhere in between the two extremes: the original proposal and Grove's definition seem to give us the "lower" and the "upper" limit for contraction. This idea could be expressed as the following set of adequacy conditions on the contraction relation:

(C1) If GR_A^-H and $A \notin L$, then there exists some maximal $\neg A$-permitting fallback K in $F(\leq_G)$ such that $K \subseteq H \subseteq G \cap (K + \neg A)$

(C2) For every maximal $\neg A$-permitting fallback K in $F(\leq_G)$, there exists some L-theory H such that GR_A^-H and $K \subseteq H \subseteq G \cap (K + \neg A)$.

(C3) If $A \in L$, then GR_A^-H iff $G = H$.

(C3) takes care of the limiting case. The figure below illustrates the principal case, in which $A \notin L$:

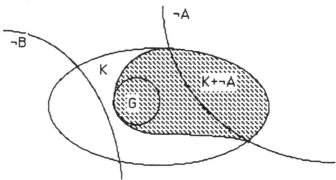

Figure 7.

As is easily seen, K and $G \cap K + \neg A$ are the lower and the upper limit for the contraction H represented by the shaded area.

Clearly, the present proposal does not imply Recovery (nor does it imply *Harper*, for that matter): in figure 7, H + A differs from the original theory G. Also, on this proposal, some propositions that are at most as entrenched as A may be retained in a contraction with A (cf. proposition B, in the figure).

Although it does not imply *Harper*, the present proposal entails the Levi identity.

LEMMA 6.1. Let $<L, \leq>$ be an entrenchment system and let **R** be the corresponding revision relation defined from $\leq$ via $(D_\leq)$. Suppose that $R^- \subseteq \mathcal{T}_L \times \Phi \times \mathcal{T}_L$ is any relation satisfying (C1) - (C3). Then **R** and **R**$^-$ satisfy *Levi*.

This fact shows that there is no fundamental incompatibility between our definition of revision from entrenchment and Levi's interpretation of revision in terms of contraction. Given that the contraction relation respects the entrenchment ordering in the way indicated by (C1) - (C3), the two interpretations of revision are going to coincide.

APPENDIX: PROOFS OF LEMMAS AND THEOREMS

Proof of Lemma 3.3: (F1) Let $\Gamma \in F(\leq)$. Suppose $\Gamma \vdash_L A$. We have to show that $A \in \Gamma$. By the compactness of L, there are $B_1,..., B_n \in \Gamma$ such that $B_1,..., B_n \vdash_L A$. By the deduction theorem and propositional logic, $\vdash_L B_1 \wedge ... \wedge B_n \rightarrow A$. That is,. $B_1 \wedge ... \wedge B_n \vdash_L A$. ($\leq$2) then yields that $B_1 \wedge ... \wedge B_n \leq A$. By the closure of Γ under $\wedge$, $B_1 \wedge ... \wedge B_n \in \Gamma$. But then, since Γ is closed upwards under $\leq$, $A \in \Gamma$.

(F2) Let $X \subseteq F(\leq)$. Consider $\cap X$. $L \subseteq \cap X$, so $\cap X \neq \emptyset$. Suppose that $A \in \cap X$ and $A \leq B$. Then $A \in H$, for all H in X. Consequently, $B \in H$, for all H in X. That is, $B \in \cap X$. We have shown that $\cap X$ is closed upwards under $\leq$. Now, let $A, B \in \cap X$. Then A and B both belong to all theories in X. Hence, the same is true for $A \wedge B$. It follows that $A \wedge B \in \cap X$. This completes the proof that $\cap X$ is a filter.

(F3) Let X be a non-empty directed set of elements in $F(\leq)$. Consider $\cup X$. Clearly, $L \subseteq \cup X$, so $\cup X \neq \emptyset$. Suppose $A \in \cup X$ and $A \leq B$. Then, for some $H \in X$, $A \in H$. Since H is a filter, $B \in H$. It follows that $B \in \cup X$. Now, let $A, B \in \cup X$. Then there are H_1 and H_2 in X such that $A \in H_1$ and $B \in H_2$. Since X is directed, there is a $K \in X$ such that $H_1 \subseteq K$ and $H_2 \subseteq K$. Hence, $A, B \in K$. But then $A \wedge B \in K$, since K is a filter. Hence, $A \wedge B \in \cup X$.

(F4) Suppose H is a proper filter. We want to show that $H \subseteq G$. If G is inconsistent, there is nothing to prove. So, we assume that $\perp \notin G$. Suppose now that $A \in H$. Since H is proper, not($A \leq \perp$). It follows by ($\leq$4) that $A \in G$. Hence, $H \subseteq G$.

(F5) Let $A \in L$ and $A \leq B$. Then $T \vdash_L A$. Using ($\leq$2) we then get $T \leq A$. ($\leq$1) yields $T \leq B$. This in turn implies $B \in L$ by means of ($\leq$5). Since L is non-empty and closed under conjunction, it follows that L is a filter.

(F6) If G is inconsistent, then clearly $G \in F(\leq)$. So assume that $\perp \notin G$. Suppose $A \in G$ and $A \leq B$. Using ($\leq$4) we conclude that not($A \leq \perp$). This together with $A \leq B$ then implies not($B \leq \perp$) (using ($\leq$1)). Applying ($\leq$4) again, we get $B \in G$. Hence, G is closed upwards under $\leq$. Since, G is an L-theory, it is non-empty and closed under conjunctions. Hence, $G \in F(\leq)$. □

Proof of Lemma 3.4: Let $\Delta = \{A: \exists\, B_1,..., B_n \in \Gamma\ (n \geq 1), B_1 \wedge ... \wedge B_n \leq A\}$. We want to show that: (i) $\Delta \subseteq \uparrow(\Gamma)$; and (ii) $\uparrow(\Gamma) \subseteq \Delta$.

(i) Let $H \in F(\leq)$ such that $\Gamma \subseteq H$. Suppose that $\exists\, B_1,..., B_n \in \Gamma\ (n \geq 1)$, $B_1 \wedge ... \wedge B_n \leq A$. Then, by by the definition of a filter, $B_1 \wedge ... \wedge B_n \in H$. Hence, once again by the definition of a filter, $A \in H$. Thus, $\Delta \subseteq \uparrow(\Gamma)$.

(ii) It suffices to prove that Δ is a filter that includes Γ. Let $A \in \Gamma$. By (≤ 2), $A \leq A$, so $A \in \Delta$, by the definition of Δ. Thus $\Gamma \subseteq \Delta$. Since $\Gamma \neq \emptyset$, it follows that $\Delta \neq \emptyset$.

Suppose that $A \in \Delta$ and $A \leq B$. Then, for some $B_1,..., B_n \in \Gamma$, $B_1 \wedge ... \wedge B_n \leq A$. By ($\leq 1$) it follows that $B_1 \wedge ... \wedge B_n \leq B$. Hence, $B \in \Delta$.

Now, let $A_1, A_2 \in \Delta$. Then there are $B_1,..., B_n, C_1,..., C_m \in \Gamma$ such that $B_1 \wedge ... \wedge B_n \leq A_1$ and $C_1 \wedge ... \wedge C_m \leq A_2$. But $B_1 \wedge ... \wedge B_n \wedge C_1 \wedge ... \wedge C_m \leq B_1 \wedge ... \wedge B_n$ and $B_1 \wedge ... \wedge B_n \wedge C_1 \wedge ... \wedge C_m \leq C_1 \wedge ... \wedge C_m$ by (≤ 2). Hence, by (≤ 1), $B_1 \wedge ... \wedge B_n \wedge C_1 \wedge ... \wedge C_m \leq A_i\ (i = 1, 2)$. It follows, using ($\leq 3$) that $B_1 \wedge ... \wedge B_n \wedge C_1 \wedge ... \wedge C_m \leq A_1 \wedge A_2$. Thus, $A_1 \wedge A_2 \in \Delta$. $\quad\square$

Proof of Theorem 3.14: Suppose that $ME(\leq) \subseteq X \subseteq E(\leq)$. That $\leq\, \subseteq \cap E(\leq)$ immediately follows from condition (i) in the definition of a minimal connected extension of $\leq$. But since $X \subseteq E(\leq)$, $\cap E(\leq) \subseteq \cap X$. Hence, $\leq\, \subseteq \cap X$.

In order to prove that $\cap X \subseteq\, \leq$, suppose that for some A and B, $A \not\leq B$. We want to show that for some $\leq' \in ME(\leq)$, $A \not\leq' B$. If $A \not\leq B$, then for some fallback $K \in F(\leq)$, $A \in K$ but $B \notin K$ (Cf. Lemma 3.6). We are now going to prove two claims:

Claim 1. If $K \in F(\leq)$, then there is some maximal chain C in $F(\leq)$ such that $K \in C$.

Claim 2. If C is a maximal chain in $F(\leq)$, then the entrenchment ordering $\leq'$ defined from C via:

(D) $\quad A \leq' B$ iff for all $H \in C$, if $A \in H$, then $B \in H$,

belongs to $ME(\leq)$.

Since we have assumed that $A \in K$ but $B \notin K$, it will follow from claims 1 and 2 that for some $\leq' \in ME(\leq)$, $A \not\leq' B$. But then, since $ME(\leq) \subseteq X$, there is some $\leq' \in X$ such that $A \not\leq' B$. It follows that $\leq\, \subseteq \cap X$.

To prove Claim 1, consider the set $\mathbf{K} = \{C:\ C$ is a chain in $F(\leq)$ and $K \in C\}$. It is easy to see that $\mathbf{K}$ is non-empty and that every chain $C \subseteq \mathbf{K}$ has an upper bound in $\mathbf{K}$ (namely, $\cap C$). Hence, by Zorn's lemma, there is a maximal element C in $\mathbf{K}$. Q.E.D.

To prove claim 2, consider a maximal chain C in $\mathbf{F}(\leq)$ and define $\leq'$ via (D). It is obvious that C is a fallback family for G. Therefore, by Lemma 3.9, $\leq'$ is an entrenchment ordering for G. Moreover, $\leq'$ is connected (cf. Lemma 3.11). It is also clear that $\leq \subseteq \leq'$. It remains to show that $\leq'$ satisfies condition (iii) in the definition of a minimal connected extension of $\leq$. Suppose it does not. Then, there is some connected entrenchment ordering $\leq''$ for G such that $\leq \subseteq \leq'' \subset \leq'$. Then, by lemma 3.11, $\mathbf{F}(\leq'')$ is a chain. Since $\leq \subseteq \leq''$, $\mathbf{F}(\leq'') \subseteq \mathbf{F}(\leq)$. Since $\leq'' \subset \leq'$, $C \, (= \mathbf{F}(\leq')) \subset \mathbf{F}(\leq')$. But this is impossible, since a maximal chain in $\mathbf{F}(\leq)$ cannot be properly included in another chain in $\mathbf{F}(\leq)$.   □

Proof of Lemma 4.3: We first show how to obtain (R8) from (R7). In (R7) replace A by A ∧ B and B by A. We then get:

If $GR_{A \wedge B}H$ and $\forall K(GR_{(A \wedge B) \vee A}K \to \neg(A \wedge B) \notin K)$, then $\exists K(GR_{(A \wedge B) \vee A}K$ and $H = K + (A \wedge B))$.

However, since $(A \wedge B) \vee A$ is tautologically equivalent to A, we have by (R5):

If $GR_{A \wedge B}H$ and $\forall K(GR_A K \to \neg(A \wedge B) \notin K)$, then $\exists K(GR_A K$ and $H = K + (A \wedge B))$.

This in turn implies (using (R2)):

If $GR_{A \wedge B}H$ and $\forall K(GR_A K \to \neg B \notin K)$, then $\exists K(GR_A K$ and $H = K + (A \wedge B))$.

Using (R2) again, we get:

If $GR_{A \wedge B}H$ and $\forall K(GR_A K \to \neg B \notin K)$, then $\exists K(GR_A K$ and $H = K + B)$,

that is, (R8).

To get (R7) from (R8), replace A by A ∨ B and B by A in (R8). We thus obtain:

If $GR_{(A \vee B) \wedge A}H$ and $\forall K(GR_{A \vee B}K \to \neg A \notin K)$, then $\exists K(GR_{A \vee B}K$ and $H = K + A)$.

Using (R5), we get:

If $GR_A H$ and $\forall K(GR_{A \vee B}K \to \neg A \notin K)$, then $\exists K(GR_{A \vee B}K$ and $H = K + A)$,

which is (R7).

Next, we derive (R9) from the other principles. First, substitute A ∨ B for A and C for B in (R7). We then get:

(*)   If $GR_{A \lor B}H$ and $\forall K(GR_{A \lor B \lor C}K \to \neg(A \lor B) \notin K)$, then
      $\exists K(GR_{A \lor B \lor C}K$ and $H = K + (A \lor B))$.

We now assume the antecedent of (R9), that is:

(i) $GR_{A \lor B}H$ and $\neg B \in H$; and
(ii) $\forall K(GR_{B \lor C}K \to \neg B \notin K)$,

in order to prove the consequent, namely: $GR_{A \lor C}H$ and $\neg C \in H$.

Claim 1: $\forall K(GR_{A \lor B \lor C}K \to \neg(A \lor B) \notin K)$.

In order to prove Claim 1, suppose that $GR_{A \lor B \lor C}K$ and $\neg(A \lor B) \in K$. Assume also that K is inconsistent. Then, by (R4), $\neg(A \lor B \lor C) \in L$. This implies that also $\neg(B \lor C) \in L$. By (R1), there is some K' such that $GR_{B \lor C}K'$. (R2) yields that $B \lor C \in K'$. Hence, K' is inconsistent and, therefore, K' = K. Thus, $GR_{B \lor C}K$. Then (ii) yields $\neg B \notin K$, contrary to the assumed inconsistency of K. Hence, K is consistent.

By the supposition and (R2), we have that $C \in K$. Hence, $B \lor C \in K$. K is consistent, so $\neg(B \lor C) \notin K$. Since $K = K + (B \lor C)$, we then get using (R1) and (R3), $GR_{B \lor C}K$. Finally, (ii) yields $\neg B \notin K$, contrary to the supposition.

From (i), Claim (1) and (*) we conclude that there is a K such that:

$$GR_{A \lor B \lor C}K \text{ and } H = K + (A \lor B).$$

Observe that it follows from Claim (1) that K is consistent.

$\neg B \in K$ implies that $A \lor B \to \neg B \in K$. But $A \lor B \to \neg B$ is tautologically equivalent to $\neg B$, so $\neg B \in K$. This in turn implies that $K + (A \lor B) = K + A$, so $H = K + A$.

Claim 2: $GR_{A \lor C}K$.

In order to prove this, we first observe that $A \lor C \in K$. This follows from the facts that $A \lor B \lor C \in K$ and $\neg B \in K$. Since K is consistent, we have that $\neg(A \lor C) \notin K$. (R1) and (R3) then yields $GR_{A \lor C}K + (A \lor C)$. But $K + (A \lor C) = K$, so $GR_{A \lor C}K$.

Claim 3: $\neg C \in K$.

Suppose $\neg C \notin K$. Then $\neg(B \lor C) \notin K$. Hence, $GR_{B \lor C}K + (B \lor C)$. (ii) then yields $\neg B \notin K + (B \lor C)$, but this contradicts the fact that $\neg B \in K$.

It follows from Claim 2 using (R2) that $A \lor C \in K$. This together with Claim 3 implies that $A \in K$. Hence, $H = K + A = K$. Thus, we have proved that $GR_{A \lor C}H$ and $\neg C \in H$.   □

Proof of Theorem 4.5: (R1). If $\neg A \in L$, then $GR_A\Phi$, by Definition 4.1. Suppose now that $\neg A \notin L$. Then L is an A-permitting fallback in $F(\leq_G)$. By

Lemma 3.13, there exists a maximal A-permitting fallback K relative to $\leq_G$. Let H = K + A. Then, by the definition of **R** and Definition 4.1, GR_AH.

(R2) Follows from Definition 4.1 and the definition of **R**.

(R3) Suppose $\neg A \notin G$ and GR_AH. All proper fallbacks are included in G (condition (F4)). Since G is A-permitting, G must be the *only* maximal A-permitting fallback for G. By the supposition, H = K + A, for some maximal A-permitting fallback for G. Hence, H = G + A.

(R4) Suppose $\neg A \notin L$ and GR_AH. Then there is some maximal A-permitting fallback K such that $H = Cn_L(K \cup \{A\})$. But if $\bot \in H$, then $(A \rightarrow \bot) \in K$, that is, $\neg A \in K$. This is contrary to K being A-permitting. Hence, $\bot \notin H$.

(R5) If $\vdash_L A \leftrightarrow B$, then the maximal A-permitting fallbacks are exactly the maximal B-permitting ones. We also have that $\neg A \in L$ iff $\neg B \in L$, in this case. Hence, GR_AH iff GR_BH.

(R6) Suppose GR_AH and $\neg B \notin H$. Then there is a maximal A-permitting fallback K in $F(\leq_G)$ such that H = K + A. Suppose $\neg(A \wedge B) \in K$. Then $A \rightarrow \neg B \in K$. The deduction theorem then yields $\neg B \in H$, contrary to the supposition. Thus K is $A \wedge B$-permitting.

Assume now that $K \subset K'$ and that K' is $A \wedge B$-permitting. Then K' is A-permitting, contrary to the assumption that K is maximal A-permitting. Hence, K is maximal $A \wedge B$-permitting. But this in turn implies that $GR_{A \wedge B}(K + (A \wedge B))$. But, $K + (A \wedge B) = (K + A) + B = H + B$. Hence, $GR_{A \wedge B}(H + B)$.

(R7) Suppose that GR_AH and $\forall K(GR_{A \vee B}K \rightarrow \neg A \notin K)$. By (R1), there exists a theory K_0 such that $GR_{A \vee B}K_0$. The supposition, then implies that $\neg A \notin K_0$. Hence, $\neg A \notin L$. It follows that there exists a maximal A-permitting fallback K_1 in $F(\leq_G)$ such that $H = K_1 + A$.

Claim: K_1 is a maximal $A \vee B$-permitting fallback.

Suppose not. Then there is a $A \vee B$-permitting fallback K_2 such that $K_1 \subset K_2$. Now, let $K = K_2 + (A \vee B)$. Then $GR_{A \vee B}K$ and $\neg A \in K$, contrary to the assumption.

Let now $K = K_1 + (A \vee B)$. Then $GR_{A \vee B}K$ and $H = K_1 + A = K_1 + (A \vee B) \wedge A = (K + (A \vee B)) + A = K + A$. That is, $\exists K(GR_{A \vee B}K$ and $H = K + A)$.

Finally, we prove the equivalence:

(D$\leq$) $A \leq_G B$ iff either $B \in L$ or $\forall H($if $GR_{\neg(A \wedge B)}H$, then $A \notin H)$.

Suppose $A \leq_G B$ and that $B \notin L$. Let $GR_{\neg(A \wedge B)}H$. $A \wedge B \notin L$, so H is consistent by (R4). It follows that there exists a maximal $\neg(A \wedge B)$-permitting fallback K in $F(\leq_G)$ such that $H = K + \neg(A \wedge B)$. Assume now that $A \in H$. Then $\neg(A \wedge B) \rightarrow A \in K$. But $\neg(A \wedge B) \rightarrow A$ is tautologically equivalent to

A, so $A \in K$. $A \leq_G B$ then implies by Lemma 3.6 that $B \in K$. It follows that $B \in H$. On the other hand, $\neg A \vee \neg B \in H$ and $A \in H$ imply that $\neg B \in H$, which contradicts the consistency of H. Hence, $A \notin H$. This concludes the proof of the left-to-right direction of $(D_\leq)$.

For the direction from right to left, we first note that $B \in L$ implies that $A \leq_G B$, by (≤ 2). Suppose A and B satisfy the condition $\forall H (\text{if } GR_{\neg(A \wedge B)}H, \text{then } A \notin H)$ and let $K \in F(\leq_G)$ be such that $B \notin K$, that is, K is $\neg B$-permitting. It follows that K is also $\neg(A \wedge B)$-permitting, so, by Lemma 3.13, there is a maximal $\neg(A \wedge B)$-permitting fallback K' in $F(\leq_G)$ such that $K \subseteq K'$. Let $H = K' + \neg(A \wedge B)$. Then $GR_{\neg(A \wedge B)}H$, so by the supposition, $A \notin H$. Since $K \subseteq K' \subseteq H$, it follows that $A \notin K$. We have shown that for all $K \in F(\leq_G)$, if $A \in K$, then $B \in K$. Finally, Lemma 3.6 yields that $A \leq_G B$.   □

Proof of Theorem 4.6: Consider any L-theory G and let $\leq$ be $\leq_G$ defined via $(D_\leq)$. We proceed to prove that $\leq$ satisfies the axioms for an entrenchment ordering (cf. Definition 3.1). We first prove Dominance.

(≤ 2) Suppose that $A \vdash_L B$. We have to show that $A \leq B$, that is, either $B \in L$ or $\forall H (\text{if } GR_{\neg(A \wedge B)}H, \text{then } A \notin H)$. Suppose $B \notin L$ and consider any H such that $GR_{\neg(A \wedge B)}H$. $\neg(A \wedge B)$ is L-consistent, since $B \notin L$. Thus, by Strong Consistency, H is L-consistent. By Success, $\neg(A \wedge B) \in H$. Suppose $A \in H$. Then $\neg B \in H$. Since $A \vdash_L B$, we also have that $B \in H$, contrary to the consistency of H. Thus, $A \notin H$.

(≤ 1) Suppose $A \leq B$ and $B \leq C$. We have to show that $A \leq C$. Suppose that the latter condition does not hold. Then by $(D_\leq)$, $C \notin L$ and there is a H such that (i) $GR_{\neg(A \wedge C)}H$ and $A \in H$. Since $C \notin L$, (≤ 2) entails that $B \notin L$. This together with $A \leq B$ implies that (ii) $\forall K (\text{if } GR_{\neg(A \wedge B)}K, \text{then } A \notin K)$. (i) and (ii) yield by (R9) that (iii) $GR_{\neg(C \wedge B)}H$ and $B \in H$. (To see this substitute in (R9) $\neg C$, $\neg A$ and $\neg B$ for A, B and C, respectively.) Given that $C \notin L$. (iii) implies via $(D_\leq)$ that not $B \leq C$, contrary to the assumption.

(≤ 3) We first prove that the following principle holds for belief revision:

(C)   If $GR_{A \vee B \vee C}H$ and $\neg C \in H$, then $GR_{A \vee C}(H+A)$ or $GR_{B \vee C}(H+B)$.

The proof of (C) mainly depends on Revision by Conjunction (R6). First, note that (C) would hold if H is L-inconsistent. To prove this, one uses Strong Consistency and Success. Hence, assume $GR_{A \vee B \vee C}H$, $\neg C \in H$ and that H is consistent. Success and the consistency of H imply that $\neg A \notin H$ or $\neg B \notin H$. Suppose that $\neg A \notin H$. Note that $\vdash_L A \vee C \leftrightarrow [(A \vee B \vee C) \wedge (A \vee C)]$. Since $\neg A \notin H$, $\neg(A \vee C) \notin H$. Thus, applying Revision by Conjunction and Substitutivity, we get $GR_{A \vee C}(H+(A \vee C))$. But $\neg C \in H$, so $H+(A \vee C) = H + A$.

By a similar reasoning, we can prove that $GR_{B \lor C}(H+B)$, if $\neg B \notin H$. This completes the proof of (C)

To prove ($\leq$3), assume that $A \leq B$ and $A \leq C$ but *not* $A \leq B \land C$. Let us first consider the case when either $B \in L$ or $C \in L$. Then $B \land C$ is tautologically equivalent to either C or B. In each case, Dominance and Transitivity will imply that $A \leq B$ and $A \leq C$ entails $A \leq B \land C$. Therefore, suppose that neither $B \in L$ nor $C \in L$. Since we have assumed that not $A \leq B \land C$, ($D_\leq$) implies that for some H, $GR_{\neg(A \land B \land C)}H$ and $A \in H$. Substituting in (C) $\neg C$ for A, $\neg B$ for B and $\neg A$ for C, we get:

If $GR_{\neg C \lor \neg B \lor \neg C}H$ and $A \in H$, then $GR_{\neg C \lor \neg A}(H+\neg C)$ or $GR_{\neg B \lor \neg A}(H+\neg B)$,

or equivalently:

If $GR_{\neg(A \land B \land C)}H$ and $A \in H$, then $GR_{\neg(A \land C)}(H+\neg C)$ or $GR_{\neg(A \land B)}(H+\neg B)$.

Since we have assumed the antecedent, the consequent holds, i.e., $GR_{\neg(A \land C)}(H+\neg C)$ or $GR_{\neg(A \land B)}(H+\neg B)$.

Since $A \in H$, $A \in H + \neg C$ and $A \in H + \neg B$. The first disjunct above therefore implies the existence of some K such that $GR_{\neg(A \land C)}K$ and $A \in K$. This, however, contradicts the assumption that $A \leq C$ and $C \notin L$. Analogously, the second disjunct contradicts the assumption that $A \leq B$ and $B \notin L$. This concludes the proof.

($\leq$4) Note that Expansion has the following special case: (T) If $\bot \notin G$ and $GR_T H$, then $H = G$. To prove ($\leq$4), we first consider the case when $\bot \notin G$ and $A \notin G$. We have to show that $A \leq \bot$, i.e., that either $\bot \in L$ (which is excluded by the assumption that L is consistent). or that $\forall H$(if $GR_{\neg(A \land \bot)}H$, then $A \notin H$). Suppose that $GR_{\neg(A \land \bot)}H$. Since $\neg(A \land \bot)$ is L-equivalent to T, (T) and Substitutivity yield that $H = G$. But then $A \notin H$, since we have assumed that $A \notin G$.

Next, we consider the case when $\bot \notin G$ and $A \leq \bot$. We have to show that $A \notin G$. Since $A \leq \bot$ and $\bot \notin L$, $\forall H$(if $GR_{\neg(A \land \bot)}H$, then $A \notin H$). By Seriality, there exists a theory H such that $GR_{\neg(A \land \bot)}H$. By the same reasoning as above, $H = G$. Since $A \notin H$, $A \notin G$.

($\leq$5) Suppose that $T \leq A$. Then by ($D_\leq$), either $A \in L$, and we are done, or $\forall H$(if $GR_{\neg(T \land A)}H$, then $T \notin H$). But $T \in H$, for every theory H, so the latter alternative contradicts Seriality. Hence, $A \in L$. □

Proof of Theorem 4.7: Suppose that **R** is functional, and that, for any G, we define $\leq_G$ in terms of **R** via ($D_\leq$). We then define $F(\leq_G)$ from $\leq_G$ and, finally, we define **S** from $F(\leq_G)$ via (D_R). We want to prove that $R \subseteq S$, that is, for all G, H and A, if GR_AH, then GS_AH. It will then follow that $S \subseteq R$. To see this, we argue as follows: Since R is functional, $\leq_G$ will be connected. It follows that also S is functional. Suppose now that GS_AH. By Seriality, GR_AK, for some K. $R \subseteq S$ then yields that GS_AK. By the functionality of S, $K = H$. Hence, GR_AH.

Suppose now that GR_AH. We want to prove that GS_AH. If $\neg A \in L$, then, by Success, H is inconsistent. It immediately follows from the definition of S, that GS_AH, in this case. Thus, we assume that $\neg A \notin L$. Now, define:

$$K = \{B: \text{not}(B \leq_G \neg A)\}.$$

We want to show that:

(1) $K \in F(\leq_G)$;

(2) $\neg A \notin K$;

(3)   for every $T \in F(\leq_G)$, if $K \subset T$, then $\neg A \in T$.

(1) -(3) imply that K is a maximal A-permitting fallback in $F(\leq_G)$. Finally, we want to prove

(4) $H = K + A$.

Then it will follow that GS_AH.

<u>Proof of (1)</u>: We first prove that K is closed upwards under $\leq_G$. Suppose that $B \in K$ (i.e., $\text{not}(B \leq_G \neg A)$) and $B \leq_G C$. We want to show that $C \in K$. If $C \notin K$, then $C \leq_G \neg A$. But then, since $B \leq_G C$ and $\leq_G$ is transitive, $B \leq_G \neg A$, contrary to the assumption.

Next, we prove that K is closed under conjunction. Suppose that $B \in K$ and $C \in K$. We want to show that $B \wedge C \in K$. Suppose that this is not the case. Then $B \wedge C \leq_G \neg A$. However, the connectedness of $\leq_G$ yields that $B \leq_G C$ or $C \leq_G B$. In the former case, $B \leq_G B$ (≤ 2) and $B \leq_G C$, so $B \leq_G B \wedge C$ (by (≤ 3)). In the latter case, we get $C \leq_G B \wedge C$ in a similar way. Hence, $B \leq_G B \wedge C$ or $C \leq_G B \wedge C$. But then, by transitivity, $B \leq_G \neg A$ or $C \leq_G \neg A$. This contradicts the assumption that $B \in K$ and $C \in K$.

<u>Proof of (2)</u>: $\neg A \notin K$, since otherwise we would have that not $\neg A \leq_G \neg A$, which is impossible given the fact that $\leq_G$ satisfies Dominance.

<u>Proof of (3)</u>: If $K \subset T$, then, for some $C \in T$, $C \notin K$. Thus, $C \leq_G \neg A$. But then, since T is closed upwards, $\neg A \in T$.

<u>Proof of (4)</u>: We want to prove that $H = K + A$, i.e.,

(i) $B \in H$ iff $A \rightarrow B \in K$.

To prove (i) it is sufficient to prove:

(ii) $B \in H$ iff $\text{not}(A \rightarrow B \leq_G \neg A)$.

Now, by $(D_\leq)$ and the fact that $\neg A \notin L$, and the fact that $\mathbf{R}$ is functional,

(iii) $\quad$ not$(A \to B \leq_G \neg A)$ iff $A \to B \in T$,

where T is the (unique!) $\mathbf{R}$-revision of G with $\neg((A \to B) \wedge \neg A)$. Now, $\neg((A \to B) \wedge \neg A)$ is L-equivalent to A. Hence, by Substitutivity, T is the $\mathbf{R}$-revision of G with A. But then, $T = H$. Thus, to prove (ii), it is sufficient to prove:

(iv) $\quad B \in H$ iff $A \to B \in H$.

But this is trivial in view of the fact that $A \in H$ (by Success). $\quad\Box$

Proof of Lemma 5.1: We first consider the limiting case, in which $\neg A \in L$. In this case, (a) GR_AH iff $\bot \in H$ (by Success and Seriality) and (b) $GR_{\neg A}^-K$ iff $G = K$, by (C3).

To prove *Levi* from right to left, assume that GR_AH. Then, by (a), $\bot \in H$. Therefore, since $\neg A \in L$, $H = G + A$. Also, by (b), $GR_{\neg A}^-G$. Hence, the r. h. s. of *Levi* is satisfied for $K = G$.

For the other direction, suppose that for some K, $GR_{\neg A}^-K$ and $H = K + A$. Since $\neg A \in L$, $\bot \in H$. But then (a) implies that GR_AH.

We now consider the principal case, in which $\neg A \notin L$. We first prove *Levi* from left to right. Suppose GR_AH. Then, by definition, there is some maximal A-permitting fallback K such that $H = K + A$. By (C2), there is some theory T such that $GR_{\neg A}^-T$ and $K \subseteq T \subseteq G \cap H$. We want to show that $H = T + A$. Since $K \subseteq T$, the monotonicity of expansion yields $K + A \subseteq T + A$, that is, $H \subseteq T + A$. Since, $T \subseteq H$ and $H + A = H$, monotonicity yields $T + A \subseteq H$.

For the other direction of *Levi*, suppose that for some K, $GR_{\neg A}^-K$ and $H = K + A$. By (C1), there is a maximal A-permitting fallback T such that $T \subseteq K \subseteq G \cap (T + A)$. By the definition of revision, $GR_A(T + A)$. Thus, GR_AH will follow if we can prove that $K + A = T + A$. Since $T \subseteq K$, $T + A \subseteq K + A$. Since $K \subseteq T + A$, $K + A \subseteq (K + A) + A = K + A$. $\quad\Box$

NOTES

[1] The inspiration for this paper comes from our discussions with the participants of the Workshop on the Logic of Theory Change — Konstanz, October 13 - 15, 1989. We want to thank them all. Special thanks go to the organizers of the conference André Fuhrmann and Michael Morreau. We are also grateful to Sven Ove Hansson and Hans Rott for their very helpful comments on an earlier version.

2 Actually, Grove works with an ordering of epistemic *plausibility*. But as Gärdenfors (1988, sect. 4.8) points out, the notions of plausibility and entrenchment are interdefinable. Thus, a proposition A is at least as plausible as a proposition B given the agent's beliefs if and only if non-B is at least as entrenched as non-A in the agent's belief set. The notion of epistemic entrenchment is primarily defined for the propositions that belong to the agent's belief set: one adopts the convention that propositions that are not believed by the agent are minimally entrenched. On the other hand, the notion of plausibility primarily applies to the propositions that are incompatible with the agent's beliefs (the propositions that are compatible with what he believes are all taken to be equally and maximally plausible). Thus, this is a notion of *conditional* plausibility. A is at least as plausible as B in this sense iff the following holds: on the condition that I would have to revise my beliefs with A ∨ B, I should change them in such a way as to allow for A.

3 Cf. our informal characterization of epistemic entrenchment above.

4 For the notion of a closure system and other basic notions from universal algebra and lattice theory that appear in this section, see for example Grätzer (1979), Chap 1 and Rasiowa & Sikorski (1970), Chap 1.

5 Rott assumes connectedness for entrenchment. Therefore, he works with nested families of fallbacks, or, as he calls them, "EE-cuts".

6 Cf. Rott (1989), for the same observation.

REFERENCES

Alchourrón, C. E., Gärdenfors, P., and Makinson, D. (1985) 'On the logic of theory change: Partial meet contraction and revision functions', *Journal of Symbolic Logic* **50**, 510-530.

Gärdenfors, P. (1988) *Knowledge in Flux: Modeling the Dynamics of Epistemic States,* Bradford Books, MIT Press.

Grove, A. (1988) 'Two modellings for theory change', *Journal of Philosophical Logic* **17**, 157-170.

Grätzer, G. (1979) *Universal Algebra* (Second Edition), Springer Verlag.

Levi, I. (1980) *The Enterprise of Knowledge,* the MIT Press.

Lindström, S. and Rabinowicz, W. (1989) 'On Probabilistic Representation of Non-Probabilistic Belief Revision', *Journal of Philosophical Logic* **18**, 69-101.

Lindström, S. and Rabinowicz, W. (1990) 'Belief Revision, Epistemic Conditionals and the Ramsey Test', *Uppsala Philosophy Reports* no 1, 1990.

Niederée, R. (1990) 'Multiple Contraction. A Further Case Against Gärdenfors' Principle of Recovery', this volume.

Rasiowa, H., and Sikorski, R. (1970) *The Mathematics of Metamathematics* (Third edition), PWN —Polish Scientific Publishers, Warsaw.

Rott, H. (1989) 'Two Methods of Contractions and Revisions of Knowledge Systems'. In Michael Morreau (ed.), *Proceedings of the Tübingen Workshop on Semantic Networks and Non-Monotonic Reasoning*, Vol. 1, SNS-Bericht 89-48, Tübingen, pp. 28-47.

The Ramsey Test
for Conditionals

The negative Ramsey test: Another triviality result

Peter Gärdenfors[1], Sten Lindström[2], Michael Morreau[3]
and Wlodzimierz Rabinowicz[2]

1. The so called *Ramsey test* is a semantic recipe for determining whether a conditional proposition is acceptable in a given state of belief. Informally, it can be formulated as follows:

(RT)   Accept a proposition of the form "if A, then C" in a state of belief K, if and only if the minimal change of K needed to accept A also requires accepting C.

In Gärdenfors (1986) it was shown that the Ramsey test is, in the context of some other weak conditions, on pain of triviality incompatible with the following principle, which was there called the *preservation criterion*:

(P)   If a proposition B is accepted in a given state of belief K and the proposition A is consistent with the beliefs in K, then B is still accepted in the minimal change of K needed to accept A.

Now, if someone wants to adhere to the Ramsey test, the preservation criterion might be attacked. On the other hand, if (P) is given up, many roads seem to be open and one may want to supplement (RT) with some other principles constraining conditionals. (RT) provides a necessary and sufficient criterion for when a 'positive' conditional should be included in a belief state, but it does not say anything about when the *negation* of a conditional sentence should be accepted. A very natural candidate for this purpose is the following *negative Ramsey test*:

(NRT)   Accept the negation of a proposition of the form "if A, then C" in a consistent state of belief K, if and only if the minimal change of K needed to accept A does not require accepting C.

[1]Cognitive Science, Dept. of Philosophy, Lund University, Kungshuset, Lundagård, S-223 50 Lund, Sweden. E-mail: Gardenfors@lumac.lu.se or Garden@seldc52.bitnet.
[2]Department of Philosophy, Uppsala University, Villavägen 5, S-752 36 Uppsala, Sweden.
[3]Seminar für natürlich-sprachliche Systeme, Universität Tübingen, Biesingerstraße 10, D-7400 Tübingen 1, West Germany. E-mail: Nffns01@dtuzdv1.bitnet.

The main purpose of this note is to show that (NRT) will lead to triviality results even in the absence of additional conditions like (P).

2.   The presentation of the results requires some minimal formal machinery. Let L be a language including truth-functional connectives and a propositional constant $\top$ (truth), as well as a conditional connective $>$. A state of belief will be modelled by sets of sentences called *belief sets* which are denoted by the letters K and H with various subscripts. For the main result of the paper, we need no assumptions at all about the underlying logic of L, nor any assumption that belief sets are closed under any particular logic. A belief set can be any set of sentences from L. L is governed by a logic $\vdash$. However, we will make no assumptions concerning the properties of $\vdash$ except that it is a relation between sets of sentences and single sentences in L. A belief set K is said to be *consistent* if there is no sentence A such that both $K \vdash A$ and $K \vdash \neg A$.

Belief revisions, as mentioned in (RT), (NRT), and (P), are modelled by a function $\mathcal{F}$, which, for every belief set K and every sentence A in L, determines a belief set K_A which represents the minimal change of K needed to include A. $K_A = \mathcal{F}(K,A)$ will be called the *revision* of K with respect to A. A *belief revision model* is an ordered pair $\langle \mathcal{K}, \mathcal{F} \rangle$, where $\mathcal{K}$ is a set of belief sets and $\mathcal{F}$ a belief revision function (not necessarily onto) with $\mathcal{K}$ as domain and range.

3.   The positive and the negative Ramsey test can now be formulated more succinctly as follows:

(RT) $A > C \in K$ if and only if $C \in K_A$.

(NRT)   If K is consistent, then $\neg(A > C) \in K$ if and only if $C \notin K_A$.

To see the power of these two principles, it can be recalled from Gärdenfors (1986) that (RT) implies the following *monotonicity* criterion:

(M)   For all belief sets K and H and all sentences A, if $K \subseteq H$, then $K_A \subseteq H_A$.

Similarly, (NRT) entails the following *inverse monotonicity* criterion:

(IM)   For all consistent belief sets K and H and all sentences A, if
         $K \subseteq H$, then $H_A \subseteq K_A$.

(*Proof*: Suppose that $K \subseteq H$ and $B \notin K_A$. By (NRT), $\neg(A > B) \in K$ and thus
$\neg(A > B) \in H$. By the other half of (NRT), we then have $B \notin H_A$ as desired).
We now want to show that (IM), and thus (NRT), cannot be satisfied in a
belief revision model except in very marginal circumstances.

A final criterion for belief revisions that will be needed for the following
result is the very weak requirement that if a consistent belief state is revised
by a tautology, nothing happens:

(T)   If K is consistent, then $K_T = K$, for all $K \in \mathcal{K}$.

Theorem: If a belief revision model $\langle \mathcal{K}, \mathcal{F} \rangle$ satisfies (NRT) and (T), then
there are no consistent belief sets K and H in $\mathcal{K}$ such that $K \subset H$.

Proof: Consider a belief revision model $\langle \mathcal{K}, \mathcal{F} \rangle$ which satisfies (NRT) and
(T). Suppose for contradiction that $\mathcal{K}$ contains some consistent belief sets K
and H in $\mathcal{K}$ such that $K \subset H$. From this it follows by (IM) (which follows
from (NRT)) that $H_T \subseteq K_T$. By (T), on the other hand, it follows that $K_T = K$
and $H_T = H$. and hence $H \subseteq K$, which contradicts $K \subset H$. *Q.E.D.*

The conclusion of the theorem – that there are no consistent belief sets K
and H in $\mathcal{K}$ such that $K \subset H$ – is clearly unreasonable. Surely, we want to
allow that some belief sets have consistent extensions in the belief revision
model.

Note that the theorem presumes nothing about the underlying logic, nor
that belief sets be closed under logical consequences. Furthermore, it
generalizes to the *relational* belief revision models of Lindström and
Rabinowicz (1989), that is models where it is not assumed that there is a
unique revision K_A but there may be several such revision sets.

4.   The theorem shows that one cannot have (NRT) together with other reasonable conditions, since any interesting belief revision model must contain some incomplete belief sets. And since (NRT) implies the highly unpalatable inverse monotonicity criterion, (NRT) must clearly be regarded as the culprit in the theorem.[1]

Nevertheless, it would be interesting to have some form of criterion for when a negative conditional can be accepted in a belief set. The following variation is a weaker version of (NRT):

(WNRT) $\neg(A > C) \in K$ if and only if $\neg C \in K_A$.

It may now be hoped that this less potent criterion may be combined peacefully with other conditions on belief revision models, for example (RT). In this final section, we assume that L is governed by classical truth-functional logic and that belief sets are closed under this logic.

However, even (WNRT) has some unappetizing consequences. To see this, first note that in the presence of (RT), (WNRT) is equivalent to:

(ST) $\neg(A > C) \in K$ if and only if $A > \neg C \in K$.

This criterion is motivated by Stalnaker's (1968) analysis of counterfactuals, in contrast to Lewis's (1973) account. On a syntactic level, the difference between the two systems is that in Stalnaker's theory the following axiom is valid, but it is not valid in Lewis's 'official' axiom system VC:

(D) $(A > C) \vee (A > \neg C)$

For the following lemma we need a weak technical assumption:

(C)   For any belief set K in a belief revision model $<\mathcal{K},\mathcal{F}>$ and every sentence A such that $\neg A \notin K$, there is a consistent belief set H in $<\mathcal{K},\mathcal{F}>$ such that and $A \in H$.

Lemma: If a belief revision model $<\mathcal{K},\mathcal{F}>$ satisfies (ST) and (C), then the formula $(A > C) \vee (A > \neg C)$ is in every belief set K in $\mathcal{K}$.

Proof: Suppose that $(A > C) \lor (A > \neg C) \notin K$, for some K in $\mathcal{K}$. By (C), there is then some consistent state H in $<\mathcal{K},\mathcal{F}>$ such that $\neg((A > C) \lor (A > \neg C)) \in$ H, which entails that $\neg(A > C) \in$ H and $\neg(A > \neg C) \in$ H. But this immediately contradicts that $<\mathcal{K},\mathcal{F}>$ satisfies (ST). Q.E.D.

It can also be noted that if $(A > C) \lor (A > \neg C)$ is in every belief set K in $\mathcal{K}$, then if $\neg(A > C) \in K$, we have immediately $A > \neg C \in K$, so one half of (ST) follows from the presence of (D).

Now, with the aid of (RT), it is shown in Gärdenfors (1978), lemma 12, that the formula $(A > C) \lor (A > \neg C)$ is in every belief set K in $\mathcal{K}$ if and only if a belief revision model $<\mathcal{K},\mathcal{F}>$ satisfies the following criterion (a belief set K is said to be *complete* if for every sentence A in *L* either $K \vdash A$ or $K \vdash \neg A$):

(E)   If K is a complete belief set, then K_A is also a complete belief set for all sentences A.

The epistemic interpretation of the criterion (E) is that if one is omniscient in the sense of being in a complete state of belief, then, no matter how one revises the belief state, one still ends up in a complete state of belief. In my opinion, this is a very strong demand on a belief revision model.

To sum up, the weaker version (WNRT) of the negative Ramsey test entails, in the presence of (RT), the criterion (ST) which in turn entails (E). And since this condition is questionable, the same judgement must fall on (WNRT).

Another reason to reject (WNRT) is the following:[1] Assume (WNRT), (RT) and the 'success' condition:

(K*2) $A \in K_A$

Let K be any belief set in a belief revision model $<\mathcal{K},\mathcal{F}>$. From (K*2) it follows that $\bot \in K_\bot$, where $\bot$ is the contradiction (the negation of $\top$). Since $K_\bot$ is a belief set $\neg A \in K_\bot$, for every A, so that by (WNRT), $\neg(\bot > A) \in K$, for every A. But also since $\bot \in K_\bot$ and $K_\bot$ is a belief set, $A \in K_\bot$, so by (RT) $\bot > A \in K$. Hence K is inconsistent. But K was an arbitrary belief set in $<\mathcal{K},\mathcal{F}>$. This result shows that (WNRT) cannot be applied using contradictions in antecedents of conditional sentences.

---

[1]This is due to David Makinson.

Acknowledgements: The authors want to thank Isaac Levi, David Makinson and Hans Rott for helpful criticism and comments. Gärdenfors' work with this article has been supported by the Swedish Council for Research in the Humanities and Social Sciences.

References:

Alchourrón, C.E., Gärdenfors, P., and Makinson, D. (1985): "On the logic of theory change: Partial meet functions for contraction and revision", *Journal of Symbolic Logic*, vol. 50, pp. 510-530.

Gärdenfors, P. (1978): "Conditionals and changes of belief", in *The Logic and Epistemology of Scientific Change*, ed. by I. Niiniluoto and R. Tuomela, *Acta Philosophica Fennica*, vol. 30, pp. 381-404.

Gärdenfors, P. (1986): "Belief revisions and the Ramsey test for conditionals", *The Philosophical Review*, vol. 95, pp. 81-93.

Gärdenfors, P. (1987): "Variations on the Ramsey test: More triviality results", *Studia Logica*, vol. 46, 321-327.

Gärdenfors, P. (1988): *Knowledge in Flux: Modeling the Dynamics of Epistemic States*, Bradford Books, MIT Press.

Levi, I. (1988): "Iteration of conditionals and the Ramsey test", *Synthese 76*, pp. 49–81.

Lewis, D.K. (1973): *Counterfactuals*, Blackwell.

Lindström, S. and Rabinowicz, W. (1989): "Belief revision, epistemic conditionals and the Ramsey test", manuscript, Department of Philosophy, Uppsala University.

Rott, H. (1989): "Conditionals and theory change: Revisions, expansions, and additions", *Synthese 81*, pp. 91-113.

Stalnaker, R. (1968): "A theory of conditionals", *Studies in Logical Theory*, (American Philosophical Quarterly Monographs Series no. 2), N. Rescher, ed., Blackwell, 98-112.

A Nonmonotonic Conditional Logic for Belief Revision

Part 1: Semantics and Logic of Simple Conditionals

Hans Rott*

Abstract

Using Gärdenfors's notion of epistemic entrenchment, we develop the semantics of a logic which accounts for the following points. It explains why we may generally infer If ¬A then B if all we know is A∨B while must not generally infer If ¬A then B if all we know is {A∨B,A}. More generally, it explains the nonmonotonic nature of the consequence relation governing languages which contain conditionals, and it explains how we can deduce conditionals from premise sets without conditionals. Depending on the language at hand, our logic provides different ways of keeping the Ramsey test and getting round the Gärdenfors triviality theorem. We indicate that consistent additions of new items of belief are not to be performed by transitions to logical expansions.

1 Introduction

1.1 An example

Imagine that you are walking along a long and lonely beach. It is a beautiful night. Still you feel somewhat uncomfortable. You are hungry. But you know that at the end of the beach there are two restaurants, one of them run

*University of Stuttgart, Institute for Computational Linguistics, Keplerstraße 17, D-7000 Stuttgart 1, West Germany

by Annie, the other one by Ben. There are no other buildings around. Now you are still far away from the restaurants, but you happen to perceive a shimmering light there, without being able to make out whether it comes from Annie's or Ben's restaurant. So you form the belief that either Annie's or Ben's restaurant is open. And also, you are willing to accept the conditional

> If Annie's restaurant is not open (then) Ben's restaurant will be open.
>
> (1)

Approaching the promising end of the beach, you see that Annie's restaurant is lit while Ben's is unlit. You form the new beliefs that Annie's but not Ben's restaurant is open. You have just learned something new, nothing causes any contradiction. But surprisingly you have lost the conditional (1). You no longer believe that if Annie's restaurant is not open then Ben's restaurant will be open, nor do you assent to the (more appropriate) subjunctive variant

> If Annie's restaurant were not open (then) Ben's restaurant would
> be open. (2)

Put in more formal terms, the premise of your belief state in the first situation may be taken to be $A \lor B$. Later on you add new pieces of information, viz., A and $\neg B$. Representing the natural language conditional 'if ... then ...' by the formal connective $\Box\!\!\rightarrow$, we find that you can infer $\neg A \Box\!\!\rightarrow B$ at the outset of your beach walk, but that you cannot infer $\neg A \Box\!\!\rightarrow B$ after spotting the light source in Annie's restaurant:

$$\neg A \Box\!\!\rightarrow B \in Cn(\{A \lor B\}) \text{ , but}$$
$$\neg A \Box\!\!\rightarrow B \notin Cn(\{A \lor B, A, \neg B\})$$
$$(\text{or } \neg A \Box\!\!\rightarrow B \notin Cn(\{A \lor B, A \& \neg B\})).$$

Conditionals thus exhibit a *non-monotonic* behaviour. That is, in the context of a language which contains conditionals, we cannot expect to have a plausible consequence relation Cn such that $\Gamma \subseteq \Gamma'$ automatically implies $Cn(\Gamma) \subseteq Cn(\Gamma')$. This is my first point. My second one is that Cn should include some kind of *conditional logic*. In the initial situation, it appears quite correct to infer the natural language conditional (1) (not just the material conditional $\neg A \rightarrow B$!) from the premises in which no conditional connective occurs.

Notice that it seems very natural to switch from considering an indicative to considering the corresponding subjunctive conditional in this example.[1] We will in fact presuppose in this paper that, roughly, both types of conditionals are susceptible to a unified account employing the so-called *Ramsey test*:[2]

(R) A□→B is accepted in a belief state if and only if updating this belief state so as to accomodate A leads to a belief state where B is accepted.

1.2 The role of consequence relations in Gärdenfors's incompatibility theorem

The points just made in the intuitive example have a counterpart in a meanwhile notorious abstract result. Gärdenfors (1986; see Gärdenfors 1988, Sections 7.4-7.7) has shown that the Ramsey test is incompatible with a small number of apparently innocuous and reasonable requirements for updating belief states. The most important one is the *preservation principle*:

(P) If a sentence A is consistent with a belief state then updating this belief state so as to add A leads to a belief state which includes all sentences accepted in the original belief state.[3]

Leaving aside technical niceties, all proofs for the Gärdenfors incompatibility theorem that can be found in the literature run like this. Start with a belief

---

[1]The example is a variation of an example to be found in Hansson (1989). The crucial difference from Hansson's hamburger example is that in my case spotting the light in Annie's restaurant completely overrides the earlier piece of information that Annie's *or* Ben's restaurant is lit. In this way my example is also meant to refute the suggestion of Morreau (1990) that the evaluation of conditionals always depends on the order of incoming information. Morreau's analysis predicts, wrongly I believe, that conditionals cannot be lost after consistent updates of belief states. See Rott (1990).

[2]Since Adams published his famous Kennedy example, most writers have refrained from venturing a unified analysis of indicative and subjunctive conditionals. I think, however, that the principle of compositionality should be applied here. If there are differences in meaning between indicative and subjunctive conditionals, they should be attributed to the different grammatical moods and/or tenses rather than to the connective 'if' itself.

[3](R) and (P) could be weakened by requiring that A and B be "objective sentences", i.e., non-conditionals. This would not make a difference for the following. However, while I reject (P), I shall accept a modified form of the preservation principle saying that *objective* sentences are preserved under consistent updates.

state K that is totally ignorant with respect to two sentences A and B. Let K' and K" be the belief states that are obtained after adding A and B to K, respectively. Now the preservation principle says that adding ¬(A&B) to K' and K" will not throw out A and B from K' and K", respectively. Applying the Ramsey test, this gives that ¬(A&B)□→A is in K' and ¬(A&B)□→B is in K". Now consider K''' which is the resulting belief state after adding A and B (or after adding A&B) to K. It is usually stipulated or just taken for granted that K''' is a superset of both K' and K". Hence both ¬(A&B)□→A and ¬(A&B)□→B are in K''', hence, by another application of the Ramsey test, A and B are in the update of K''' which is necessary in order to accomodate ¬(A&B). But of course, ¬(A&B) should be in this update as well. So this update is inconsistent, in contradiction to a quite modest principle of consistency maintenance.

The reader will already have guessed the point where I do not agree. It is the stipulation that K''' be a superset of K' and K". Actually, most writers identify consistent additions of beliefs with logical *expansions*:

$$K' = Cn(K \cup \{A\})$$
$$K'' = Cn(K \cup \{B\})$$
$$K''' = Cn(K \cup \{A,B\})$$
$$(or \ K''' = Cn(K \cup \{A\&B\})).$$

It follows that K''' is a superset of both K' and K", if one can presuppose that Cn is monotonic, or respectively, if it satisfies the similar, slightly weaker principle of *classical monotonicity*: if $Cn_0(\Gamma) \subseteq Cn_0(\Gamma')$ then $Cn(\Gamma) \subseteq Cn(\Gamma')$. But we saw in the introductory example that neither monotonicity nor classical monotonicity is warranted in languages containing conditionals.

Another way to make precise the intuitive idea behind the proofs of the Gärdenfors incompatibility theorem is to keep the expansion idea for K' and K" but to identify K''' with $Cn(K' \cup \{B\})$ and $Cn(K'' \cup \{A\})$. This would guarantee that K''' is a superset of K' and K"; but it of course assumes that $Cn(K' \cup \{B\})$ and $Cn(K'' \cup \{A\})$ are the same set. We shall see below, however, that this identification is not valid either in our modelling of Cn, as long as we are concerned with the language L_1 specified below. In the more comprehensive language L_2, $Cn(K' \cup \{B\})$ and $Cn(K'' \cup \{A\})$ will be identical, but only at the expense of inconsistency.[4]

---

[4]In anticipation of things to be explained below: In L_1, $Cn(Cn(\{A\}) \cup \{B\})$ corresponds to the sentences satisfied by the E-relation based on $\bot \prec B \prec A \prec \top$, $Cn(Cn(\{B\}) \cup \{A\})$ cor-

It is, however, utterly implausible to assume that adding B after A (or adding A after B) to a belief state that is totally ignorant about A and B leads to an inconsistent belief state. In Rott (1989a) I argued that the right lesson to be drawn from the Gärdenfors incompatibility result is that *consistent revisions* by new items of belief, which I call *additions*, are not to be identified with expansions. Now let us write K°_A for the result of adding A to K. In the final analysis, we see how the puzzle caused by the Gärdenfors incompatibility theorem gets resolved. We will develop an account of how consistent additions of sentences are possible by adding new pieces of information to some set of premises from which a belief state is generated. What we then get is that $(K^\circ_A)^\circ_B$ equals $(K^\circ_B)^\circ_A$ but that no longer $(K^\circ_A) \subseteq (K^\circ_A)^\circ_B$ or $(K^\circ_B) \subseteq (K^\circ_B)^\circ_A$. We summarize our preliminary overview of the different possiblities of cutting the chain of proof of the Gärdenfors incompatibility theorem in the table on the next page.[5]

1.3 Program

This paper is intended to be the first part of a trilogy. We shall base the notion of a belief revision model on the concept of a relation of epistemic entrenchment ("E-relation"). We discuss the properties, the motivation and the finite representability of E-relations. Then we say what it means that a relation of epistemic entrenchment satisfies a sentence. Sentences of four different languages will be considered.[6] First, we have the purely "truth-functional" language L_0 of propositional logic with the symbols $\neg$, &, $\vee$, $\rightarrow$, $\perp$ and $\top$. In the present paper we will then examine the language L_1 with an additional binary conditional operator $\square\!\!\rightarrow$ which connects sentences from L_0. In the second part, we extend L_1 to L_2 by admitting the possibility that L_1-sentences are connected by the classical operators of L_0; in particular L_1 allows for negations and disjunctions of conditionals. Finally, in the third part of the trilogy, we shall make some comments on L_3 which extends L_2 by permitting nested conditionals. This last part will largely be devoted

---

responds to $\perp \prec A \prec B \prec \top$. In L_2, however, B cannot be consistently added to $Cn(\{A\})$ at all.

[5]Admittedly, it is unlikely that the full meaning of this table is transparent for the reader at the present stage. I apologize for this.

[6]We identify a language with the set of its sentences.

Proving Gärdenfors's theorem

Let K be "totally ignorant" about A and B.

Proof idea:

$$\neg(A\&B)\Box\!\!\to A \in K^\circ_A \subseteq K^{??}_{??} \supseteq K^\circ_B \ni \neg(A\&B)\Box\!\!\to B$$

If so, $(K^{??}_{??})^*_{\neg(A\&B)}$ would be inconsistent.

Ideas to get this to work:

$K^{??}_{??} = \ldots$	theory addition		base addition	
	$K \mapsto K^\circ_A = Cn(K \cup \{A\})$		$\begin{array}{c} \Gamma \mapsto \Gamma \cup \{A\} \\ Cn \downarrow \quad \downarrow Cn \\ K \mapsto K^\circ_A \end{array}$	
	L_1	L_2	L_1	L_2
$K^\circ_{\{A,B\}} \supseteq K^\circ_A, K^\circ_B$	no	no	no	no
		since Cn is nonmonotonic		
$K^\circ_{A\&B} \supseteq K^\circ_A, K^\circ_B$	no	no	no	no
		since Cn is not classically monotonic		
$(K^\circ_A)^\circ_B = (K^\circ_B)^\circ_A$	no	yes	yes	yes
		inconsistent		
$(K^\circ_A)^\circ_B \supseteq K^\circ_A$	yes	yes	no	no
Proof of theorem	fails	succeeds	fails	fails

to the application of the present logic Cn in belief revision. It is due to the fact that we can model belief revisions and keep the Ramsey test for conditionals without falling prey to the Gärdenfors incompatibility theorem that the present logic is called a logic *for belief revision*. We shall mainly be concerned with belief *additions*, and it will turn out that the method of belief revision advocated violates the preservation principle. We treat additions and revisions not only by "objective" sentences from L_0, but also by conditionals and compounds of conditionals.

In the present paper we confine ourselves to L_1. In order to develop a logic which suits our purposes we do not explicate the relation

$$\Gamma \models A \text{ , or equivalently, } A \in Cn(\Gamma)$$

in the usual way as meaning that *every E-relation which satisfies Γ also satisfies A*. This would give us too few consequences of Γ. We restrict the class of E-relations that are suitable for Γ and adopt the following criterion of the preferential-models-approach: *every E-relation that "minimally", or "preferentially", satisfies Γ also satisfies A*. In so doing we make Cn nonmonotonic.

The main task then will be to find the right notion of minimality. Three candidates will be considered. The first one will turn out to be insufficient, the second one is quite satisfactory. But we will choose a third one which gives us a unique minimal (in fact a smallest) E-relation for every consistent finite and what is more, for every "well-founded" premise set Γ. In the last section of this paper we examine the inference patterns validated by the resulting conditional logic Cn. In particular we show that the so-called "counterfactual fallacies" (see Lewis 1973, Section 1.8) are *defeasibly valid*, or *valid by default*.

2 Belief revision systems and epistemic entrenchment

Gärdenfors (1988, p. 148) defined a *belief revision system* as a pair $\langle \mathcal{K}, * \rangle$ where $\mathcal{K}$ is a set of *belief sets*, i.e., a set of sets of sentences that are closed under the consequence relation Cn_0 of classical propositional logic, and where * is a *belief revision function* taking any belief set K from $\mathcal{K}$ and any L_0-sentence A to the new belief set $*(K,A) \in \mathcal{K}$, or simply $K*_A$, which is to be interpreted as the minimal revision of K needed to accept A. Moreover, it is required that a belief revision system is rational in the sense that it satisfies a set of rationality postulates originally specified by Gärdenfors in 1982 (see Gärdenfors 1988, Section 3.3). Equivalently, we can say that a belief revision system is a set $\{\langle K,*_K \rangle : K \in \mathcal{K}\}$, where $*_K$, the revision function associated with K, is obtained by putting $*_K(A) = *(K,A)$ for each $K \in \mathcal{K}$.

Now let $K \in \mathcal{K}$ be fixed. Gärdenfors showed that it is, in a very strict sense of the term, the same thing to have a belief revision function $*_K$ for K as it is to have a *belief contraction function* $-_K$ for K satisfying another set of rationality postulates. The relevant connections are furnished by the so-called Levi identity

$$*_K = R(-_K) \text{ is defined by } K*_A = Cn_0(K^-_{\neg A} \cup \{A\})$$

and the so-called Harper identity

$$-_K = C(*_K) \text{ is defined by } K^-_A = K \cap K^*_{\neg A}$$

(see Gärdenfors 1988, Section 3.6). More recently, Gärdenfors and Makinson (1988) showed that it is the same thing to have a contraction function $-_K$ satisfying the relevant set of rationality postulates as it is to have a *relation of epistemic entrenchment*, or shortly an *E-relation*, with respect to K. Now, what are E-relations? An E-relation with respect to K, denoted by $\leq_K$, is a relation holding between L_0-sentences. For $A,B \in L_0$, $A \leq_K B$ is supposed to mean that *B is at least as firmly entrenched in K as A* or, better, *Withdrawing A from K is not harder than withdrawing B*. This can be made quite precise by an idea again due to Gärdenfors. Suppose you are pressed to give up either A or B (where $\nvdash A\&B$), which appears to be the same as to give up A&B. Now you decide to give up A *just in case* B is at least as firmly entrenched in K as A. Since by supposition you have to retract either A or B, this explication clearly entails that $A \leq_K B$ or $B \leq_K A$.

E-relations $\leq_K$ are to satisfy the following conditions (we drop the subscript '$_K$' when there is no danger of confusion):

(E1) If $A \leq B$ and $B \leq C$ then $A \leq C$		(Transitivity)
(E2) If $\emptyset \neq \Gamma \vdash A$ then $B \leq A$ for some $B \in \Gamma$		(Entailment)
(E3) If $B \leq A$ for every B then $\vdash A$		(Maximality)
(E4) If $K \neq L_0$ then $A \leq B$ for every B iff $A \notin K$		(Minimality)

Here and throughout this paper, $\Gamma \vdash A$ is short for $A \in Cn_0(\Gamma)$, $A \vdash B$ is short for $\{A\} \vdash B$ and $\vdash A$ is short for $\emptyset \vdash A$. Condition (E4) expresses the fact that the relation $\leq_K$ of epistemic entrenchment is interesting only within the set K. Outside K, all sentences have equal — viz., minimal — epistemic entrenchment. Condition (E2) replaces Gärdenfors's conditions

(E2a) If $A \vdash B$ then $A \leq B$		(Dominance)
(E2b) $A \leq A\&B$ or $B \leq A\&B$		(Conjunctiveness).

(compare Gärdenfors 1988, Section 4.6, and Gärdenfors and Makinson 1988). It is easily verified that in the presence of (E1) and when applied to belief sets, (E2) is equivalent to the conjunction of (E2a) and (E2b). Apart from reducing the number of postulates, (E2) has two more advantages. First, it has a very clear motivation. For suppose that $\Gamma \vdash A$ and $B \nleq A$ for all $B \in \Gamma$. The latter means, roughly, that it is easier to give up A than give up any B in Γ, which is to say that we may keep all of Γ when removing A. But as A is derivable from Γ by classical propositional logic, we cannot really, or *rationally*, remove A while keeping Γ. In this sense (E2) may be called a rationality criterion. But secondly, note that (E2) makes sense even when K is not closed under Cn_0. Consider for example the set K={A,B,C,A&B&C}. While (E2b) does not apply here, (E2) says that A&B&C is at least as firmly entrenched in K as A or B or C. This is, I believe, in accordance with our intuitions about the rational removal of sentences.

From ≤, we define the strict relation < and the equivalence relation ≐ in the usual way: A<B iff A≤B and B≰A, and A≐B iff A≤B and B≤A. Notice that the connectivity condition A≤B or B≤A follows from (E1) and (E2). Thus A<B is equivalent to B≰A. Other well-known properties of E-relations are the substitutivity of Cn_0-equivalents and the useful

$$A≤B \quad iff \quad A≤A\&B \quad iff \quad A≐A\&B .$$

We say that an E-relation ≤ is *finite* iff ≐ partitions L_0 into finitely many equivalence classes, and we say that ≤ is a *well-ordering E-relation* iff every non-empty set of L_0-sentences has a smallest element under ≤. Of course, the well-ordering E-relations include the finite ones. Well-ordering E-relations will play a key role in later sections of this paper. The epistemological drawback of E-relations which are not well-ordering is evident in the case of *multiple* contractions and revisions. When one is forced to give up at least one of the sentences in some set Γ which possesses no smallest element, it is very difficult to see what should be done. No decision to give up one or more certain sentences can be the best decision. People having coarser but well-ordering E-relations are better off.

We have to say how contraction functions $-_K$ are constructed with the help of epistemic entrenchment relations $≤_K$. In Gärdenfors and Makinson (1988) it is shown that the definitions

$$-_K = C(≤_K) \text{ is given by } K^-_A = \begin{cases} K \cap \{B: A <_K A \vee B\} & \text{if } \nvdash A, \\ K & \text{otherwise.} \end{cases}$$

and

$$≤_K = E(-_K) \text{ is given by } A ≤_K B \text{ iff } A \notin K^-_{A\&B} \text{ or } \vdash A\&B.$$

just do the right thing and fit together perfectly. As we will be concerned with revisions only, we take down the direct link between revisions and relations of epistemic entrenchment.

Observation 1 *Let $R(\leq_K)=_{df}R(C(\leq_K))$ and $E(*_K)=_{df}E(C(*_K))$. Then*

(i) *If* $*_K=R(\leq_K)$ *then* $K*_A = \begin{cases} \{B: \neg A <_K \neg A \vee B\} & \text{if } \not\vdash \neg A, \\ L_0 & \text{otherwise.} \end{cases}$

(ii) *If* $\leq_K=E(*_K)$ *then* $A \leq_K B$ *iff* $A \notin K*_{\neg A \vee \neg B}$ *or* $\vdash A\&B$.

(iii) *$R(\leq_K)$ satisfies the Gärdenfors postulates for revisions if $\leq_K$ is an E-relation with respect to K, and $E(*_K)$ is an E-relation with respect to K if $*_K$ satisfies the Gärdenfors postulates for revisions. Finally, $R(E(*_K))=*_K$ and $E(R(\leq_K))=\leq_K$.*

Proofs of the Observations are collected in an appendix at the end of the paper.

It is of crucial importance for the success of this paper that the reader accepts the notion of epistemic entrenchment as a useful and well-considered tool of analysis. First, he or she is recommended to consult the seminal discussions in Gärdenfors (1988, Chapter 4) and Gärdenfors and Makinson (1988). Secondly, it is shown in Rott (1989b) and (1989c) that contractions constructed from relations of epistemic entrenchment are equivalent in a very strict sense to both partial meet contractions (see Alchourrón, Gärdenfors and Makinson 1985) and safe contractions (see Alchourrón and Makinson 1985, 1986). And thirdly, Lindström and Rabinowicz (1990) develop an interesting liberalized notion of epistemic entrenchment with incomparabilies. We take it for granted that contractions and revisions using epistemic entrenchment have a proper standing by now.

So far we have seen that a Gärdenfors belief revision system can be represented by a set $\{\langle K, \leq_K\rangle: K \in \mathcal{K}\}$, where $\mathcal{K}$ is a set of belief sets and $\leq_K$ is an E-relation with respect to K, for each $K \in \mathcal{K}$. To reach our final definition of a belief revision system, we make two more adjustments. In the first step, we note that we can recover every consistent belief set K from $\leq_K$ through

$$K = K_0(\leq_K) =_{df} \{A: \perp <_K A\} \ (\neq \emptyset).$$

That this is true is clear from (E4). So a belief revision system can be represented as $\{\leq_K: K \in \mathcal{K}\}$. $\mathcal{K}$ can be treated as an arbitrary index set as long as we remember that for $K \neq K'$ we have $K_0(\leq_K) \neq K_0(\leq'_K)$. It is hard, however, to think of a motivation for this restriction. An E-relation mirrors a person's "objective" beliefs (i.e., beliefs expressible in L_0) as well as his dispositions to change his objective beliefs in response to incoming objective information (recall the definition of $R(\leq_K)$). Two persons then with different relations of epistemic entrenchment are in different epistemic states, even if they agree on the objective beliefs they currently hold. So I suggest as my second step to give up this restriction. Taking E-relations as primitive and belief sets as derived by the equation just mentioned, we can do without belief sets at all. Furthermore, we can drop (E4) from the set of requirements for E-relations. E-relations are no longer E-relations *with respect to some belief set K*, but belief sets are belief sets *obtained from some E-relation* $\leq$. We do not need the index set $\mathcal{K}$ any more. My official definition of a belief revision system reads thus:

Definition 1 *A belief revision system is any set $\mathcal{E}$ of E-relations, i.e., binary relations over L_0 satisfying (E1) through (E3). We say that a belief revision system $\mathcal{E}$ is* Gärdenforsian *if and only if for every $\leq$ and $\leq'$ in $\mathcal{E}$, if $K_0(\leq)= K_0(\leq')$ then $\leq=\leq'$.*[7]

3 Bases for relations of epistemic entrenchment

In the course of this paper we shall often want to discuss concrete examples of E-relations. As E-relations are infinite subsets of $L_0 \times L_0$, this is not a completely trivial matter. What we need is a finite representation of some interesting E-relations which enables us to retrieve the full E-relations in a canonical and easily understandable way. We shall introduce the appropriate means in this section.

Definition 2 *A base for an E-relation, or simply, an E-base, is a pair $\langle \mathcal{B}, \preceq \rangle$ where $\mathcal{B}$ is a set of L_0-sentences and $\preceq$ is a non-strict weak ordering of, i.e., a reflexive, transitive and connected relation over, $\mathcal{B}$.*

---

[7]We might also call such belief revision systems *functional*. For they specify a unique revision K^*_A for every $A \in L_0$ and every belief set K such that $\mathcal{E}_K =_{df} \{\leq \in \mathcal{E}: K_0(\leq)=K\}$ is not empty. In general belief revision systems, there are several candidate revisions, one for each $\leq \in \mathcal{E}_K$. This perspective invites interesting comparisons with the work of Lindström and Rabinowicz (1990). For non-empty $\mathcal{E}_K$, for instance, we find that $\bigcap \mathcal{E}_K$ is no E-relation in our sense, but an epistemic entrenchment ordering in the sense of Lindström and Rabinowicz's Definition 3.1. Also see their representation Theorem 3.14. Notice, however, that the "skeptical" intersection of all candidate revisions $\bigcap \{\{B: \neg A < \neg A \vee B\}: \leq \in \mathcal{E}_K\}$ is representable as $\{B: \neg A \vee B \not\leq^* \neg A\}$ where $\leq^* = \bigcup \mathcal{E}_K$. $\leq^*$ is yet another kind of relation (cf. Observation 7 below).

Note that $\mathcal{B}$ need not be consistent and that $\preceq$ need not be antisymmetrical. Given an E-base $\langle \mathcal{B}, \preceq \rangle$, a $\mathcal{B}$-cut is any subset S of $\mathcal{B}$ such that if A∈S and A$\preceq$B then B∈S. Since $\preceq$ is connected, $\mathcal{B}$-cuts are nested.

Definition 3 *Let* $\langle \mathcal{B}, \preceq \rangle$ *be an E-base. Then* the E-relation $\leq = E(\preceq)$ *gener-ated by* $\langle \mathcal{B}, \preceq \rangle$ *is given by*

$A \leq B$ *iff for all* $\mathcal{B}$-cuts S, if $A \in Cn_0(S)$ then $B \in Cn_0(S)$,

for all L_0-*sentences A and B.*

We have to verify that this definition really does what we want.

Observation 2 *Let* $\langle \mathcal{B}, \preceq \rangle$ *be an E-base. Then* $E(\preceq)$ *is an E-relation.*

An E-base $\langle \mathcal{B}, \preceq \rangle$ can rightly be called a base *for the generated E-relation* $E(\preceq)$ only if the relationships as specified by $\preceq$ are preserved in $E(\preceq)$. That is, with $\leq = E(\preceq)$, if for every A and B in $\mathcal{B}$, A$\leq$B if and only if A$\preceq$B, or more succinctly, if $\leq \cap \mathcal{B} \times \mathcal{B} = \preceq$. We would like to know under what circumstances an E-base is a base for its generated E-relation. The following observation demonstrates the usefulness of the Entailment condition.

Observation 3 *An E-base* $\langle \mathcal{B}, \preceq \rangle$ *is a base for* $E(\preceq)$ *if and only if* $\preceq$ *satisfies (E2) over* $\mathcal{B}$.

Notice that if $\preceq$ satisfies (E2) over $\mathcal{B}$ there are in general many E-relations besides $E(\preceq)$ which preserve the relationships as specified by $\preceq$. These re-lationships between the sentences in $\mathcal{B}$ might be viewed as providing *partial information* about some underlying full relation of epistemic entrenchment. An E-base $\langle \mathcal{B}, \preceq \rangle$, however, is intended to be a means for discussing the unique E-relation $E(\preceq)$ generated by it.

In the following, we shall use, without any further indication, only E-bases satisfying (E2).

An E-base $\langle \mathcal{B}, \preceq \rangle$ is called *finite* if $\mathcal{B}$ is finite. In this case, the relation $\simeq = \preceq \cap \preceq^{-1}$ obviously partitions $\mathcal{B}$ into finitely many equivalence classes. Let the number of equivalence classes be n. We denote the equivalence classes by $\mathcal{B}_i$. The indices are chosen so as to ensure that i$\leq$j iff A$\preceq$B for every A∈$\mathcal{B}_i$ and B∈$\mathcal{B}_j$. We employ the following convenient string notation for $\preceq$:

$$\underbrace{\perp \simeq A_{01} \simeq \ldots \simeq A_{0n_0}}_{\mathcal{B}_0} \prec \underbrace{A_{11} \simeq \ldots \simeq A_{1n_1}}_{\mathcal{B}_1} \prec \ldots$$

$$\ldots \prec \underbrace{A_{m1} \simeq \ldots \simeq A_{mn_m}}_{\mathcal{B}_m} \prec \underbrace{\top}_{\mathcal{B}_{m+1}}$$

where $\prec = \preceq - \simeq$, $m \geq 0$, $n_0 \geq 0$ and $n_i \geq 1$ for $i=1,\ldots,m$. It is understood that $(\mathcal{B}-\mathrm{Cn}_0(\emptyset)) \cup \{\perp, \top\} = \mathcal{B}_0 \cup \mathcal{B}_1 \cup \ldots \cup \mathcal{B}_m \cup \mathcal{B}_{m+1}$. If $\mathcal{B} \cap \mathrm{Cn}_0(\emptyset)$ is empty (this will be the case in the intended applications), then $\mathcal{B}_0 = \{\perp\}$ and $m=n$ if $\mathcal{B}$ is consistent, but $m=n-1$ if $\mathcal{B}$ is inconsistent. If $\mathcal{B} \cap \mathrm{Cn}_0(\emptyset)$ is non-empty, then $\mathcal{B}_0 = \{\perp\}$ and $m=n-1$ if $\mathcal{B}$ is consistent, but $m=n-2$ if $\mathcal{B}$ is inconsistent. It is easy to check that the equivalence classes with respect to $\doteq = E(\preceq) \cap (E(\preceq))^{-1}$ are given by $\mathrm{Cn}_0(\mathcal{B}_i \cup \mathcal{B}_{i+1} \cup \ldots \cup \mathcal{B}_m) - \mathrm{Cn}_0(\mathcal{B}_{i+1} \cup \mathcal{B}_{i+2} \cup \ldots \cup \mathcal{B}_m)$ for $i=0,\ldots,m$, and $\mathrm{Cn}_0(\emptyset)$.

4 Epistemic entrenchment semantics for conditionals

4.1 Monotonic semantics

Having a precise notion of a belief revision system at his disposal, Gärdenfors was able to develop a formal epistemic semantics for conditionals with the help of the following version of the Ramsey test (R):

(R′) Let $\langle \mathcal{K}, * \rangle$ be a belief revision system in the sense of Gärdenfors. Then, for every $K \in \mathcal{K}$ and every $A, B \in L_0$, $A \square\!\!\!\rightarrow B \in K$ iff $B \in *(K, A)$.

By Observation 1, this is equivalent to

$$A \square\!\!\!\rightarrow B \in K \quad \text{iff} \quad \neg A <_K \neg A \vee B \quad \text{or} \quad \vdash \neg A.$$

With Definition 1 we modified the concept of a belief revision system by considering E-relations as primitive* and allowing one and the same belief set to be associated with several E-relations. Therefore, we will not speak of the inclusion of a conditional in a belief set but of the satisfaction of a conditional by an E-relation.[8]

---

[8]The following definition is formally more similar to Lewis's (1973) evaluation of conditionals than appears at first sight. See Grove (1988) and Gärdenfors (1988, Section 4.8).

Definition 4 *An E-relation* $\leq$ *satisfies a conditional* $A\square\!\!\rightarrow\!B$ *iff* $\neg A < \neg A \lor B$ *or* $\vdash \neg A$.

The principal condition $\neg A < \neg A \lor B$, i.e., $\neg A < A \rightarrow B$, can be motivated as follows. When an E-relation $\leq$ says that the material conditional $A \rightarrow B$ is more firmly entrenched than $\neg A$, this can be taken to mean that the material conditional is accepted not just because the negation of the antecedent is accepted. And more, if a person in epistemic state $\leq$ should come to learn that A is in fact true, this would not destroy his or her belief in $A \rightarrow B$. Put as a slogan, a natural language conditional is the corresponding material conditional believed more firmly than the negation of its antecedent. Note that conditionals express strict $<$-relationships, not non-strict $\leq$-relationships. In view of Observation 1, $A < B$ is expressible by means of the L_1-sentence If $\neg A \lor \neg B$ then B. But only in L_2 will we dispose of a linguistic expression for $A \leq B$.

An E-relation $\leq$ is said to *satisfy an L_0-sentence* A iff A is in $K_0(\leq)$, i.e., iff $\perp < A$.[9] By (E1)–(E3), $K_0(\leq)$ is consistent and closed under Cn_0, for every E-relation $\leq$. E-relations are *non-classical models*, since, e.g., it is not the case that $\leq$ satisfies $\neg A$ iff $\leq$ does not satisfy A. Nor can E-relations be regarded as the models of a three-valued "truth-functional" logic with the values 'accepted', 'rejected' and 'undecided', because it is impossible to determine the value of $A \lor B$ from the values of A and B if the latter are both 'undecided'. It is either 'undecided' or 'accepted'.[10]

If an E-relation $\leq$ satisfies an L_1-sentence A we write $\leq \models A$, and we set

$$K(\leq) =_{df} \{A \in L_1 : \leq \models A\}.$$

Sometimes we say that $K(\leq)$ is the *belief set* or the *theory* associated with the E-relation $\leq$. Obviously, $K(\leq) \cap L_0 = K_0(\leq)$. An E-relation *satisfies a set* Γ *of L_1-sentences* if it satisfies every element of Γ, i.e., if $\Gamma \subseteq K(\leq)$. Sometimes, when Γ is a given premise set, we say that $\leq$ is an *E-relation for* Γ iff $\leq$ satisfies Γ. More semantic concepts are readily defined along the standard lines:

---

[9]As regards satisfaction, an "objective" L_0-sentence A is equivalent to the conditional $\top\square\!\!\rightarrow\!A$. But they differ in syntactic behaviour. In L_1, we have for instance $A\square\!\!\rightarrow\!A$ but not $(\top\square\!\!\rightarrow\!A)\square\!\!\rightarrow\!(\top\square\!\!\rightarrow\!A)$. Moreover, in Part 2, we shall argue that $\neg A$ differs from $\neg(\top\square\!\!\rightarrow\!A)$ in meaning.

[10]Like belief sets, E-relations seem to obey the logic of supervaluations instead. Cf. Martin (1984).

Definition 5 *An L_1-sentence A is called* satisfiable *or* consistent *if it is satisfied by some E-relation,*[11] *and A is called* (monotonically) valid, *in symbols $\models_1 A$, if it is satisfied by every E-relation. Γ is said to be* consistent *if there is an E-relation for Γ. An L_1-sentence A is* (monotonically) entailed *by a set Γ of L_1-sentences, in symbols $\Gamma \models_1 A$ or equivalently $A \in Cn_1(\Gamma)$, if every E-relation satisfying Γ also satisfies A.*

Example 1 Now, at last, we are able to deal with the introductory beach walk and the generalizations we drew from it. Remember that we have set out to find a way to get (no — not a hamburger, but) the paradigmatic inference[12]

$$\{A \lor B\} \models \neg A \,\square\!\!\rightarrow B \tag{3}$$

and yet block the inference

$$\{A \lor B, A, \neg B\} \models \neg A \,\square\!\!\rightarrow B \tag{4}$$

Let us see if our logic Cn_1 is appropriate. The inference (4) is indeed blocked. Consider the E-relation $\leq$ generated by the E-base

$$\bot \prec A \lor B \simeq A \simeq \neg B \prec \top$$

Obviously, $\leq$ satisfies all the premises of (4), and it does so in an intuitively plausible way. In order to satisfy the conclusion of (4), $\leq$ would have to be such that $A < A \lor B$ holds. There would have to be a $\mathcal{B}$-cut S such that $A \lor B$ but not A is in $Cn_0(S)$. But there is none.

Next consider (3). The most natural E-relation for the single premise $A \lor B$, viz., that generated by the E-base

$$\bot \prec_1 A \lor B \prec_1 \top \,,$$

behaves well. It indeed yields $A <_1 A \lor B$, since $A \lor B$ but not A is a Cn_0-consequence of $S_{A \lor B} =_{df} \{C \in \mathcal{B}: A \lor B \preceq_1 C\} = \{A \lor B\}$. But of course there are more E-relations satisfying $A \lor B$, for example the one generated by the E-base

$$\bot \prec_2 A \prec_2 \top \,.$$

---

[11]Recall that E-relations themselves, or rather their L_0-images $K_0(\leq)$, are always consistent.

[12]In these and all similar considerations to follow, it is understood that A and B are contingent L_0-sentences which are independent with respect to Cn_0.

And it gets clear immediately that the E-relation $E(\preceq_2)$ does not satisfy $\neg A \square\!\!\rightarrow B$. So we cannot validate (3), if $\models_1$ is substituted for $\models$. (End of example)

The objection to this last line of reasoning is that there is nothing which could justify the E-base $\langle\{A\},\preceq_2\rangle$ if all we know is $A \vee B$. In every conceivable sense, the E-base $\langle\{A\vee B\},\preceq_1\rangle$ is much more natural for the singleton premise set $\{A\vee B\}$ than $\langle\{A\},\preceq_2\rangle$. Among the E-relations satisfying some premise set Γ, it appears, there are E-relations that are appropriate for Γ and E-relations that are inappropriate for Γ. There exists, one may suppose, a *preference ordering* among the E-relations satisfying Γ. And only the best E-relations matter. If all of the best ones satisfy the conclusion of the inference, then the inference may be called "valid". Section 4.2 will reveal that we have just argued for employing the techniques of a quite well-known kind of non-monotonic logic.

Before turning to this abstract topic, let us remain at the paradigmatic infernce patterns (3) and (4) for a moment. The problem was found to lie in the validation of (3). What is it that makes $E(\preceq_2)$ so much worse for the single premise $A \vee B$ than $E(\preceq_1)$? It is safe to assume that in this particular case where $A \vee B$ is supposed to be *all one knows*, the relationship $\perp < A$ is not warranted. But what is the general mistake? Three suspicions come to one's mind.

- $E(\preceq_2)$ satisfies *too many sentences*. In order not to invoke "beliefs" that are not justified by the premise set, we should try to minimize the set of sentences satisfied by an appropriate E-relation for the premise set. Just as in usual monotonic logics the deductive closure of a set Γ is the minimal theory including Γ, we should opt for minimal theories (associated with some E-relation) including Γ in the present case.

- $E(\preceq_2)$ satisfies *too many L_0-sentences*. The motivation for this idea is the same as for the last one. If it should turn out insufficient to minimize the number of L_1-sentences (L_1 is the language under consideration), it seems plausible to attribute a preferred status to the "objective" L_0-sentences.

- $E(\preceq_2)$ assigns to some L_0-sentence, for example to A, a *gratuitously high "rank" of epistemic entrenchment* which is not justified by the single premise $A \vee B$. It seems prudent not to attribute a greater degree of irremovability to any objective sentence than is explicitly warranted by the premise set. A believer should be prepared to give up his or her beliefs by minimizing epistemic entrenchments.

I think that all three of these suggestions have a sound basis. In Sections 5–7, we shall examine the consequences of taking them into accout within the framework of nonmonotonic reasoning we are now going to introduce.

4.2   Nonmonotonic semantics

We said that when inquiring whether A follows from a given premise set Γ we only want to consider the *preferred* E-relations satisfying Γ. In the three informal objections against the inadequate E-base which invalidates (3) we found that we wanted to *minimize* certain parameters of E-relations satisfying Γ. These formulations will ring a bell in the ears of those acquainted with the work that has been done in the field of nonmonotonic reasoning. In fact, we can draw on the *minimal models approach* or *preferential models approach* which was developed in its general form by Shoham (1987, 1988). Makinson (1989) generalized it to cases in which the models considered are allowed to be, like E-relations, non-classical. We now adapt some of their central definitions to our purposes of providing an epistemic semantics for conditionals.

Definition 6 *Let $\sqsubset$ be a strict partial ordering of (i.e., an asymmetric and transitive relation over) the class of all E-relations. Then an E-relation $\leq$ is called* minimal *(or preferred) iff there is no E-relation $\leq'$ such that $\leq'\sqsubset\leq$.[13] Let Γ be a set of L_1-sentences. An E-relation $\leq$ is called* minimal for Γ *if $\leq\models\Gamma$ and there is no E-relation $\leq'$ such that $\leq'\models\Gamma$ and $\leq'\sqsubset\leq$. In this case we say that $\leq$ minimally (or preferentially) satisfies Γ (with respect to $\sqsubset$) and write $\leq\models_\sqsubset\Gamma$. We say that A is* minimally valid, *in symbols $\models_\sqsubset A$, if every minimal E-relation satisfies A. We say that Γ minimally entails A, in symbols $\Gamma\models_\sqsubset A$, if every minimal E-relation for Γ satisfies A. We also write $\mathrm{Cn}_\sqsubset(\Gamma)$ for $\{A\in L_1:\Gamma\models_\sqsubset A\}$.*

Be aware that if $\sqsubset\subseteq\sqsubset'$ then there are at least as many $\sqsubset$-minimal E-relations as $\sqsubset'$-minimal ones, and hence $\mathrm{Cn}_\sqsubset(\Gamma)\subseteq\mathrm{Cn}_{\sqsubset'}(\Gamma)$. The intuitive idea behind

---

[13]This is not a very interesting definition. With respect to the three orderings for E-relations suggested in the next section, there is only one smallest E-relation, viz., that generated by the E-base $\bot\prec\top$.

preferential entailment in our case is that only a minimal E-relation for Γ is an epistemic state which is warranted if all the items one explicitly knows are given by Γ. And only warranted belief states should be called upon when determining the consequences of a premise set. The task before us now is to explicate what features can make an E-relation count as "minimal" or "preferred".

From the non-monotonic point of view, it is interesting to enquire the circumstances under which an inference is *robust* (or *persistent* or *stable*) under possible enrichments of the premise set. We say that Γ *robustly entails* A (with respect to some given $\sqsubset$), in symbols $\Gamma \models\!\!\!\models_\sqsubset A$, iff $\Gamma \models_\sqsubset A$ and for every superset Σ of Γ, $\Sigma \models_\sqsubset A$. It turns out that normally, and in particular in our concrete instantiations of $\sqsubset$ presented below, $\models\!\!\!\models_\sqsubset$ is just identical with the old monotonic consequence relation $\models_1$:

Observation 4 *Let $\sqsubset$ be a strict partial ordering of the class of E-relations, Γ be a set of L_1-sentences and A an L_1-sentence. Then*

(i) If $\Gamma \models_1 A$ then $\Gamma \models\!\!\!\models_\sqsubset A$.

(ii) If every E-relation $\leq$ is $\sqsubset$-minimal for $K(\leq)$, then if $\Gamma \models\!\!\!\models_\sqsubset A$ then $\Gamma \models_1 A$.

It is natural to assume that every E-relation $\leq$ is among the preferred E-relations for the total set $K(\leq)$ of sentences satisfied by $\leq$. We shall find that this assumption is fulfilled in all three orderings of E-relations to be discussed in the next section.[14]

5   Three orderings for relations of epistemic entrenchment

In this section, we are going to work out the details of the three suggestions that were made in response to the failure of (3) in the monotonic setting of Cn_1. The first one was that an E-relation which is "grounded in" or "induced by" a given premise set Γ should not satisfy more sentences than necessary. That is, an E-relation $\leq$ for Γ is better than another E-relation $\leq'$ for Γ if $K(\leq)$ is a proper subset of $K(\leq')$.

---

[14]See Definition 7, Observation 6, Observation 13 and its corollary.

Definition 7 *Let $\leq$ and $\leq'$ be E-relations. Then $\leq$ is at least as K-good as $\leq'$, in symbols $\leq \sqsubseteq_K \leq'$, if and only if $K(\leq) \subseteq K(\leq')$. $\leq$ is K-preferred over $\leq'$, in symbols $\leq \sqsubset_K \leq'$, if and only if $\leq \sqsubseteq_K \leq'$ and not $\leq' \sqsubseteq_K \leq$.*[15]

As we are taking E-relations, rather than belief sets, as primary representations of epistemic states, it is desirable to replace this metamathematical definition referring to sets of sentences and satisfaction by a purely mathematical condition.

Observation 5 *Let $\leq$ and $\leq'$ be E-relations. Then the following conditions are equivalent:*

(i) $\leq \sqsubseteq_K \leq'$;
(ii) $\leq' \subseteq \leq$;
(iii) $< \subseteq <'$;
(iv) $\doteq' \subseteq \doteq$.

An obvious corollary is

Corollary *Let $\leq$ and $\leq'$ be E-relations. Then the following conditions are equivalent:*

(i) $\leq \sqsubset_K \leq'$;
(ii) $\leq' \subset \leq$;
(iii) $< \subset <'$;
(iv) $\doteq' \subset \doteq$.

Now we have got quite a good picture of what K-preference consists in. An E-relation $\leq$ satisfies less L_1-sentences than another E-relation $\leq'$ if and only if $\doteq' \subset \doteq$. This means that whenever two L_0-sentences A and B are in the same equivalence class with respect to $\doteq'$ then they are in the same equivalence class with respect ot $\doteq$, and besides there are L_0-sentences A and B which are equivalent with respect to $\doteq$ but not with respect to $\doteq'$. $\doteq$ is a coarsening of $\doteq'$. If $\doteq'$ is given by an E-base in string notation, then a K-preferred $\doteq$ is obtained by replacing one or more occurances of $\prec$ in the string by $\simeq$. We can rephrase the idea of K-preference as follows: *Choose as coarse an E-relation (for a given premise set Γ) as possible! Do not impose unnecessary differences in the degrees of epistemic entrenchment!*

---

[15]The reader be warned that the direction of '$\sqsubseteq$' and '$\sqsubset$' may be the reverse of what he or she has expected. The reason for this is that the preferred E-relations are, in some intuitive as well as formal sense, minimal.

Plausible as all this may be, it is not sufficient. This is borne out dramatically by our paradigm Example 1, where for $\Gamma=\{A\vee B\}$ the E-bases $\bot\prec_1 A\vee B\prec_1\top$ and $\bot\prec_2 A\prec_2\top$ both generate minimal E-relations for Γ with respect to $\sqsubseteq_K$. For any attempt to extend $\simeq_1$ and $\simeq_2$ will result in the trivial base $\bot\prec\top$ and thus fail to satisfy Γ. Note in particular that $E(\prec_1)$ and $E(\prec_2)$ are incomparable with respect to $\sqsubseteq_K$, since $\neg A\Box\!\!\rightarrow B$ is in $K(E(\preceq_1))-K(E(\preceq_2))$ and A is in $K(E(\preceq_2))-K(E(\preceq_1))$. We do not get $\Gamma\models_{\sqsubseteq_K}\neg A\Box\!\!\rightarrow B$. Preference with respect to $\sqsubseteq_K$, therefore, cannot be the key for the validation of (3).

But clearly, $E(\preceq_1)$ should be preferred to $E(\preceq_2)$ in Example 1. It seems obvious that the defect of $\preceq_2$ as an E-base for $\Gamma=\{A\vee B\}$ lies in the fact that $\bot\prec_2 A$, i.e., that A is satisfied by $E(\preceq_2)$. There is no reason for this to be found in Γ. So we turn to the second idea propounded at the end of Section 4.1, namely that $E(\preceq_2)$ satisfies too many L_0-sentences. In order to further compare the E-relations $E(\preceq_1)$ and $E(\preceq_2)$ even though $K(E(\preceq_1))$ and $K(E(\preceq_2))$ are not related by set inclusion, we adopt the following maxim: *Among the K-minimal E-relations, choose only those that commit us to as few L_0-sentences as possible! Do not adopt unwarranted "objective" beliefs!*

Definition 8 *Let $\leq$ and $\leq'$ be E-relations. Then $\leq$ is at least as K_0-good as $\leq'$, in symbols $\leq\sqsubseteq_{K_0}\leq'$, if and only if $\leq\sqsubseteq_K\leq'$, or $\leq$ and $\leq'$ are $\sqsubseteq_K$-incomparable and $K_0(\leq)\subseteq K_0(\leq')$. $\leq$ is K_0-preferred over $\leq'$, in symbols $\leq\sqsubset_{K_0}\leq'$, if and only if $\leq\sqsubseteq_{K_0}\leq'$ and not $\leq'\sqsubseteq_{K_0}\leq$.*

The definition of $\sqsubseteq_{K_0}$ is a bit complicated. Fortunately, the strict version $\sqsubset_{K_0}$ which is the one that in fact enters into the nonmonotonic semantical apparatus, is captured by a nice and easy condition.

Observation 6 *Let $\leq$ and $\leq'$ be E-relations. Then $\leq\sqsubset_{K_0}\leq'$ iff $K(\leq)\subset K(\leq')$ or $K_0(\leq)\subset K_0(\leq')$.*

Note that $\sqsubset_{K_0}$ is transitive because $K(\leq)\subset K(\leq')$ implies $K_0(\leq)\subseteq K_0(\leq')$. Being an extension of $\sqsubset_K$, $\sqsubset_{K_0}$ allows us to compare more E-relations than the former. As a consequence, $\mathrm{Cn}_{\sqsubset_{K_0}}(\Gamma)$ is a superset of $\mathrm{Cn}_{\sqsubset_K}(\Gamma)$ for every premise set Γ. In most cases, the latter will be a *proper* subset of the former. This is true in Example 1, which K_0-preference gets right. It is evident that $\bot\prec_1 A\vee B\prec_1\top$ is the base of the only minimal E-relation for $\Gamma=\{A\vee B\}$ with respect to $\sqsubseteq_{K_0}$, so we have $\Gamma\vdash_{\sqsubset_{K_0}}\neg A\Box\!\!\rightarrow B$. We have managed to find a plausible way of validating the desired inference (3).

It is an interesting and important question whether K_0-preference gives, as in Example 1, always a unique E-relation for a (finite) premise set Γ. The answer is no:

Example 2 Let $\Gamma=\{A,B,\neg A\square\!\!\rightarrow B\}$. Then the E-bases $\bot\prec A\simeq B\prec A\vee B\prec\top$ and $\bot\prec'A\prec'B\simeq'A\vee B\prec'\top$ both generate E-relations $\leq=E(\preceq)$ and $\leq'=E(\preceq')$ for Γ. Both $\leq$ and $\leq'$ are K-minimal for Γ. Any attempt to reduce the number of equivalence classes of $\leq$ and $\leq'$ will result in a violation of either $\bot<^{(\prime)}A$, $\bot<^{(\prime)}B$ or $A<^{(\prime)}A\vee B$. In particular, $\leq$ and $\leq'$ are incomparable with respect to $\sqsubseteq_K$. On the one hand, $\leq$ satisfies but $\leq'$ does not satisfy $\neg B\square\!\!\rightarrow A$, on the other hand, $\leq'$ satisfies but $\leq$ does not satisfy $\neg A\vee\neg B\square\!\!\rightarrow B$. Furthermore, $K_0(\leq)=Cn_0(\{A\&B\})=K_0(\leq')$, and obviously any E-relation for Γ must satisfy $Cn_0(\{A\&B\})$. Hence both $\leq$ and $\leq'$ are K_0-minimal for Γ. It is straightforward to check that $\leq$ and $\leq'$ are the only K_0-preferred E-relations for Γ. (End of example)

Intuitively, K_0-preference seems to be a very natural ordering of E-relations. Still there is an objection. We know from Example 2 that in general there is more than one minimal E-relation with respect to $\sqsubseteq_{K_0}$ for a given premise set Γ. The consequences of Γ, according to $Cn_{\sqsubseteq_{K_0}}$, are those L_1-sentences which are satisfied by all $\sqsubseteq_{K_0}$-minimal E-relations for Γ, i.e., $\cap\{K(\leq):\leq$ is $\sqsubseteq_{K_0}$-minimal for $\Gamma\}$. The question arises as to what *the* epistemic state is, if Γ is all one explicitly knows and Γ admits various $\sqsubseteq_{K_0}$-minimal candidates. It turns out that in most cases it cannot be an E-relation. To see this, we define $K(\leq)=\{A\in L_1:\leq\models A\}$ for an *arbitrary* binary $\leq$ over L_0, to be the set $\{A\in L_0:A\not\leq\bot\}\cup\{B\square\!\!\rightarrow C\in L_1:\neg B\vee C\not\leq\neg B\}$.[16]

Observation 7 *Let $\leq_1,\ldots,\leq_n$ be E-relations and $\leq\ =\ \leq_1\cup\ldots\cup\leq_n$. Then*
   (i) $K(\leq)\ =\ K(\leq_1)\cap\ldots\cap K(\leq_n)$.
   (ii) If $\leq^*$ is an E-relation such that $K(\leq^*)\ =\ K(\leq_1)\cap\ldots\cap K(\leq_n)$, then $\leq^*=\leq$.
   (iii) $\leq$ fails to be an E-relation iff there are sentences A,B,C in L_0 such that $A<_iB\leq_iC$ and $C\leq_jA<_jB$ for some $1\leq i,j\leq n$, and $A<_kB$ for every $1\leq k\leq n$.

From this observation it is clear that if there are multiple $\sqsubseteq_{K_0}$-minimal E-relations for a premise set Γ, we cannot expect to have a unique E-relation $\leq^*$

---

[16]I always presuppose that the satisfaction of an L_1-sentence is defined for non-E-relations $\leq$ in the same way as for E-relations. Different, more complicated definitions of satisfaction may make a big difference.

that satisfies exactly all those sentences satisfied by each of them. Given two E-relations Γ_1 and Γ_2, in particular, we will in most cases find L_0-sentences A,B,C such that $A<_1B\leq_1C$ and $C\leq_2A<_2B$ (or vice versa). For $\leq^*=E(\preceq)\cup E(\preceq')$, we have in Example 2 $A\lor B\leq^*B$ and $B\leq^*A$, but not $A\lor B\leq^*A$, and, for the sake of illustration, in Example 1 we find that for $\leq^*=E(\preceq_1)\cup E(\preceq_2)$ $A\lor B\leq^*A$ and $A\leq^*\bot$, but not $A\lor B\leq^*\bot$. Violation of transitivity seems to be the rule rather than the exception.

We would like to identify $Cn(\Gamma)$ with the set of sentences accepted by an idealized "rational" believer whose only explicit information is given by Γ. We have seen, however, that if we take $Cn_{\sqsubseteq K_0}$ as Cn, there is in general no E-relation satisfying all and only the sentences in $Cn_{\sqsubseteq K_0}(\Gamma)$. Hence the believer's beliefs cannot be mirrored by an E-relation. This is an abstract problem as yet, concerning the formal representation of belief states. Why not just give up the doctine that an epistemic state is best represented by a single relation of epistemic entrenchment? In fact, in Part 2 of the present trilogy, we shall have to give up this doctrine anyway when considering disjunctions of conditionals. Moreover, in Part 3, we shall argue that when it comes to belief revision, it is not E-relations but premise sets which should be taken as the primary objects of revision.

Yet we stick to the thesis that an epistemic state should be represented by a single E-relation in this paper. First, it seems reasonable to assume that something like a measure of the firmness of belief is transitive. Secondly, it is easily verified that in terms of the conditionals satisfied, the transitivity condition (E1) is equivalent to

$$\text{If } \leq\ \models A\lor C\,\square\!\!\!\rightarrow\neg C \text{ and } \leq\ \not\models B\lor C\,\square\!\!\!\rightarrow\neg C \text{ then } \leq\ \models A\lor B\,\square\!\!\!\rightarrow\neg B.$$
(Transitivity by Conditionals)

Substituting D for A, $\neg E$ for B and $D\&\neg E$ for C, we see that Transitivity by Conditionals entails

$$\text{If } \leq\ \models D\,\square\!\!\!\rightarrow E \text{ and } \leq\ \not\models \neg E\,\square\!\!\!\rightarrow\neg D \text{ then } \leq\ \models D\lor\neg E\,\square\!\!\!\rightarrow E.$$
(Failure of Contraposition[17])

If one wants to retain these conditions *for epistemic states*, then one cannot opt for the transition to unions of E-relations. In Example 2, for instance,

---

[17]Notice that $\leq\models D\,\square\!\!\!\rightarrow E$ iff $\leq\models D\,\square\!\!\!\rightarrow\neg D\lor E$. — We shall return to the failure of contrapostion for conditionals in Section 7 below and in Part 2 of the trilogy.

we find that $\leq^*=E(\preceq)\cup E(\preceq')$ satisfies $\neg A\square\rightarrow B$, but neither $\neg B\square\rightarrow A$ nor $\neg A\vee\neg B\square\rightarrow B$. I have to admit, though, that the intuitions behind such inference patterns are not very strong.

The main reason for my tentative insistence on the *one E-relation doctrine* derives from the third idea put forward at the end of Section 4.1. We shall presently show that if we do not assign greater ranks of epistemic entrenchment to L_0-sentences than is explicitly required by a given (well-behaved) premise set Γ, then Γ "induces" a *unique* minimal, and in fact a smallest, E-relation for Γ. In sum, then, I do not want to say that K_0-preference is not good, but I put it aside only because I think that there is a more promising alternative.

In a way, this alternative just generalizes on the idea of K_0-preference. Opting for an E-relation which is minimal with respect to $\sqsubseteq_{K_0}$ means opting for a maximal set of sentences with the lowest epistemic rank possible, viz., the rank of $\perp$. But why follow the prudent strategy of accepting things just to the degree they are explicitly warranted only at this lowest level? It seems to me that believers are well-advised if they adopt the distrustful *maxim of universal minimality: Do not have more confidence in your items of belief than is assured by your premises! Assign to all sentences the lowest epistemic rank possible!*

In order to make this idea more precise we need the notion of the *rank of epistemic entrenchment* of a sentence A according to an E-relation $\leq$. This notion makes sense for well-ordering E-relations.

Definition 9 *Let $\leq$ be a well-ordering E-relation. Then we define for any ordinal α*

$$\alpha(\leq) = \{A\in L_0-\overleftarrow{\alpha}(\leq): A\leq B \text{ for all } B\in L_0-\overleftarrow{\alpha}(\leq)\},$$

where $\overleftarrow{0}(\leq) =_{df} \emptyset$ and $\overleftarrow{\alpha}(\leq) =_{df} \bigcup\{\beta(\leq):\beta<\alpha\}$ for $\alpha>0$.
Then for every L_0-sentence A, $\text{rank}_\leq(A)=\alpha$ iff $A\in\alpha(\leq)$.

As we can go on with this construction up to any arbitrary ordinal, $\text{rank}_\leq$ is well-defined for well-ordering E-relations even if L_0 is supposed to have non-denumerably many atoms. And by construction, if there is no $A\in L_0$ such that $\text{rank}_\leq(A)=\alpha$ for an ordinal α, then there is no $B\in L_0$ such that $\text{rank}_\leq(B)=\beta$ for any $\beta>\alpha$. All ranks are "occupied". It is also easy to see that $A\leq B$ if and only if $\text{rank}_\leq(A)\leq\text{rank}_\leq(B)$. If a finite E-relation is generated by an E-base

$$\underbrace{\perp \simeq A_{01} \simeq \ldots \simeq A_{0n_0}}_{\mathcal{B}_0} \prec \underbrace{A_{11} \simeq \ldots \simeq A_{1n_1}}_{\mathcal{B}_1} \prec \ldots$$

$$\ldots \prec \underbrace{A_{m1} \simeq \ldots \simeq A_{mn_m}}_{\mathcal{B}_m} \prec \underbrace{\top}_{\mathcal{B}_{m+1}}$$

satisfying (E2) over $\mathcal{B}$ then $\mathrm{rank}_{\leq}(A_{ij})=i$, as expected. More generally, $\mathrm{rank}_{\leq}(A)=i$ for any A in $\mathrm{Cn}_0(\mathcal{B}_i \cup \mathcal{B}_{i+1} \cup \ldots \cup \mathcal{B}_m) - \mathrm{Cn}_0(\mathcal{B}_{i+1} \cup \mathcal{B}_{i+2} \cup \ldots \cup \mathcal{B}_m)$. We can now formulate a precise definition for the new maxim.

Definition 10 *Let $\leq$ and $\leq'$ be E-relations. Then $\leq$ is at least as E-good as $\leq'$, in symbols $\leq \sqsubseteq_E \leq'$, if and only if $\leq$ is well-ordering and $\leq'$ is not, or both $\leq$ and $\leq'$ are well-ordering and $\mathrm{rank}_{\leq}(A) \leq \mathrm{rank}_{\leq'}(A)$ for every L_0-sentence A. $\leq$ is E-preferred over $\leq'$, in symbols $\leq \sqsubset_E \leq'$, if and only if $\leq \sqsubseteq_E \leq'$ and not $\leq' \sqsubseteq_E \leq$.*

It is easy to check that $\sqsubseteq_E$ is antisymmetrical. Now our first task is to explore the relationship between E-preference and K-preference and K_0-preference.

Observation 8 *Within the class of well-ordering E-relations, $\sqsubseteq_K \subseteq \sqsubseteq_E$.*

Corollary *Within the class of well-ordering E-relations, $\sqsubset_K \subseteq \sqsubset_E$.*

$\sqsubset_E$ is an extension of $\sqsubset_K$ just as $\sqsubset_{K_0}$ was. The relation between $\sqsubset_E$ and $\sqsubset_{K_0}$, on the other hand, is more delicate. There are examples of E-relations $\leq$ and $\leq'$, for which $\leq \sqsubset_{K_0} \leq'$ but not $\leq \sqsubset_E \leq'$, such as those based on

$$\perp \prec \quad A \quad \prec B \prec \top \quad \text{and}$$
$$\perp \prec' B \simeq' C \quad \prec' A \quad \prec' \top \ ,$$

and also examples where the converse holds, such as those based on

$$\perp \prec \quad A \simeq B \quad \prec \quad C \quad \prec \top \quad \text{and}$$
$$\perp \prec' \quad A \quad \prec' B \simeq' C \quad \prec' \top \ .$$

The best we can do is state is the following

Observation 9 *Within the class of well-ordering E-relations, $\sqsubseteq_E \subseteq \sqsubseteq_{K_0}$.*

6 Constructing E-minimal relations of epistemic entrenchment for well-founded premise sets

We decide to base the following considerations on $\sqsubseteq_E$. In this section we are going to show that with respect to $\sqsubseteq_E$, every consistent finite set of L_1-premises possesses a unique minimal, and in fact a smallest, E-relation satisfying it. This allows us to keep the one-E-relation doctrine for all practical applications of L_1. We shall also consider the case of an infinite Γ.

An arbitrary set Γ of L_1-sentences can be given the following format. It divides into a set Γ_0 of L_0-premises A_i and a set Γ_1 of conditionals from L_1–L_0 of the form $B_j \square\!\!\rightarrow C_j$. When trying to find an E-relation satisfying Γ, one can regard the premises as providing partial information about the set of E-relations — or preferably, about *the* E-relation — constituting the epistemic state of an individual whose only explicit information consists in Γ. For the sake of simplicity, we cancel all conditionals $B_i \square\!\!\rightarrow C_i$ for which $\neg B_i \in Cn_0(\emptyset)$. By Definition 4, these conditionals are satisfied by every E-relation, so they do not matter. Recalling how satisfaction of L_1-sentences by E-relations has been defined, we can now describe the situation with the following figure:

Γ	$\longmapsto$	$\leq$
A_1	$\longmapsto$	$\bot < A_1$
A_2	$\longmapsto$	$\bot < A_2$
A_3	$\longmapsto$	$\bot < A_3$
$\vdots$	$\vdots$	$\vdots$
$B_1 \square\!\!\rightarrow C_1$	$\longmapsto$	$\neg B_1 < B_1 \rightarrow C_1$
$B_2 \square\!\!\rightarrow C_2$	$\longmapsto$	$\neg B_2 < B_2 \rightarrow C_2$
$B_3 \square\!\!\rightarrow C_3$	$\longmapsto$	$\neg B_3 < B_3 \rightarrow C_3$
$\vdots$	$\vdots$	$\vdots$

Evidently, an L_0-sentence A_i has the same satisfaction condition as the corresponding L_1-sentence $\top \square\!\!\rightarrow A_i$. Another simplifying move consists in identifying objective sentences with their conditional counterparts. We can therefore assume that every premise set Γ in L_1 is a set $\{A_i \square\!\!\rightarrow B_i : i \in I\}$ of conditionals where I is a possibly infinite index set and $\neg A_i \notin Cn_0(\emptyset)$ for every $i \in I$. It will be helpful to have in mind a seperate picture for the simplified format:

Γ	$\longmapsto$	$\leq$
$A_1 \square\!\!\rightarrow B_1$	$\longmapsto$	$\neg A_1 < A_1 \rightarrow B_1$
$A_2 \square\!\!\rightarrow B_2$	$\longmapsto$	$\neg A_2 < A_2 \rightarrow B_2$
$A_3 \square\!\!\rightarrow B_3$	$\longmapsto$	$\neg A_3 < A_3 \rightarrow B_3$
$\vdots$	$\vdots$	$\vdots$

Now the construction of an E-minimal E-relation for Γ, i.e., of an E-relation which assigns to all sentences the lowest epistemic rank possible, is pretty obvious. In the first step we note that the partial information about admissible E-relations provided by Γ "forces" all material conditionals $A_i \rightarrow B_i$ to be more entrenched than something, hence to be more entrenched than $\bot$. Remembering that the Entailment condition (E2) must be respected by all E-relations, we know that all Cn_0-consequences of the $A_i \rightarrow B_i$'s must also be more entrenched than $\bot$. Abbreviating the "L_0-counterpart" $\{A_i \rightarrow B_i : A_i \square\!\!\rightarrow B_i \in \Gamma\}$ of Γ by $L_0(\Gamma)$, we now know that all sentences in $\Delta_1 =_{df} Cn_0(L_0(\Gamma))$ obtain at least the first rank of epistemic entrenchment. In the second step, we collect all those $\neg A_j$'s which are in Δ_1. The corresponding inequalities $\neg A_j < A_j \rightarrow B_j$ are triggered and force all the $A_j \rightarrow B_j$'s to be more entrenched than the rest — except for the Cn_0-consequences of the $A_j \rightarrow B_j$'s, which are also lifted up to the second rank of epistemic entrenchment by (E2). This process of raising epistemic entrenchments as required by the "$\leq$-translations" of Γ and subsequent closing under Cn_0 is repeated time and again. In the limit, we take intersections. Roughly, we are ready if no inequality is triggered any longer. There may arise serious complications but they cannot be examined without a formal definition.

Definition 11 *Let* $\Gamma = \{A_i \square\!\!\rightarrow B_i : i \in I\}$ *be a set of L_1-sentences. Then* $\leq_\Gamma = E(\Gamma)$ *is defined as follows. Put*

$$\Delta_0 = L_0$$
$$\Delta_{\alpha+1} = Cn_0(\{A_i \to B_i : \neg A_i \in \Delta_\alpha\})$$
$$\Delta_\alpha = \cap\{\Delta_\beta : \beta < \alpha\} \quad \text{for limit ordinals } \alpha$$

and

$$\alpha(\Gamma) = \begin{cases} \emptyset, & \text{if } \Delta_\alpha = Cn_0(\emptyset) \text{ and} \\ & \Delta_\beta = Cn_0(\emptyset) \text{ for some } \beta < \alpha, \\ \Delta_\alpha, & \text{if } \Delta_\alpha = Cn_0(\emptyset) \text{ and} \\ & \Delta_\beta \neq Cn_0(\emptyset) \text{ for all } \beta < \alpha, \\ \Delta_\alpha - \Delta_{\alpha+1}, & \text{otherwise.} \end{cases}$$

Then for every L_0-sentence C, $\text{rank}_\Gamma(C)=\alpha$ iff $C \in \alpha(\Gamma)$, and for every pair of L_0-sentences C and D, $C \leq_\Gamma D$ iff $\text{rank}_\Gamma(C) \leq \text{rank}_\Gamma(D)$.

A number of tasks lies before us. First, we have to check whether the definition makes sense at all, i.e., whether every L_0-sentence gets a unique rank number α. We shall see that the definition works fine and terminates after a finite number of steps if Γ is consistent and finite. It is no real disadvantage that it fails for inconsistent premise sets, but it will be interesting to observe in which of the infinite cases it fails. Secondly, we verify that in all successful cases, the definition actually generates an E-relation for Γ. Thirdly and lastly, we show that $E(\Gamma)$ is the $\sqsubseteq_E$-smallest E-relation for Γ.

The primary case in the definition of $\alpha(\Gamma)$ is of course captured by the last line. The worst thing that can happen in the construction process is that for some ordinal α, $\Delta_{\alpha+1}$ is identical with $\Delta_\alpha \neq Cn_0(\emptyset)$. For that would mean that not only $\Delta_{\alpha+1} = Cn_0(\{A_i \to B_i : \neg A_i \in \Delta_\alpha\}) = Cn_0(\{A_i \to B_i : \neg A_i \in \Delta_{\alpha+1}\})$ $= \Delta_{\alpha+2}$, but, by the same argument, that $\Delta_\gamma = \Delta_\alpha$ for every $\gamma > \alpha$. As a consequence, $\gamma(\Gamma)$ would be empty for $\gamma > \alpha$, and the processing of the $\leq$-translations of the premises in Γ would be interrupted. Consider two examples for illustration.

Example 3 Let $\Gamma = \{A\square\!\!\to B\&C, B\square\!\!\to A\&\neg C\}$. The translation in terms of epistemic entrenchment is

$$\neg A < A \to (B\&C) \quad \text{and} \quad \neg B < B \to (A\&\neg C).$$

Now Δ_0 is L_0, and Δ_1 is $Cn_0(\{A \to (B\&C), B \to (A\&\neg C)\})$, but this again is L_0. So $\neg A$ and $\neg B$ are in Δ_1, so Δ_2 is again $Cn_0(\{A \to (B\&C), B \to (A\&\neg C)\})$ $= L_0$, and so on for every Δ_α. We never get an acceptable result.

Example 4 Another problematic case is $\Gamma = \{A_i \vee A_{i+1}\square\!\!\to\neg A_i : i=1,2,$ $3,\dots\}$. The $\leq$-translations are

$$\neg A_i \& \neg A_{i+1} < (A_i \vee A_{i+1}) \rightarrow \neg A_i, \quad i=1,2,3,\ldots,$$

or equivalently,

$$\neg A_{i+1} < \neg A_i, \quad i=1,2,3,\ldots.^{18}$$

As always, Δ_0 is L_0. Δ_1 is $Cn_0(\{(A_i \vee A_{i+1}) \rightarrow \neg A_i : i=1,2,3,\ldots\}) = Cn_0(\{\neg A_i : i=1,2,3,\ldots\})$. But then, for every $i=1,2,3,\ldots$, $\neg A_i \& \neg A_{i+1}$ is in Δ_1, so Δ_2 is again $Cn_0(\{\neg A_i : i=1,2,3,\ldots\})$, and the same for every Δ_α. We never manage to exploit the information provided by Γ. (End of examples)

It turns out that the two premise sets have a different status. In Example 3, Γ is inconsistent, and we shall see presently that every *finite* premise set which leads into this problem is inconsistent. So we need not bother about the problem for finite premise sets too much. In Example 4, on the other hand, Γ is consistent, since it is satisfied e.g. by the E-relation generated by the base

$$\bot \prec \ldots \prec \neg A_3 \prec \neg A_2 \prec \neg A_1 \prec \top.$$

The point illustrated by Example 4 is that there are premise sets which do not admit well-ordering E-relations. Since Γ translates to $\neg A_{i+1} < \neg A_i$, $i=1,2,3,\ldots$, it is clear that no E-relation $\leq$ for Γ can pick out an $\leq$-minimal sentence from the set $\{\neg A_i : i=1,2,3,\ldots\}$. But as our definition is made for well-ordering E-relations only, it is to be expected that it does not work fine in cases like Example 4. We suggest the following well-behavedness criterion for infinite premise sets:

Definition 12 *A premise set* $\Gamma = \{A_i \square\!\!\rightarrow B_i : i \in I\}$ *is called* well-founded *iff it satisfies the condition*

$$\{\neg A_j : j \in J\} \not\subseteq Cn_0(\{A_j \rightarrow B_j : j \in J\}), \text{ for every non-empty } J \subseteq I.$$

Observe that only well-founded premise sets Γ admit well-ordering E-relations for Γ. For assume Γ is not well-founded and $J \neq \emptyset$ is such that $\{\neg A_j : j \in J\} \subseteq Cn_0(\{A_j \rightarrow B_j : j \in J\})$. Suppose for reductio that $\leq$ is well-ordering and satisfies Γ. Consider $\{A_j \rightarrow B_j : j \in J\}$, and take a smallest element $A_k \rightarrow B_k$ of this set. By assumption, $\neg A_k \in Cn_0(\{A_j \rightarrow B_j : j \in J\})$. So, by (E2), $A_j \rightarrow B_j \leq \neg A_k$ for some $j \in J$. But $A_k \rightarrow B_k \leq A_j \rightarrow B_j$, so by (E1) $A_k \rightarrow B_k \leq \neg A_k$,

---

[18]Examples like this have been the subject of considerable discussion in the literature. Measure again Lewis's (1973, p. 20) line and instantiate A_i as 'Lewis's line is $1+(1/i)$ inches long.'

so $\leq$ fails to satisfy $A_k \square \rightarrow B_k \in \Gamma$, so $\leq$ is no E-relation for Γ, and we have a contradiction.

Now let us carefully collect some basic facts concerning the construction of $E(\Gamma)$.

Observation 10 *Let $\Gamma = \{A_i \square \rightarrow B_i : i \in I\}$ be a set of L_1-sentences. Then*

(i) for all α, $Cn_0(\emptyset) \subseteq \Delta_{\alpha+1} \subseteq \Delta_\alpha$;

(ii) for all ordinals α such that $\alpha(\Gamma) = \Delta_\alpha - \Delta_{\alpha+1}$, $\overleftarrow{\alpha}(\Gamma) =_{df} \bigcup \{\beta(\Gamma) : \beta < \alpha\} = L_0 - \Delta_\alpha$;

(iii) if Γ is finite and consistent then Γ is well-founded.

Furthermore, if Γ is well-founded, then

(iv) for all α, if $\Delta_\alpha \subseteq \Delta_{\alpha+1}$ then $\Delta_\alpha = Cn_0(\emptyset)$;

(v) for all α, $\{A_i \rightarrow B_i : \neg A_i \in \Delta_{\alpha+1}\} \subseteq \{A_i \rightarrow B_i : \neg A_i \in \Delta_\alpha\}$, and if $\{A_i \rightarrow B_i : \neg A_i \in \Delta_{\alpha+1}\} = \{A_i \rightarrow B_i : \neg A_i \in \Delta_\alpha\}$, then $\{A_i \rightarrow B_i : \neg A_i \in \Delta_\alpha\} = \emptyset$;

(vi) there is an α such that $\top \in \alpha(\Gamma) = Cn_0(\emptyset)$; in particular, if Γ is finite and has n elements then $\top \in \alpha(\Gamma)$ for some $\alpha \leq n+1$;

(vii) for every L_0-sentence A, there is exactly one α such that $A \in \alpha(\Gamma)$;

(viii) for every α, Δ_α is an L_0-cut with respect to $\leq_\Gamma$, and for every non-empty L_0-cut S with respect to $\leq_\Gamma$, $S = \Delta_\alpha$ for some α;

(ix) for all L_0-sentences A and B, $A \leq_\Gamma B$ iff $A \in \Delta_\alpha$ implies $B \in \Delta_\alpha$ for every α.

Part (iii) of Observation 10 shows that we will have no problems if Γ is finite, and part (vi) shows that in this case the number of steps to be performed in the construction does not essentially exceed the number of conditionals in Γ. Part (vii) shows that $rank_\Gamma$ is a function assigning to every L_0-sentence an ordinal. So $A \leq_\Gamma B$ iff $rank_\Gamma(A) \leq rank_\Gamma(B)$. We shall make use of this in the following. Parts (i) and (iv) make clear that this function is onto some initial segment $\{\beta : \beta < \alpha\}$ of the ordinals. All ranks are occupied. Parts (viii) and (ix) exhibit a similarity of the construction of an E-relation $E(\Gamma)$ from a given set of premises Γ with the construction of $E(\preceq)$ from a given E-base $\langle B, \preceq \rangle$. In fact, the whole construction of Definition 11 may be viewed as the establishment of an E-base with $B = L_0(\Gamma)$ and $\preceq = \leq_\Gamma \cap B \times B$. The $\neg A_i$'s just help us to determine the relations between the $A_i \rightarrow B_i$'s under minimalization. After these preparations, the following result will hardly be surprising.

Observation 11 *Let $\Gamma=\{A_i\square\!\!\rightarrow B_i : i\in I\}$ be a well-founded set of L_1-sentences. Then*

(i) $E(\Gamma)$ is a well-ordering E-relation.

(ii) $E(\Gamma)$ satisfies Γ, i.e., $\Gamma\subseteq K(E(\Gamma))$.

We see that what we have constructed is in fact an E-relation for Γ. To substantiate that we reach our final aim, we need a further technical lemma.

Observation 12 *Let $\Gamma=\{A_i\square\!\!\rightarrow B_i : i\in I\}$ be a well-founded set of L_1-sentences. Then for every L_0-sentence A, $rank_{E(\Gamma)}(A) = rank_\Gamma(A)$.*

Now we can prove what we have been after in this section.

Observation 13 *Let $\Gamma=\{A_i\square\!\!\rightarrow B_i : i\in I\}$ be a well-founded set of L_1-sentences. Then for every E-relation $\leq$ satisfying Γ, $E(\Gamma)\sqsubseteq_E\leq$ or $\leq=E(\Gamma)$.*

Corollary *For well-ordering E-relations $\leq$, $E(K(\leq))=\leq$.*

7 The logic of E-minimality

We propose to use $Cn_{\sqsubseteq_E}$ as the right consequence relation for conditionals.

Definition 13 *Let Γ be a set of L_1-sentences and A an L_1-sentence. Then $\Gamma\models A$, or equivalently $A\in Cn(\Gamma)$, iff $\Gamma\models_{\sqsubseteq_E} A$. Furthermore, $\Gamma\mathrel{\vert\!\equiv} A$ iff $\Gamma\mathrel{\vert\!\equiv}_{\sqsubseteq_E} A$.*

Recall that we just instantiate here the scheme of preferential entailment in the sense of Makinson (1989; 1990), with the underlying preferential model structure being $(\mathcal{E},\models,\sqsubseteq_E)$ where $\mathcal{E}$ is the set of all E-relations over L_0 and $\models$ and $\sqsubseteq_E$ are as determined in Definitions 4 and 10. We allow infinite sets of premises, which will often give rise to infinite ranks of epistemic entrenchment. It is an effect of having done the whole thing for ordinals rather than for natural numbers that we can apply Cn to infinite sets of sentences. As usual, we may say that a set K of L_1-sentences is a *theory* or a *belief set* in L_1 if $K=Cn(K)$.

In the well-behaved — i.e., well-founded — cases, $\sqsubseteq_E$ will perform interesting comparisons. But there are non-well-founded premise sets Γ which do not permit well-ordering E-relations, for instance that of Example 4, viz., $\Gamma=\{A_i\vee A_{i+1}\square\!\!\rightarrow\neg A_i : i=1,2,3,\dots\}$. In this case, $\Gamma\models A$ coincides with $\Gamma\models_1 A$. On the other hand, recall that by the definition of $\sqsubseteq_E$, if there is one well-ordering E-relation $\leq$ for Γ then we need not consider any E-relations for Γ that are not well-ordering, because $\leq$ is $\sqsubseteq_E$-preferred to all of these. Moreover, if Γ is well-founded we know that there are well-ordering E-relations for Γ and that there is a $\sqsubseteq_E$-smallest among them, viz., $E(\Gamma)$. So for a well-founded Γ, $\Gamma \models A$ iff $E(\Gamma) \models A$, or in other words, $Cn(\Gamma) = K(E(\Gamma))$. It is no problem to determine the consequences of many suspicuous-looking infinite premise sets like e.g. $\Gamma = \{A_i \vee A_{i+1} \square \!\!\rightarrow \neg A_{i+1} : i = 1,2,3, \dots \}$.

Our consequence relation accounts for the paradigm example presented in the introduction and Example 1 in a satisfactory and almost trivial way. If all we know is given by $\Gamma = \{A \vee B\}$, then the unique $\sqsubseteq_E$-minimal E-relation for Γ is given by the E-base $\bot \prec A \vee B \prec \top$, which satisfies $\neg A \square \!\!\rightarrow B$. But if we then learn that A (and $\neg B$) then all we know is $\Gamma = \{A \vee B, A(,\neg B)\}$, so the unique $\sqsubseteq_E$-minimal E-relation is given by $\bot \prec A \vee B \simeq A(\simeq \neg B) \prec \top$ which fails to satisfy $\neg A \square \!\!\rightarrow B$. That is, $Cn_{\sqsubseteq_E}$ in fact validates (3) and invalidates (4) mentioned in the discussion of Example 1. It is obvious but notable that Cn is *nonmonotonic* and allows the *inference of conditionals from non-conditional knowledge bases*.

In Example 2, the second E-base is discarded, so we get for instance that $\Gamma = \{A, B, \neg A \square \!\!\rightarrow B\}$ entails the contraposed conditional $\neg B \square \!\!\rightarrow A$.

Besides the performance of Cn in examples, its abstract properties are of interest.[19]

Observation 14 *Cn satisfies*

    (i) $Cn_0(\Gamma) \cap L_1 \subseteq Cn(\Gamma) \cap L_1$ *(Restricted Supraclassicality)*

    (ii) *for all* L_0-*sentences A and B,* $\Gamma \cup \{A\} \models B$ *iff* $\Gamma \models A \rightarrow B$ *(Restricted Deduction Theorem)*

  (iii) $\Gamma \subseteq Cn(\Gamma)$ *(Inclusion)*

  (iv) $Cn(Cn(\Gamma)) = Cn(\Gamma)$ *(Idempotence)*

   (v) *if* $\Gamma \subseteq \Sigma \subseteq Cn(\Gamma)$ *then* $Cn(\Sigma) \subseteq Cn(\Gamma)$ *(Cut)*

  (vi) *if* $\Gamma \subseteq \Sigma \subseteq Cn(\Gamma)$ *then* $Cn(\Gamma) \subseteq Cn(\Sigma)$ *(Cautious Monotony)*

 (vii) *if* $\Gamma_2 \subseteq Cn(\Gamma_1)$, $\Gamma_3 \subseteq Cn(\Gamma_2), \dots, \Gamma_n \subseteq Cn(\Gamma_{n-1})$,
      $\Gamma_1 \subseteq Cn(\Gamma_n)$ *then* $\Gamma_i = \Gamma_j$ *for every* $i,j \leq n$ *(Loop)*

Parts (iii)–(vi) mean that Cn is a *cumulative* inference relation in Makinson's sense. We point out that the restriction of Supraclassicality is severe. For example, if we have $\Gamma \models A \square \!\!\rightarrow B$ and $\Gamma \models C \square \!\!\rightarrow D$, we would certainly like to take over the classical step to $\Gamma \models (A \square \!\!\rightarrow B) \& (C \square \!\!\rightarrow D)$, but this already transcends the bounds of the language L_1. A similar restriction applies to the Deduction

---

[19] The names of the conditions to be discussed are taken from Makinson(1989; 1990).

Theorem. In Part 2 of the present trilogy we shall extend L_1 in order to attain full Supraclassicality and give a treatment of negations and disjunctions of conditionals as well.

Observation 14 shows where Cn behaves well. But there are also less mannerly features.

Observation 15 *Cn does not satisfy*

    (i) *if* $\Gamma\cup\{A\}\models C$ *and* $\Gamma\cup\{B\}\models C$ *then* $\Gamma\cup\{A\vee B\}\models C$ *(Disjunction in the Antecedent)*

    (ii) *if* $\Gamma\cup\{A\}\models B$ *and* $\Gamma\cup\{\neg A\}\models B$ *then* $\Gamma\models B$ *(Proof by Cases)*

    (iii) *if* $\Gamma\models B$ *then* $\Gamma\cup\{A\}\models B$ *or* $\Gamma\cup\{\neg A\}\models B$ *(Negation Rationality)*

    (iv) *if* $\{A,B\}\not\models\bot$ *then* $Cn(\{A\})\cup\{B\}\not\models\bot$ *(Consistency Preservation)*

I feel that I should give an example that makes the case for at least one of these results. Let me explain how Disjunction in the Antecedent can fail.

Example 5 We consider another restaurant example and assume now that there is a third restaurant which is run by Debbie. Let $\Gamma=\{\neg A\square\!\!\rightarrow B\vee D, \neg B\square\!\!\rightarrow A\vee D\}$. Now suppose you (only) know that either Annie's or Ben's restaurant is open. In this situation, Γ adds nothing new, since the information provided by

> If Annie's restaurant is not open (then) Ben's or Debbie's restaurant will be open.

and

> If Ben's restaurant is not open (then) Annie's or Debbie's restaurant will be open.

is already contained in the information provided by $A\vee B$. But suppose you (only) know that Annie's restaurant is open. In this case the first element in Γ, now read as

> If Annie's restaurant were not open (then) Ben's or Debbie's restaurant would be open.

does contain additional information. In particular, it seems justified to infer from $\Gamma\cup\{A\}$ the following conditional:

> If neither Annie's nor Ben's restaurant were open (then) Debbie's restaurant would be open.   (5)

By an analogous argument, we can infer (5) from the premise set $\Gamma\cup\{B\}$. From $\Gamma\cup\{A\vee B\}$, on the other hand, we saw that we cannot get anything over and above the conclusions which can be drawn from $\{A\vee B\}$ alone, so in particular we cannot get (5).[20] (End of example)

The failure of Disjunction in the Antecedents and Proof by Cases is neither very common nor very uncommon in nonmonotonic logics. The failure of Negation Rationality which is common in nonmonotonic logics implies the failure of more non-Horn conditions for Cn (see Makinson 1990, Section IV.1). The failure of Consistency Preservation is perhaps the most striking deviation from usual patterns. In fact, the proof shows that for arbitrary independent L_0-sentences A and B, $Cn(\{A\})$ and $Cn(\{B\})$ are not satisfiable simultaneously. This already indicates that the addition of new items of belief should not be performed by taking the logical expansion of the current theory, but by generating a new theory from the augmented premise set. Belief change based on Cn will be the topic of Part 3 of the trilogy.

For reasons of language restriction, we cannot directly compare our logic with Lewis's "official" logic **VC**. With the plausible consistency condition for L_2

$$\text{if} \leq\; \models \neg(A\square\!\!\rightarrow B) \quad\text{then}\quad \leq\; \not\models A\square\!\!\rightarrow B\;,$$

however, we get the following translations of the prominent **VC**-axioms into robust inferences. We refer to the axiomatization of **VC** given by Gärdenfors (1988, Section 7.2).

Observation 16 *Let A,B,C range over L_0-sentences. Then the following sentence schemes of the form $(A_0\&\ldots\&A_n)\rightarrow B$ $(n\geq 0)$, which are axioms for* **VC***, are translatable into valid robust inferences of the form $\{A_0,\ldots,A_n\}\models B$:*

(i) A, for $A\in Cn_0(\emptyset)$;
(ii) $((A\square\!\!\rightarrow B)\&(A\square\!\!\rightarrow C))\rightarrow(A\square\!\!\rightarrow B\&C)$;
(iii) $A\square\!\!\rightarrow\top$;
(iv) $A\square\!\!\rightarrow A$;
(v) $(A\square\!\!\rightarrow B)\rightarrow(A\rightarrow B)$;
(vi) $(A\&B)\rightarrow(A\square\!\!\rightarrow B)$;

---

[20]For details, see the proof of Observation 15(i). — Notice that the switch from indicative to subjunctive mood seems to produce some change in the meaning of the conditionals in question. Both types of conditionals (if they constitute any clear-cut types at all) are covered by our analysis.

(vii) $(A\square\!\!\rightarrow\neg A) \rightarrow (B\square\!\!\rightarrow\neg A)$;

$(viii)$ $((A\square\!\!\rightarrow B)\&(B\square\!\!\rightarrow A)\&(A\square\!\!\rightarrow C)) \rightarrow (B\square\!\!\rightarrow C)$;

(ix) $((A\square\!\!\rightarrow C)\&(B\square\!\!\rightarrow C)) \rightarrow (A\vee B\square\!\!\rightarrow C)$;

(x) $((A\square\!\!\rightarrow C)\&\neg(A\square\!\!\rightarrow\neg B)) \rightarrow (A\&B\square\!\!\rightarrow C)$.

Furthermore, the **VC-rule** *"from $B\rightarrow C$, to infer $(A\square\!\!\rightarrow B)\rightarrow(A\square\!\!\rightarrow C)$" is translatable into the valid robust inference*

(xi) *if $C\in Cn_0(B)$ then $A\square\!\!\rightarrow B \models A\square\!\!\rightarrow C$.*

When pressed to name the most distinctive feature of natural language conditionals as opposed to "conditionals" encountered in logic and mathematics, I think the best thing one can do is point out that natural language conditionals fail to satisfy some cherished inference patterns. There is a canon of three arguments which have become known as the *counterfactual fallacies* (see Lewis 1973, Section 1.8):

Strengthening the Antecedent (SA)	*Transitivity* (Tr)	*Contraposition* (Cp)
$\dfrac{A\square\!\!\rightarrow B}{A\&C\square\!\!\rightarrow B}$	$\dfrac{A\square\!\!\rightarrow B \quad B\square\!\!\rightarrow C}{A\square\!\!\rightarrow C}$	$\dfrac{A\square\!\!\rightarrow B}{\neg B\square\!\!\rightarrow\neg A}$

Most writers agree that these schemes are not universally valid for conditionals. Yet there seem to be many contexts in which one may safely make use of them. The present logic accounts for this fact by construing conditionals in such a way that (SA), (Tr) and (Cp) are *valid by default*. That is, the relevant premises taken in isolation entail the respective conclusions, but the inference is not robust, since it can be spoilt by augmenting the premise set. We can give a precise description of the contexts in which the so-called counterfactual fallacies fail.

Observation 17

(i) $\{A\square\!\!\rightarrow B\}\models A\&C\square\!\!\rightarrow B$, but not $\{A\square\!\!\rightarrow B\}\mathrel{\|\!\!\!\approx} A\&C\square\!\!\rightarrow B$;

$\{A\square\!\!\rightarrow B,\ B\square\!\!\rightarrow C\}\models A\square\!\!\rightarrow C$, but not $\{A\square\!\!\rightarrow B, B\square\!\!\rightarrow C\}\mathrel{\|\!\!\!\approx} A\square\!\!\rightarrow C$;

$\{A\square\!\!\rightarrow B\}\models\neg B\square\!\!\rightarrow\neg A$, but not $\{A\square\!\!\rightarrow B\}\mathrel{\|\!\!\!\approx}\neg B\square\!\!\rightarrow\neg A$.

(ii) *In particular,* $\{A\square\!\!\rightarrow B,\ A\square\!\!\rightarrow\neg C\}\mathrel{\|\!\!\!\not\approx} A\&C\square\!\!\rightarrow B$;

$\{A\square\!\!\rightarrow B,\ B\square\!\!\rightarrow C,\ B\square\!\!\rightarrow\neg A\}\mathrel{\|\!\!\!\not\approx} A\square\!\!\rightarrow C$;

$\{A\square\!\!\rightarrow B,\ B\}\mathrel{\|\!\!\!\not\approx}\neg B\square\!\!\rightarrow\neg A$.

(iii) For every E-relation ≤, if ≤ satisfies the premise but not the conclusion of (SA) then ≤ satisfies $A\square\!\!\!\rightarrow\neg C$; if ≤ satisfies the premises but not the conclusion of (Tr) then ≤ satisfies $B\square\!\!\!\rightarrow\neg A$; if ≤ satisfies the premise but not the conclusion of (Cp) then ≤ satisfies B.

Some comments are in order. In order to have a proper understanding of what is "counterfactual" in these inference schemes, we should introduce the appropriate terms in our setting.

Definition 14 *Let ≤ be an E-relation and A and B L_0-sentences. Then the conditional $A\square\!\!\!\rightarrow B$ is called* open *(with respect to ≤) if $A\leq\bot$ and $\neg A\leq\bot$; it is called* (weakly) counterfactual *(with respect to ≤) if $\bot<\neg A$ and* strongly counterfactual *(with respect to ≤) if $\bot<\neg A$ and $\bot<\neg B$; it is called* factual *(with respect to ≤) if $\bot<A$; it is called* even if type *(with respect to ≤) if $\bot<B$.*

The positive parts of Observation 17(i), are, as they stand, about open conditionals. But it is easy to verify that they are extendable to counterfactual and strongly counterfactual conditionals, in the sense that the pertinent conditions of Definition 14 are added to the premise set. Note, however, the exceptional status of (Cp). If both the premise and the conclusion of (Cp) are to be counterfactual, then they are also **even if** type. If the premise is to be strongly counterfactual, then the conclusion is a factual **even if** conditional.

Parts (ii) and (iii) of Observation 17 are more interesting. Considering the proof, we discover that (SA), (Tr) and (Cp) only fail if counterfactual conditionals are involved. As to (SA), the conclusion must be counterfactual; as to (Tr), the first premise and the conclusion must be counterfactual, and, by the same token, $B\square\!\!\!\rightarrow\neg A$ is **even if** type; as to (Cp), again the conclusion must be counterfactual while the premise is **even if** type. So there is no failure of the "counterfactual fallacies" if all conditionals involved are open. This is what justifies the predicate 'counterfactual'. The predicate 'fallacy' is, as Part (i) of Observation 17 shows, not quite appropriate.

Appendix: Proofs of Observations

Proof of Observation 1 (i) The limiting case $\vdash \neg A$ is immediate. So let $\nvdash \neg A$; then, by the definition of $*_K = R(C(\leq_K))$, an L_0-sentence C is in $K*_A$ iff it is in $Cn_0((K \cap \{B: \neg A <_K \neg A \vee B\}) \cup \{A\})$, i.e., iff $A \to C \in K \cap \{B: \neg A <_K \neg A \vee B\}$, i.e., by (E4), iff $\bot <_K A \to C$ and $\neg A <_K \neg A \vee (A \to C)$, i.e., by the properties of E-relations, iff $\neg A <_K \neg A \vee C$, i.e., iff C is in $\{B: \neg A <_K \neg A \vee B\}$.

(ii) By the definition of $\leq_K$, $A \leq_K B$ iff $A \notin (K \cap K*_{\neg(A\&B)})$ or $\vdash A\&B$. It remains to be shown that in the case where $\nvdash A\&B$, $A \notin K$ implies $A \notin K*_{\neg A \vee \neg B}$. Now if $A \notin K$, then, by the Gärdenfors postulates for revisions of belief sets in L_0, $K*_{\neg A \vee \neg B} = Cn_0(K \cup \{\neg A \vee \neg B\})$. But since belief sets are closed under Cn_0, $A \notin K$ is equivalent to $A \notin Cn_0(K)$, which in turn is equivalent to $A \notin Cn_0(K \cup \{\neg A \vee \neg B\}) = K*_{\neg A \vee \neg B}$, so we are done.

(iii) Immediate from the results in Gärdenfors (1988, Section 3.6) and Gärdenfors and Makinson (1988). □

Proof of Observation 2 Let $\leq = E(\preceq)$. Transitivity (E1) is trivial. — For Entailment (E2), assume that $\emptyset \neq \Gamma \vdash A$. We have to show that $B \leq A$ for some $B \in \Gamma$. Since classical propositional logic is compact, there is a finite $\Gamma_0 \subseteq \Gamma$ such that $\Gamma_0 \vdash A$. Now suppose for reductio that $B \nleq A$ for every $B \in \Gamma$. Hence $B \nleq A$ for every $B \in \Gamma_0$, i.e., by the definition of $E(\preceq)$, there is a $\mathcal{B}$-cut S_B for every $B \in \Gamma_0$ such that $S_B \vdash B$ but $S_B \nvdash A$. Consider $\bigcup\{Cn_0(S_B): B \in \Gamma_0\}$. Clearly, Γ_0 is included in $\bigcup\{Cn_0(S_B): B \in \Gamma_0\}$. Since $\mathcal{B}$-cuts are nested, the $Cn_0(S_B)$'s are nested, so, since Γ_0 is finite, $\bigcup\{Cn_0(S_B): B \in \Gamma_0\}$ is identical with $Cn_0(S_B)$ for some $B \in \Gamma_0$. For this B then, we have $\Gamma_0 \subseteq Cn_0(S_B)$ and $S_B \nvdash A$. But this contradicts $\Gamma_0 \vdash A$. — For Maximality (E3), assume that $B \leq A$ for every B. By definition, this means that for every B and every $\mathcal{B}$-cut S, if $B \in Cn_0(S)$ then $A \in Cn_0(S)$. Choose $B = \top$ and $S = \emptyset$. This gives us $\vdash A$, as desired. □

Proof of Observation 3 It is clear that (E2) for $\preceq$ is a necessary condition for $E(\preceq) \cap \mathcal{B} \times \mathcal{B} = \preceq$. For otherwise $E(\preceq)$ could not be an E-relation, in contradiction to Observation 2. To show conversely that (E2) for $\preceq$ is sufficient, assume that $\preceq$ satisfies (E2) over $\mathcal{B}$. We have to show that for all A and B in $\mathcal{B}$, $A \preceq B$ iff $A \in Cn_0(S)$ entails $B \in Cn_0(S)$ for all $\mathcal{B}$-cuts S. The direction from left to right follows immediately from the definition of a $\mathcal{B}$-cut and the monotonicity of Cn_0. For the direction from right to left, assume that $A \npreceq B$. It remains to show that there is a $\mathcal{B}$-cut S such that $A \in Cn_0(S)$

but $B\notin Cn_0(S)$. Now consider $S_A =_{df} \{C\in\mathcal{B}: A\preceq C\}$. S_A is a $\mathcal{B}$-cut, since $\preceq$ is transitive. $A\in S_A$, since $\preceq$ is reflexive, so $S_A\neq\emptyset$ and $A\in Cn_0(S_A)$. $A\not\preceq B$ by assumption, so, since $\preceq$ is transitive, $C\not\preceq B$ for every C in S_A. Hence, by (E2) for $\preceq$ over $\mathcal{B}$, $B\notin Cn_0(S_A)$, and we are done. $\square$

Proof of Observation 4 (i) Let $\Gamma\models_1 A$, i.e., every E-relation satisfying Γ satisfies A. This implies that every $\sqsubseteq_E$-minimal E-relation for some superset Σ of Γ satisfies A, i.e., $\Gamma\models_c A$.

(ii) Let $\Gamma\models_c A$. Assume that $\Gamma\not\models_1 A$, i.e., there is an E-relation $\leq$ which satisfies Γ without satisfying A. That is, $\Gamma\subseteq K(\leq)$ and $A\notin K(\leq)$. But by hypothesis, every Σ such that $\Gamma\subseteq\Sigma$ minimally implies A. So in particular every minimal E-relation for $K(\leq)$ must satisfy A. But since $\leq$ does not satisfy A, it cannot be minimal for $K(\leq)$. Therefore, the antecedent of (ii) is false. $\square$

Proof of Observation 5 (i)$\Leftrightarrow$(ii): We have to show that $K(\leq)\subseteq K(\leq')$ iff $\leq'\subseteq\leq$. As remarked above, L_0-sentences A are satisfaction-equivalent to conditionals $\top\square\!\!\rightarrow A$, so $K(\leq)$ and $K(\leq')$ can be thought of as consisting of conditionals only. We have to show that for all L_0-sentences A and B,

  if $\neg A < \neg A\vee B$ then $\neg A <' \neg A\vee B$,

   i.e., by the connectivity of E-relations,

    if not $\neg A\vee B\leq\neg A$ then not $\neg A\vee B\leq'\neg A$, i.e.,

 (*) if $\neg A\vee B\leq'\neg A$ then $\neg A\vee B\leq\neg A$,

iff for all L_0-sentences C and D,

 (**) if $C\leq'D$ then $C\leq D$.

The direction from (**) to (*) is immediate. To see that the converse also holds, substitute $\neg(C\&D)$ for A and C for B in (*). This gives us

  if $\neg\neg(C\&D)\vee C\leq'\neg\neg(C\&D)$ then $\neg(C\&D)\vee C\leq\neg\neg(C\&D)$,

i.e., by (E2),

  if $C\leq'C\&D$ then $C\leq C\&D$.

But since for every E-relation $\leq$, $C\leq C\&D$ is equivalent to $C\leq D$, the latter condition is equivalent to (**).

(iii)$\Leftrightarrow$(ii): This is immediate from the connectivity of E-relations which gives us $<=(L_0\times L_0)-\leq$ and $<'=(L_0\times L_0)-\leq'$.

(iv)$\Leftrightarrow$(ii): That $\leq\subseteq\leq'$ implies $\doteq\subseteq\doteq'$ is clear from the definitions $\doteq=\leq\cap\leq^{-1}$ and $\doteq'=\leq'\cap(\leq')^{-1}$. To verify the converse, assume that $\leq\not\subseteq\leq'$, i.e., that there are L_0-sentences A and B such that $A\leq B$ but not $A\leq'B$. By the properties of E- relations, this implies that $A\doteq A\&B$ but not $A\doteq'A\&B$, so $\doteq\not\subseteq\doteq'$, and we are done. $\square$

Proof of Observation 6 By a number of Boolean transformations of the definition of $\sqsubseteq_{K_0}$. $\square$

Proof of Observation 7 (i) As to conditionals, we show that for every B and C in L_0,

$\neg B \lor C \not\leq \neg B$ iff $\neg B \lor C \not\leq_i \neg B$ for all i, i.e.,

$\neg B \lor C \leq \neg B$ iff $\neg B \lor C \leq_i \neg B$ for some i.

But this immediate from the definition of $\leq$. The case of L_0-sentences is similar.

(ii) Let $\leq^*$ be as indicated. Then, just as before, for every B and C in L_0,

$\neg B \lor C \leq^* \neg B$ iff $\neg B \lor C \leq_i \neg B$ for some i.

Substituting $\neg(D \& E)$ for B and D for C gives us

$\neg\neg(D \& E) \lor D \leq^* \neg\neg(D \& E)$ iff $\neg\neg(D \& E) \lor D \leq_i \neg\neg(D \& E)$ for some i, i.e.,

as all relations involved are E-relations,

$D \leq^* D \& E$ iff $D \leq_i D \& E$ for some i.

But again, since all relations involved are E-relations, this is equivalent to

$D \leq^* E$ iff $D \leq_i E$ for some i,

i.e., since D and E were chosen arbitrarily, $\leq^* = \leq_1 \cup \ldots \cup \leq_n = \leq$, as desired.

(iii) Clearly, any union of E-relations satisfies Entailment (E2) and Maximality (E3). So $\leq = \leq_1 \cup \ldots \cup \leq_n$ is an E-relation iff it satisfies Transitivity (E1), i.e., iff for all $A, B, C \in L_0$,

if $B \leq_i C$ for some i and $C \leq_j A$ for some j, then $B \leq_k A$ for some k.

By a simple Boolean transformation, we see that this is violated iff $A <_i B \leq_i C$ for some i and $C \leq_j A <_j B$ for some j, and $A <_k B$ for every k, as desired. $\square$

Proof of Observation 8 Let $\leq \sqsubseteq_K \leq'$. From Observation 5 we know that this is equivalent to $\leq' \subseteq \leq$.

We first show by transfinite induction on α that for any ordinal α, $\overleftarrow{\alpha}(\leq') \subseteq \overleftarrow{\alpha}(\leq)$.

- $\overleftarrow{0}(\leq') \subseteq \overleftarrow{0}(\leq)$: $\overleftarrow{0}(\leq') = \emptyset = \overleftarrow{0}(\leq)$.

- $\overleftarrow{\alpha+1}(\leq') \subseteq \overleftarrow{\alpha+1}(\leq)$: The induction hypothesis is $\overleftarrow{\beta}(\leq') \subseteq \overleftarrow{\beta}(\leq)$ for every $\beta < \alpha+1$. So in particular $\overleftarrow{\alpha}(\leq') \subseteq \overleftarrow{\alpha}(\leq) \subseteq \overleftarrow{\alpha+1}(\leq)$. As $\overleftarrow{\alpha+1}(\leq') = \overleftarrow{\alpha}(\leq') \cup \alpha(\leq')$, it remains to show that $\alpha(\leq') \subseteq \overleftarrow{\alpha+1}(\leq)$:

$$\alpha(\leq') =$$
$$= \{B \in L_0 - \overleftarrow{\alpha}(\leq') : B \leq' C \text{ for every } C \in L_0 - \overleftarrow{\alpha}(\leq')\} =$$
$$= (\{B \in L_0 - \overleftarrow{\alpha}(\leq') : B \leq' C \text{ for every } C \in L_0 - \overleftarrow{\alpha}(\leq')\} \cap \overleftarrow{\alpha}(\leq)) \cup$$
$$(\{B \in L_0 - \overleftarrow{\alpha}(\leq') : B \leq' C \text{ for every } C \in L_0 - \overleftarrow{\alpha}(\leq')\} \cap L_0 - \overleftarrow{\alpha}(\leq)) \subseteq$$

$\subseteq \overleftarrow{\alpha}(\leq) \cup \{B \in (L_0 - \overleftarrow{\alpha}(\leq')) \cap (L_0 - \overleftarrow{\alpha}(\leq)) : B \leq' C \text{ for every } C \in L_0 - \overleftarrow{\alpha}(\leq')\} \subseteq$
(by the induction hypothesis)

$\subseteq \overleftarrow{\alpha}(\leq) \cup \{B \in L_0 - \overleftarrow{\alpha}(\leq) : B \leq' C \text{ for every } C \in L_0 - \overleftarrow{\alpha}(\leq)\} \subseteq$ (by $\leq' \subseteq \leq$)

$\subseteq \overleftarrow{\alpha}(\leq) \cup \{B \in L_0 - \overleftarrow{\alpha}(\leq) : B \leq C \text{ for every } C \in L_0 - \overleftarrow{\alpha}(\leq)\} =$

$= \overleftarrow{\alpha}(\leq) \cup \alpha(\leq) =$

$= \overleftarrow{\alpha+1}(\leq).$

• $\overleftarrow{\alpha}(\leq') \subseteq \overleftarrow{\alpha}(\leq)$ for limit ordinals α: The induction hypothesis is $\overleftarrow{\beta}(\leq') \subseteq \overleftarrow{\beta}(\leq)$ for every $\beta < \alpha$. But since $\overleftarrow{\alpha}(\leq') = \bigcup\{\beta(\leq') : \beta < \alpha\} = \bigcup\{\overleftarrow{\beta+1}(\leq') : \beta < \alpha\}$, and similarly for $\leq$, we get the claim immediately from the induction hypothesis. Having shown that for any ordinal α, $\overleftarrow{\alpha}(\leq') \subseteq \overleftarrow{\alpha}(\leq)$, we can rerun the argument establishing $\alpha(\leq') \subseteq \overleftarrow{\alpha+1}(\leq)$, this time for any ordinal α. But this just means that for every L_0-sentence A, if $\text{rank}_{\leq'} = \alpha$ then $\text{rank}_{\leq} \leq \alpha$, and we are done. □

Proof of the Corollary Immediate from the Observation and the fact $\leq \sqsubseteq_E \leq'$ and $\leq' \sqsubseteq_E \leq$ implies $\leq = \leq'$. □

Proof of Observation 9 Let $\leq \sqsubseteq_E \leq'$. If also $\leq' \sqsubseteq_E \leq$, then, by the antisymmetry of $\sqsubseteq_E$, $\leq = \leq'$, so $\leq \sqsubseteq_{K_0} \leq'$ is trivial. Now consider the principal case where $\leq' \not\sqsubseteq_E \leq$. By Observation 8, this gives us $\leq' \not\sqsubseteq_K \leq$. Hence either $\leq \sqsubseteq_K \leq'$ or $\leq$ and $\leq'$ are incomparable with respect to $\sqsubseteq_K$. In the former case, $\leq \sqsubseteq_{K_0} \leq'$ is immediate. In the latter case, we have to show the $K_0(\leq) \subseteq K_0(\leq')$. But this just means that $L_0 - 0(\leq) \subseteq L_0 - 0(\leq')$ which is entailed by $\leq \sqsubseteq_E \leq'$. □

Proof of Observation 10 (i) As Cn_0 is monotonic, $Cn_0(\emptyset)$ is included in Δ_α for every α. $\Delta_{\alpha+1} = Cn_0(\{A_j \rightarrow B_j : \neg B_j \in \Delta_\alpha\}) \subseteq Cn_0(\{\neg B_j : \neg B_j \in \Delta_\alpha\}) \subseteq Cn_0(\Delta_\alpha) = \Delta_\alpha$, since Δ_α is closed under Cn_0.

(ii) By definition, $\overleftarrow{\alpha}(\leq) = \bigcup\{\beta(\Gamma) : \beta < \alpha\} = \bigcup\{\Delta_\beta - \Delta_{\beta+1} : \beta < \alpha\}$. We show by transfinite induction that the latter set equals $L_0 - \Delta_\alpha$.

$\alpha = 0$: $\bigcup\{\Delta_\beta - \Delta_{\beta+1} : \beta < 0\} = \emptyset = L_0 - \Delta_0$.

$\alpha + 1$: $\bigcup\{\Delta_\beta - \Delta_{\beta+1} : \beta < \alpha+1\} = (\bigcup\{\Delta_\beta - \Delta_{\beta+1} : \beta < \alpha\}) \cup (\Delta_\alpha - \Delta_{\alpha+1}) =$ (by induction hypothesis) $(L_0 - \Delta_\alpha) - (\Delta_\alpha - \Delta_{\alpha+1}) = L_0 - \Delta_{\alpha+1}$.

Limit ordinals α: $\bigcup\{\Delta_\beta - \Delta_{\beta+1} : \beta < \alpha\} =$ (by set theory) $\bigcup\{\bigcup\{\Delta_\gamma - \Delta_{\gamma+1} : \gamma < \beta\} : \beta < \alpha\} =$ (by induction hypothesis) $\bigcup\{L_0 - \Delta_\beta : \beta < \alpha\} = L_0 - \bigcap\{\Delta_\beta : \beta < \alpha\} =$ (by definition) $L_0 - \Delta_\alpha$.

(iii) Let $\Gamma = \{A_i \rightarrow B_i : i \in I\}$ be finite and consistent, and let $\leq$ be an E-relation for Γ. Now assume for reductio that there is a non-empty $J \subseteq I$ such that $\{\neg A_j: j \in J\}$ is contained in $Cn_0(\{A_j \rightarrow B_j: j \in J\})$. Observe that J is finite. So $\{A_j \rightarrow B_j: j \in J\} \vdash \& \{\neg A_j: j \in J\}$, where $\& \{\neg A_j: j \in J\}$ is the conjunction of the elements of $\{\neg A_j: j \in J\}$. Thus, by (E2), $A_k \rightarrow B_k \leq \& \{\neg A_j: j \in J\} \leq \neg A_k$ for some k in J. That is $\neg A_k \not< A_k \rightarrow B_k$, but this means that $\leq$ does not satisfy $A_k \square \rightarrow B_k \in \Gamma$, contradicting our assumption that $\leq$ is an E-relation for Γ.

For the following, assume that Γ is well-founded.

(iv) Let α be such that $\Delta_\alpha \subseteq \Delta_{\alpha+1}$. Hence, by (i), $\Delta_\alpha = \Delta_{\alpha+1}$. By definition then, $\Delta_{\alpha+1} = Cn_0(\{A_j \rightarrow B_j: \neg A_j \in \Delta_\alpha\}) = Cn_0(\{A_j \rightarrow B_j: \neg A_j \in \Delta_{\alpha+1}\})$. Set $J=\{j \in I: \neg A_j \in \Delta_{\alpha+1}\}$. Then $\{\neg A_j: j \in J\} = \{\neg A_j: \neg A_j \in \Delta_{\alpha+1}\} \subseteq \Delta_{\alpha+1} = Cn_0(\{A_j \rightarrow B_j: \neg A_j \in \Delta_{\alpha+1}\}) = Cn_0(\{A_j \rightarrow B_j: j \in J\})$. Hence, by the well-foundedness of Γ, $J=\{j \in I: \neg A_j \in \Delta_{\alpha+1}\}=\emptyset$. That is, since $\Delta_\alpha = \Delta_{\alpha+1}$, $\{j \in I: \neg A_j \in \Delta_\alpha\}=\emptyset$, i.e., by definition, $\Delta_{\alpha+1}=Cn_0(\emptyset)$, hence, by $\Delta_\alpha = \Delta_{\alpha+1}$ again, $\Delta_\alpha = Cn_0(\emptyset)$.

(v) The first part of (v) follows immediately from (i). For the second part, suppose that $\{A_i \rightarrow B_i: \neg A_i \in \Delta_{\alpha+1}\} = \{A_i \rightarrow B_i: \neg A_i \in \Delta_\alpha\}$. So, by definition, $\Delta_{\alpha+2} = \Delta_{\alpha+1}$, hence, by (iv), $\Delta_{\alpha+1}=Cn(\emptyset)$. Since we presuppose that all conditionals with antecedents A such that $\vdash \neg A$ have been deleted from Γ in advance, it follows that $\{A_i \rightarrow B_i: \neg A_i \in \Delta_{\alpha+1}\} = \emptyset$, so by supposition $\{A_i \rightarrow B_i: \neg A_i \in \Delta_\alpha\} = \emptyset$.

(vi) From (v), we know that $\{A_i \rightarrow B_i: \neg A_i \in \Delta_\alpha\} - \{A_i \rightarrow B_i: \neg A_i \in \Delta_{\alpha+1}\} \neq \emptyset$, unless $\{A_i \rightarrow B_i: \neg A_i \in \Delta_\alpha\}=\emptyset$. That is, each step in the construction process reduces the number of conditionals to be taken into account by at least one. Let β be the smallest cardinal that is greater than the cardinal number of Γ. Since there is no bijective mapping between β and Γ, then $\{A_i \rightarrow B_i: \neg A_i \in \Delta_\beta\}=\emptyset$, so $\Delta_{\beta+1}=Cn(\emptyset)$. Hence the set of ordinals $\gamma \leq \beta+1$ such that $\Delta_\gamma=Cn(\emptyset)$ is non-empty. Let α be the smallest ordinal of that set. Then, by definition, $\top \in \alpha(\Gamma)=Cn_0(\emptyset)$. In particular, let Γ be finite and $|\Gamma|=n$; then $|\{A_i \rightarrow B_i: \neg A_i \in \Delta_0\}|=n$, and hence, since each step in the construction reduces the number of conditionals to be taken into account by at least one, $|\{A_i \rightarrow B_i: \neg A_i \in \Delta_n\}| = 0$. Thus $\Delta_{n+1} = Cn_0(\{A_i \rightarrow B_i: \neg A_i \in \Delta_n\}) = Cn_0(\emptyset)$, i.e., $\top \in \alpha(\Gamma)$ for some $\alpha \leq n+1$.

(vii) If $A \in Cn_0(\emptyset)$, then $A \in \alpha(\Gamma)$ if and only if α is the smallest ordinal such that $\Delta_\alpha=Cn_0(\emptyset)$, which exists, as shown above. If $A \notin Cn_0(\emptyset)$, then $A \notin \Delta_\alpha$ for those α such that $\Delta_\alpha=Cn_0(\emptyset)$. So the set of all ordinals β such that $A \notin \Delta_\beta$ is non-empty. Let γ be the smallest ordinal of that set. γ cannot be 0, for $\Delta_0=L_0$; γ cannot be a limit ordinal for if $A \notin \Delta_\gamma$ for a limit ordinal γ then, by the construction of Δ_γ, there must be a $\gamma'<\gamma$ such that $A \notin \Delta_{\gamma'}$; so γ is a successor number. So $A \in \Delta_{\gamma-1} - \Delta_{\gamma}$, i.e., $A \in \gamma\text{-}1(\Gamma)$. To show uniqueness, suppose for reductio that $A \in \alpha(\Gamma)$ and $A \in \beta(\Gamma)$ with $\alpha < \beta$. From $A \in \alpha(\Gamma)$, it follows that $A \notin \Delta_{\alpha+1}$, hence, since $\Delta_\beta \subseteq \Delta_{\alpha+1}$, $A \notin \Delta_\beta$, contradicting $A \in \beta(\Gamma)$.

(viii) Let $A \in \Delta_\alpha$ and $A \leq_\Gamma B$. From $A \in \Delta_\alpha$, we get that $A \in \beta(\Gamma)$ for some $\beta \geq \alpha$, and from $A \leq_\Gamma B$ we then get that $B \in \gamma(\Gamma) = \Delta_\gamma - \Delta_{\gamma+1}$ for some $\gamma \geq \beta \geq \alpha$, hence, by (i), $B \in \Delta_\alpha$. So Δ_α is an L_0-cut with respect to $\leq_\Gamma$. To show that the Δ_α's are the only non-empty cuts with respect to $\leq_\Gamma$, suppose that $S \neq \emptyset$ is a cut with respect to $\leq_\Gamma$. Consider the set of ordinals β such that there is an $A \in S$ with $A \in \beta(\Gamma)$, and take the smallest ordinal α from this class. We show that $\Delta_\alpha = S$. Select some $A \in S$ with $A \in \alpha(\Gamma)$. Since S is a cut, $B \in L_0$ is in S iff $A \leq_\Gamma B$, i.e., iff $B \in \beta(\Gamma)$ for some $\beta \geq \alpha$, i.e., iff $B \in \bigcup \{\beta(\Gamma): \beta \geq \alpha\} = \Delta_\alpha$, by (vii) and (ii).

(ix) From left to right: Let $A \leq_\Gamma B$ and $A \in \Delta_\alpha$. From the latter, we get that $A \in \beta(\Gamma)$ for some $\beta \geq \alpha$, then the former gives us that $B \in \gamma(\Gamma)$ for some $\gamma \geq \beta \geq \alpha$, hence $B \in \Delta_\gamma \subseteq \Delta_\alpha$, as desired. From right to left: Let $A \not\leq_\Gamma B$, i.e., by (vii), there are β and γ such that $A \in \beta(\Gamma)$, $B \in \gamma(\Gamma)$ and $\gamma < \beta$. But then, $A \in \Delta_\beta$ and $B \notin \Delta_{\gamma+1} \supseteq \Delta_\beta$, so A, but not B is in Δ_β, and we are done. $\square$

Proof of Observation 11 (i) That $E(\Gamma)$ satisfies Transitivity (E1) follows immediately from the transitivity of $\leq$ on the ordinals.

For Entailment (E2), suppose that $\emptyset \neq \Sigma \vdash A$ Consider the set of ordinals β such that there is a $B \in \Sigma$ with $\text{rank}_\Gamma(B) = \beta$, take the smallest ordinal α from this class and select some $B \in \Sigma$ with $\text{rank}_\Gamma(B) = \alpha$. Now since for all $C \in \Sigma$, $\text{rank}_\Gamma(C) \geq \alpha$, they are in Δ_γ for some $\gamma \geq \alpha$, hence, by part (i) of Observation 10, each $C \in \Sigma$ is in Δ_α, so $\Sigma \subseteq \Delta_\alpha$. But Δ_α is closed under Cn_0 by definition. Hence $A \in \Delta_\alpha$, hence $A \in \gamma(\Gamma)$ for some $\gamma \geq \alpha$, hence $B \leq_\Gamma A$.

For Maximality (E3), suppose that $B \leq_\Gamma A$ for all B. That is, $\text{rank}_\Gamma(B) \leq \text{rank}_\Gamma(A)$ for all B, so in particular $\text{rank}_\Gamma(\top) \leq \text{rank}_\Gamma(A)$. Let $\alpha = \text{rank}_\Gamma(\top)$. Then, by part (vi) of Observation 10, $\Delta_\alpha = \text{Cn}_0(\emptyset)$, and we have $\Delta_\beta = \text{Cn}_0(\emptyset)$ for $\beta > \alpha$, so, since $\text{rank}_\Gamma(A) \geq \alpha$, $A \in \text{Cn}_0(\emptyset)$.

To show that $E(\Gamma)$ is well-ordering, let Σ be a non-empty set of L_0-sentences. Consider the set $\{\alpha: \text{rank}_\Gamma(A) = \alpha \text{ for some } A \in \Sigma\}$, select the smallest ordinal β from that set and a $B \in \Sigma$ such that $\text{rank}_\Gamma(B) = \beta$. Since $\beta \leq \text{rank}_\Gamma(A)$ for all $A \in \Sigma$, $B \leq_\Gamma A$ for all $A \in \Sigma$, so B is a smallest element in Σ, and we are done.

(ii) Suppose for reductio that there is an $A_i \square \rightarrow B_i \in \Gamma$ which $\leq_\Gamma$ does not satisfy. Then $A_i \rightarrow B_i \leq_\Gamma \neg A_i$, i.e., $\text{rank}_\Gamma(A_i \rightarrow B_i) \leq \text{rank}_\Gamma(\neg A_i)$. Let $\text{rank}_\Gamma(\neg A_i) = \alpha$, i.e., $\neg A_i \in \Delta_\alpha - \Delta_{\alpha+1}$. As $\neg A_i \in \Delta_\alpha$, we get, by definition,

$A_i \rightarrow B_i \in \Delta_{\alpha+1} = Cn_0(\{A_j \rightarrow B_j : \neg A_j \in \Delta_\alpha\})$. So $rank_\Gamma(A_i \rightarrow B_i) \geq \alpha+1 > rank_\Gamma(\neg A_i)$, and we have a contradiction. $\square$

Proof of Observation 12 Let $rank_{E(\Gamma)}(A) = \alpha$, i.e., by definition $A \in L_0 - \overleftarrow{\alpha}(\leq_\Gamma)$ and $A \leq_\Gamma B$ for every $B \in L_0 - \overleftarrow{\alpha}(\leq_\Gamma)$. By part (ii) of Observation 10, this means that $A \in \Delta_\alpha$ and $A \leq_\Gamma B$ for every $B \in \Delta_\alpha$. Thus, by part (ix) of Observation 10, $A \in \Delta_\alpha$ and for every β and $B \in \Delta_\alpha$, if $A \in \Delta_\beta$ then $B \in \Delta_\beta$. But we know from parts (i) and (iv) of Observation 10 that $\alpha(\Gamma)$ is non-empty, i.e., that there is a $B \in \Delta_\alpha - \Delta_{\alpha+1}$. So $A \notin \Delta_{\alpha+1}$, so $A \in \alpha(\Gamma)$, so $rank_\Gamma(A) = \alpha$. $\square$

Proof of Observation 13 Let Γ be as indicated and $\leq$ an E-relation satisfying Γ. If $\leq$ is not well-ordering, then $E(\Gamma) \sqsubset_E \leq$ by definition, since $E(\Gamma)$ is well-ordering by Observation 11. So let $\leq$ be well-ordering. As $\sqsubseteq_E$ is antisymmetrical, it suffices to show that $E(\Gamma) \sqsubseteq_E \leq$. We show that for every L_0-sentence A, $rank_{E(\Gamma)}(A) \leq rank_\leq(A)$ by transfinite induction on $rank_\leq(A)$.

Let, as induction hypothesis, $rank_{E(\Gamma)}(A) \leq rank_\leq(A)$ be established for all A with $rank_\leq(A) < \alpha$. Now let $rank_\leq(C) = \alpha$. We have to verify that $rank_{E(\Gamma)}(C) \leq \alpha$, i.e., by Observation 12, $rank_\Gamma(C) \leq \alpha$, i.e., $C \in U\{\beta(\Gamma) : \beta \leq \alpha\} = L_0 - \Delta_{\alpha+1}$, by part (ii) of Observation 10.

Suppose for reductio that $C \in \Delta_{\alpha+1}$, i.e., by construction, $C \in Cn_0\{A_i \rightarrow B_i : \neg A_i \in \Delta_\alpha\}$. Since $\leq$ is an E-relation, so by (E2), $A_i \rightarrow B_i \leq C$ for some i such that $\neg A_i \in \Delta_\alpha$. As $\leq$ satisfies Γ, we have $\neg A_i < A_i \rightarrow B_i$, so by (E1), $\neg A_i < C$. Hence, $rank_\leq(\neg A_i) < rank_\leq(C) = \alpha$. But $\neg A_i \in \Delta_\alpha$, so $rank_{E(\Gamma)}(\neg A_i) = rank_\Gamma(\neg A_i) \geq \alpha > rank_\leq(\neg A_i)$, which contradicts the induction hypothesis. $\square$

Proof of the Corollary First we recall that any set of sentences satisfied by a well-ordering E-relation $\leq$ is well-founded, so in particular $K(\leq)$ is well-founded and the construction of $E(K(\leq))$ yields a well-ordering E-relation, by Observation 11(i). In view of Observation 13 and the antisymmetry of $\sqsubseteq_E$, it suffices to show that $\leq \sqsubseteq_E E(K(\leq))$.

We show that $rank_\leq(A) \leq rank_{E(K(\leq))}(A)$ for every A by induction on $rank_\leq(A)$. Let, as induction hypothesis, $rank_\leq(A) \leq rank_{E(K(\leq))}(A)$ be established for every A with $rank_\leq(A) < \alpha$. Now let $rank_\leq(A) = \alpha$. For $\alpha = 0$, the claim is trivial. For $\alpha > 0$, choose representatives B_β with $rank_\leq(B_\beta) = \beta$ for all $\beta < \alpha$ (such B_β's exist!). Now clearly $B_\beta < A$ for all $\beta < \alpha$, hence $\leq$ satisfies $\neg A \vee \neg B_\beta \square \rightarrow A$ for all $\beta < \alpha$. By Observation 11(ii), $E(K(\leq))$ satisfies $K(\leq)$, so $E(K(\leq))$ satisfies in particular $\neg A \vee \neg B_\beta \square \rightarrow A$ for every $\beta < \alpha$, so $B_\beta \leq_{K(\leq)} A$ for every $\beta < \alpha$, so by induction hypothesis $\beta=\text{rank}_{\leq}B_\beta\leq\text{rank}_{E(K(\leq))}B_\beta<\text{rank}_{E(K(\leq))}A$ for every $\beta<\alpha$, so $\text{rank}_{\leq}(A)=\alpha\leq\text{rank}_{E(K(\leq))}A$.

Proof of Observation 14 (i) Let $A\in\text{Cn}_0(\Gamma)\cap L_1$. As Cn_0 does not operate on the internal structure of conditionals, they may be regarded as atoms when applying Cn_0 to Γ. Note that since Γ is an L_1-set, these new atoms do not appear in any complex sentence. Therefore, if A is a conditional, i.e., if A is in L_1-L_0, it can only be a Cn_0-consequence of Γ if $A\in\Gamma$, and the claim reduces to Inclusion which will be proved as (iii). On the other hand, if A is in L_0, then, by the same argument, it must be a Cn_0-consequence of $\Gamma\cap L_0$. But as $K_0(\leq)$ is a Cn_0-theory for every E-relation $\leq$, every E-relation satisfying $\Gamma\supseteq\Gamma\cap L_0$ satisfies $\text{Cn}_0(\Gamma\cap L_0)$, so every E-relation for Γ satisfies A.

(ii) Let $B\in L_0\cap\text{Cn}(\Gamma\cup\{A\})$. As $B\in L_0$, this means that $B\in K_0(E(\Gamma\cup\{A\}))$ $=\text{Cn}_0(L_0(\Gamma\cup\{A\}))$, by construction. But this is equivalent to $A\to B\in$ $\text{Cn}_0(L_0(\Gamma))=K_0(E(\Gamma))$, i.e., $A\to B\in\text{Cn}(\Gamma)$.

(iii)–(v) Immediate from the general results of Makinson (1989; 1990) for arbitrary preferential model structures.

(vi) As Makinson points out, it suffices to show that $(\mathcal{E},\models,\sqsubseteq_E)$ is "stoppered" in the sense that for all E-relations $\leq\in\mathcal{E}$ and all L_1-premise sets Γ, if $\leq\models\Gamma$ then there is a $\leq'$ such that either $\leq'\sqsubseteq_E\leq$ or $\leq'=\leq$, and $\leq'$ satisfies Γ $\sqsubseteq_E$-minimally. Let $\leq\models\Gamma$. In the first case, assume that there are only non-well-ordering E-relations for Γ. Then we are immediately done, since, by the definition of $\sqsubseteq_E$, non-well-ordering E-relations are incomparable with respect to $\sqsubseteq_E$, so $\leq'=\leq$ will do. So assume, as the second case, that there is a well-ordering E-relation for Γ. So Γ is well-founded. Hence $E(\Gamma)$ is the smallest E-relation with respect to $\sqsubseteq_E$, so $\leq'=E(\Gamma)$ will do.

(vii) Drawing again on Makinson's work, we only have to verify that $\sqsubseteq_E$ is transitive. But this follows trivially from the definition of $\sqsubseteq_E$. □

Proof of Observation 15 By giving counterexamples.

(i) Let $\Gamma=\{\neg A\square\!\!\to B\vee D, \neg B\square\!\!\to A\vee D\}$; the $\leq$-translations are $A<A\vee B\vee D$ and $B<A\vee B\vee D$. $E(\Gamma\cup\{A\})$ has the E-base $\bot\prec A\prec A\vee B\vee D\prec\top$, $E(\Gamma\cup\{B\})$ has the E-base $\bot\prec B\prec A\vee B\vee D\prec\top$; in both cases, it follows that $A\vee B<A\vee B\vee D$, so both $\Gamma\cup\{A\}$ and $\Gamma\cup\{B\}$ entail $\neg(A\vee B)\square\!\!\to D$ $(\equiv C)$. But $E(\Gamma\cup\{A\vee B\})$ has the E-base $\bot\prec A\vee B\prec\top$ which does not give $A\vee B<A\vee B\vee D$, so $\Gamma\cup\{A\vee B\}$ does not entail $\neg(A\vee B)\square\!\!\to D$.

(ii) Let $\Gamma=\{\neg C, A\vee C\square\!\!\to D, \neg A\vee C\square\!\!\to D\}$; the $\leq$-translations are $\bot<\neg C$, $\neg A\&\neg C<(\neg A\&\neg C)\vee D$ and $A\&\neg C<(A\&\neg C)\vee D$. $E(\Gamma\cup\{A\})$ has the E-base $\bot\prec A\simeq\neg C\simeq D\prec(A\&\neg C)\vee D\prec\top$, $E(\Gamma\cup\{\neg A\})$ has the E-base

$\perp \prec \neg A \simeq \neg C \simeq D \prec (\neg A \& \neg C) \vee D \prec T$; in both cases, it follows that $\neg C < \neg C \vee D$, so both $\Gamma \cup \{A\}$ and $\Gamma \cup \{\neg A\}$ entail $C \square \rightarrow D$ ($\equiv B$). But $E(\Gamma)$ has the E-base $\perp \prec \neg C \simeq D \prec T$ which does not give $\neg C < \neg C \vee D$, so Γ does not entail $C \square \rightarrow D$.

(iii) Let $\Gamma = \{C, D, \neg D \square \rightarrow C, \neg A \vee \neg C \square \rightarrow C, A \vee \neg C \square \rightarrow C\}$; the $\leq$-translations are $\perp < C, \perp < D, D < C \vee D, A < C$ and $\neg A < C$. $E(\Gamma)$ has the E-base $\perp \prec C \simeq D \prec C \vee D \prec T$, so Γ entails $\neg C \square \rightarrow D$ ($\equiv B$). But $E(\Gamma \cup \{A\})$ has the E-base $\perp \prec A \simeq D \prec C \simeq C \vee D \prec T$, and $E(\Gamma \cup \{\neg A\})$ has the E-base $\perp \prec \neg A \simeq D \prec C \simeq C \vee D \prec T$, so neither gives $C < C \vee D$, so neither $\Gamma \cup \{A\}$ nor $\Gamma \cup \{\neg A\}$ entails $\neg C \square \rightarrow D$.

(iv) Let $\Gamma = \{A, \neg A \vee \neg C \square \rightarrow C\}$. Γ is consistent and has the E-base $\perp \prec A \prec C \prec T$. $Cn(\{A\})$ is the set of all sentences satisfied by $E(\{A\})$ which has the E-base $\perp \prec A \prec T$. Now $\neg A \vee \neg C \square \rightarrow A \in Cn(\{A\})$. So both $\neg A \vee \neg C \square \rightarrow A$ and $\neg A \vee \neg C \square \rightarrow C$ ($\equiv B$) are in $Cn(\{A\}) \cup \{\neg A \vee \neg C \square \rightarrow C\}$. But there is no E-relation satisfying these two sentences, for the first one translates to $A < C$ while the second one translates to $C < A$ which contradicts the definition of $<$ from $\leq$. $\square$

Proof of Observation 16 We restrict our attention to the principal cases with antecedents the negations of which are not in $Cn_0(\emptyset)$; the limiting cases are all trivial. In view of Observation 4, we can replace $\models$ by $\models_1$.

(i) $\models_1 A$ for $A \in L_0 \cap Cn_0(\emptyset)$: $\perp < T \doteq A$ for such an A and every E-relation $\leq$, by (E3).

(ii) $\{A \square \rightarrow B, A \square \rightarrow C\} \models_1 A \square \rightarrow (B \& C)$: Let $\leq$ satisfy the premises, i.e., $\neg A < \neg A \vee B$ and $\neg A < \neg A \vee C$. By (E2) then, $\neg A \vee B \leq A \vee (B \& C)$ or $\neg A \vee C \leq A \vee (B \& C)$, so, by (E1) and (E2), $\neg A < \neg A \vee (B \& C)$, i.e., $\leq \models_1 A \square \rightarrow (B \& C)$.

(iii) $\models_1 A \square \rightarrow T$: like (i), $\neg A < \neg A \vee T$ is immediate, provided that $\neg A \notin Cn_0(\emptyset)$.

(iv) $\models_1 A \square \rightarrow A$: like (i), $\neg A < \neg A \vee A$ is immediate, provided that $\neg A \notin Cn_0(\emptyset)$.

(v) $\{A \square \rightarrow B)\} \models_1 A \rightarrow B$: Let $\leq$ satisfy the premise, i.e., $\neg A < \neg A \vee B$. Thus $\perp \leq \neg A < \neg A \vee B$, so $\perp < A \rightarrow B$, i.e., $\leq \models A \rightarrow B$.

(vi) $\{A \& B\} \models_1 A \square \rightarrow B$: Let $\leq$ satisfy the premise, i.e., $\perp < A \& B$. Then, by (E2), $\neg A \leq \perp < A \& B \leq \neg A \vee B$, so $\leq \models A \square \rightarrow B$.

(vii) $\{A \square \rightarrow \neg A\} \models_1 B \square \rightarrow \neg A$: Immediate, since there is no $\leq$ satisfying $A \square \rightarrow \neg A$ which would mean $\neg A < \neg A \vee \neg A$, a contradiction with (E2).

(viii) $\{A \square \rightarrow B, B \square \rightarrow A, A \square \rightarrow C\} \models_1 B \square \rightarrow C$: Let $\leq$ satisfy the premises, i.e., $\neg A < \neg A \vee B$, $\neg B < \neg B \vee A$, and $\neg A < \neg A \vee C$. The first term implies, with the help of (E2), that $\neg B \leq \neg A$. Also by (E2), either $\neg B \vee A \leq \neg B \vee C$ or

$\neg A \lor C \leq \neg B \lor C$. In the former case, we get $\neg B < \neg B \lor A \leq \neg B \lor C$, in the latter case we get $\neg B \leq \neg A < \neg A \lor C \leq \neg B \lor C$, so in any case $\leq \models B\square\!\!\rightarrow C$.

(ix) $\{A\square\!\!\rightarrow C, B\square\!\!\rightarrow C\} \models_1 A \lor B\square\!\!\rightarrow C$: Let $\leq$ satisfy the premises, i.e., $\neg A <$ $\neg A \lor C$ and $\neg B < \neg B \lor C$. By (E2), either $\neg A \lor C \leq (\neg A \& \neg B) \lor C$ or $\neg B \lor C \leq$ $(\neg A \& \neg B) \lor C$. In the former case, $\neg A \& \neg B \leq \neg A < \neg A \lor C \leq (\neg A \& \neg B) \lor C$, in the latter case similarly $\neg A \& \neg B \leq \neg B < \neg B \lor C \leq (\neg A \& \neg B) \lor C$, so in any case $\leq \models (A \lor B)\square\!\!\rightarrow C$.

(x) $\{A\square\!\!\rightarrow C, \neg(A\square\!\!\rightarrow \neg B)\} \models_1 A \& B\square\!\!\rightarrow C$: Let $\leq$ satisfy the premises, so $\neg A < \neg A \lor C$ and, by the consistency condition for L_2, $\neg A \lor \neg B \leq \neg A$. Hence, by (E1) and (E2), $\neg A \lor \neg B \leq \neg A < \neg A \lor C \leq (\neg A \lor \neg B) \lor C$, so $\leq \models (A \& B)\square\!\!\rightarrow C$.

(xi) If $C \in Cn_0(B)$ then $A\square\!\!\rightarrow B \models_1 A\square\!\!\rightarrow C$: Let $C \in Cn_0(B)$ and let $\leq$ satisfy the premise, i.e., $\neg A < \neg A \lor B$. Since $C \in Cn_0(B)$, also $\neg A \lor C \in Cn_0(\neg A \lor B)$, so, by (E2), $\neg A \lor B \leq \neg A \lor C$, hence $\neg A < \neg A \lor C$, i.e., $\leq \models A\square\!\!\rightarrow C$. $\square$

Proof of Observation 17 (i) We show the positive claims concerning $\models$; the negative claims concerning $\not\models$ follow from (ii). The E-relations $E(\Gamma)$ generated by the respective premise sets of (SA), (Tr) and (Cp) have the following E-bases:

$\perp \prec \neg A \lor B \prec \top$,

$\perp \prec \neg A \lor B \simeq \neg B \lor C \prec \top$,

$\perp \prec \neg A \lor B \prec \top$, respectively.

Clearly, for these E-relations it holds that $\neg A \lor \neg C < \neg A \lor \neg C \lor B$, $\neg A < \neg A \lor C$, and $B < \neg A \lor B$, respectively. So they satisfy the desired conclusions.

(ii) The E-relations $E(\Gamma)$ generated by the augmented premise sets have the following E-bases:

$\perp \prec \neg A \lor B \simeq \neg A \lor \neg C \prec \top$,

$\perp \prec \neg A \simeq \neg B \lor C \prec \neg A \lor B \prec \top$,

$\perp \prec B \prec \top$, respectively.

It is easy to see that for these E-relations it holds that $\neg A \lor \neg C \lor B \leq \neg A \lor \neg C$, $\neg A \lor C \leq \neg A$, and $\neg A \lor B \leq B$, respectively. So they do not satisfy the desired conclusions.

(iii) Let in the following $\leq$ satisfy the premise(s) but not the conclusion of our inference patterns.

In the case of (SA), we have $\neg A < \neg A \lor B \leq \neg A \lor \neg C \lor B \leq \neg A \lor \neg C$, so $\leq$ satisfies $A\square\!\!\rightarrow \neg C$.

In the case of (Tr), we have, first, $\neg A < \neg A \lor B$, secondly, $\neg B < \neg B \lor C$, and thirdly, $\neg A \lor C \leq \neg A$. From (E2), we know that either $\neg A \lor B \leq \neg A \lor C$ or $\neg B \lor C \leq \neg A \lor C$. But the former cannot be, since it would imply, with the help of the first and third condition, $\neg A < \neg A$. So $\neg B \lor C \leq \neg A \lor C$. But by the second and the third condition and by (E2) this gives us the chain $\neg B < \neg B \lor C \leq \neg A \lor C \leq \neg A \leq \neg B \lor \neg A$, so $\leq$ satisfies $B \square \!\!\rightarrow \neg A$.

In the case of (Cp), we have $\bot \leq \neg A < \neg A \lor B \leq B$, so $\leq$ satisfies B. $\square$

References

Alchourrón, Carlos, Peter Gärdenfors and David Makinson: 1985, "On the Logic of Theory Change: Partial Meet Contraction Functions and Their Associated Revision Functions", *Journal of Symbolic Logic* **50**, 510–530.

Alchourrón, Carlos, and David Makinson: 1985, "On the Logic of Theory Change: Safe Contraction", *Studia Logica* **44**, 405–422.

Alchourrón, Carlos, and David Makinson: 1985, "Maps Between Some Different Kinds of Contraction Function: The Finite Case", *Studia Logica* **45**, 187–198.

Gärdenfors, Peter: 1986, "Belief Revisions and the Ramsey Test for Conditionals", *Philosophical Review* **95**, 81–93.

Gärdenfors, Peter: 1988, *Knowledge in Flux: Modeling the Dynamics of Epistemic States*, Bradford Books, MIT Press, Cambridge, Mass.

Gärdenfors, Peter, and David Makinson: 1988, "Revisions of Knowledge Systems Using Epistemic Entrenchment', in M. Vardi(ed.), *Theoretical Aspects of Reasoning About Knowledge*, Morgan Kaufmann, Los Altos, 83–95.

Grove, Adam: 1988, "Two Modellings for Theory Change", *Journal of Philosophical Logic* **17**, 157–170.

Hansson, Sven O.: 1989, "New Operators for Theory Change", *Theoria* **55**, 114–136.

Lewis, David: 1973, *Counterfactuals*, Harvard UP, Cambridge, Mass.

Lindström, Sten, and Wlodzimierz Rabinowicz: 1990, "Epistemic Entrenchment with Incomparabilities and Relational Belief Revision", *this volume.*

Makinson, David: 1989, "General Theory of Cumulative Inference', in M. Reinfrank a.o. (eds.), *Non-Monotonic Reasoning – Proceedings of the 2nd International Workshop 1988*, Springer, Berlin, 1–18.

Makinson, David: 1990, "General Patterns in Nonmonotonic Reasoning", in D.M. Gabbay a.o. (eds.), *Handbook of Logic in Artificial Intelligence and Logic Programming, Vol. II: Non-Monotonic and Uncertain Reasoning*, Oxford UP, Oxford, to appear.

Martin, John N.: 1984, "Epistemic Semantics for Classical and Intuitionistic Logic, *Notre Dame Journal of Formal Logic* 25, 105–116.

Morreau, Michael: 1990, "Epistemic Semantics for Counterfactuals", in H. Kamp (ed.), *Conditionals, Defaults and Belief Revision*, DYANA Deliverable R2.5.A, ESPRIT Basic Research Action BR3175, Edinburgh, 1–27.

Rott, Hans: 1989a, "Conditionals and Theory Change: Revisions, Expansions, and Additions", *Synthese* 81, 91–113.

Rott, Hans: 1989b, "Two Methods of Constructing Contractions and Revisions of Knowledge Systems", *Journal of Philosophical Logic*, to appear.

Rott, Hans: 1989c, "On the Logic of Theory Change: More Maps Between Different Kinds of Contraction Function", to appear.

Rott, Hans: 1990, "Updates, Conditionals and Non-monotonicity: Introductory Comments on Veltman and Morreau", in H. Kamp (ed.), *Conditionals, Defaults and Belief Revision*, DYANA Deliverable R2.5.A, ESPRIT Basic Research Action BR3175, Edinburgh, 65–78.

Shoham, Yoav: 1987, "Nonmonotonic Logics: Meaning and Utility", *Proceedings 10th IJCAI–87*, 388–393.

Shoham, Yoav: 1988, *Reasoning about Change – Time and Causation from the Standpoint of Artificial Intelligence*, MIT Press, Cambridge, Mass.

Theory Change and
Nonmonotonic Reasoning

Relations between the Logic of Theory Change and Nonmonotonic Logic

David Makinson[1] and Peter Gärdenfors[2]

Abstract

The purpose of this paper is to investigate the close relations between the logic of theory change (alias belief revision) on the one hand, and nonmonotonic logic on the other. The connection is most manifest at the level of general conditions on nonmonotonic inference operations, compared to those on theory revision operations. It also appears between some of the specific constructions that have been used in the literature to generate such operations.

After discussing the connection in intuitive terms, we express it as a formal translation procedure, and examine the outcome of translating well-known postulates and conditions from one domain to the other. On the level of specific constructions, we show the exact relationship, which is very close to identity, between the procedure of theory revision known as "full meet revision" and Poole's procedure for generating "default" inference operations.

Several illustrations are given of how results already known in one of the two domains throw light on the other domain, and also how they may suggest interesting open questions.

1 Introduction

Anyone familiar with the logic of conditional propositions as developed in the late 60's and 70's using "possible worlds semantics", or the logic of theory change (alias belief revision) as developed in the early 80's using notions such as "partial meet contraction and revision", finds that many things in nonmonotonic logic as studied at present are "strangely familiar".

The sense of similarity arises for certain of the specific constructions that have been used to generate nonmonotonic logics. In particular, the version of "default reasoning" presented by Makinson (to appear) as an expression of Poole's (1988) proposal, which is based upon a procedure of intersecting maximally consistent

---

[1] Les Etangs B2, La Ronce, F-92410 Ville d'Avray, France. E-mail: Shmak@frunes21.bitnet.

[2] Cognitive Science, Dept. of Philosophy, Lund University, Kungshuset, Lundadård, S-223 50 Lund, Sweden. E-mail: Gardenfors@lumac.lu.se (internet), Garden@seldc52.bitnet.

sets of propositions, is evidently very close to the "full meet revision" defined in the logic of theory change by Alchourrón and Makinson (1982), and also to the conditional logic constructions of Ginsberg (1986). Further, the approach to nonmonotonic logic known as preferential entailment, due to Shoham (1988) and further generalized by Makinson (1989) and Kraus, Lehmann and Magidor (1990), using an ordering among models to determine those that are minimal, is reminiscent of orderings in the possible worlds semantics for conditional logic of Lewis (1973) and others. It is also reminiscent of the orderings used in the logic of theory change by Alchourrón, Gärdenfors and Makinson (1985) to determine transitively relational partial meet contraction and revision functions.

This is not to say that the correspondences are always exact. Nor does it mean that every approach to, say, nonmonotonic logic already has a counterpart in the literature on theory change. For example, there is nothing in the logic of theory change, as it presently exists, that corresponds in any natural way with the default constructions of Reiter (1980). Nor is there anything in the literature on nonmonotonic logic that corresponds to the "safe revisions" of Alchourrón and Makinson (1985) or the "revision via epistemic entrenchment" of Gärdenfors and Makinson (1988).

Moreover, the different motivations of the three domains give rather different ambitions to the theories developed. For example, the logic of conditional propositions has always reflected a desire to understand the import of "if ... then ..." locutions of ordinary language. Nonmonotonic reasoning has been studied with hopes for use in artificial intelligence, with consequent attention to the requirements of finitude and eventual practical computability. On the other hand, the logic of theory change, as developed for example in Alchourrón, Gärdenfors and Makinson (1985) and Gärdenfors (1988), has been quite unconcerned by such constraints.

In order not to become lost in the thicket of variant generating constructions, we shall in this paper look at the question of connections from a more abstract standpoint. We shall examine the relations that exist between *general conditions* that are often regarded as desirable (or at least interesting) for nonmonotonic inference relations, and similarly general conditions that have been suggested for operations of theory revision.

We shall not look in detail into conditional logics, although it is evident, as has been noted by Lehmann and Magidor (to appear) and others, that the "flat" formulas of conditional propositional logic (i.e those formulas of the form x > y where neither x nor y contains any occurrences of the conditional connective >) can be seen as expressing a range of possible conditions on inference relations. (Cf. also Arló Costa and Carnota (1989a,b) who establish a correspondence between Delgrande's semantics for conditionals and a particular class of preferential models for nonmonotonic logic).

The possibility of iterating the connective > in well-formed formulas of conditional logic gives rise to a range of problems well beyond those of either nonmonotonic inference or theory revision. It is curious that the most complex of the three domains was, historically, the first to be tackled.

2 The Central Idea

The logic of theory change studies two principal processes – in addition to the familiar one of the *expansion* of a set A of propositions by a proposition x, understood as $Cn(A \cup \{x\})$ where Cn is the classical consequence operation. These two additional notions are *contraction* and *revision*.

Contraction is the process of removing a proposition x from a theory A, in such a way that the outcome theory $A \doteq x$ no longer implies x (unless, of course, x is itself a tautology) but is not gratuitously impoverished or distorted. Revision is the process of adding a proposition y to a theory A, in such a way that the outcome theory $A*y$ contains y, and yet is consistent (unless, of course, y is itself inconsistent) despite possible inconsistency between y and A.

These two processes are not so much specific, well-defined constructions as general *kinds* of operations, that can take various forms. In some of these forms, at least, they are interdefinable: revision can be defined from contraction by the "Levi identity" $A*x = Cn((A \doteq \neg x) \cup \{x\})$, and when A is already closed under classical consequence, i.e. when $A = Cn(A)$, we can define contraction by the "Harper identity" $A \doteq x = A \cap A*\neg x$. These concepts are studied in the book Gärdenfors (1988), which draws upon earlier papers of Alchourrón, Gärdenfors and/or Makinson listed in the bibliography.

There are two ways in which theory change can be said to be nonmonotonic. Firstly, if one sees the revision of a theory A by a proposition x as an *operation on A modulo x*, it is much "worse" than merely nonmonotonic. It does indeed fail monotony: we may have $A \subseteq B$ but $A*x \not\subseteq B*x$. At least we may have such failure if revision is taken to satisfy certain of the postulates of Alchourrón, Gärdenfors and Makinson (1985). But, and this is our main point, on all variants the operation fails an even more fundamental condition, of reflexivity or inclusion. This is the condition that if A is any set of propositions then each element of A may be inferred from A, i.e. that $A \vdash\!\!\sim x$ for all $x \in A$ where $\vdash\!\!\sim$ is the nonmonotonic inference relation; or in other notation, that $A \subseteq C(A)$ where $C(A)$ is $\{x: A \vdash\!\!\sim x\}$. Relations $\vdash\!\!\sim$ or operations C failing this condition may well represent processes of reasoning, but they hardly deserve to be called inferences, monotonic or otherwise. And such is the case of revision. We may very well have $A \not\subseteq A*x$; indeed, this will happen *whenever* the proposition x is consistent but is inconsistent with A.

On the other hand, if we change our *gestalt* and see the revision of a theory A by a proposition x as an *operation on x modulo A*, we get a quite different picture and a second sense in which theory revision is nonmonotonic. The revision of A by x always contains x (on the postulates presented by Gärdenfors (1988)) and so we have $x \in C(\{x\})$. In other words, the revision of a theory by a proposition x can be seen as an inference — but as *inference from the proposition x* rather than from the theory A. This inference operation will moreover be nonmonotonic, in that we may have $x \vdash y$ (where $\vdash$ is classical consequence), but not $A*x \vdash A*y$. For example, suppose we put $x = a\&b$ and $y = a$, where a, b are elementary propositions, and take $A = Cn(\{\neg a \vee \neg b\})$. Then (at least on the postulates for revision presented by Gärdenfors (1988)), $A*x = A*(a\&b)$ will be a consistent theory containing a&b. On the other hand, since a is consistent with $\neg a \vee \neg b$, we have $A*y = Cn(\{\neg a \vee \neg b\}) \cup \{a\}) = Cn(\{a\&\neg b\})$. Thus although $x \vdash y$ we do not have $A*x \vdash A*y$.

With this *gestalt*, we are in a position to understand the link between nonmonotonic logic and the logic of theory change. The key idea is:

(1)   See the revision of a theory A by a proposition x, forming a theory A*x, as a form of nonmonotonic inference *from x*;

(2)   Conversely, see a nonmonotonic inference of a proposition y from a proposition x as a discovery that y is contained in the result of revising a *fixed background theory* A so as to integrate x. In this way, the nonmonotonic relation x $\vdash$ y serves as a shorthand for x $\vdash_A$ y which indicates that the nonmonotonic inference is dependent on the background theory A.

The next section expresses this intuitive idea in formal terms. As the details of the formal expression are fastidious, some readers may prefer to proceed directly to sections 4 and 5 to see the translation in action, returning to section 3 later as desired.

3 The Formal Translation

The simple idea outlined above can be expressed as a formal procedure for translating conditions about one of the two concepts into conditions on the other. We assume that these conditions are first written in purely first-order terms, with elementary ingredients of the form x $\vdash$ y in the one case, where $\vdash$ is the nonmonotonic inference relation, and the form y $\in$ A*x in the other. We then proceed as follows.

*From $\vdash$ to *:*
Simply replace each elementary part of the form x $\vdash$ y by y $\in$ A*x, where A is an arbitrary but fixed background theory.

*From * to $\vdash$:*
This translation is more fastidious, due to the elimination of the variable A. There are three steps:

1.   Inspect the condition on * to see whether it involves considering the revision of two theories A and A'. If so, stop: the condition cannot in general be translated. If not, continue.

2.   Inspect the condition on * to see whether it involves reference to a theory in both its unrevised form A and a revised form A*x for one or more

propositions x. If not, continue. If so, first break the condition up into a principal case that A is consistent and a limiting case that A is inconsistent. In the first case, replace all "unrevised" occurrences of A by A∗τ, where τ is an arbitrarily chosen tautology. In the second case, eliminate all "unrevised" occurrences of A by treating elementary parts x ∈ A of the condition to be translated as true.

3.   Taking the output(s) of step 2, translate by replacing all elementary parts of the form y ∈ A∗x by x ⊢ y.

Comments on the ⊢ to ∗ Translation.

Note that the ⊢ to ∗ translation is formulated for inference between *individual propositions* only. Clearly, when X is a finite set of propositions, it is natural to translate X ⊢ y by first re-expressing it as &X ⊢ y, where &X is the conjunction (in some conventional order) of all the propositions in X. When X is an infinite set of properties, this trick is of course no longer available (unless we move to a language admitting infinitely long conjunctions). In principle, one can still translate X ⊢ y *directly* as y ∈ A∗X, where A∗X is understood as the result of revising the theory A so as to integrate simultaneously and consistently *all* the propositions in X. "In principle", because although the idea of infinitary revision functions seems to make good intuitive sense, the formal study of revision has to date been almost entirely limited to the case where propositions are introduced one (or finitely many) at a time. An exception is Fuhrmann (1988) who presents postulates for generalised forms of contractions.

Comments on the ∗ to ⊢ Translation.

Revision is an operation of two arguments, forming A∗x out of theory A and proposition x. On the other hand, nonmonotonic inference conceived as an operation C(x) defined as {y: x ⊢ y} is a function of only one argument x. For this reason the logic of theory change is potentially more general than the logic of nonmonotonic inference, in that it allows the possibility of *variation* in the other argument, A. "Potentially", because this possibility has hardly been explored. The postulates for revision presented by Gärdenfors (1988) all concern the case where the theory A is held *constant*. Moreover, the semantic notion of "partial meet revision", to which those postulates correspond, does not easily suggest plausible principles in which A varies. However, one context in which such principles have been formulated and proven is that of the notion of "safe contraction"; see the last section of Alchourrón and Makinson (1985). Furthermore, Hansson (1989a,b) and Lindström and Rabinowicz (1990) investigate some postulates which utilize varying theories.

The * to ⊢ translation eliminates all occurrences of the theory variable. If the translation were applied to a condition on * referring to two theories, it would, by thus eliminating them, implicitly identify them or at least treat their difference as without significance, thereby distorting the sense of the condition. This is the reason for the first clause of the translation procedure. The restriction to conditions on * involving only a single theory variable A bars from translation any conditions that relate A*x to B*x when A ⊆ B. It also rules out the translation of conditions on iterated revision, e.g. relating (A*x)*y to A*(x&y) and to (A*y)*x.

The second step of the * to ⊢ translation prescribes a preliminary "doctoring" of all "unrevised" occurrences of the theory variable A. This is because the suppression of the theory parameter in its "revised" occurrences will distort meaning unless the unrevised ones are also got out of the way. The trick adopted, suggested to the authors by Hans Rott, is to identify unrevised A with A*⊤. This is legitimate (on the postulates for revision presented by Gärdenfors (1988)) whenever A is consistent, for then ⊤ will be consistent with A and A*⊤ = Cn(A ∪ {⊤}) = Cn(A) = A using also the background assumption that A is closed under Cn. But it is not legitimate when A is inconsistent, for then (on the postulates presented by Gärdenfors (1988)) since ⊤ is consistent A*⊤ will be consistent, so A ≠ A*⊤. This is why the limiting case is treated separately in the translation process.

4 Translating the Postulates for Revision

Despite the various limitations to their applicability, as noticed in the previous section, the translation procedures cover considerable ground. In this section we look at the result of translating the postulates presented by Gärdenfors (1988) for * into the language of ⊢. These postulates are presented in e.g. Alchourrón,

Gärdenfors and Makinson (1985) and Gärdenfors (1988). The main difference between those presentations is that in Alchourrón, Gärdenfors and Makinson (1985) the variable A is taken to stand for any *set* of propositions, with the hypothesis A = Cn(A) written explicitly into such of the postulates that need it (most of them do), whilst in Gärdenfors (1988), A is assumed throughout to be restricted to the *theories* in the sense of sets of propositions A with A = Cn(A).

Here we follow the presentation (and numbering) of Gärdenfors (1988). For each postulate we state the postulate itself, state its translation, comment, if appropriate, on the translation process (which may be skipped by readers who have skipped section 3), and finally comment on the translation output.

Postulate (K∗1):	A∗x = Cn(A∗x)
Translation:	C(x) = CnC(x)

Remarks on the Translation Process: The postulate (K∗1) needs first of all to be put in pure first order form, without identity between theories, as $y \in$ A∗x iff $y \in$ Cn(A∗x) and then again, to get all elementary parts into requisite shape, by using the compactness theorem for Cn to get $y \in$ A∗x iff there are $z_1, \ldots, z_n \in$ A∗x with $y \in$ Cn($\{z_1, \ldots, z_n\}$). This is now ready for step 3 of the translation process, giving us x ⊢ y iff there are $z_1, \ldots, z_n$ with x ⊢ z_1, ... , x ⊢ z_n and $y \in$ Cn($\{z_1, \ldots, z_n\}$). Using compactness of Cn again and the usual definition of C(x) as {y: x ⊢ y} this is equivalent to x ⊢ y iff $y \in$ CnC(x), i.e. C(x) = CnC(x).

Comments on the Translational Output: This is a familiar principle of non-monotonic inference, holding of the inference operations generated by most of the constructions in the literature, including e.g. the generally rather irregularly behaved Reiter default systems, with "skeptical" reading. See Makinson (to appear) for details.

Postulate (K∗2):	x ∈ A∗x
Translation:	x ⊢ x

Comments: The translation process is direct as the source condition is already in suitable form. The output holds of all nonmonotonic inference relations currently in the literature and indeed, as remarked earlier, should hold of any relation that deserves the name of "inference relation".

Postulate (K∗3): $\quad$ A∗x ⊆ Cn(A ∪ {x})

Translation: $\quad$ Whenever x ⊢ z then ⊤ ⊢ (x → z)

Remarks on the Translation Process: First get the postulate into appropriate first-order form rewriting as: z ∈ A∗x implies z ∈ Cn(A ∪ {x}), then as: z ∈ A∗x implies x → z ∈ Cn(A), and then breaking this into two cases, following step 2 of the translation process. The limiting case, where Cn(A) = A is inconsistent, is the vacuous condition z ∈ L∗x implies x → z ∈ L, where L is the set of all formulas, which translates to the vacuous condition x ⊢ z implies x → z ∈ L. The principal case, where A is consistent, is the condition z ∈ A∗x implies x → z ∈ A∗⊤ which translates to x ⊢ z implies ⊤⊢ (x → z) as claimed.

Comments on the Translation Output: Although postulate (K∗3) occupies a central place in the logic of theory change, its translation has not played an explicit role in nonmonotonic logic, and does not have much intuitive resonance. It is, however, a particular case of the general principle that whenever y&x ⊢ z then y ⊢ x → z (put y = ⊤), known as the principle of *conditionalization*, and which holds in many systems of nonmonotonic logic, notably in all classical preferential entailment relations in the sense of Kraus, Lehmann, and Magidor (1990) and Makinson (1989), even when not stoppered. And conditionalization, as we shall shortly see, is itself the translation of postulate (K∗7), of which (K∗3) is also a particular case.

Postulate (K∗4): $\quad$ If ¬x ∉ Cn(A), then Cn(A ∪ {x}) ⊆ A∗x

Translation: $\quad$ If ⊤ ⊬ ¬x and ⊤ ⊢ (x → z), then x ⊢ z

Remarks on the Translation Process: Postulate (K∗4) is of course a conditional converse of (K∗3), so similar remarks apply to its translation process.

Comments on the Translation Output: The source postulate uses a negative hypothesis ¬x ∉ Cn(A) and its translation likewise involves the negative hypothesis that ⊤ ⊬ ¬x. The translation is thus a *non-Horn* condition on ⊢. It does not figure explicitly in discussions of nonmonotonic logic. It does, however, hold for some nonmonotonic relations considered in the literature; namely those determined by classical stoppered preferential model structures satisfying the condition that every minimal model is less than every non-minimal model.

It also follows from the condition of "rational monotony", to which we shall return when considering the translation of postulate (K*8).

*Postulate (K*5):*   If Cn(x) ≠ L, then A*x ≠ L
Translation: If Cn(x) ≠ L, then C(x) ≠ L

Remarks on the Translation Process: Again, L is the set of all formulas. To translate A*x ≠ L we first put it in the first order form: there is a y with y ∉ A*x, which translates as: there is a y such that x ⊬ y, i.e. y ∉ C(x).

Comments on the Translation Output: An equivalent formulation of the output is, if x ⊢ ⊥, then x ⊦ ⊥, where ⊥ is an arbitrary contradiction..This condition on nonmonotonic inference operations is sometimes called "consistency preservation". It does not hold for many kinds of nonmonotonic inference. It does not hold, in general, for preferential entailments – even when these are classical, stoppered and ranked. Classical stoppered preferential entailments do however satisfy a weaker condition of "relative consistency preservation": There is a consequence operation Cn' (in the sense of Tarski) with Cn ⊆ Cn' ⊆ C such that whenever Cn'(x) ≠ L then C(x) ≠ L. Consistency preservation does hold for the skeptical inference relation generated by any Poole system *without* constraints – but can fail when the system involves constraints. For Reiter default inferences, the situation is rather more complex. Consistently preservation holds for the skeptical inference operation generated by any *normal* Reiter default system, but may fail for the non-normal ones. Nevertheless, an analysis of the ways in which this failure can take place reveals that it can happen only in two limiting cases: when the set {$b_1, ..., b_n$} of all "justifications" of some default rule a; $b_1, ..., b_n/c$ of the system is empty, and when the set of all extensions of the system is empty. Accordingly, minor modifications to the definitions in these two limiting cases suffice to guarantee consistency preservation for all skeptical Reiter default inference operations, without giving rise to any visible undesirable failure of other properties. The exact modifications are described in section III.2 of Makinson (to appear).

*Postulate (K*6):*   If Cn(x) = Cn(y), then A*x = A*y
Translation: If Cn(x) = Cn(y), then C(x) = C(y)

Comments on the Translation Output: This holds for all main nonmonotonic inference operations in the literature: Reiter default, preferential models, Poole systems with or without constraints, and epsilon entailments in the style of Adams and Pearl. See Makinson (to appear) for details.

The postulates (K∗1) to (K∗6) are generally referred to as the "basic" postulates presented by Gärdenfors (1988) for theory revision, whilst the following two, (K∗7) and (K∗8) are called the "supplementary" postulates. This is because the former have a simplicity that permits a clear intuitive grasp of their meaning. The supplementary postulates are a little more complex and more difficult to understand. The distinction reflects itself on the semantic side. There is a natural model-theoretic construction (partial meet revision) which, as shown in Alchourrón, Gärdenfors and Makinson (1985), is characteristic for theory revision operations satisfying postulates (K∗1) to (K∗6), and by imposing an additional requirement on this construction ("transitive relationality") we can characterize (K∗1) - (K∗8). It is still not known whether the requirement of relationality alone characterizes exactly the postulates (K∗1) - (K∗7), although it is known to satisfy them.

On the other hand, when we translate from the language of ∗ to the language of ⊢, this natural heuristic distinction between basic and supplementary conditions disappears. Indeed, the translations of postulates (K∗3) and (K∗4), which make use of a tautology ⊤, acquire a clear intuitive meaning only when seen as special cases of the translations of (K∗7) and (K∗8).

Postulate (K∗7): $A*(y\&x) \subseteq Cn((A*y) \cup \{x\})$
Translation: If $y \& x \vdash z$ then $y \vdash (x \rightarrow z)$

Remarks on the Translation Process: Essentially the same as for postulate (K∗3).

Comments on the Translation Output: As already observed when discussing postulate (K∗3), that postulate is a special case of (K∗7) (putting y = ⊤), and the translation of (K∗3) is likewise the same special case of the translation of (K∗7). And as already observed, the translation of (K∗7) is known as the principle of conditionalization, and holds of all classical preferential entailment relations. See Kraus, Lehmann, and Magidor (1990), or Makinson (1989, to appear) for details.

Postulate (K*8):   If ¬x ∉ A*y then Cn((A*y) ∪ {x}) ⊆ A*(y&x)

Translation: If y ⊬ ¬x and y ⊢ (x → z) then y & x ⊢ z

Comments on the Translation Output: Postulate (K*4) is a special case of postulate (K*8), putting y = ⊤, and likewise for their respective translations. Note that the translation of (K*8) is equivalent (given some background conditions) to the following: If y ⊬ ¬x and y ⊢ z then y & x ⊢ z, which is the condition known in nonmonotonic logic as *rational monotony*. This is of course a non-Horn condition, as was the translation of (K*4). It holds for the inference relation generated by any classical stoppered preferential model structure that is "ranked" in the sense that there is a function r from the set of all models of the model structure into a totally ordered set, such that m < m′ iff r(m) < r(m′) for all models m and m' in the model structure. See Lehmann and Magidor (to appear) or Makinson (to appear) for details. The restriction of the condition to the case y = ⊤ corresponds to the following special case of the special case of the rankedness condition: Every minimal model in the model structure is less than every non-minimal one.

In summary: Every postulate on * from Gärdenfors (1988) translates into a condition on ⊢ that is valid in *some* kinds of nonmonotonic inference in the literature. In particular, all of the postulates (K*1) to (K*7) (resp. (K*1) to (K*8)) *except* consistency preservation hold, when translated, in all classical stoppered (resp. and ranked) preferential model structures. The significance of the exception is not entirely clear.

5 Translating Conditions on Nonmonotonic Inference

We may now look briefly at some of the more important conditions on ⊢ to see how they translate. For reasons explained in section 3, we consider only "unit" forms of these conditions, i.e. with individual propositions (rather than sets of propositions) on the left.

As the translation introduces a (fixed) parameter A (assumed closed under Cn) rather than eliminate one, the translation process is straightforward.

Moreover, it is evident from the translations themselves that if $C(*)$ is a condition on $*$ that can be put into translatable form $C'(*)$ following steps (1) and (2), which is then translated into a condition $C''(\vdash)$ on $\vdash$, which is finally translated back to a condition $C'''(*)$ on $*$, then $C'''(*)$ is the very same condition as $C'(*)$, so that given the principle $A = A*\top$ for consistent theories A, $C'''(*)$ is equivalent to the original condition $C(*)$.

Thus conditions like consistency preservation and rational monotony for $\vdash$ translate back into the conditions on $*$ from which they were obtained in section 4, and there is no need to review them again. We consider only some important conditions on $\vdash$ that did not emerge explicitly as outputs of the $*$ to $\vdash$ translation. These include: supraclassicality, cut, cautious monotony, cumulativity, reciprocity, distribution, and loop (see Makinson (1989) for a presentation of these conditions). We shall see that their translations are *all* consequences of the postulates presented by Gärdenfors (1988) for $*$ (basic plus supplementary postulates).

Supraclassicality: If $x \vdash y$, then $x \vdash y$
Translation: If $x \vdash y$, then $y \in A*x$

Remarks on the Translation Output: Immediate consequence of postulates $(K*1)$ and $(K*2)$.

Unit Version of Cut: If $x \vdash y$ and $x \& y \vdash z$, then $x \vdash z$.
Translation: If $y \in A*x$ and $z \in A*(x\&y)$, then $z \in A*x$.

Remarks on the Translation Output: Derivable using basic postulates plus supplementary postulate $(K*7)$, as follows. Suppose $y \in A*x$ and $z \in A*(x \& y)$. By $(K*7)$ the latter gives us $z \in Cn(A*x \cup \{y\}) = A*x$ by the supposition and $(K*1)$ as desired. It appears that the translation output may be rather weaker than $(K*7)$, in the sense that $(K*7)$ may not be itself derivable from the translation output together with the basic postulates $(K*1)$ to $(K*6)$ on $*$. See the discussion of distribution below.

Unit Version of Cautious Monotony: If $x \vdash y$ and $x \vdash z$, then $x \& y \vdash z$.
Translation: If $y \in A*x$ and $z \in A*x$, then $z \in A*(x\&y)$.

Remarks on the Translation Output: This can be derived using basic postulates together with (K∗8). It is perhaps worth noting that we do not need the full force of (K∗8). The following principle (K∗C), which can be shown to be weaker than (K∗8) (it follows immediately from lemma 3.16 in Gärdenfors (1988)), suffices: Either $A*x \subseteq A*(x\&y)$ or $A*x \subseteq A*(x\&\neg y)$. The derivation is as follows. Suppose $y \in A*x$ and $z \in A*x$. Then using (K∗C) we have either $y, z \in A*(x\&y)$ or $y, z \in A*(x\&\neg y)$. The first case gives our desired conclusion. The second case implies, using (K∗5), that $x \vdash y$ so $Cn(x) = Cn(x\&y)$ so $z \in A*x = A*(x\&y)$ using (K∗6).

Unit Cumulativity:	If $x \vdash y$, then $x \vdash z$ iff $x\&y \vdash z$.
Translation:	If $y \in A*x$, then $A*x = A*(x\&y)$.

Remarks on the Translation Output: Unit cumulativity is just unit cut and unit cautious monotony together. The translation is derivable by simply combining the derivations of two components.

Unit Reciprocity:	If $x \vdash y$ and $y \vdash x$, then $C(x) = C(y)$.
Translation:	If $y \in A*x$ and $x \in A*y$, then $A*x = \dot{A}*y$.

Remarks on the Translation Output: This is a well known principle of the logic of revision, discussed in Alchourrón and Makinson (1982) in the context of maxichoice revision and in Gärdenfors (1988) for any revision function satisfying the postulates (K∗1) to (K∗8). It also has a well known analogue in conditional logic, discussed by Stalnaker (1968). In nonmonotonic logic, reciprocity is equivalent to cumulativity (given supraclassicality), and in the logic of theory change the reciprocity condition is derivable from postulates (K∗7) and (K∗8) (it does not seem, conversely, to imply them). For a derivation see lemma (3.13) in Gärdenfors (1988).

Unit Distribution:	If $x \vdash z$ and $y \vdash z$, then $x \vee y \vdash z$
Translation:	If $z \in A*x$ and $z \in A*y$, then $z \in A*(x \vee y)$.

Remarks on the Translation Output: This can be derived using (K∗7). By (K∗6), $A*x = A*((x \vee y) \& x)$ and $A*y = A*((x \vee y) \& y)$, so by (K∗7) and our hypotheses, $x \to z \in A*(x \vee y)$ and $y \to z \in A*(x \vee y)$ so using (K∗1) and (K∗2), $z \in A*(x \vee y)$ as desired.

Unit Loop:	If $x_1 \vdash x_2, x_2 \vdash x_3, \ldots, x_n \vdash x_1$ $(n \geq 2)$, then $C(x_i) = C(x_j)$, for all $i, j \leq n$.
Translation:	If $x_2 \in A*x_1, \ldots, x_n \in A*x_{n-1}, x_1 \in A*x_n$ $(n \geq 2)$, then $A*x_i = A*x_j$ for all $i, j \leq n$.

Remarks on the Translation Output: This principle is quite unknown in the literature on theory change. Its obvious analogue for conditional logic appears to be unknown to the literature on that subject too. The loop principle first made its appearance in nonmonotonic logic in work of Kraus, Lehmann and Magidor (1990), where it serves as a syntactic counterpart of a condition of transitivity in preferential model structures. The translation output (call it loop for $*$) can be derived from the postulates (K$*$1) to (K$*$8). The derivation below parallels the derivation of Makinson (to appear) section II.2 of loop for $\vdash$ from cumulativity and distribution.

First we need a *lemma*: If $y \in A*x$ then $A*y = A*(x \vee y)$. This is an interesting application of the translation of unit distribution. By reciprocity for $*$ it suffices to show $x \vee y \in A*y$ and $y \in A*(x \vee y)$.

The former is immediate from postulates (K$*$1) and (K$*$2). For the latter we have by hypothesis $y \in A*x$ and clearly $y \in A*y$ so by the translation of unit distribution, $y \in A*(x \vee y)$ as desired.

For the derivation of loop itself, we induce on n. The basis $n=2$ is just reciprocity, already established. Suppose the principle holds for $n=k$, and suppose $x_2 \in A*x_1$, $\ldots, x_{k+1} \in A*x_k, x_1 \in A*x_{k+1}$. We want to show $A*x_i = A*x_j$, for all $i, j \leq k+1$. Since $x_1 \in A*x_{k+1}$, our lemma gives us $A*x_1 = A*(x_{k+1} \vee x_1)$. Since $x_{k+1} \in A*x_k$ we also have $x_{k+1} \vee x_1 \in A*x_k$. Putting this together, we have: $x_2 \in A*(x_{k+1} \vee x_1)$, $x_3 \in A*x_2, \ldots, (x_{k+1} \vee x_1) \in A*x_k$ which is a k-term loop, so by the induction hypothesis: $A*x_i = A*x_j = A*(x_{k+1} \vee x_1)$ for all i, j with $2 \leq i, j \leq k$, so that, since we also have $A*x_1 = A*(x_{k+1} \vee x_1)$, $A*x_i = A*x_j = A*(x_{k+1} \vee x_1)$ for all i, j with $1 \leq i, j \leq k$.

To complete the proof it thus suffices to show that $A*x_{k+1} = A*(x_{k+1} \vee x_1)$. Clearly, $x_{k+1} \vee x_1 \in A*x_{k+1}$. Also by hypothesis $x_{k+1} \in A*x_k = A*(x_{k+1} \vee x_1)$ as just shown. Hence by reciprocity $A*x_{k+1} = A*(x_{k+1} \vee x_1)$ and the proof is complete.

In summary: Every condition on $\sim$ from Makinson (1989, to appear) translates into a condition on $*$ that is a consequence of the postulates in Gärdenfors (1988). In this direction the translation thus works without any exceptions.

6 Poole Inference Systems Compared to Full Meet Revision

On the level of particular constructions, there is one of the approaches to nonmonotonic inference that is clearly very close, even in its formulation, to an earlier approach to the logic of revision. These are the "default logic" of Poole (1988) and the "full meet revision" of Alchourrón and Makinson (1982).

Full meet revision is a limiting case of partial meet revision. If A is a set of propositions and x a proposition, A$*$x is defined by the equation:

(1) $A*x = Cn(\{x\} \cup \cap\{D: D \in A\bot\neg x\})$

where $A\bot\neg x$ is the collection of all maximal subsets D of A that are consistent with x, i.e. such that $\neg x \notin Cn(D)$.

Poole's terminology and notation are different, but his idea is essentially the same. Let Δ be a set of propositions, called the "default set". The (skeptical) inference operation C: $2^L \rightarrow 2^L$ generated by the default set Δ, without constraints, is defined by the equation:

(2∞) $C(X) = \cap\{Cn(X \cup D): D$ is a maximal subset of Δ consistent with X$\}$.

Restricting this equation to singletons $\{x\}$, and for uniformity using the Alchourrón/Makinson notation $A\bot\neg x$, with A in place of Δ, this becomes:

(2) $C(x) = \cap\{Cn(\{x\} \cup D): D \in A\bot\neg x\}$

Equations (1) and (2) are evidently very close: they differ only in the order in which the operations of intersecting, forming union, and closing are performed. A routine verification shows that for all $A \subseteq L, x \in L$:

(2') $C(x) = Cn(\{x\} \cup \cap\{Cn(D): D \in A\bot\neg x\})$

so that clearly $A*x \subseteq C(x)$. The converse is not in general true in the case that the "default set" A is not closed under Cn. When $A = Cn(A)$, it is easy to verify that $D = Cn(D)$ for all $D \in A\perp\neg x$, so that in that case $A*x = C(x)$ and the two constructions coincide.

In their treatment of the logic of theory change in their (1982), Alchourrón and Makinson focussed principally on the case that the "theory" A is closed under Cn, i.e. that $A = Cn(A)$. In his approach to nonmonotonic inference in his (1988), Poole evidently regarded the principal case as that in which the default set A (alias Δ) is *not* closed under Cn, i.e. in which $A \neq Cn(A)$.

Comparison of the two constructions helps throw light on each. Reflection on the skeptical Poole construction suggests that whilst the definition of theory revision $A*x$ given by equation (1) may be quite adequate when A is closed under Cn, it may perhaps not be the best definition in the case that $A \neq Cn(A)$ – in that case the right hand side of (2') may perhaps be marginally more suitable. If so, then we would in effect be restricting the legitimacy of the Levi identity $A*x = Cn((A \dotminus \neg x) \cup \{x\})$ to the case $A = Cn(A)$, or else forcing a modification of the notion of full meet theory contraction from $A \dotminus \neg x = \bigcap\{D: D \in A\perp\neg x\}$ to $A \dotminus \neg x = \bigcap\{Cn(D): D \in A\perp\neg x\}$, in which situation the inclusion principle $A \dotminus x \subseteq A$ would need to be modified to $A \dotminus x \subseteq Cn(A)$. Without going further into the consequences and options arising from such a modification of the notion of full meet revision, we merely remark that consideration of the nonmonotonic construction helps appreciate the range of possible options in the theory change context.

Conversely, comparison of the two constructions permits us to translate an interesting formal result from the theory change context to the nonmonotonic one. It was shown by Alchourrón and Makinson (1982) that when $A = Cn(A)$ then full meet revision collapses into Cn itself in the sense that:

$$A*x = \begin{cases} Cn(x) & \text{when } \neg x \in A \\ \\ Cn(A \cup \{x\}) & \text{when } \neg x \notin A \end{cases}$$

Given the identity of $A*x$ and $C(x)$ when $A = Cn(A)$ we thus have a similar result for the skeptical inference operations for singleton sets generated by default sets Δ where $\Delta = Cn(\Delta)$:

$$C(x) = \begin{cases} Cn(x) & \text{when } \neg x \in \Delta \\ \\ Cn(\Delta \cup \{x\}) & \text{when } \neg x \notin \Delta. \end{cases}$$

Indeed, we can generalize this result from singletons to arbitrary sets $X \subseteq L$. If Δ is a default set with $\Delta = Cn(\Delta)$, and C is the (skeptical) inference operation defined by equation (2∞) above, then for all $X \subseteq L$:

$$C(X) = \begin{cases} Cn(X) & \text{when } \Delta \cup X \text{ is inconsistent} \\ \\ Cn(\Delta \cup X) & \text{when } \Delta \cup X \text{ is consistent.} \end{cases}$$

The proof is as follows: Suppose that $\Delta \cup X$ is consistent. Then clearly by definition (2∞), $C(X) = \bigcap\{Cn(X \cup D): D = \Delta\} = Cn(X \cup \Delta)$ as desired. Suppose for the principal case that $\Delta \cup X$ is inconsistent; we want to show $C(X) = Cn(X)$. Clearly by (2∞), $Cn(X) \subseteq C(X)$ so it suffices to prove the converse. Suppose $y \notin Cn(X)$, we want to show $y \notin C(X)$, i.e. by the definition (2∞) we want to show that $y \notin Cn(D \cup X)$ for some D that is a maximal subset of Δ consistent with X.

Since $\Delta \cup X$ is inconsistent, we have by the compactness of Cn that there are $x_1, \ldots, x_n \in X$ with $\Delta \cup \{x_1, \ldots, x_n\}$ inconsistent, so that $\Delta \cup \{x_1, \ldots, x_n, y\}$ is inconsistent, so that $\neg x_1 \vee \ldots \vee \neg x_n \vee \neg y \in Cn(\Delta) = \Delta$ by hypothesis.

Also, since $y \notin Cn(X)$, $X \cup \{\neg y\}$ is consistent, so $X \cup \{\neg x_1 \vee \ldots \vee \neg x_n \vee \neg y\}$ is consistent. Putting the above together, we may conclude by the compactness of Cn that there is a maximal subset D of Δ with $\neg x_1 \vee \ldots \vee \neg x_n \vee \neg y \in D$ such that $X \cup D$ is consistent. Since $\neg x_1 \vee \ldots \vee \neg x_n \vee \neg y \in D$ we have $\neg y \in Cn(D \cup \{x_1, \ldots, x_n\}) \subseteq Cn(D \cup X)$. So since $D \cup X$ is consistent, $y \notin Cn(D \cup X)$ and the proof is complete.

7 Some General Remarks and An Open Question

The above verification also illustrates a heuristic point. In the logic of theory change we have two principal operations: contraction $\doteq$ and revision $*$. If we have to prove something about $*$ we may do so either directly (using the postulates presented by Gärdenfors (1988) for $*$ or a semantic characterization), or indirectly via $\doteq$ and the Levi identity $A*x = Cn((A \doteq \neg x) \cup \{x\})$. Quite often, as with the above "collapse" theorem for full meet revision, it is easier to grasp intuitively what is going on if we follow the route via contraction. But in nonmonotonic logic, there has been no formulation or exploitation of a counterpart of contraction. It is in this kind of situation that we may expect the insights gained in the logic of theory change to be particularly helpful in the theory of nonmonotonic logic.

This suggests the question of whether we may usefully *introduce* into the nonmonotonic context some sort of counterpart to contraction. One avenue that suggests itself is to define an operation C^- on individual propositions by mimicking the Harper identity, already mentioned in section 2, that is by putting $C^-(x) = C(\top) \cap C(\neg x)$ for any proposition x. However, it is not clear whether this operation C^- has much significance in the nonmonotonic context. It seems to lack any direct intuitive motivation. Moreover, it has the technical limitation that it is defined only for individual propositions as arguments, rather than arbitrary sets of propositions, and it is not clear how one might transcend this limitation.

It is perhaps worth noting, finally, that whilst the operation of theory contraction satisfies, as one of its most important postulates, the condition of "success" that $x \notin A \doteq x$ unless $x \in Cn(\emptyset)$, the operation C^- defined above does not in general satisfy the corresponding condition that $x \notin C^-(x)$ unless $x \in Cn(\emptyset)$. This is because, as we have already observed in section 4 when discussing the translation of postulate (K*5), several important kinds of nomonotonic inference operation C fail consistency preservation. It can thus happen that we have $x \in C(\top)$ and also $x \in C(\neg x) = L$ although $Cn(\neg x) \neq L$, that is $x \notin Cn(\emptyset)$, so that $x \in C^-(x) = C(\top) \cap C(\neg x)$.

We end with an important open question. In their (1985), Alchourrón, Gärdenfors and Makinson established a representation theorem for theory revision operations * satisfying conditions (K*1) to (K*8), in terms of "transitively relational partial meet revisions". The proof went via a representation theorem for a contraction function $\doteq$ satisfying certain conditions (K$\doteq$1) to (K$\doteq$8). On the other hand, Kraus, Lehmann and Magidor (1990) have established a representation theorem for supraclassical, cumulative and distributive nonmonotonic inference relations $\vdash$ defined between individual propositions, in terms of classical stoppered preferential model structures. The former proof is relatively short and abstract; the latter seems more complex. Also, the latter has not been generalized to a representation theorem for supraclassical, cumulative and distributive inference operations C: $2^L \to 2^L$ (see Makinson (to appear) for further background). Does the representation theorem for theory change hold the key for a solution to this problem of extending the Kraus/Lehmann/Magidor representation theorem to the infinite case – despite the failure of consistency preservation for preferential model structures? Or do we have two essentially different representation problems?

References

Alchourrón, C.E., P. Gärdenfors, and D. Makinson (1985): "On the logic of theory change: Partial meet contraction and revision functions", *The Journal of Symbolic Logic 50*, 510-530.

Alchourrón, C.E. and D. Makinson (1982): "On the logic of theory change: Contraction functions and their associated revision functions", *Theoria 48*, 14-37.

Alchourrón, C.E. and D. Makinson (1985): "The logic of theory change: Safe contraction", *Studia logica 44*, 405-422.

Arló Costa, H. and R. Carnota (1989a): "Non monotonic preferential models and conditional logic", manuscript, Depto. de Filosofía, Univ. de Buenos Aires.

Arló Costa, H. and R. Carnota (1989b): "Non monotonic logics: Consequence relations and conditional operators", manuscript, Depto. de Filosofía, Univ. de Buenos Aires.

Fuhrmann, A. (1988): *Relevant Logics, Modal Logics and Theory Change* (Australian National University: Dept. of Philosophy and Automated Reasoning Project, RSSS).

Gärdenfors P. (1988): *Knowledge in Flux: Modeling the Dynamics of Epistemic States* (Cambridge, MA: The MIT Press, Bradford Books).

Gärdenfors, P. and D. Makinson. (1988): "Revisions of knowledge systems using epistemic entrenchment", in M. Vardi ed., *Proceedings of the Second Conference on Theoretical Aspects of Reasoning about Knowledge*. (Los Altos, CA: Morgan Kaufmann).

Ginsberg, M. (1986): "Counterfactuals", *Artificial Intelligence 30*, 35-79.

Hansson, S.O. (1989a): "New operators for theory change", *Theoria 55*, 114-136.

Hansson, S.O. (1989b): "A dyadic representation of belief", manuscript, Department of Philosophy, Uppsala University.

Kraus, S., D. Lehmann, and M. Magidor, (1990): "Nonmonotonic reasoning, preferential models and cumulative logics", to appear in *Artificial Intelligence*. A preliminary version appeared as Technical Report TR 88-15 of the Dept. of Computer Science, Hebrew University of Jerusalem, November 1988.

Lehmann, D. and M. Magidor (to appear): "Rational logics and their models: A study in cumulative logics". A preliminary version appeared as Technical Report TR 88-16 of the Dept. of Computer Science, Hebrew University of Jerusalem, November 1988.

Lewis, D. (1973): *Counterfactuals* (Oxford: Blackwell).

Lindström, S. and Rabinowicz, W. (1990): "Epistemic entrenchment with incomparabilities and relational belief revision", this volume.

Makinson, D. (1989): "General theory of cumulative inference", in M. Reinfrank, J. de Kleer, M.L. Ginsberg, and E. Sandewall, eds., *Non-Monotonic Reasoning* (Berlin: Springer Verlag, Lecture Notes on Artificial Intelligence nº 346).

Makinson, D. (to appear): "General patterns in nonmonotonic reasoning", to appear as chapter 2 of *Handbook of Logic in Artificial Intelligence and Logic Programming, Volume II: Non-Monotonic and Uncertain Reasoning*. (Oxford: Oxford University Press).

Poole, D. (1988): "A logical framework for default reasoning", *Artificial Intelligence 36*, 27-47.

Reiter R. (1980): "A logic for default reasoning", *Artificial Intelligence 13*, 81-132.

Shoham, Y. (1988): *Reasoning about Change*. (Cambridge: Cambridge University Press).

Stalnaker, R. (1968): "A theory of conditionals", in *Studies in Logical Theory* (American Philosophical Quarterly Monograph Series nº 2), ed. N. Rescher. (Oxford: Blackwell) .

Belief Revision in a Framework for Default Reasoning

Gerhard Brewka

Gesellschaft für Mathematik und Datenverarbeitung

Postfach 12 40, D-5305 Sankt Augustin, Fed. Rep. of Germany

Abstract:

We present an approach which provides a common solution to problems recently addressed in two different research areas: nonmonotonic reasoning and theory revision. We define a framework for default reasoning based on the notion of preferred maximal consistent subsets of the premises. Contrary to other formalizations of default reasoning, this framework is able to handle also unanticipated inconsistencies. This makes it possible to handle revisions of default theories by simply adding the new information. Contractions require the introduction of constraints, i.e. formulas used to determine preferred maximal consistent subsets but not used to determine the derivable formulas. Both, revisions and contractions, are totally incremental, i.e. old information is never forgotten and may be recovered after additional changes. Moreover, the order of changes is - in a certain sense - unimportant.

1. Introduction

In this paper we present an approach which provides a common solution to some problems which recently have been addressed in two different research areas: nonmonotonic reasoning and theory revision.

In commonsense additional information often leads to the retraction of former conclusions, i.e. the accepted conclusions do not grow monotonically with the available information. Researchers in Artificial Intelligence therefore have put much effort into formalizing nonmonotonic forms of reasoning. The main focus was on default reasoning, i.e. reasoning based on general rules for which exceptions may exist. Without such a formalization the goal of modeling human reasoning on a computer seems unachievable.

In the last decade a number of different logics and frameworks for nonmonotonic reasoning have been developed in Artificial Intelligence, e.g. Reiter´s default logic (Reiter 80), autoepistemic logic (Moore 84) or circumscription (McCarthy 80, 84). For an overview see (Brewka 90). It is common to all these approaches that they require an exact specification of those parts of the knowledge which possibly can be retracted. Let´s illustrate this with default logic.

In default logic the user has to specify a set D of defaults of the form A:B/C with the intuitive meaning "if A is provable and $\neg B$ is not, then derive C". [1] A is called the prerequisite, B the justification, and C the consequent of the default. A set of defaults D together with a set of first order formulas W form a default theory (D,W). Default theories induce sets of "acceptable beliefs", so-called extensions. The extensions of closed default theories (i.e. default theories where the defaults contain no free variables) are defined as fixed points of an operator Γ:

Definition 1 (Reiter): *Let (D,W) be a (closed) default theory, S a set of formulas. $\Gamma(S)$ is the smallest set such that*

D1   *W is a subset of $\Gamma(S)$,*

D2   *$\Gamma(S)$ is deductively closed,*

D3   *If $(A:B/C) \in D$, $A \in \Gamma(S)$, and $\neg B \notin S$, then $C \in \Gamma(S)$.*

E is an extension of (D,W) iff $\Gamma(E)=E$, i.e. E is a fixed point of Γ.

According to Reiter each arbitrary chosen extension can be seen as an acceptable set of beliefs. Extensions, however, can also be used to define a sceptical notion of inference where a formula is derivable iff it is contained in all extensions.

It is not difficult to see how the addition of information may lead to the retraction of former conclusions. This is for instance the case if we add the negation of the justification of an otherwise applicable default to W. However, if information is added to a default theory which is inconsistent with W, then the set of all formulas is the single extension obtained, i.e. whether we take the sceptical view regarding multiple extensions or not, we end up with an inconsistent belief state. In this sense possible inconsistencies have to be anticipated. We have to know in advance where possible exceptions may arise. Only if

---

[1] For sake of simplicity we only consider defaults with one justification in this paper.

we have represented our information adequately the logical machinery accomodates new conflicting information. In case of an unanticipated inconsistency the approach breaks down to inconsistency.

This observation also holds in a similar way for the other nonmonotonic logics mentioned above. In circumscription explicit abnormality predicates are introduced, in autoepistemic logic conclusions may be based on disbelief in certain formulas. In each case it is not possible to handle arbitrary inconsistent information.

Research in the area of theory revision, e.g. (Gärdenfors 88) (Gärdenfors, Makinson 88), has been performed mainly by logicians and philosophers. This research is based on somewhat different intuitions. The basic question here is: given an epistemic state S and an arbitrary piece of information p, what is the epistemic state S′ a rational agent should be in after p is added to or removed from S. Epistemic states are often modeled as belief sets, i.e. deductively closed sets of logical formulas, and p is taken to be a logical formula. Note that, contrary to what we saw in the nonmonotonic logics, there is no distinction between expected and unforeseen inconsistencies: p can be an arbitrary formula.

At least from the standpoint of Artificial Intelligence, however, the description of an epistemic state in terms of logical theories is somewhat unsatisfactory. First of all, AI is interested in finite descriptions of the beliefs of an agent. Moreover, there seems to be an important distinction missing from this characterization of epistemic states: the distinction between derived and underived beliefs. Researchers in theory revision have felt this lack (Gärdenfors 88, p 67):

> However, belief sets cannot be used to express that some beliefs may be reasons for other beliefs. ... And intuitively, when we compare degrees of similarity between different epistemic states, we want the structure of reasons or justifications to count as well.

In AI the standard way to obtain finite descriptions of an agent′s beliefs is to use finite sets of premises instead of their deductive closure. Moreover, the distinction between underived and derived beliefs is, often implicitly, introduced by interpreting these premises as underived and their theorems as derived beliefs. We will adopt this simple view in this paper. However, instead of a classical logic we will use a nonmonotonic formalism: our premises, i.e. underived beliefs, will be default theories in a nonmonotonic formalism. The epistemic states are the "theorems" of these premises. As in Reiter′s default logic some sets of premises will give rise to different extensions, i.e. alternative possible epistemic states. This makes it possible to adopt either a sceptical or a credulous view: we can either take the intersection of all extensions as "the" epistemic state, or we can pick out an arbitrary extension.

Our nonmonotonic formalism has earlier been presented in (Brewka 89). In Section 2 we describe again the basic concepts and definitions of the approach which is based on the notion of preferred maximal consistent subsets of the premises, or simpler: preferred subtheories. The main difference between this and the other nonmonotonic logics described above is that there is no need to anticipate possible inconsistencies. Every possible additional information can be integrated without the risk of inconsistency.

In Section 3 we discuss the problem of changing default theories. The just mentioned property of our formalism is what makes the task of revising default theories, i.e. adding possibly inconsistent information, indeed trivial. It turns out that revisions are implicitly handled by the available mechanisms. New, possibly inconsistent information simply can be added. Moreover, a certain degree of reliability of the new information can be specified. An additional advantage of this approach is that old information is never forgotten. This leads to a certain independence from the order of incoming information.

The contraction of a piece of information, i.e. its deletion without the assertion of its negation, is somewhat more difficult. However, with a slight extension of our general framework which introduces constraints, also contractions can be modeled quite easily. The constraints are an additional type of premises which are used to determine preferred maximal consistent subsets of the premises, but which are not used in the definition of derivable formulas. It is shown how they can be used to make certain formulae underivable without asserting their negation. Again the order of contractions is - in a certain sense - unimportant.

2. Preferred Subtheories: A Framework for Default Reasoning

We saw in the introduction that the "standard" approaches to formalize nonmonotonic and in particular default reasoning start from a consistent set of premises (otherwise no interesting result at all is obtained) and extend the inference relation to get more than just the classically derivable formulas. Here we will present an approach based on an alternative view. What makes a default a default? What distinguishes it from a fact? Certainly our attitude towards it in case of a conflict, i.e. an inconsistency. If we take this view serious then the idea of default reasoning as a special case of inconsistency handling seems quite natural. There is no problem with inconsistent premises as long as we provide ways to handle the inconsistency adequately (in other words, if we modify the inference relation such that in case of an inconsistency fewer, i.e. not all formulas are derivable).

In this section we will first present a simple general framework for defining nonmonotonic systems based on this view. We then show that Poole´s approach to default reasoning (Poole 88) is a simple instance of this framework and discusse the limitations of his approach which are due to the inability of representing priorities between defaults. Sect. 2.3 presents a generalization of Poole´s approach which introduces several layers of possible hypotheses representing different degrees of reliability. A second further generalization based on a partial ordering between premises is described in Sect. 2.4. In both approaches a formula is provable from a theory if it is possible to construct a consistent argument for it based on the most reliable hypotheses.

2.1 A Framework for Nonmonotonic Systems

A standard way of handling inconsistent premise sets uses maximal consistent subsets of the premises at hand. Since, in general, there is more than one such maximal consistent subset, provability is defined as provability in all such sets. The idea behind the "maximal" is clear: we want to modify the available information as few as possible. The notion of maximal consistent subsets per se, however, does not allow to express, say, that *Tweety flies* should be given up instead of *Tweety is a penguin*, if we know that penguins don´t fly. To be able to express such preferences we have to consider not all maximal consistent subsets, but only some of them, the preferred maximal consistent subsets, or simpler: *preferred subtheories*. This idea is similar to preferential entailment where not all, but only a subset of the models is taken into account.

The notion of a preferred maximal consistent subset is not new: it dates back to (Rescher 64). Rescher has defined a particular ordering of subtheories for hypothetical reasoning. He did, however, not apply this idea to default reasoning.

We are now in a position to define a weak and a strong notion of provability:

Definition 2: *A formula p is weakly provable from a set of premises T iff there is a preferred subtheory S of T such that S /- p.*

Definition 3: *A formula p is strongly provable from a set of premises T iff for all preferred subtheories S of T we have S /- p.*

These notions, roughly, correspond to containment in at least one or in all extensions in the fixed point approaches to default reasoning. In fact, we can also introduce the notion of extension in the following way:

Definition 4: *E is an extension of a set of premises T iff there is a preferred subtheory S of T and E = Th(S).*

To specify what exactly the preferred subtheories are we will impose in the rest of the paper a certain structure on the premises T. In one approach (Section 2.2), for instance, we will split T into several levels $T_1, ..., T_n$. This additional structure will be used to define the preferred subtheories of T. For sake of simplicity we will also speak of preferred subtheories (and extensions) of these structures and leave the premise set T implicit.

One important aspect of this approach should be noted: the provable formulas of our theories depend on the syntactic form of the premises. It makes an important difference whether, for instance, a set of premises contains both A and B, or the equivalent single formula $A \wedge B$. Assume there is a preferred subtheory S inconsistent with A, but not with B. If both A and B are given, then B must be contained in S. If, however, our premise is $A \wedge B$, then this is not the case.

We could avoid this by introducing a certain normal form for formulas. However, we don´t see this unusual behaviour as a drawback at all. It increases the expressiveness. We can express that two formulas A and B should be accepted or given up together. It makes perfect sense to distinguish between situations where A as well as B are possible, unrelated hypotheses or where $A \wedge B$ is one hypothesis.

Consider the following example: someone tells you that Michael was sitting in a bar drinking bear. Call "Michael was in the bar" A and "Michael was drinking bear" B. Now someone else gives you the more reliable information "Michael was working at the university". Call this information C. Clearly, C is inconsistent with A, but not with B. However, it seems reasonable to give up also B in this case. In our approach this can be achieved by using the premise $A \wedge B$. Note that replacing a single premise P by an equivalent single premise Q does not change the resulting preferred subtheories.

What we have so far is just a general framework. To obtain a specific instance of the framework, i.e. a real nonmonotonic system, it remains to be defined what the preferred subtheories are. We will first show that Poole´s approach can be seen as such an instance.

2.2 Poole´s System: Default Reasoning as Theory Construction

David Poole (Poole 88) recently presented a simple and elegant, yet quite expressive approach to default reasoning. In Poole´s framework it is assumed that the user provides

1)   a consistent set F of closed formulas, the facts about the world,

2)   a set Δ of, possibly open, formulas, the possible hypotheses.

Definition 5 (Poole): A *scenario* of F and Δ is a set $D \cup F$ where D is a set of ground instances of elements of Δ such that $D \cup F$ is consistent.

Definition 6 (Poole): A formula g is *explainable* from F and Δ iff there is a scenario of F and Δ which implies g.

Definition 7 (Poole): An *extension* of F and Δ is the set of logical consequences of a (set inclusion) maximal scenario of F and Δ.

The terminology reflects that Poole uses his framework not only for prediction, but also for explanation of observed facts. Since our main interest here is default reasoning we will also call Δ the set of defaults. Poole has shown that many of the standard examples involving defaults can be handled adequately with this simple framework (Poole 88). He uses the following naming technique: for a hypothesis $w(x) \in \Delta$ with free variables x a new predicate symbol p_W of the same arity is introduced. Poole shows that $w(x)$ can equivalently be replaced by $p_W(x)$, if the formula

$$\forall x. p_W(x) \supset w(x)$$

is added to F. Poole uses the notation $p_W(x):w(x)$ as an abbreviation for that case. Thus, the power of the system is not restricted if only atoms are allowed in Δ.

The use of names allows to block the applicability of a default when needed. If we want a default $p_W(x)$ to be inapplicable in situation s we simply have to add $\forall x.\ s \supset \neg p_W(x)$ to our facts. (Poole 88) contains many nice examples of how this technique can be used.

It is not difficult to see that Poole's approach can be obtained as a simple instance of our preferred subtheory framework: if we define the preferred subtheories of $\Delta' \cup F$ (Δ' is obtained from Δ by replacing open formulas with all of their ground instances) as those subtheories containing F, then weak provability and Poole's explainability coincide.

Poole's approach is simple and elegant, and its expressiveness is astonishing. Moreover, an efficient Prolog-implementation exists (Poole et al. 86). However, as shown in (Brewka 89), there is no simple way of representing priorities between defaults: This motivated the generalizations presented in the rest of this section.

2.3. First Generalization: Levels of Reliability

The following figure illustrates the basic idea of Poole's approach: we have two levels of theories, the basic level can be seen as premises which must be true (and be consistent), the second level is a level of hypotheses which are less reliable.

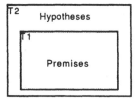

We generalize these ideas in two respects. First, we do not require the most reliable formulas (i.e. T1) to be consistent. In our generalization every formula is in principle refutable. And second, we introduce more than just two levels. This can be illustrated by the following graphic:

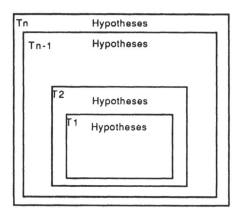

The idea is that the different levels of a theory represent different degrees of reliability. The innermost part is the most reliable one. If inconsistencies arise the more reliable information is preferred. Intuitively, a formula is provable if we can construct an argument for it from the most reliable available information. Of course, there may be conflicting information with the same reliability. In this case we get multiple extensions, i.e. two contradicting formulas can be provable in the weak sense. The fact that there are no in principle unrefutable "premises" makes it possible to treat all levels uniformly. For instance, we can add to any theory information which is even more reliable than the current innermost level.

We now show how these intuitive ideas can be made precise in the preferred subtheory approach.

Definition 8: *A default theory T is a tuple $(T_1, ..., T_n)$, where each T_i is a set of classical first order formulas.*

Intuitively, information in T_i is more reliable than that in T_j if $i<j$. A default like *birds fly* can be represented as the set of all ground instances of a schema $BIRD(x) \supset FLIES(x)$. For sake of simplicity we will write $T_i = \{..., P(x), ...\}$ if we want to express that T_i

contains all ground instances of $P(x)$. Note again the important difference between universally quantified formulas and schemata containing free variables.

It remains to define the preferred subtheories:

Definition 9: *Let $T=(T_1,...,T_n)$ be a default theory. $S = S_1 \cup...\cup S_n$ is a preferred subtheory of T iff for all k ($1 \leq k \leq n$) $S_1 \cup...\cup S_k$ is a maximal consistent subset of $T_1 \cup ... \cup T_k$.*

In other words, to obtain a preferred subtheory of T we have to start with any maximal consistent subset of T_1, add as many formulas from T_2 as consistently can be added (in any possible way), and continue this process for T_3, ..., T_n.

The following simple examples show how the different levels can be used to express priorities between defaults:

T1 = {BIRD(TWEETY), $\forall$x.PENGUIN(x) $\supset$ ¬FLIES(x)}

T2 = {BIRD(x) $\supset$ FLIES(x)}

FLIES(TWEETY) is strongly provable.

T1 = {BIRD(TWEETY), $\forall$x.PENGUIN(x) $\supset$ ¬FLIES(x), PENGUIN(TWEETY)}

T2 = {BIRD(x) $\supset$ FLIES(x)}

¬FLIES(TWEETY) is strongly provable. This example also illustrates the importance of the distinction between schemata and universally quantified formulas. If we wouldn´t use a schema in T2 but instead a quantified formula, then this formula wouldn´t be usable if there is a single nonflying bird.

If there is a penguin who does fly, then we can use the following representation where *penguins don´t fly* is given higher priority than *birds fly*:

T1 = {BIRD(TWEETY), PENGUIN(TWEETY), PENGUIN(TIM), FLIES(TIM)}

T2 = {PENGUIN(x) $\supset$ ¬FLIES(x)}

T3 = {BIRD(x) $\supset$ FLIES(x)}

2.4 Second Generalization: Partially Ordered Defaults

For many problems the introduction of levels of reliability as described above is sufficient to express the necessary priorities between defaults. Sometimes, however, we want to leave open whether a formula p is of more, less or the same reliability as another formula q. Here is a political example that reflects the ideas of different groups (in Germany) of how to handle unemployment. The social democrats (SPD) usually believe that there are not enough jobs and we simply should share the rest, i.e. everybody should work less.

However, reducing everybody's salary is bad for economy. There is a subgroup of the social democrats around the politician Lafontaine, however, which agree with the first, but not with the second position since, according to their view, working less without reducing the salaries makes work too expensive. According to company owners the problem is not that we have not enough to do. They believe that the salaries are too high. These ideas could be formalized using the following defaults:

(1)   SPD ⊃ LESS-WORK ∧ ¬LESS-MONEY

(2)   LAF ⊃ LESS-WORK ∧ LESS-MONEY

(3)   COMP-OWNER ⊃ ¬LESS-WORK ∧ LESS-MONEY

LAF is a subclass of SPD, i.e. information about Lafontaine-supporters is more specific than information about social democrats in general. We certainly want to give (2) priority over (1) in this case. But how about (3)? The approach from the last section forces us to choose exactly one level for each formula, i.e. to specify a priority either between (1) and (3) or between (2) and (3). There seems to be no reason why we should want this.

This problem can be avoided if we allow the degrees of reliability to be represented via an arbitrary (strict) partial ordering of the premises instead of the different levels. A default theory now is a pair $(T, <)$, where the relation $<$ is defined over T, and $p < q$, intuitively, states that p is more reliable than q. Again we have to define the preferred subtheories to obtain weak and strong provability based on such a partial ordering:

Definition 10: *Let $<$ be a strict partial ordering on a (finite) set of premises T. S is a preferred subtheory of a default theory $(T, <)$ iff there exists a strict total ordering $(t_1, t_2, ..., t_n)$ of T respecting $<$ (i.e. $t_j < t_k => j < k$) such that $S = S_n$ with*

$S_0 := \{\}$, and for $0 \leq i < n$

$S_{i+1} := $ if t_{i+1} consistent with S_i then $S_i \cup \{t_{i+1}\}$ else S_i.

The generalization to the infinite case is straightforward if we forbid infinite descending chains in the orderings.

If we define in our above example the ordering to be $(2) < (1)$, then LESS-WORK ∧ LESS-MONEY is strongly provable from SPD and LAF ("from some formulas" here means that these formulas are smaller than (1), (2) and (3) with respect to $<$). From SPD and COMP-OWNER both LESS-WORK ∧ ¬LESS-MONEY and ¬LESS-WORK ∧ LESS-MONEY are weakly provable. The two corresponding preferred subtheories are generated from different total orderings respecting $<$. Similarly, we obtain two preferred subtheories given LAF and COMP-OWNER. In this case LESS-WORK ∧ ¬LESS-MONEY is provable from one preferred subtheory.

The example shows that we were able to express the wanted preference between (2) and (1) without having to introduce any unwanted preference involving (3).

There is obviously a common intuition behind our approach, in particular the last generalization, and the notion of epistemic entrenchment in (Gärdenfors, Makinson 88) and (Gärdenfors 88). As mentioned in the introduction, these authors, however, are interested in belief sets, i.e. deductively closed sets of formulas, and the changes of such states when new information is obtained. They are not interested in deriving plausible conclusions from, possibly inconsistent, premises. Therefore epistemic entrenchment is defined for the whole logical language whereas for our purposes it is sufficient to order premises. Moreover, they require the new knowledge state after the addition of new information to be uniquely determined by the epistemic entrenchment whereas we allow multiple preferred subtheories whenever no priority between conflicting defaults is specified.

See (Brewka 89) for a discussion of other related work and more motivating examples for both generalizations.

In this section we presented two generalizations of Poole's approach to default reasoning as particular instances of a general nonmonotonic framework. The first generalization extends his original approach in two respects: 1) we allow several levels of reliability instead of only two and 2) treat all levels uniformly, i.e. there are no unrefutable premises. The second generalization introduces a partial ordering on the premises instead of the levels. In Poole's theory the applicability of a default can be blocked, but there is no way of representing priorities between defaults in the sense that one of two conflicting defaults is not applied if the other one can be applied. Our systems provide a natural means of representing such priorities.

There is always a tradeoff between expressiveness and simplicity. Obviously, we had to give up some of the simplicity and elegance of Poole's system in order to increase expressiveness and to allow for the representation of default priorities. But still we are much closer to classical logic than many other systems: we don't need modal operators, nonstandard inference rules, fixed point constructions, second order logic or abnormality predicates. This should make it simpler to integrate default reasoning with other forms of commonsense reasoning.

We see as the main advantage of this approach to default reasoning that the problem of handling inconsistent information - a problem every commonsense reasoner has to deal with anyway - is implicitly solved.

3. Changing Default Theories

As motivated in the introduction we will see epistemic states as implicitly given in the form of a default theory. The problem of revising and contracting epistemic states therefore reduces to the problem of revising and contracting default theories. For sake of simplicity we will base our presentation here on the approach using levels of reliability (Section 2.3). All necessary generalizations to partially ordered defaults (Section 2.4) are straightforward.

3.1 Revisions

We will start with revisions, i.e. the addition of possibly inconsistent information. We are looking for a function, *, which, given a default theory T and a formula p, produces a default theory "containing" p. As usual we will use infix notation and denote this new default theory with T*p.

Since our default theories consist of several layers of formulas there is some additional expressiveness not available in standard approaches to theory revision: we can specify a degree of reliability of the information to be added. We will express this by indexing p accordingly.

Definition 11: *Let $T = (T_1,...,T_n)$ be a default theory, p a formula, j a natural number.*

The revision of T with respect to p, T*p, is the default theory $(\{p\}, T_1, ...,T_n)$.

The (insert-) revision of T with respect to p at degree j, $T^{*(j)}p$, is the default theory

$$(T_1,.., T_j \cup \{p\}, ... , T_n)$$

The (minus-) revision of T with respect to p at degree -j, $T^{*(-j)}p$, is the default theory

$$(T_1,.., T_{j-1}, \{p\}, T_j, ... ,T_n)$$

Note that, among others, Gärdenfors´ postulate K*2 (Gärdenfors 88) for revisions does not generally hold in our approach. This postulate requires that the new information p is believed in the new epistemic state. In our approach the new information may be less reliable than conflicting old information. Even if we revise without specifying a degree of reliability the postulate is violated if p is inconsistent.

Of course, all the above definitions are very straightforward. Everything is left to the logical machinery of the underlying nonmonotonic formalism. However the approach has some other nice features, besides the additional expressiveness. First, it is totally incremental. Earlier information is never forgotten, even if it is currently ruled out by more reliable conflicting information. This is very useful since it is always possible that this conflicting information itself is overridden. Let's illustrate this with the following example:

$T = (T_1, T_2)$ with

$$T_2 = \{B\}$$
$$T_1 = \{A\}$$

We revise this default theory with respect to $\neg A \vee \neg B$. According to Definition 11 this yields

$T * \neg A \vee \neg B = (T'_1, T'_2, T'_3)$ with

$$T'_3 = T_2 = \{B\}$$
$$T'_2 = T_1 = \{A\}$$
$$T'_1 = \{\neg A \vee \neg B\}$$

This new default theory has a single extension: $Th(\{A, \neg A \vee \neg B\})$. If we now revise with respect to $\neg A$ we obtain

$(T * \neg A \vee \neg B) * \neg A = (T''_1, T''_2, T''_3, T''_4)$ with

$$T''_4 = \{B\}$$
$$T''_3 = \{A\}$$
$$T''_2 = \{\neg A \vee \neg B\}$$
$$T''_1 = \{\neg A\}$$

This default theory again has a single extension: $Th(\{\neg A, B\})$. Note that B is recovered.

Generally, a formula which is not contained in any extension of a default theory may become weakly or even strongly provable if, as a consequence of some revisions, arguments against this formula are themselves overridden by better information.

As another advantage we like to mention that sequences of revisions are, up to the needed degrees of the revisions, order-independent.

Proposition 1: *Let T be a default theory, $A_1, ..., A_n$ formulas, and $j_1, ..., j_n$ integers. For every permutation $A_{k1}, ..., A_{kn}$ of the formulas $A_1, ..., A_n$ there exist integers $i_1, ..., i_n$ such that*

$$T *^{(j1)} A_1 * ... *^{(jn)} A_n = T *^{(i1)} A_{k1} * ... *^{(in)} A_{kn}.$$

Proof: obvious

3.2 Contractions

Revisions turned out in the last section to be handled easily within our framework. Contractions are somewhat more difficult. The basic idea behind contraction is that a formula is removed from a belief set without assertion of its negation. We would like to handle this kind of change in a way as simple as revisions and without destroying the incrementality of the whole approach with its nice consequences discussed in the last section.

It turns out that a simple generalization of our framework achieves this goal. Poole (Poole 88) introduced so-called constraints to avoid undesired consequences of contrapositions of defaults. A constraint in Poole's approach, basically, is a formula which is used for checking consistency, i.e. for determining scenarios, but which is not used for derivations. We adopt this idea and extend our general framework in the following way

Definition 12: *Let P and C be sets of formulas. A formula p is weakly provable from the premises P with constraints C iff there is a preferred subtheory S of P and C such that $S \cap P \vdash p$.*

Definition 13: *Let P and C be sets of formulas. A formula p is strongly provable from the premises P with constraints C iff for all preferred subtheories S of P and C we have $S \cap P \vdash p$.*

Definition 14: *Let P and C be sets of formulas. E is an extension of a set of premises P with constraints C iff there is a preferred subtheory S of P and C and $E = Th(S \cap P)$.*

We next introduce the necessary modifications of the reliability level approach. Again we split premises and constraints into several levels. The different levels of a default theory now consist of pairs of sets of formulas, the first element of each pair will be treated as premises, the second element as constraints:

Definition 15: *A default theory with constraints is a tuple $(T_1, ..., T_n)$ where each T_i is a pair (P_i, C_i) of sets of formulas.*

Definition 16: *Let $T = ((P_1, C_1), ..., (P_n, C_n))$ be a default theory with constraints. S is a preferred subtheory of T iff it is a preferred subtheory (in the sense of Definition 9) of $(P_1 \cup C_1, ..., P_n \cup C_n)$.*

Definition 18: *Let $T = ((P_1, C_1), ..., (P_n, C_n))$ be a default theory with constraints. Let $P = P_1 \cup ... \cup P_n$. E is an extension of T iff there is a preferred subtheory S of T and $E = Th(S \cap P)$.*

We will not use the premise/constraint pair notation in the rest of the paper, instead we underline formulas to distinguish constraints from premises in each reliability level. This should make the examples more readable.

With these extensions we can easily define a contraction function, $-$, for default theories.

Definition 19: *Let $T = (T_1,...,T_n)$ be a default theory with constraints, P a formula, j a natural number.*

The contraction of T with respect to p, $T-p$, is the default theory $(\{\underline{\neg P}\}, T_1, ...,T_n)$.

The (insert-) contraction of T with respect to p at degree j, $T\text{-}^{(j)}p$, is the default theory

$$(T_1,.., T_j \cup \{\underline{\neg P}\}, ... , T_n).$$

The (minus-) contraction of T with respect to p at degree -j, $T\text{-}^{(-j)}p$, is the default theory

$$(T_1,.., T_{j-1}, \{\underline{\neg P}\}, T_j, ... ,T_n).$$

Thus, the basic idea of contracting p is to insert $\neg p$ as a constraint in the right level. Here is a simple example:

T=(T1,T2) with

    T2 = $\{\forall x.\text{BIRD}(x) \supset \text{FLIES}(x)\}$

    T1 = $\{\text{BIRD}(\text{TWEETY}), \text{BIRD}(\text{POLLY})\}$

This default theory has a single extension Th(T1 $\cup$ T2) which contains FLIES(TWEETY). Now let´s contract this theory with respect to FLIES(TWEETY):

T$-$FLIES(TWEETY) = (T´1,T´2,T´3) with

    T´3 = $\{\forall x.\text{BIRD}(x) \supset \text{FLIES}(x)\}$

    T´2 = $\{\text{BIRD}(\text{TWEETY}), \text{BIRD}(\text{POLLY})\}$

    T´1 = $\{\underline{\neg\text{FLIES}(\text{TWEETY})}\}$

The new default theory has a single preferred subtheory:

$\{\underline{\neg\text{FLIES}(\text{TWEETY})}, \text{BIRD}(\text{TWEETY}), \text{BIRD}(\text{POLLY})\}$

The single extension is:

Th($\{\text{BIRD}(\text{TWEETY}), \text{BIRD}(\text{POLLY})\}$)

Again we have the additional expressiveness to contract at a certain degree. And we keep the incrementality of the whole approach with its nice consequences. For instance, information is never "forgotten". Assume we revise T$-$FLIES(TWEETY) with respect to FLIES(TWEETY). The resulting default theory T$-$FLIES(TWEETY)*FLIES(TWEETY) has a single extension containing FLIES(POLLY). Moreover, the order of sequences of contractions and - more general - sequences of contractions and revisions is unimportant up to the indices. We have the following generalization of Proposition 1:

Proposition 2: *Let T be a default theory with constraints, A_1, ..., A_n formulas, j_1, ..., j_n integers, and op_1, ..., op_n a sequence of * or − operations. For every permutation A_{k1}, ..., A_{kn} of the formulas A_1, ..., A_n there exist integers i_1, ..., i_n such that*

$$T \; op_1^{(j1)} \; A_1 \; op_2^{(j2)} \; A_2 \; ... \; op_n^{(jn)} \; A_n = T \; op_{k1}^{(i1)} \; A_{k1} \; op_{k2}^{(i2)} \; A_{k2} \; ... \; op_{kn}^{(in)} \; A_{kn}.$$

Proof: obvious

We discussed in Section 3.1 already that not all of the Gärdenfors rationality postulates for revisions (Gärdenfors 88) hold in our approach. The same is true for his rationality postulates for contraction. Of course, these postulates cannot directly be applied, they have to be reformulated to make sense for our default theories at all. One of the difficulties of this reformulation is that there is no analogon to the +-operation used in the original postulates. This operation adds information regardless whether an inconsistency results or not. Such an addition is not possible in the preferred subtheory approach since the logical machinery guarantees consistency.

But even in cases where the corresponding reformulation seems obvious some of the reformulated postulates do not hold. Take as an example Gärdenfors´ postulate (−2). It requires that, for any belief set K and formula A, $K−A \subseteq K$. The natural reformulation for default theories would be: every extension of a default theory T−A is contained in an extension of T. This requirement is clearly violated since, as discussed above, the approach is able to memorize currently unused information and T−A may have extensions containing formulas not contained in any extension of T. As a consequence the relation between revisions and contractions known as the Harper identity, $K−A = K*¬A \cap K$, is also violated.

We do, however, not consider this as a sign for any kind of irrationality of our approach. The Gärdenfors postulates are particularly devised for changes of epistemic states seen as deductively closed theories. The distinction between derived and underived beliefs, and the view of epistemic states as implicitly given as the nonmonotonic consequences of a set of premises seem to require different rationality criteria.

Acknowledgments

Thanks to Ulrich Junker and Hans Rott for various helpful comments.

References

(Brewka 89) Brewka, Gerhard: Preferred Subtheories - An Extended Logical Framework for Default Reasoning, Proc. IJCAI-89, 1989

(Brewka 90) Brewka, Gerhard: Nonmonotonic Reasoning - Logical Foundations of Commonsense, Cambridge University Press, to appear

(Gärdenfors 88) Gärdenfors, Peter: Knowledge in Flux, MIT Press, Cambridge, MA, 1988

(Gärdenfors, Makinson 88) Gärdenfors, Peter, Makinson, David: Revisions of Knowledge Systems Using Epistemic Entrenchment. In: Vardi, M. (ed): Proceedings of the Second Conference on Theoretical Aspects of Reasoning about Knowledge, Morgan Kaufmann, Los Altos, 1988

(McCarthy 80) McCarthy, John: Circumscription - A Form of Nonmonotonic Reasoning, Artificial Intelligence 13, 1980

(McCarthy 84) McCarthy, John: Applications of Circumscription to Formalizing Common Sense Knowledge, Proc. AAAI-Workshop Non-Monotonic Reasoning, 1984 (also in Artificial Intelligence 28, 1986)

(Moore 85) Moore, Robert C.: Semantical Considerations on Nonmonotonic Logic, Artificial Intelligence 25, 1985

(Poole 88) Poole, D.: A Logical Framework for Default Reasoning, Artificial Intelligence 36, 1988

(Reiter 80) Reiter, Raymond: A Logic for Default Reasoning, Artificial Intelligence 13, 1980

(Rescher 64) Rescher, Nicholas: Hypothetical Reasoning, North-Holland Publ., Amsterdam. 1964

Preferential Cumulative Reasoning and Nonmonotonic Semantic Nets

Klaus U. Schulz
Seminar für natürlich-sprachliche Systeme (SNS)
University of Tübingen
Biesingerstr. 10
D-7400 Tübingen
nfseja1@dtuzdv1.bitnet

Abstract: We first describe a decision procedure for purely cumulative and preferential cumulative reasoning which is based on a completion algorithm and computationally very simple: if a system of axioms is given, the completion leads to a canonical representation (called pool table) which organizes knowledge in the style of an encyclopedia. With this table, the decision whether an implication holds or not is trivial. We show in the second part of the paper that it is possible to assign in a natural way an inheritance graph structure to the columns of the table. Then usual network inheritance techniques may be applied and lead to a rather strong notion of consequence. Such network structures on encyclopaedias are interesting for natural language processing since nontrivial techniques for reasoning on the base of a background encyclopaedia would have various applications in text understanding and related areas.

Introduction

In the absence of probabilistic arguments, common sense reasoning is typically based on a "consistent view of the world" (Gabbay, [Ga1]). The hypothesis which we make about the world in the presence of some explicitly given data do not conflict with each other: if we learn that one of our assumptions is in fact true, then we do not withdraw another. Non-monotonic reasoning, as a formalization of non-probabilistic common sense reasoning, should reflect this situation. Gabbay [Ga2] suggests the following definition: a *non-monotonic consequence relation* is a binary relation $\vdash \subseteq P(L) \times L$ which satisfies Reflexivity, Cut and the following rule of Restricted Monotonicity:

If $\Delta \vdash x$ and $\Delta \vdash y$, then $\Delta, y \vdash x$ (RM).

Restricted Monotonicity, also called Cautious or *Cumulative* Monotonicity has - in combination with Cut - the effect that explicit addition or erasure of derivable information does not change the set of consequences. Besides its intuitive justification, the study of cumulative (i.e. non-monotonic) consequence relations is interesting for two reasons. First, a general study of cumulative reasoning on an abstract level may help to clarify the formal differences between existing systems of non-monotonic logic in terms of their consequence relation (Makinson [Mak], Kraus, Lehmann, Magidor [KLM]).

The second idea, also present in [KLM], is more practically oriented: if $\vdash$ is internalized, Reflexivity, Cut and Cumulative Monotonicity may be regarded as inference rules of a Gentzen-style system **C** of *purely* cumulative inference which deals with sequents of the form $\Delta \vdash x$. A related proof system may be formulated for the language and background logic of propositional calculus. Such systems of purely cumulative or preferential cumulative reasoning (the system **PC** has one additional inference rule called Loop) are interesting for their own. They have only "Horn-clause" inference rules and the derivability of a sequent never depends from the non-derivability of another sequent. One intuition behind such systems is the idea to allow only steps which are *not* defeasible, thus to characterize the small subpart of nonmonotonic reasoning where conflicting arguments (should) yet not appear. It is clear that these systems are very weak. Does it make sense to investigate them? The answer depends from several questions:

(1) Is it possible to formalize nontrivial knowledge in terms of the sequents of the systems?
(2) Are there decision procedures for these systems which work efficiently for all practically interesting cases?
(3) Is it possible to use these decision procedures as a submodule of a more powerful systems?
(4) Do we draw any benefit from such a modular structure of the inference mechanism?

The first question has an affirmative answer. Sequents may be used to formalize at least the type of knowledge occurring in semantic networks. If we use the language of propositional calculus, then the expressiveness of sequents even exceeds the possibilities of simple networks: we may formulate not only "Bird $\vdash$ Flying" or "Penguin $\vdash$ ~Flying", but also "Human $\vdash$ Male $\vee$ Female" and "~Startup $\vdash$ ~Gas $\vee$ ~Batteryok" (modifying an example from [KLM]). Thus nontrivial conditional databases may be formalized by means of sequents which may be regarded as axioms (or as one-step derivations which do not need any further justification).

In our paper [Sch] it was shown that for a finite set of axioms the system **C** allows a simple decision procedure which is based on the computation of a so-called pool-table. The algorithm is first formulated for connective-free language. Then set theoretical inclusion is translated into logical implication and the same method yields a decision procedure for purely cumulative reasoning based on propositional calculus. In the first part of this paper, we continue this work and give a similar decision procedure for the system **PC** of (purely) preferential cumulative reasoning ([KLM]). Again results may be formulated both for connective-free language and for the language and background logic of propositional calculus. For realistic systems of axioms, the decision procedures seem in fact to work efficiently, an example is discussed.

In the second part of the paper we give a partial answer to questions (3) and (4). A pool table represents implicational knowledge just in the way knowledge is represented in an encyclopaedia: each *column* of the table has one or several head lines, called *sources*. In general we have a *principal* source which may be regarded as definiendum ("Bird", for example) of the column. If further headlines exist, they represent default definitions (like "Flying,Animal" or "Feathered,Animal"). The remaining part of the column (the *pool*) contains a list of typical properties or features of the definiendum. Purely cumulative (or preferential cumulative) reasoning can roughly be described as the strategy to decide an implication on the base of a single column only. Thus, even if we know that birds are animals it is not allowed to go to the column with headline "Animal" in order to find typical properties of "Bird". In some sense, the systems **C** and **PC** should in fact rather be regarded as rules which organize implicational knowledge than as (powerful) inference rules.

Returning to question (3): can we use the tables for a more powerful deduction mechanism? Here we suddenly find a question with immediate practical relevance: a reasonable deduction mechanism which uses the information offered by an encyclopaedia would be very interesting for text understanding and various related areas of natural language processing. We want to show that network inheritance techniques may be applied to the pool tables which we get via preferential cumulative reasoning if the columns are regarded as the nodes of a graph. Since every column represents a complete equivalence class of information states (where equivalence means to have the same consequences) we may regard it as a single object of higher category and the assignment of a network structure turns out to be very natural. The problem is, of course, how to properly define IS-A and IS-NOT-A links between columns. Our suggestion works well for simple examples but is open for discussion. Pool tables, however, are only primitive variants of real-life enyclopaedias. It has still to be studied more thoroughly how network techniques may be used for reasoning with real encyclopaedias.

Question (4) reads now as follows: is it really necessary to compute the pool table or is it possible to apply network arguments directly? The direct use of network arguments presupposes that the net is already completely specified and that there are no cyclic IS-A relationships. Both assumptions are not realistic for typical natural language applications. If definitions are used, we have immediately a cyclic IS-A relationship between definiendum and definiens. If we want to handle such cyclic information, nodes necessarily get an internal structure. Moreover, for text understanding systems it would be a highly undesirable constraint if we had to specify a complete net at the beginning of a session. There should rather be a mechanical device which allows to correctly incorporate new instances of IS-A information at any moment of the session, taking into account the inherent structure of labels. The pool table constructing algorithm is such a device. Its role is not a dramatic, but in fact a useful and necessary one.

Part 1   Decision Procedures for Cumulative Inference and Preferential
Cumulative Inference

The Language of Literals

Let $L = C \cup \{\sim c; c \in C\}$ be the language of complementary literals over a set C of
sentential constants. Suppose that we are given a system of axioms of type $\Delta \vdash^{(0)} x$,
where $\Delta \subseteq L$ and $x \in L$. The system C of cumulative inference for literals over C has
(the trivial rule $\Delta \vdash x$ if $\Delta \vdash^{(0)} x$ and) the three inference rules Reflexivity, Restricted
Monotonicity and Cut:

$$\Delta \vdash x \text{ if } x \in \Delta \qquad\qquad\qquad \text{(Refl)},$$
$$\text{if } \Delta \vdash x \text{ and } \Delta \vdash y, \text{ then } \Delta,y \vdash x \qquad \text{(RM)},$$
$$\text{if } \Delta \vdash x \text{ and } \Delta,x \vdash y, \text{ then } \Delta \vdash y \qquad \text{(Cut)}.$$

$\Delta \vdash \Gamma$ is an abbreviation for $\Delta \vdash x$ for all $x \in \Gamma$, we write Δ,x for the set $\Delta \cup \{x\}$. In
the following letters $\Delta, \Gamma, \ldots$ stand always for sets of literals of L and letters $x,y,z,x_1,\ldots$
denote single literals of L.

Lemma 1: The following rule Reciprocity is a derived rule in S_{ci}:
For finite sets Δ_1 and Δ_2: If $\Delta_1 \vdash x$, $\Delta_1 \vdash \Delta_2$ and $\Delta_2 \vdash \Delta_1$, then $\Delta_2 \vdash x$ (Rec)

Proof (Sketch): First use $\Delta_1 \vdash x$, $\Delta_1 \vdash \Delta_2$, (RM) and (Cut) to find derivations of
$\Delta_1,\Delta_2 \vdash x$. Then use $\Delta_2 \vdash \Delta_1$, $\Delta_2,\Delta_1 \vdash x$, (RM) and (Cut) to find $\Delta_2 \vdash x$. ♦

Definition 2: A *pool table* for S_{ci} is a finite set $PT = \{<S_i,\Pi_i>; 1 \leq i \leq n\}$ of ordered
pairs, called *columns*. Each *pool* Π_i is a finite set of literals, S_i is a finite collection of
subsets of Π_i, called the *sources* of Π_i. Conversely Π_i is called the pool of each $\Sigma \in S_i$
$(1 \leq i \leq n)$. The following conditions must be satisfied:
   (pt1) $\Sigma \subseteq \Pi_i$ for all $\Sigma \in S_i$ $(1 \leq i \leq n)$.
   (pt2) If $\Sigma_1, \Sigma_2 \in S_i$, then Σ_1 is not a subset of Σ_2 $(1 \leq i \leq n)$.
A set $I \subseteq L$ is called an *intermediate set* of column i if $\Sigma \subseteq I \subseteq \Pi_i$ for a $\Sigma \in S_i$. PT is a
completed pool table if two different columns of PT never share a common intermediate
set. A column $<S_i,\Pi_i>$ of PT is called *trivial* if $\Pi_i \in S_i$.

Definition 3: Let $PT = \{<S_i,\Pi_i>; 1 \leq i \leq n\}$ be a pool table. A formula x is called
derivable from Ω *according to PT* (symbolically $\Omega \vdash^{(PT)} x$) iff $x \in \Omega$ or Ω is an
intermediate set of a column $<S_i,\Pi_i>$ such that $x \in \Pi_i$, for some $1 \leq i \leq n$.

Theorem 4: Let PT = {<S_i,Π_i>; $1 \leq i \leq n$} be a completed pool table. Then $\vdash^{(PT)}$ satisfies (Refl), (RM) and (Cut).

Proof: Trivial. ◆

A system of axioms $\vdash^{(0)}$ will be called finite, if the number of axioms of $\vdash^{(0)}$ is finite and all premises of the axioms are finite.

Definition 5: Let $\vdash^{(0)}$ be a finite system. A completed pool table PT is called a *pool table for* $\vdash^{(0)}$ if and only if $\vdash^{(PT)} = \vdash$.

The decision whether or not an implication $\Omega \vdash x$ is valid can be made on the base of set theoretical inclusion only if a completed pool table PT = {<S_i,Π_i>; $1 \leq i \leq n$} for $\vdash^{(0)}$ is given. The algorithm is trivial:

Algorithm 1

```
Begin
    if x ∈ Ω
    then print "Yes" and Halt.
    For i := 1 until n do
    if Ω is an intermediate set of <Sᵢ,Πᵢ> and x ∈ Πᵢ,
        then print "Yes" and Halt.
    Print "No".
end of algorithm 1.
```

The pool table constructing algorithm may in described in different ways. We want to use Buchberger´s [Buc] abstract concept of a critical pair/completion procedure in order to stress the fact that the algorithm may be seen as a particular instance of a whole class of related algorithms. The primitive objects of the pool table constructing algorithm are columns, i.e. pairs <S_i,Π_i> as in definition 2. For this purpose, axioms $\Delta \vdash^{(0)} x$ are represented as columns <{Δ},$\Delta \cup \{x\}$>. In the basic step, two columns <T,Θ> and <S,Π> are compared - if there is a critical interaction, i.e. a common intermediate set, then <T,Θ>,<S,Π> is called a *critical pair*. Critical pairs are merged and give the new column <Min(S,T),$\Pi \cup \Theta$>, where Min(S,T) is the set of all elements of $S \cup T$ which are minimal with respect to inclusion. As a matter of fact the algorithm terminates after a finite number of merge-steps.

Algorithm 2

Begin

PT := ∅.

While $\vdash^{(0)}$ has an element $\Delta \vdash^{(0)} x$ such that $x \notin \Delta$, do

    begin

        Merge(PT,$<\{\Delta\},\Delta \cup \{x\}>$).

        $\vdash^{(0)} := \vdash^{(0)} - \{\Delta \vdash^{(0)} x\}$.

    end.

Print PT and halt.

Procedure Merge(PT,$<T,\Theta>$)

Begin

    If there exists $<S,\Pi> \in$ PT such that $<S,\Pi>$, $<T,\Theta>$ is a critical pair,

        then Merge$((PT - \{<S,\Pi>\})$, $<Min(S,T),\Pi \cup \Theta>)$

    else PT := PT $\cup \{<T,\Theta>\}$.

End of Merge.

End of Algorithm 2.

It is not difficult to prove that the output PT of algorithm 2 is in fact a completed pool table for $\vdash^{(0)}$ without trivial columns and that such a pool table is unique. The proof in [Sch] is more complicated than necessary since (Rec) is not used explicitly there. See the corresponding proof of theorem 9 below.

Preferential Cumulative Inference over Literals

The system **PC** of preferential cumulative inference for literals over C has all rules of C and in addition Loop:

If $\Delta_1 \vdash \Delta_2, \Delta_2 \vdash \Delta_3, \dots , \Delta_{k-1} \vdash \Delta_k$ and $\Delta_k \vdash \Delta_1$, then $\Delta_1 \vdash \Delta_k$ (k > 1).   (Loop)

Definition 6: Let PT = $\{<S_i,\Pi_i>; 1 \leq i \leq n\}$ be a pool table. The column $<S_i,\Pi_i>$ *dominates* the column $<S_j,\Pi_j>$ ($i \neq j$) if S_j contains a source $\Sigma \subseteq \Pi_i$. PT is *acyclic* if there does not exist a *domination-cycle*, i.e. a sequence of columns $<S_{i1},\Pi_{i1}>$, ..., $<S_{ik},\Pi_{ik}>$ (k > 1) such that every $<S_{ir},\Pi_{ir}>$ dominates $<S_{i(r+1)},\Pi_{i(r+1)}>$ ($1 \leq r \leq k-1$) and that $<S_{ik},\Pi_{ik}>$ dominates $<S_{i1},\Pi_{i1}>$.

Remark: If two columns of a pool table have a common intermediate set, then they dominate each other. Thus every acyclic pool table is in particular completed.

Theorem 7: Let PT = $\{<S_i,\Pi_i>; 1 \leq i \leq n\}$ be an acyclic pool table. Then $\vdash^{(PT)}$ satisfies (Refl), (RM), (Cut) and (Loop).

Proof: The proofs for Reflexivity, Restricted Monotonicity and Cut are trivial. To prove Loop, suppose $\Delta_1 \mathrel{\vdash} {}^{(PT)} \Delta_2$, $\Delta_2 \mathrel{\vdash} {}^{(PT)} \Delta_3$, ... , $\Delta_{k-1} \mathrel{\vdash} {}^{(PT)} \Delta_k$ and $\Delta_k \mathrel{\vdash} {}^{(PT)} \Delta_1$. We use induction on k and show that $\Delta_i \mathrel{\vdash} {}^{(PT)} \Delta_j$ $(1 \leq i,j \leq k)$. For $k = 2$ there is nothing to show. Let $k > 2$. If each Δ_i, $1 \leq i \leq k$, is an intermediate set of a column $<S_{1,i},\Pi_{1,i}>$, then (the column is unique and) these columns are necessarily identical - otherwise we would have a domination-cycle. Thus $\Delta_i \mathrel{\vdash} {}^{(PT)} \Delta_j$ holds trivially $(1 \leq i,j \leq k)$. If some set Δ_{i0}, $1 \leq i0 \leq k$, does not occur as an intermediate set of a column, then $\Delta_{i0+1} \subseteq \Delta_{i0}$ (respectively $\Delta_1 \subseteq \Delta_k$ if $i0 = k$) and $\Delta_{i-1} \mathrel{\vdash} {}^{(PT)} \Delta_{i+1}$ (respectively $\Delta_{k-1} \mathrel{\vdash} {}^{(PT)} \Delta_1$) gives a shorter cycle. By induction hypothesis, $\Delta_i \mathrel{\vdash} {}^{(PT)} \Delta_j$ for $i,j \neq i0$. A simple application of (Rec) shows that in addition $\Delta_j \mathrel{\vdash} {}^{(PT)} \Delta_{i0}$ and $\Delta_{i0} \mathrel{\vdash} {}^{(PT)} \Delta_j$ $(1 \leq j \leq k)$. ◆

Theorem 8: There exists a unique acyclic pool table without trivial elements for any finite system $\mathrel{\vdash} {}^{(0)}$. The table is computed by the following algorithm 3:

Algorithm 3

```
Begin
    n:= 0.
    PT := ∅.
    Domination-Table = ∅.
    While ⊢ (0) has an element Δ ⊢ (0) x such that x ∉ Δ, do
        begin
            n:=n+1.
            Merge(PT,<n,{Δ},Δ ∪ {x}>).
            ⊢ (0) :=⊢ (0) - {Δ ⊢ (0) x}.
        end.
    While PT has columns <i1,Si1,Πi1>,....,<ik,Sik,Πik> such that the
    Domination-Table contains the cycle <i1,i2>,...<ik-1,ik>,<ik,i1> do
        begin
            replace all occurrences of i1,....,ik in the Domination-Table by i1.
            erase all entries <i1,i1> in the Domination Table.
            Merge(PT-{<i1,Si1,Πi1>,....,<ik,Sik,Πik>},
                              <i1,Min(Si1,...,Sik),Πi1 ∪ ... ∪ Πik>).
        end.
    Print PT and halt.

Procedure Merge(PT,<i,T,Θ>)
    Begin
        for every <j,S,Π> ∈ PT do
        begin
            if <S,Π>, <T,Θ> is a critical pair, then do
                begin
                    replace in the Domination-Table all occurrences of i by j.
                    erase entries <j,j> in the Domination Table.
                    Merge((PT- {<j,S,Π>}),<j,Min(S,T),Π ∪ Θ>).
                end
```

else if <S,Π> dominates <T,Θ>, then
    add <j,i> to the Domination-Table
else if <T,Θ> dominates <S,Π>, then
    add <i,j> to the Domination-Table.
PT := PT $\cup$ {<i,T,Θ>}.
End of Merge.

End of Algorithm 3.

Proof: We say that a pool table PT_j occurs during the execution of the algorithm

(1) if there is any call Merge(PT_j',<n,{Δ},Δ $\cup$ {x}>) where
$$PT_j = PT_j' \cup \{<n,\{\Delta\},\Delta \cup \{x\}>\}, \text{ or}$$
(2) if there is any call
Merge(PT_j'-{<i_1,S_{i1},Π_{i1}>,....,<i_k,S_{ik},Π_{ik}>},<i_1,Min(S_{i1},...,S_{ik}),$\Pi_{i1}\cup$...$\cup\Pi_{ik}$>).),
where
$PT_j = (PT_j'$-{<i_1,S_{i1},Π_{i1}>,....,<i_k,S_{ik},Π_{ik}>}) $\cup$ {<i_1,Min(S_{i1},...,S_{ik}),$\Pi_{i1}\cup$...$\cup\Pi_{ik}$>} or
(3) if there is any call Merge((PT_j'- {<j,S,Π>}),<j,Min(S,T),Π $\cup$ Θ>)
where $PT_j = PT_j' \cup$ {<j,Min(S,T),Π $\cup$ Θ>}.

(It is trivial to verify that all these objects are in fact pool tables.) The pool tables occuring during the execution may be ordered in a sequence $\emptyset = PT_1,PT_2,...,PT_m = PT$ corresponding to the order of their natural occurrence. It is simple to see that $\vdash^{(PTj)} \subseteq \vdash^{(PT(j+1))}$ ($1 \leq j \leq m$). Since every nontrivial axiom $\Delta \vdash^{(0)} x$ is eventually introduced as a new column <n,{Δ},Δ $\cup$ {x}> it follows easily that $\vdash \subseteq \vdash^{(PT)}$. Thus algorithm 3 (in connection with algorithm 1) is complete. It is also simple to see that the final pool table PT is acyclic. Uniqueness may be proved straightforward, see [Sch]. It remains to prove correctness, i.e. $\vdash^{(PT)} \subseteq \vdash$. We show by induction that $\vdash^{(PTj)} \subseteq \vdash$, for all j = 1,...,m. This is trivial for j = 1. Suppose that $\vdash^{(PTj)} \subseteq \vdash$, for some j < m. If PT_{j+1} has the form $PT_j \cup$ {<n,{Δ},Δ $\cup$ {x}>}, then $\Omega \vdash^{(PTj+1)} y$ iff $\Omega \vdash^{(PTj)} y$ or $\Omega = \Delta$ and y = x. Hence $\vdash^{(PTj+1)} \subseteq \vdash$. If PT_{j+1} has the form

$$PT_{j+1} = (PT_{j+1}' \cup \{<i_1,\text{Min}(S_{i1},...,S_{ik}),\Pi_{i1}\cup...\cup\Pi_{ik}>\},$$

then PT_j has the form

$$PT_{j+1}' \cup \{<i_1,S_{i1},\Pi_{i1}>,....,<i_k,S_{ik},\Pi_{ik}>\}.$$

The columns <S_{i1},Π_{i1}>,....,<S_{ik},Π_{ik}> represent a domination-circle, thus it is possible to find sources $\Sigma_{i1} \in S_{i1}$,...,$\Sigma_{ik} \in S_{ik}$ such that $\Sigma_{ir} \vdash^{(PTj)} \Sigma_{i(r+1)}$ for all $1 \leq r \leq k-1$ and that $\Sigma_{ik} \vdash^{(PTj)} \Sigma_{i1}$. By induction hypothesis and (Loop), $\Sigma_{ir} \vdash \Sigma_{is}$ for all $1 \leq r,s \leq k$. If $x \in \Pi_{ir}$, then $\Sigma_{ir} \vdash x$, $\Sigma_{ir} \vdash \Sigma_{is}$ and $\Sigma_{is} \vdash \Sigma_{ir}$. Thus, by (Rec), $\Sigma_{is} \vdash x$. Thus $\Sigma_{is} \vdash \Pi_{i1}\cup$...$\cup\Pi_{ik}$ and $\vdash^{(PTj+1)} \subseteq \vdash$. The situation $PT_{j+1} = PT_j' \cup$ {<j,Min(S,T),Π $\cup$ Θ>} with $PT_j = PT_j' \cup$ {<j,S,Π>},<i,T,Θ>} may be regarded as a special case of the previous situation. The same arguments give $\vdash^{(PTj+1)} \subseteq \vdash$. ◆

Definition/Remark 9: Let $\vdash^{(o)}$ be a finite system of axioms, suppose that PT is an acyclic pool table for $\vdash^{(o)}$ without trivial columns. Let us call two sets of formulas *equivalent* if exactly the same formulas are derivable from both sets. It is trivial to see that Δ has a nontrivial equivalence class iff Δ occurs as an intermediate set of a column of PT. The formulas which are derivable from Δ are exactly the formulas of the pool of the column. The sources are the elements of equivalence classes which are minimal with respect to set theoretical inclusion. To have a uniform formulation, we say that for trivial equivalence classes source and pool are identical.

Remark: It should be clear there are various similar algorithms which compute a completed or acyclic pool table for finite systems of axioms. A more homogenious formulation in the acyclic case is possible, for example, if we use the fact that critical pairs are special cases of domination cycles and eliminate one while-loop. Any implementation of the procedure for **PC** must incorporate some means of detecting loops in a graph. For this purpose, several algorithms exist. Szwarcfiter and Lauer [SzL] give an algorithm which enumerates the simple loops of a graph in $O(v + e)$ per cycle, where e (v) is the numbers of edges (vertices) of the graph.

An Example

Suppose we have the following database.

(1) Animal $\vdash^{(o)}$ Living, (2) Bird $\vdash^{(o)}$ Animal, (3) Bird $\vdash^{(o)}$ Flying, (4) Bat $\vdash^{(o)}$ Animal, (5) Bat $\vdash^{(o)}$ Flying, (6) Penguin $\vdash^{(o)}$ Bird, (7) Penguin $\vdash^{(o)}$ ~Flying, (8) Bird $\vdash^{(o)}$ Feathered, (9) Animal,Feathered $\vdash^{(o)}$ Bird, (10) Bat $\vdash^{(o)}$ Mammal, (11) Mammal,Flying $\vdash^{(o)}$ Bat, (12) Animal, Flying $\vdash^{(o)}$ Bird, (13) Bat $\vdash^{(o)}$ ~Bird.

After axioms (1)-(8) are included, the actual table is still trivial (sources in bold):

1	2	3	4
<{{**Animal**}}, {Animal, Living}>	<{{**Bird**}}, {Bird, Animal, Flying, Feathered}>	<{{**Bat**}}, {Bat, Animal, Flying}>	<{{**Penguin**}}, {Penguin, ~Flying, Bird}>

Then axiom (9) is called. The columns <{{Bird}},{Bird,Animal,Flying,Feathered}> and <{{Animal,Feathered}},{Animal,Feathered,Bird}> have the common intermediate set {Bird,Animal,Feathered} and are merged. We get
<{{Bird},{Animal,Feathered}},{Bird,Animal,Flying,Feathered}> which has two sources. After the first while-loop of algorithm 2, the actual pool table is completed and may be represented (modulo simplification of numbers, omitting brackets and commas) as

1	2	3	4
Animal	Bird	Bat	Penguin
	Animal,Feathered	Mammal,Flying	
	Animal,Flying		
Animal	Bird	Bat	Penguin
Living	Flying	Flying	~Flying
	Animal	Animal	Bird
	Feathered	Mammal	
		~Bird	

The domination table has the entries <2,1>,<3,1>,<4,2> and <3,2>. Thus there is no domination cycle and the algorithm stops. Derivable implications are, for example, "Animal,Feathered ⊢~ Flying", "Animal,Feathered,Flying ⊢~ Bird" and "Mammal,Bat ⊢~ Flying".

Now consider the similar system where (3) is omitted and (9) is replaced by (9⁄): Animal,Feathered ⊢~ (o) Fly. After the first while-loop, we get (modulo numbers) columns <2,{{Bird}},{Bird,Animal,Feathered}>, <5,{{Animal,Feathered}},{Animal,Flying,Feathered}> and <6,{{Animal,Fly}},{Animal,Flying,Bird}>. The domination table has the cycle <2,5>, <5,6>, <6,2>. The second while-loop produces the complex column <2,{{Bird},{Animal,Feathered},{Animal,Flying}},{Bird,Animal,Flying,Feathered}> and we get the same final table.

Propositional Calculus as Background Logic

Let L be the set of wff over a set of propositional variables. Validity (with respect to the propositional calculus) ⊨ is defined as usual. Similar as in the first section, suppose that a set ⊢~ (o) ⊆ L × L of axioms is given. The system C (PC) uses the inference rules Reflexivity, Left Logical Equivalence, Right Weakening, And, Restricted Monotonicity, Cut (and Loop):

$$\alpha \mathrel{\vdash\mkern-7mu\sim} \alpha \qquad\qquad \text{(Refl)}$$

$$\frac{\alpha \mathrel{\vdash\mkern-7mu\sim} \beta, \ \models \alpha \leftrightarrow \gamma}{\gamma \mathrel{\vdash\mkern-7mu\sim} \beta} \qquad\qquad \text{(LLE)}$$

$$\frac{\alpha \mathrel{\vdash\mkern-7mu\sim} \beta, \ \models \beta \rightarrow \gamma}{\alpha \mathrel{\vdash\mkern-7mu\sim} \gamma} \qquad\qquad \text{(RW)}$$

$$\frac{\alpha \mathrel{\vdash\mkern-7mu\sim} \beta, \ \alpha \mathrel{\vdash\mkern-7mu\sim} \gamma}{\alpha \mathrel{\vdash\mkern-7mu\sim} \beta \wedge \gamma} \qquad\qquad \text{(And)}$$

$$\frac{\alpha \mathrel{\vrule height 1.2ex depth 0pt width 0pt}\!\!\sim \gamma,\ \alpha \mathrel{\vrule}\!\!\sim \gamma}{\alpha \wedge \beta \mathrel{\vrule}\!\!\sim \gamma} \qquad \text{(RM)}$$

$$\frac{\alpha \mathrel{\vrule}\!\!\sim \beta,\ \alpha \wedge \beta \mathrel{\vrule}\!\!\sim \gamma}{\alpha \mathrel{\vrule}\!\!\sim \gamma} \qquad \text{(Cut)}$$

$$\frac{\alpha_1 \mathrel{\vrule}\!\!\sim \alpha_2,\ \alpha_2 \mathrel{\vrule}\!\!\sim \alpha_3, \dots \alpha_{k-1} \mathrel{\vrule}\!\!\sim \alpha_k,\ \alpha_k \mathrel{\vrule}\!\!\sim \alpha_1}{\alpha_1 \mathrel{\vrule}\!\!\sim \alpha_k} \qquad \text{(Loop)}$$

Lemma 10: The following rule Reciprocity is a derived rule in **C**:

if $\alpha \mathrel{\vrule}\!\!\sim \eta$, $\alpha \mathrel{\vrule}\!\!\sim \beta$ and $\beta \mathrel{\vrule}\!\!\sim \alpha$ then $\beta \mathrel{\vrule}\!\!\sim \eta$.   (Rec)

Proof: By (RM) and (LLE) $\beta \wedge \alpha \mathrel{\vrule}\!\!\sim \eta$, by (Cut) $\beta \mathrel{\vrule}\!\!\sim \eta$. ◆

As mentioned in the introduction, definitions, algorithms and proofs for the systems **C** and **PC** for the language of propositional calculus may be translated almost literally by replacing set theoretical inclusion by logical implication:

Definition 11: A pool table for propositional logic as background logic is a finite set PT $= \{<S_i,\Pi_i>;\ 1 \le i \le n\}$ of ordered pairs, called *columns*. Each *pool* Π_i is a formula and the S_i are finite sets of formulas called the *sources* of the pool Π_i. Conversely Π_i is called the pool of each $\sigma \in S_i$ $(1 \le i \le n)$. The following conditions must be satisfied:

(pt1) $\Pi_i \models \sigma$ for each $\sigma \in S_i$ $(1 \le i \le n)$.

(pt2) if $\sigma_1, \sigma_2 \in S_i$, then $\not\models \sigma_1 \to \sigma_2$ $(1 \le i \le n)$.

A formula α is called an *intermediate formula* of column i if $\Pi_i \models \alpha$ and $\alpha \models \sigma$ for a $\sigma \in S_i$. PT is a *completed* pool table if two different columns of PT never have a common intermediate formula. A column $<S_i,\Pi_i>$ of PT is called *trivial*, if Π_i is logically equivalent to a source σ in S_i. The column $<S_i,\Pi_i>$ *dominates* the column $<S_j,\Pi_j>$ $(i \ne j)$ if S_j contains a source σ such that $\models \Pi_i \to \sigma$. PT is *acyclic* if there does not exist a *domination-cycle*, i.e. a sequence of columns $<S_{i1},\Pi_{i1}>,\dots,<S_{ik},\Pi_{ik}>$ $(k > 2)$ such that every $<S_{ir},\Pi_{ir}>$ dominates $<S_{i(r+1)},\Pi_{i(r+1)}>$ $(1 \le r \le k-1)$ and that $<S_{ik},\Pi_{ik}>$ dominates $<S_{i1},\Pi_{i1}>$.

Definition 12: Let PT $= \{<S_1,\Pi_1>,\dots,<S_n,\Pi_n>\}$ be a pool table. A formula γ is called *derivable* from the formula θ *according to PT*, symbolically $\theta \mathrel{\vrule}\!\!\sim^{(PT)} \gamma$ iff $\models \theta \to \gamma$ or θ is an intermediate formula of a column $<S_i,\Pi_i>$ such that $\models \Pi_i \to \gamma$, for some $1 \le i \le n$.

Theorem 13: Let PT $= \{<S_1,\Pi_1>,\dots,<S_n,\Pi_n>\}$ be a completed (acyclic) pool table. Then $\mathrel{\vrule}\!\!\sim^{(PT)}$ satisfies all rules of **C** (**PC**).

Proof: Straightforward. ◆

Definition 14: Let $\vdash^{(0)}$ be a finite system of axioms. A completed (acyclic) pool table PT is called a *pool table for* $\vdash^{(0)}$ in **C** (**PC**) if and only if $\vdash^{(PT)} = \vdash$ (where $\vdash$ denotes derivability in **C** (**PC**)).

The structure of the pool table constructing algorithms remains the same. We just have to modify the notions of a critical pair in the obvious way: $<S,\Pi>$, $<T,\Theta>$ is a *critical pair* if Π logically implies a source of T and if Θ logically implies a source of S. Critical pairs (domination cycles) are merged and give $<Min(S,T),\Pi \wedge \Theta>$ (respectively $<Min(S_{i1},...,S_{ik}),\Pi_{i1} \wedge ... \wedge \Pi_{ik}>$) where $Min(S,T)$ $(Min(S_{i1},...,S_{ik}))$ is the set of all sources in $S \cup T$ $(S_{i1} \cup ... \cup S_{ik})$ which are not implied by another source of the same set. Elements are unique up to logical equivalence.

Hard Implications

For various applications it is very natural to distinguish between "soft" axioms and "hard" axioms. Soft axioms, like "Bird $\vdash^{(0)}$ Flying" have a nonmonotonic behaviour - additional information in the antecedent may destroy the conclusion, as in the example "Bird,Penguin$\vdash^{(0)}$ ~Flying". Hard axioms, like "Bird $\vdash^{(0)}$ Animal" have a monotonic behaviour - for every set Δ of formulas, "Δ,Bird $\vdash^{(0)}$ Animal" has to be true. It is simple to generalize definitions and algorithms for the corresponding systems **C′** (**PC′**) with the following additional rules of inference:

(1) $\Delta \vdash x$ implies $\Delta \vdash x$ and

(2) If $\Delta \vdash x$ and $\Delta \subseteq \Gamma$, then $\Gamma \vdash x$ (Monotonicity for hard sequents)

(Similar for language of propositional calculus). The modifications are straightforward.

Part 2 Combining Preferential Cumulative Reasoning with Inheritance Network Techniques

Inheritance Nets

An inheritance net is a set of positive (IS-A-) links $p \rightarrow_{+} q$ and negative (IS-NOT-A-) links $r \rightarrow$. s. The labels p,q,r,s,... are elements of a set L which is sometimes divided into $L = P \cup I$. In this case, the elements of I (the individual constants) are not allowed to occur on the right side of a link.

A (generalized) path is a sequence $l_1,...,l_n$ of links ($n \geq 1$) such that the right element of l_i is the left element of l_{i+1} ($1 \leq i \leq n-1$). The sequence $l_1,...,l_n$ is a positive (negative) path if every link l_i is a link of type $\rightarrow_+$ (if all links have type $\rightarrow_+$ but l_n which has type $\rightarrow_-$).

For deduction, the notion of a (positive or negative) path which is supported by the net is central. The idea is that supported paths allow flow of information: if TWEETY $\rightarrow_+...$ $\rightarrow_+$ FLYING is supported, then we may conclude by inheritance along the path that Tweety is a flying thing, whereas a supported negative path TWEETY $\rightarrow_+ ... \rightarrow_-$ FLYING would express that Tweety does not fly.

To define the notion of supported paths, two principal approaches may be distinguished: the extension approach (see [Tou], [San]) and the sceptical approach ([HTT]). Both share some principal ideas: single links are always supported (thus, it might be that we have a local inconsistency). A positive (negative) path $x \rightarrow_+ \sigma \rightarrow_+ y \rightarrow_+ z$ ($x \rightarrow_+ \sigma \rightarrow_+ y \rightarrow_-$ z) is *not* supported by the net if already an initial segment is rejected or there exists a path which is based on more specific information and leads to the conclusion that x is not a z (that x is a z). Schematically such a situation can be described as follows (σ and τ are possibly empty paths):

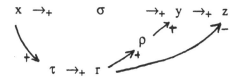

respectively

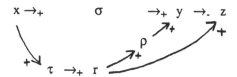

In both cases, to be an r is a more specific property than to be a y. But it is clear that the lower path may only override the upper path if it is not refuted itself by another path. Thus the exact definition of supported paths is not trivial. A reasonable definition is only possible if (at least) positive paths do not contain cycles.

If conflicting paths appear none of which is more specific than the other, the two approaches have a different strategy: in the extension approach, one path is just taken to be stronger and therefore supported. Thus we get different ways to extend the basic set of supported paths (the set of links). In the sceptical approach, both paths neutralize each other and are not supported.

We do not go into the details of inheritance techniques but refer to [HTT],[San],[Tou] for central definitions and ideas and to [MaS] for some problems. We are mainly concerned with the question how to define nets over pool tables in the appropriate way and do not touch the question of an optimal evaluation.

Inheritance Nets Defined on Pool Tables

To get an intuition for the relationship between inheritance nets and acyclic pool tables, let us give a reformulation of a prominent net. The Nixon-diamond

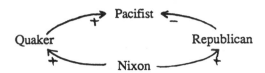

may be described by means of the following pool table (we just translate links x →$_+$ y (x →$_-$ y) into axioms x $\vdash$ (o) y (x $\vdash$ (o) ~y) and compute then the pool table for $\vdash$ (o)):

1 Pacifist	2 Quaker	3 Republican	4 Nixon
Pacifist	Quaker	Republican	Nixon
	Pacifist	~Pacifist	Quaker
			Republican

An IS-A relationsship of the net manifests itself in domination of the corresponding columns, as we may seen by the domination table <2,1>,<3,1>,<4,2>,<4,3>. An IS-NOT-A relationsship is indicated by columns <Π_i,S_i> and <Π_j,S_j> such that the pool Π_i contains a literal which is complementary to a literal of a (the) source of S_j. This is the case, in our example, (only) for columns 3 and 1.

We now want to convert the view and to assign an inheritance graph structure to acyclic pool tables. If all columns of PT have a unique source with a single element, then we may define an inheritance graph as follows: we introduce a node for every source and for every sentential constant which occurs (in positive or negated version) in a pool. We introduce a positive link from the node of source x to node y iff y is in the pool of Σ. We introduce a negative link iff the complement of y is in the pool of x. The resulting graph does not have a cyclic IS-A path since PT is acyclic. Thus, for example

1 Animal	2 Bird	3 Bat	4 Penguin
Animal	Bird	Bat	Penguin
Living	Animal	Animal	~Fly
	Fly	Fly	Bird
	Feathered		

is translated into

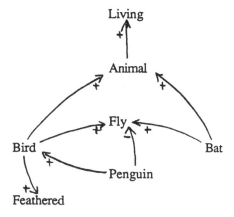

It is clear that the retranslation of the graph into a pool table is - modulo trivial columns - identical to the pool table from which we started.

For tables which have columns with several sources, the best translation is not so obvious. Consider the following example PT1:

1	2	3	4
Animal	**Bird**	**Bat**	**Penguin**
	Animal,Feathered	**Mammal,Flying**	
	Animal,Flying		
Animal	Bird	Bat	Penguin
Living	Flying	Flying	~Flying
	Animal	Animal	Bird
	Feathered	Mammal	
		~Bird	

First it is clear that we may not use different nodes for different sources of a column - we would immediately get a cyclic IS-A path. Thus the net has to be defined on the columns of the table and nodes get an internal structure. This is quite natural since columns represent equivalence classes of information states (remember Definition/Remark 10) and may be regarded as single objects of higher order. (The elements of such an equivalence class may be regarded as the members of a "subgalaxy" which are all connected by a trivial IS-A relationship.) The straightforward idea would now be to translate domination of columns into IS-A relationship. But this idea is too naive: consider, for example, PT1: column 3 has the representant {Bat,Flying,Animal} and dominates column 2 with source {Animal,Flying}. But, there is hardly a IS-A relationship since it is explicitly mentioned that Bats are not Birds. The latter information is stronger since "Bird" is the definiendum of the column and may be regarded as a *principal source*: since "Flying Animal" serves as a default definition of "Bird", but not vice versa. For all examples which we found multiple sources of a column relied on the same phenomenon. Thus it is reasonable to distinguish between principal source(s) (several principal sources may only occur if synonymous expressions are used) and non-principal sources in order to define IS-S links and IS-NOT-A links. The following definition 15 is a suggestion. The intuitions should be selfexplaining. For any set Δ of formulas, cl(Δ) and P(Δ) denote the equivalence class of Δ respectively the pool of cl(Δ).

Definition 15: Let PT be an acyclic pool table without trivial columns, representing derivability $\vdash$. The inheritance net N(PT) for PT is defined as follows: the set of labels is the set of all equivalence classes cl(Δ) which correspond to columns of PT. N(PT) has a link

(i) cl(Δ) →+ cl(Γ) iff
- P(Δ) contains a (the) principal source of cl(Γ), or
- P(Δ) contains a source of cl(Γ) and does not contain a literal which is complementary to a literal of a source of cl(Γ).

(ii) cl(Δ) →_ cl(Γ) iff
- P(Δ) contains a literal which is complementary to a literal of a (the) principal source cl(Γ), or
- P(Δ) does not contain a source of cl(Γ) and has a literal which is complementary to a source of cl(Γ).

Lemma 16: The IS-A subgraph of N(PT) is acyclic.

Proof: Suppose that we have links cl(Δ₁) →+ cl(Δ₂) →+ ... →+ cl(Δ$_k$) →+ cl(Δ₁) in N($\vdash$). Then there exist representants Δᵢ′ ∈ cl(Δᵢ) (1 ≤ i ≤ k) such that Δ₁′ $\vdash$ Δ₂′ $\vdash$ ... $\vdash$ Δ$_k$′ $\vdash$ Δ₁′. By (Loop) we easily get cl(Δ₁) = cl(Δ₂) = ... = cl(Δ$_k$), a contradiction. ♦

Definition 17: The formula x (~x) is derivably from Δ by inheritance, in symbols Δ $\vdash$ (Inh) x (Δ $\vdash$ (Inh) ~x) if there exists a supported positive (negative) path in N(PT) from cl(Δ) to cl({x}).(The notion of a supported path may be defined in any reasonable way.).

Example: The following net is assigned to PT 1:

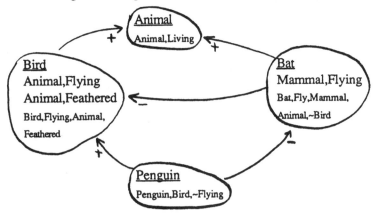

To bring more colour into the picture, we may allow arbitrary queries $\Delta \hspace{0.1em}\vdash\hspace{-0.3em}\sim x$. If $cl(\Delta)$ is trivial and does not correspond to a column, then we introduce a new node with principal source and pool Δ. Similar a node for $cl(\{x\})$ is introduced if $\{x\}$ is not an intermediate set of any column. Then the additional positive and negative links are introduced according to definition 15 and derivability is tested according to definition 17. (It may be shown that this strategy has a natural interpretation: if we would draw all trivial equivalence classes $cl(\Delta)$ for finite Δ, then we would get an infinite net (for an infinite set of proposition symbols). For this net, links can be defined exactly as in definition 15. The IS-A subgraph of the net is acyclic. For a given query $\Delta \hspace{0.1em}\vdash\hspace{-0.3em}\sim x$, the evaluation may be done in the finite subraph which is described above. The proof of this correpondence is very technical and omitted.)

If we use the notion of a supported path of the sceptical approach, for example, then we get the following consequences (all formulas of the right side are derivable via inheritance):

Tweety,Royal,Flying,Penguin $\hspace{0.1em}\vdash\hspace{-0.3em}\sim^{(Inh)}$ Bird,Feathered,Animal,Living,~Bat,

Animal,~Flying,Heavy $\hspace{0.1em}\vdash\hspace{-0.3em}\sim^{(Inh)}$ Living,~Bird,~Bat,

Strong,Flying,Mammal $\hspace{0.1em}\vdash\hspace{-0.3em}\sim^{(Inh)}$ Bat,Animal,Living,~Bird.

It is obvious that nets defined on pool tables have applications in the natural language area. They may help, for example, to find in DRT the correct anaphoric links for sentence combinations. (As an example, consider the sentences "-my dog does not like my bird. This morning it barked and that stupid animal flew out of the window -".) But the range of such applications is restricted. Compared with real encyclopaedias, pool tables are very primitive. It is an interesting question which type of structures may be used to model existing encyclopaedias in a more realistic way and how evaluation techniques for such structures could look like.

References

[Buc]   Buchberger, B., *History and Basic Features of the Critical-Pair/Completion Procedure*, J. Symbolic Computation 3 (1987), 3-38.

[Ga1]   Gabbay, D.M., The Tübingen Lectures 1988 on The Logics of Practical Reasoning, to appear as SNS-Bericht, Seminar für natürlich-sprachliche Systeme, Universität Tübingen 1989.

[Ga2]   Gabbay, D.M., *Theoretical foundations for non-monotonic reasoning in expert systems*, Research Report DoC 84/11, Department of Computing, Imperial College of Science and Technology, 1984.

[HTT]   Horty, J.F., Thomason, R.H. and Touretzky, D.S., *A Skeptical Theory of Inheritance in Nonmonotonic Semantic Networks*, Proceedings of the AAAI-87 (1987), 358-363.

[KLM]   Kraus, S.,Lehmann, D. and Magidor, M., *Preferential models and cumulative logics*, to appear in Artificial Intelligence.

[Mak]   Makinson, D., *General Theory of Cumulative Inference*, in Proceedings of the Second International Workshop on Non-Monotonic Reasoning, Springer Lecture Notes on Computer Science, subseries on Artificial Intelligence Vol. 346 (1989), 1-19.

[MaS]   Makinson, D.,Schlechta, K., *On Some Difficulties in the Theory of Defeasible Inheritance Nets*, Proceedings of the Tübingen Workshop on Semantic Networks and Nonmonotonic Reasoning, Vol. 2, Morreau, M., (editor), SNS-Bericht, Seminar für natürlich-sprachliche Systeme, Universität Tübingen 1989.

[San]   Sandewall, E., *Nonmonotonic inference rules for multiple inheritance with exceptions*, Proceedings if the IEEE 74 (1986), 1345-1353.

[Sch]   Schulz, K.U., *A Decision Procedure for Two Systems of Cumulative Inference*, Proceedings of the Tübingen Workshop on Semantic Networks and Nonmonotonic Reasoning, Vol. 2, Morreau, M., (editor), SNS-Bericht, Seminar für natürlich-sprachliche Systeme, Universität Tübingen 1989.

[SzL]   Szwarcfiter, J.L. and Lauer, P.E., *Finding the elementary cycles of a directed graph in $O(n+m)$ per cycle*, Tech. Rep. No. 60, Univ. of Newcastle upon Tyne, England, May 1974.

[Tou]   Touretzky, D.S., *The Mathematics of Inheritance Systems*, Morgan Kaufmann, Los Altos and Pitman, London 1986.

Reformulations
and Extensions

Propositional Logic Based on the Dynamics of Disbelief

David Pearce*and Wolfgang Rautenberg†

Abstract

Gärdenfors' (1984) epistemic modelling of intuitionistic propositional logic interprets propositions as functions from belief states to belief states. In this paper we generalise his approach by including also disbelief, or rejection, as a basic epistemic attitude. Propositions are here defined as ordered pairs of functions on belief states, representing the attitudes of acceptance and rejection, respectively. For this semantics we obtain strong completeness results wrt the constructive logics of Nelson (1949) and Almukdad and Nelson (1984).

1   Introduction

In [Grd 84,Grd 88] Peter Gärdenfors has provided an epistemic basis for logic, by interpreting propositions not as sets of possible worlds but rather as functions from epistemic states to epistemic states. This idea is appealing in that it grounds logic on a rather meagre ontology, it is simple and natural and it offers an interesting alternative to the customary view that the content of a proposition is characterised by the possible worlds in which the proposition is true. On Gärdenfors' approach, the content of a proposition A is expressed in terms of the impact it has on any given state of knowledge or belief, in other words, what change if any in one's total state of belief would result from coming to accept A as true. In this manner, if $\mathbf{K}$ is the set of states of belief (in short: *epistemic states*), then a proposition A is simply a function from $\mathbf{K}$ into $\mathbf{K}$, where for any $K \in \mathbf{K}$, $A(K)$ is the epistemic state

*Institut für Philosophie, Freie Universität Berlin, Habelschwerdter Allee 30, D-1000 Berlin 33

†Institut für Mathematik II, Freie Universität Berlin, Arnimallee 3, D-1000 Berlin 33

that results from adjusting the state of belief K so as to accommodate A.

A further feature of the epistemic approach to logic concerns the mathematical setting in which it is naturally cast. On the usual possible worlds or set-theoretic modelling of propositions, the logical connectives are characterised by standard set-theoretic operations like union, intersection, complementation, etc. The basic constructions employed by the epistemic model, instead, are those of function *composition* and (in Gärdenfors' terminology) function *equaliser* (or *pullback*). This in turn makes a difference to the type of logic that is determined in each case. The usual set-theoretic operations determine classical logic, whereas under quite natural assumptions the epistemic model leads, as Gärdenfors shows, to intuitionistic logic.

One is easily drawn to ask whether this is the only or the most natural outcome of basing logic on an epistemic model. Clearly, which logic is determined by the model will depend on a combination of two sets of assumptions, regarding: (a) the basic nature of epistemic states and operations on them, and (b) the way in which compound propositions are characterised in terms of their constituents. The aim of this note is to show how some subtle but important modifications in the assumptions made by Gärdenfors lead to what may be viewed as a more natural epistemic modelling of logic. The logic determined, moreover, is a version of constructive propositional logic. The alternative account proposed here is largely motivated by what seems to be an unnatural feature of Gärdenfors' approach to negation. On his account, the content of the proposition $\neg A$ ("not A") is not expressed in the most natural manner as the firm epistemic *rejection* of A. Rather negation is a derivative concept, defined by the identity $\neg A \equiv A \to \bot$. In other words, to explain the meaning of "not", one must first explain the implication connective and postulate the existence of a falsity proposition $\bot$ (a constant function on epistemic states). Moreover, it follows from Gärdenfors' postulates that $\neg A$ is accepted in a state K if and only if the acceptance of A would lead to a contradiction; formally: $\neg A(K) = K$ iff $A(K) = K_\bot$, where $K_\bot$ is the "absurd" or "contradictory" state whose existence must also be postulated. This seems to be a more restrictive way of handling negation than by using the notion of rejection, which is a natural epistemic attitude. Our approach below will therefore be to generalise (a) so as to obtain more natural assumptions governing (b).

2   Some Philosophical Motivation

We begin with some general remarks to motivate our treatment of the dynamics of epistemic states. In logic, semantics and epistemology one customarily focuses on representing and processing the 'positive' dimensions of knowledge, belief, information, evidence and inference. In both philosophy and in cognitive science there is a strong tendency to represent first and foremost what is known or believed to be true or probable, rather than what is known or believed to be false or improbable. Knowledge of what is not the case has a kind of secondary status as that which is definitely excluded by what we know. Disbeliefs are understood as the negations of beliefs, and 'negative' information, or evidence against a hypothesis, is treated as 'positive' information or evidence in favour of its formal negation. Logical inference may run 'downwards', deductively, or 'upwards', inductively, but the rules of logical inference preserve truth or (degrees of) acceptability, so that inference to the falsity of A is merely inference to the truth of $\neg A$.

The standard approach presents an idealised and in many respects impoverished view of knowledge and inference. It works well in certain contexts, for instance when our language consists of fully decidable predicates, when sentences are determinately true-or-false, when predicate or sentence negation is unambiguous, when knowledge and information is consistent and exhaustive. But in general these contexts are not typical of human action, cognition and problem-solving, where often 'negative' reasoning may be direct and unmediated, and information can be partial or even 'contradictory'. Nor does this approach mesh well with any epistemology that admits refutation as a direct and decisive procedure, allowing verification and corroboration to come only in degrees.

[PeWag 89] defend the view that for many purposes a more satisfactory approach to knowledge representation and processing can be achieved by explicitly modelling the 'negative' dimensions of knowledge, information and inference alongside the usual 'positive' dimensions. Whatever type of knowledge system or information structure might be involved, the essential point is that what is denied should find a place alongside what is asserted, that negative information should be distinguished from positive information, and so forth. Moreover, since positive and negative information may arise from different and independent sources, it is important in the first instance to treat them as separate items. Ultimately, the underlying language will provide for explicit links between the positive and negative items, but the type and strength of the links will depend in general on the kind of system that is being modelled.

The natural generalisation of Gärdenfors' approach to an epistemic interpretation of logic therefore amounts to regarding epistemic states as comprising information about what is disbelieved as well as what is believed; in short it amounts to constructing a belief-disbelief model of logic. Moreover, in this model the meaning of the logical connectives should be explained not merely by properties of the dynamics of belief and acceptance, but by those of disbelief and rejection, too. Before we develop the model at any length, let us briefly review Gärdenfors' method.

3 Gärdenfors' Dynamics of Belief

The central concept of Gärdenfors' approach is that of a *belief model* $< \mathbf{K}, \mathbf{P} >$ in the sequel also referred to as a Gärdenfors frame. $\mathbf{K}$ is a set of *epistemic states* and $\mathbf{P}$ is a class of functions from $\mathbf{K}$ into $\mathbf{K}$. The elements of $\mathbf{P}$ are called *propositions*, and A, B, C,... are used as variables ranging over propositions. Epistemic states are denoted by K, K',...; they are equipped with no particular structure, but can be read intuitively as representing an agent's state of belief. Thus, for any proposition A and epistemic state K, $A(K)$ is construed as the state of belief which results from expanding the state K so as firmly to accept the proposition A. Moreover, in any belief model, two propositions A and B are identified if they are identical as functions, ie. if $A(K) = B(K)$ for all states K. A proposition is already known (firmly believed or accepted) in K if $A(K) = K$, ie. if $K \in Fix_A$, where Fix_f denotes the set of fixed points of a function f, ie. $\{x : f(x) = x\}$

Though, in this fashion, propositions are functions, rather than linguistic entities, they can be endowed with a certain 'logical form' by postulating special closure properties to hold for the class $\mathbf{P}$. In the first place, it is assumed that the identity function $\top$ on $\mathbf{K}$, representing the tautologies of $< \mathbf{K}, \mathbf{P} >$, is in $\mathbf{P}$ and moreover that $\mathbf{P}$ is closed under function composition, which is interpreted as logical *conjunction*, ie. the proposition $A \wedge B$ is identified with the function composition $A \cdot B$. Though it is an epistemic idealisation, in line with ordinary logic it is assumed that the order of inputs can be ignored and iterations of the same input have no bearing on the resulting output. In other words, function composition, besides being associative, is also commutative and idempotent. Thus Gärdenfors' first four postulates can be summarised as follows:

For any belief model $< \mathbf{K}, \mathbf{P} >$,

G0 $\top \in \mathbf{P}$, where $\top$ denotes the identity function on $\mathbf{K}$.

G1 If $A, B \in \mathbf{P}$ then $A \cdot B \in \mathbf{P}$, and, for all $A, B \in \mathbf{P}$, $A \cdot A = A$ and $A \cdot B = B \cdot A$.

By **G1**, composition is a semilattice operation on $\mathbf{P}$ which hence induces a partial order $\leq$ on $\mathbf{P}$, defined by $A \leq B \Leftrightarrow B \cdot A = A$. Moreover, $A \cdot B$ is the infimum of A, B in this order.[1] It is important to observe that $A \leq B$ is equivalent to $Fix_A \subseteq Fix_B$. Indeed, if $B \cdot A = A$ then $A(K) = K$ yields $B(K) = B(A(K)) = A(K) = K$, and, similarly, the converse is derivable using **G1**. Thus, $A \leq B$ is equivalent to $A(K) = K \Rightarrow B(K) = K$, for all K, which is to mean that if K firmly accepts A then K firmly accepts B, in short, A *implies* B. From $A \leq B \Leftrightarrow Fix_A \subseteq Fix_B$ it readily follows that $Fix_{A \cdot B} = Fix_A \cap Fix_B$ and that $A = B \Leftrightarrow Fix_A = Fix_B$, so that A is completely determined by the set of states in which it is firmly accepted.

The characterisation of $A \leq B$ by $Fix_A \subseteq Fix_B$ extends in a natural way to pairs (S, A), $S \subseteq \mathbf{P}$, $A \in \mathbf{P}$, allowing one to define a consequence relation by setting $S \leq A$ iff $\bigcap_{B \in S} Fix_B \subseteq Fix_A$. The meaning of $S \leq A$ is therefore that if a state K accepts all $B \in S$, ie. $B(K) = K$, then it also accepts A, ie. $A(K) = K$. For $S = \emptyset$, we obtain $\bigcap_{B \in S} Fix_B = \mathbf{K}$, so that $\emptyset \leq A \Rightarrow A = \top$.

Gärdenfors proceeds by postulating certain classes of propositions to possess strongest or weakest elements (under his ordering), and thereby obtains a functional interpretation for the implication and disjunction connectives. The following approach, making use of the above partial ordering $\leq$, yields an equivalent but somewhat more perspicuous set of postulates.

---

[1] Gärdenfors actually considers the inverse order, in which $A \cdot B$ is the supremum.

G2 For every A and B in a belief model $< \mathbf{K}, \mathbf{P} >$, the supremum of A and B under the partial ordering $\leq$ exists in $\mathbf{P}$ and is denoted by $A \vee B$.

G3 If $A, B \in \mathbf{P}$ then of all elements $C \in \mathbf{P}$ with $A \cdot C \leq B$ there is a largest one in $\mathbf{P}$, denoted by $A \to B$. Thus, $A \cdot C \leq B \Leftrightarrow C \leq A \to B$.

By **G2**, $\leq$ is a lattice order with greatest element $\top$. By **G3**, $\leq$ is relatively pseudo- complemented and, hence in particular, a *distributive lattice* order; see, eg., [Ras 74]. We shall make essential use of this fact in §4 below.

It is readily seen that **G0-G3** are equivalent to the postulates P1-P7 of [Grd 88], minus postulate P6 requiring the existence of a constant function $\perp$ on $\mathbf{K}$. As already remarked, Gärdenfors treats negation via the notion of an *absurd* epistemic state, $K_\perp$, assumed to be present in any belief model. He requires the constant function $\perp$ to have the property $\perp(K) = K_\perp$, for all $K \in \mathbf{K}$, and on this basis identifies $\neg A$ with the proposition $A \to \perp$.

Once the general structure of belief models has been settled, one can turn to the question: Which logic do they determine? The idea here is that the logic is to be characterised by those propositional forms that are known in all epistemic states, in short, that are tautologies (ie. equal to $\top$) in any belief model. In Gärdenfors' case, a correspondence between belief models and Heyting algebras serves to show that the epistemic model determines precisely intuitionistic propositional logic.

4 Dynamic Belief Semantics

On the above approach, therefore, a proposition A is regarded as an input on epistemic states K, K', etc. whose resulting outputs $A(K)$, $A(K')$ are new epistemic states in which A is firmly accepted. We can generalise this framework by admitting also disbelief and rejection as basic epistemic attitudes. As before, a belief state K will be an idealised abstract entity, having no specific structure; but let us assume that disbeliefs as well as beliefs are to be thought of as in some sense 'embodied' in a state K. Moreover, we now require a proposition to produce two basic kinds of outputs on states, corresponding respectively to acceptance and to rejection. Thus we can regard a proposition A as an ordered pair $< a, b >$ of functions on states (equivalently denoted by $< A^+, A^- >$), where now $A^+(K)$ represents the expansion of K

in which the proposition A is accepted, and $A^-(K)$ represents the expansion of K in which A is *firmly rejected* or definitely *known to be false*. Clearly, $A = B$ iff $A^+ = B^+$ and $A^- = B^-$.

To make this idea precise, let us start with any Gärdenfors frame, ie. a belief model $< \mathbf{K}, \mathbf{P} >$ satisfying postulates G0-G3 above.

Definition 1 A *dynamic belief frame* is a pair $\mathcal{E} =< \mathbf{K}, \mathbf{Q} >$, where $\mathbf{Q} = \mathbf{P} \times \mathbf{P}$ and $< \mathbf{K}, \mathbf{P} >$ is a Gärdenfors frame. The elements $K \in \mathbf{K}$ are called *states*, the elements $A =< a, b >=< A^+, A^- >$ are called the *propositions* of $\mathcal{E}$.

In the obvious manner, a proposition A is said to be *accepted* (resp. *rejected*) in K, if $A^+(K) = K$ (resp. $A^-(K) = K$). Though in general A^+ and A^- represent epistemically different attitudes, we make no assumption to the effect that the two outputs must be distinct states. Thus, in particular, there could be a state K for which $A^+(K) = A^-(K) = K$, ie. in which A is both accepted and rejected, without us having to assume that K is an absurd state. For this reason we prefer to speak here of *belief* state and *belief* frame, reserving the name *epistemic* frame for structures containing an absurd state, $K_\perp$, and a constant function $\perp$, to be discussed in §5 below. Additionally, in the light of our general philosophical standpoint, we shall assume that acceptance and rejection are quite independent attitudes in the following sense: in dynamic belief semantics two propositions A and B in a frame $\mathcal{E}$, could have the same impact viewed in the sense of acceptance (ie. $A^+(K) = B^+(K)$ for all $K \in \mathbf{K}$), yet have different effects when being rejected (ie. for some $K \in \mathbf{K}$, $A^-(K) \neq B^-(K)$), or conversely. We can, however, express the idea that two propositions are equivalent in either the acceptance or the rejection sense. Let us say that A and B are acceptance or *a-equivalent* (in symbols $A \equiv_a B$) in a frame $< \mathbf{K}, \mathbf{Q} >$, if $A^+(K) = B^+(K)$ for all $K \in \mathbf{K}$, and rejection or *r-equivalent* (in symbols $A \equiv_r B$) if $A^-(K) = B^-(K)$, for all $K \in \mathbf{K}$. Clearly, $A = B$ iff $A \equiv_a B$ and $A \equiv_r B$.

Since a dynamic belief frame $\mathcal{E} =< \mathbf{K}, \mathbf{Q} >$ is obtained directly from a Gärdenfors frame satisfying G0-G3, the closure properties on $\mathbf{Q}$ are already fixed by those postulates. In particular, for any $a, b \in \mathbf{P}$, $a \vee b$ and $a \to b$ are defined as above, as is the partial ordering $\leq$. As far as the semantics is concerned, however, we shall need to extend the operations already defined on $\mathbf{P}$ so as to obtain appropriate operations on function pairs, ie. on elements of $\mathbf{Q}$.

In the first place, in contrast to Gärdenfors, we want to give a direct interpretation to negation in terms of the epistemic attitude of rejection. Let $A = < A^+, A^- >$ be an arbitrary proposition. Now let us suppose that the firm and unconditional rejection of A, represented by the function A^-, corresponds to the firm acceptance of the proposition *not* A (to be denoted by $\sim A$) in other words $(\sim A)^+ = A^-$. Similarly, firmly to reject $\sim A$ as false should amount to the same as accepting A as true, in short $(\sim A)^- = A^+$. So if $A = < a, b >$, we put $\sim A = < b, a >$, and, in this manner, acceptance and rejection can be taken on an equal footing as basic epistemic attitudes, thereby establishing a simple relation between a proposition and its negation. As a consequence of this definition it is immediate that $\sim\sim A = A$ and that for any A and B, $\sim A$ and $\sim B$ are a- (resp. r-) equivalent iff A and B are r- (resp. a-) equivalent.

Following Gärdenfors, we shall assume that the result of accepting the conjunction $A \wedge B$ of two propositions is the same as the result of accepting one of them, say B, and later accepting the other, A; in short, we define $(A \wedge B)^+ := A^+ \cdot B^+$. Similarly, for disjunction and implication we want to have $(A \vee B)^+ := A^+ \vee B^+$ and $(A \to B)^+ := A^+ \to B^+$.

It remains to consider which operations should correspond to the rejection of propositions. Here too we can to a large extent follow the intuitions underlying Gärdenfors' semantics. Take, for instance, his postulate governing disjunction. It is motivated by the idea that if one has accepted $A \vee B$ and later comes to accept A, the "net effect is the same as merely addding A to what one accepts (and analogously for B)" [Grd 88, p. 138]. Assuming $A \vee B$ to be the strongest proposition with this property, then, under our partial ordering $\leq$, $A \vee B$ is identified with the supremum of A and B. However, once rejection is admitted as a fundamental input on epistemic states, a completely analogous consideration applies to conjunction-rejection. Suppose one has rejected the conjunction $A \wedge B$ of two propositions. If one later comes to reject one of them, say A, the net effect should be the same as merely rejecting A. So, by analogy with the earlier argument, we should set $(A \wedge B)^- = A^- \vee B^-$.

The introduction of rejection as an epistemic input enables us to exploit a further duality between conjunction and disjunction. This time it concerns disjunction-rejection. Suppose that one first rejects the proposition B and later comes to reject also the proposition A. The net effect is to have rejected the proposition $A \vee B$, since the information that both A is false and B is false should amount to the same as the information that the disjunction $A \vee B$ is false. This motivates the definition $(A \vee B)^- = A^- \cdot B^-$.

Let us turn lastly to the interpretation of logical implications of the form $A \rightarrow B$. Gärdenfors' treatment of implication is motivated by a familiar intuition about what it means to *accept* the proposition $A \rightarrow B$. The acceptance of 'if A, then B' does not commit one, either now or later, to the acceptance of either A or of B. However, if one were later to accept A as certain, the prior acceptance of $A \rightarrow B$ would then commit one to the acceptance of B. Postulate **G3** provides a precise rendering of this idea. However, we are still faced with the task of explaining the meaning of $A \rightarrow B$ under the epistemic attitude of *rejection*, that is, to interpret $(A \rightarrow B)^-$. Notice that if rejection of a proposition in a belief state were the same as the non-acceptance of that proposition, we could simply 'negate' the above criterion of acceptance. That says that $A \rightarrow B$ is not accepted in a belief state if we could conceivably reach a state in which the acceptance of A does not commit us to the acceptance of B. Rejection, however, is a far stronger attitude than mere non-acceptance. Firmly to reject $A \rightarrow B$ as false means that we exclude, now and forever, that A could in the above sense imply B, ie. that the acceptance of A could ever commit us to the acceptance of B. Yet to be absolutely certain of this, it seems we must already be in the state of taking a definite stance on A and on B, namely that we have in fact already accepted A and rejected B. In other words, if rejection is interpreted in the strongest possible terms as something like 'direct and undefeasible refutation', then $A \rightarrow B$ will be rejected just in case A is already accepted and B rejected. If for example one of the propositions, say B, were merely undecided in a state K where the other proposition A is accepted, we would scarcely have grounds for the firm rejection of $A \rightarrow B$ in K, since we could not exclude that in all future states B might be found to be true. Combining these considerations leads us to define $(A \rightarrow B)^- = A^+ \cdot B^-$.

Summarising the above remarks, we arrive at

Definition 2 Let $\mathcal{E} =< \mathbf{K}, \mathbf{Q} >$ be a dynamic belief frame. We define the operations $\sim$, $\wedge$, $\vee$, $\rightarrow$ on $\mathbf{Q}$ as follows:

$$\sim< a, a' >:=< a', a >,$$

$$< a, a' > \wedge < b, b' >:=< a \cdot b, a' \vee b' >,$$

$$< a, a' > \vee < b, b' >:=< a \vee b, a' \cdot b' >,$$

$$< a, a' >\rightarrow< b, b' >:=< a \rightarrow b, a \cdot b' > .$$

It is easily verified that the following equations hold in any dynamic belief frame:

$$\sim\sim A = A; \sim (A \wedge B) =\sim A \vee \sim B; \sim (A \vee B) =\sim A \wedge \sim B; \sim (A \rightarrow B) = A \wedge \sim B.$$

We now turn to the question of which logic is determined by dynamic belief frames. Let $\mathcal{L} = \mathcal{L}(\sim, \wedge, \vee, \rightarrow)$ be the propositional language based on a (not necessarily countable) set V of variables, denoted by $p, q, \ldots$. Let $\alpha, \beta, \ldots$ denote formulas of $\mathcal{L}$. An assignment $v : V \rightarrow \mathbf{Q}$, where $v(p) =< v^+p, v^-p >$, extends to a valuation $v : \mathcal{L} \rightarrow \mathbf{Q}$ such that v is a homomorphism; ie. $v\sim\alpha =\sim v\alpha$, $v(\alpha \wedge \beta) = v\alpha \wedge v\beta$, etc. Thus, $v\alpha =< v^+\alpha, v^-\alpha >$, with $v^+\alpha$, $v^-\alpha \in \mathbf{P}$.

Let $\Phi \subseteq \mathcal{L}$, $\alpha \in \mathcal{L}$, and $\mathcal{E} =< \mathbf{K}, \mathbf{Q} >$ be a dynamic belief frame.

Definition 3 $\Phi \models_\mathcal{E} \alpha$ iff for all $K \in \mathbf{K}$ and all valuations v
$(\forall \phi \in \Phi)(K \in Fix_{v^+\phi}) \Rightarrow K \in Fix_{v^+\alpha}$. Moreover, $\Phi \models \alpha$ iff $\Phi \models_\mathcal{E} \alpha$ for all $\mathcal{E}$.

In particular, we obtain $\models \alpha$ (ie. $\emptyset \models \alpha$, or α is a tautology) iff $v^+\alpha = \top$ for all $\mathcal{E}$ and valuations $v : \mathcal{L} \rightarrow \mathbf{Q}$. Note also that $\alpha \models \beta$ (ie. $\{\alpha\} \models \beta$) iff $v^+\alpha \leq v^+\beta$ for all v and $\mathcal{E}$. More generally,

$$\{\alpha_1, \ldots, \alpha_n\} \models \beta \text{ iff } \{v^+\alpha_1, \ldots, v^+\alpha_n\} \leq v^+\beta,$$

for all valuations v.

Lemma 1 $\Phi \models \alpha$, $\alpha \rightarrow \beta$ *imply* $\Phi \models \beta$

Lemma 2 *Let Φ be finite. Then $\Phi, \alpha \models \beta$ implies $\Phi \models \alpha \to \beta$.*

We omit the simple proofs. As regards Lemma 2 (the Deduction Theorem), there is no direct argument confirming the claim for arbitrary Φ, though it is in fact a consequence of Theorem 1 below.

Lemma 3 $\models \phi$, *where ϕ is any of the following formulas (N1)-(N12):*
N1. $\alpha \to (\beta \to \alpha)$
N2. $(\alpha \to (\beta \to \gamma)) \to ((\alpha \to \beta) \to (\alpha \to \gamma))$
N3. $\alpha \to (\beta \to \alpha \wedge \beta)$
N4. $(\alpha \wedge \beta) \to \alpha$
N5. $(\alpha \wedge \beta) \to \beta$
N6. $\alpha \to (\alpha \vee \beta)$
N7. $\beta \to (\alpha \vee \beta)$
N8. $(\alpha \to \gamma) \to ((\beta \to \gamma) \to (\alpha \vee \beta \to \gamma))$
N9. $\sim(\alpha \to \beta) \leftrightarrow \alpha \wedge \sim\beta$
N10. $\sim(\alpha \wedge \beta) \leftrightarrow \sim\alpha \vee \sim\beta$
N11. $\sim(\alpha \vee \beta) \leftrightarrow \sim\alpha \wedge \sim\beta$
N12. $\alpha \leftrightarrow \sim\sim\alpha$.

Proof. $(N1)$ follows from the fact that $\{\alpha, \beta\} \models \alpha$, applying Lemma 2 twice. Similarly one proves $(N2)$. For $(N3) - (N5)$ one applies Lemmas 1 and 2. $(N6)$ and $(N7)$ follow immediately from $a \leq a \vee b$, and $b \leq a \vee b$. For $(N8)$ observe first that

$$(*) \ \{d, a\} \leq c, \ \{d, b\} \leq c \Rightarrow \{d, a \vee b\} \leq c$$

Indeed, the assumptions are equivalent to $d \cdot a \leq c, d \cdot b \leq c$; hence $d \cdot (a \vee b) = d \cdot a \vee d \cdot b \leq c$. Thus, $\{d, a \vee b\} \leq c$. Now, since $\{a \to c, b \to c, a\} \leq c$ and $\{a \to c, b \to c, b\} \leq c$, by $(*)$ and Lemma 1 we can infer $\{a \to c, b \to c, a \vee b\} \leq c$; whence $\{\alpha \to \gamma, \beta \to \gamma, \alpha \vee \beta\} \models \gamma$. This establishes $(N8)$, applying Lemma 1 three times. For$(N9)$ observe that $v^+ \sim (\alpha \to \beta) = v^-(\alpha \to \beta) = v^+\alpha \cdot v^-\beta = v^+\alpha \cdot v^+\sim\beta = v^+(\alpha \wedge \sim\beta)$. Similarly one can verify $(N10) - (N12)$. $\square$

With modus ponens as the only inference rule, $(N1) - (N12)$ provide an axiomatisation of the logic N^- of [AlNel 84]. This is a weak version of Nelson's constructive logic, or logic with constructible falsity [Nel 49]. Apropos of N^-, Almukdad and Nelson remark that it "is a constructive logic which may be applied to inconsistent subject matter without necessarily generating a trivial theory" [AlNel 84, p. 231]. In fact, in N^- there is no axiom to ensure that an arbitrary formula β is derivable from a contradiction $\alpha \wedge \sim\alpha$.

Let $\vdash$ denote the derivability relation for N^-; more precisely, we write $\Phi \vdash \alpha$ if α is derivable from $\Phi \cup \{N^-\}$ by means of modus ponens. Notice that by $(N1), (N2)$ the deduction theorem holds for $\vdash$, ie.

$$\Phi; \alpha \vdash \beta \;\Rightarrow\; \Phi \vdash \alpha \to \beta.$$

To establish that N^- is complete wrt dynamic belief semantics we shall define a canonical belief model. Consider the collection $\mathbf{K_c}$ of all deductively closed sets of $\mathcal{L}$-formulas, ie.

$$\mathbf{K_c} = \{\Delta \subseteq \mathcal{L} \mid \Delta = \Delta^\vdash\},$$

where $\Delta^\vdash := \{\phi \in \mathcal{L} \mid \Delta \vdash \phi\}$. Let $\bar{\alpha} : \mathbf{K_c} \to \mathbf{K_c}$ be defined by $\bar{\alpha}(\Delta) = (\Delta \cup \{\alpha\})^\vdash$. Let $\mathbf{P_c} = \{\bar{\alpha} \mid \alpha \in \mathcal{L}\}$, then the following holds:

Lemma 4 $< \mathbf{K_c}, \mathbf{P_c} >$ is a Gärdenfors frame.

Proof (Sketch) First notice that $\mathbf{P_c}$ is closed under composition in virtue of

$$\bar{\alpha} \cdot \bar{\beta}(\Delta) = (\Delta \cup \{\alpha, \beta\})^\vdash = (\Delta \cup \{\alpha \wedge \beta\})^\vdash = \overline{\alpha \wedge \beta}(\Delta).$$

Since eg. $\overline{p \to p} = \top$, **G0** is satisfied, as is **G1**. Moreover, we have

$$\bar{\alpha} \le \bar{\beta} \Leftrightarrow \alpha \vdash \beta \tag{1}$$

in particular, $\bar{\alpha} = \bar{\beta} \Leftrightarrow \vdash \alpha \leftrightarrow \beta$. Now, (1) implies that $\overline{\alpha \vee \beta}$ is the supremum of $\bar{\alpha}, \bar{\beta} \in \mathbf{P_c}$ under $\le$ and that $\overline{\alpha \to \beta}$ is the largest $\bar{\gamma}$ with $\bar{\alpha} \cdot \bar{\gamma} \le \bar{\beta}$. In other words,

$$\bar{\alpha} \cdot \bar{\beta} = \overline{\alpha \wedge \beta}, \; \bar{\alpha} \vee \bar{\beta} = \overline{\alpha \vee \beta}, \; \bar{\alpha} \to \bar{\beta} = \overline{\alpha \to \beta}. \tag{2}$$

This establishes that $< \mathbf{K_c}, \mathbf{P_c} >$ is a Gärdenfors frame satisfying (G0)-(G3).
$\square$

Now put $\mathbf{Q_c} = \mathbf{P_c} \times \mathbf{P_c}$. $< \mathbf{K_c}, \mathbf{Q_c} >$ will be called the *canonical frame*. Let $w : \mathcal{L} \to \mathbf{Q_c}$ be defined by $w(p) = < \bar{p}, \overline{\sim p} >$. We call w the *canonical valuation* and $\mathcal{C} = < \mathbf{K_c}, \mathbf{Q_c}, w >$ the *canonical model*.

Lemma 5 *(Canonical model lemma)* $w(\alpha) = < \bar{\alpha}, \overline{\sim\alpha} >$ for all $\alpha \in \mathcal{L}$.

Proof By induction on the complexity of α. Observe in particular $(N9) -$ $(N12)$.

Theorem 1 *(Completeness)* $\Phi \vdash \alpha \Leftrightarrow \Phi \models \alpha$.

Proof Soundness, ie. $\Phi \vdash \alpha \Rightarrow \Phi \models \alpha$, is readily shown by induction on the length of a proof of α from Φ. For the induction start, consider Lemma 3. To prove the converse, suppose that $\Phi \nvdash \alpha$. Let $\mathcal{C}$ be the canonical model, with $\Delta = \Phi^{\vdash}$. If $\phi \in \Delta$ then $w^+\phi = \overline{\phi}$ and so $\overline{\phi}(\Delta) = \Delta$. Since $\alpha \notin \Delta$ we have $w^+\alpha(\Delta) = \overline{\alpha}(\Delta) \neq \Delta$, hence $\Phi \nvDash \alpha$. $\square$

In particular, $\vdash \alpha \Leftrightarrow \models \alpha$, ie. N^- characterises the tautologies of dynamic belief semantics. It is interesting to note that the completeness theorem entails the non-trivial fact that $\models$ is finitary and, as remarked earlier, satisfies the deduction theorem. The above proof also yields an alternative method of showing the completeness of Gärdenfors' semantics. In fact, we can in this manner obtain a strong completeness result for Gärdenfors' semantics, without any appeal to Heyting algebras. Moreover, in neither case does one need recourse to Zorn's Lemma, even for uncountable $\mathcal{L}$, due to the 'functional' character of the semantics.

5 Dynamic Epistemic Semantics

It is easy to see why an axiom of the form:

$$N13. \quad \alpha \wedge \sim\alpha \rightarrow \beta$$

will not, without further assumptions, be valid in every dynamic belief model, since we have not postulated any special properties to govern the case that a proposition is both accepted and rejected in some state K. In short, we have not specified further the nature of inputs of the form $A^+ \cdot A^-(K)$.

We can, however, borrow one additional concept from Gärdenfors, namely that of a falsity function $\perp$ and an *absurd* state $K_\perp$.

Definition 4 A *dynamic epistemic frame* is a pair $< \mathbf{K}, \mathbf{Q} >$ such that $< \mathbf{K}, \mathbf{P} >$ is a Gärdenfors frame containing the constant function $\perp$ and a state $K_\perp$ such that $\perp(K) = K_\perp$ for all $K \in \mathbf{K}$, and $\mathbf{Q} = \{< a, b > \in \mathbf{P} \times \mathbf{P} \mid Fix_{a \cdot b} = \{K_\perp\}\}$.

Intuitively, the latter means that a proposition can be simultaneously accepted and rejected in the same state K only if K is the absurd state $K_\perp$, remembering that $Fix_{a \cdot b} = Fix_a \cap Fix_b$. The main property we need to show is that the notion of dynamic epistemic frame is indeed well-formed:

Lemma 6 *Let* $< \mathbf{K}, \mathbf{Q} >$ *be a dynamic epistemic frame. Then* $\mathbf{Q}$ *is closed under the operations* $\sim$, $\wedge$, $\vee$, $\rightarrow$.

Proof Clearly, $Fix_{a \cdot b} = \{K_\perp\}$ iff $a \cdot b \leq c$ for all $c \in \mathbf{P}$. Now, if $a \cdot a' \leq c$ for all c, then also $a' \cdot a \leq c$, since $a \cdot a' = a' \cdot a$. Thus, $\mathbf{Q}$ is closed under $\sim$. Now, suppose $a \cdot a' \leq c$, $b \cdot b' \leq c$. Then

$$(a \cdot b)(a' \vee b') = a \cdot b \cdot a' \vee a \cdot b \cdot b' \leq a \cdot a' \vee b \cdot b' \leq c \vee c = c.$$

This shows that $\mathbf{Q}$ is closed under $\wedge$. Likewise, the fact that $\leq$ is a distributive lattice order implies that $\mathbf{Q}$ is closed under $\vee$. To establish closure under $\rightarrow$ we have to show

$$a \cdot a', \ b \cdot b' \leq c \Rightarrow (a \rightarrow b) \cdot a \cdot b' \leq c.$$

In fact, it suffices to assume $b \cdot b' \leq c$ for all c. Then, since $(a \rightarrow b) \cdot a \leq b$, we obtain by monotonicity $(a \rightarrow b) \cdot a \cdot b' \leq b \cdot b' \leq c$. □

Henceforth, let $\models$ be defined as in §4, but restricted to dynamic epistemic frames. Note that $\models \alpha \wedge \sim\alpha \rightarrow \beta$, because $v^+(\alpha \wedge \sim\alpha) = v^+\alpha \cdot v^-\alpha \leq b$ for all $b \in \mathbf{P}$. Let $\vdash$ now be the derivability relation for Nelson's constructive logic N, ie. the logic based on N^- plus axiom $(N13)$. We have

Theorem 2 *(Completeness)* $\Phi \vdash \alpha \Leftrightarrow \Phi \models \alpha$.

The method of proof is exactly as before. The canonical model $\mathcal{C}$ is defined as before, with $K_\perp = \mathcal{L}$ and $\mathbf{Q_c} = \{< a, b > \in \mathbf{P_c} \times \mathbf{P_c} \mid Fix_{a \cdot b} = \{K_\perp\}\}$. In particular, $\perp := \overline{p \wedge \sim p}$ belongs to $\mathbf{P_c}$ and $w : p \rightarrow < \overline{p}, \overline{\sim p} >$ is indeed a valuation into $\mathbf{Q_c}$ because

$$\overline{p} \cdot \overline{\sim p}(\Delta) = (\Delta \cup \{p, \sim p\})^\vdash = \mathcal{L}$$

for all $\Delta \in \mathbf{K}$. Hence, if $\overline{p} \cdot \overline{\sim p}(\Delta) = \Delta$, then $\Delta = \mathcal{L} = K_\perp$.

6 Concluding Remarks

By generalising Gärdenfors' concept of belief model so as to include disbeliefs as well as beliefs, we have shown how acceptance and rejection, as
natural epistemic attitudes, can be placed on an equal footing to yield an
alternative basis for logic. In this respect, it seems that **G0-G3**, together
with the operations given in Definition 2, form a rather natural 'minimal'
set of assumptions, which, moreover, tollerate 'conflicting' epistemic attitudes towards propositions, without leading to epistemic 'absurdity'. The logic
thereby obtained is N^- which looks to be a promising formal foundation for
the processing of incomplete and possibly inconsistent information; it should
have useful applications in semantics, in cognitive science and in artificial intelligence, especially in the areas of knowledge-based systems, belief revision
and logic programming.[2]. It would be an interesting exercise to try to model
weaker implications and other forms of conditionals by suitably modifying
the above assumptions, but it remains to be seen to what extent this can
be achieved without departing from the natural 'functional' perspective on
propositions inherent in the present approach.

The additional assumptions imposed in §5 lead to a system that might be
said to reflect closer the epistemic attitudes of an 'ideally rational' agent,
or alternatively, to reflect better the notion of knowledge state rather than
belief state. It should come as no suprise that the logic thereby generated is the constructive logic N. Nelson's (strong) negation has a clearly
constructive character that is missing from ordinary intuitionistic negation.
Just as Gärdenfors' approach, based on the epistemic attitude of acceptance,
provides a foundation for intuitionistic logic, it is a natural consequence of
extending his method to handle the attitude of rejection (or falsity as an
independent concept) that the 'logic of constructible falsity' is the resulting
outcome. At the same time, in a dynamic epistemic frame an additional
intuitionistic negation can, if required, easily be defined, as in the case of
Nelson's system N.

Finally, it should be noted that the present framework is restricted to that
of monotonic reasoning. In particular, negatively signed functions $A^-(K)$
represent the rejection of a proposition A in a state K, rather than the

---

[2]For some applications of systems of strong negation to natural language semantics and
to logic programming, see [Ro 90,PeWag 89]

'contraction' of A out of K or the 'revision' of K wrt A. The operations of contraction and revision, whose study forms the backbone of [Grd 88], belong to a broader framework whose logic is in general non-monotonic. To extend the present approach to this more general area of belief revision one would have to endow states with a suitable internal structure to represent beliefs and disbeliefs alike. One can then formulate postulates for disbelief revision that parallel those for belief revision. This, however, will be the topic of a future paper.

7 Acknowledgements

The first-named author would like to thank the participants of the Konstanz workshop on The Logic of Theory Change for helpful comments. Suggestions and advice from Marcus Kracht and Sten Lindström led to considerable improvements in a preliminary version of the paper.

References

[Grd 84]   P. Gärdenfors, The Dynamics of Belief as a Basis for Logic, *Brit. J. Phil. Sci.* **35** (1984): 1-10.

[Grd 88]   P. Gärdenfors, *Knowledge in Flux*, MIT Press, Cambridge and London, 1988.

[PeWag 89] D. Pearce & G. Wagner, Reasoning with Negative Information, I: Strong Negation in Logic Programs, *Berichte der Gruppe Logik, Wissenstheorie und Information* 4/1989, Freie Universität Berlin.

[Ro 90]   A. Rossdeutscher, Ereignisfilter und -ideale. Zur algebraischen und topologischen Repräsentation der semantischen Leistung der negation und aspektueller Partikeln wie *schon* und *noch*, *Berichte der Gruppe Logik, Wissenstheorie und Information*, 1990, Freie Universität Berlin (to appear).

[Nel 49]   D. Nelson, Constructible Falsity, *JSL* **14** (1949): 16-26.

[AlNel 84] A. Almukdad & D. Nelson, Constructible Falsity and Inexact Predicates, *JSL* **49** (1984): 231-233.

[Ras 74]   H. Rasiowa, *An Algebraic Approach to Non-Classical Logics*, PWN and North-Holland, Warsaw and Amsterdam, 1974.

On the Modal Logic
of Theory Change

André Fuhrmann*

1 Background

Carlos Alchourron, Peter Gärdenfors and David Makinson (henceforth AGM) have studied in a number of papers the formal aspects of certain changes of theories.[1] The units of change, theories, are thought of as sets of sentences (in a language containing the usual connectives $\neg, \wedge, \vee, \rightarrow$ and a falsum constant $\perp$) closed under truth-functional consequence, Cn. The objects under investigation, change operations, are mappings from theories and sentences to theories. I shall use $T, T', \ldots$ as variables ranging over theories and $A, B, C, \ldots$ will stand variably for sentences of the formal language under consideration.

The simplest kind of change operation is an *expansion*. The expansion of a theory T by a sentence A, $T + A$, is the closure of $T \cup \{A\}$ under logical consequence:

$$T + A := Cn(T \cup \{A\}).$$

The *contraction* of a theory T should be a theory $T - A$ which does not contain A and is otherwise as much like T as is compatible with the purpose of a contraction. Clearly, contractions are not as straightforwardly definable as expansions. AGM offer two approaches to the problem of characterizing contraction operations: a direct approach, proceeding by explicit

*Department of Philosophy, University of Konstanz, P.O.B. 5560, 7750 Konstanz, W.Germany; pifuhrma@dknkurz1.BITNET.
[1]See e.g. [1], [14] or [9].

constructions, and an indirect approach in terms of a set of postulates every (rational) contraction operation ought to satisfy. The following postulates have been proposed.

Basic postulates for contraction

(-1) $T - A = Cn(T - A)$ (closure)

(-2) $T - A \subseteq T$ (inclusion)

(-3) $A \notin T \Rightarrow T \subseteq T - A$ (vacuity)

(-4) $A \notin Cn(\emptyset) \Rightarrow A \notin T - A$ (success)

(-5) $T \subseteq T - A + A$ (recovery)

(-6) $Cn(A) = Cn(B) \Rightarrow T - A = T - B$ (extensionality)

Supplementary postulates for contraction

(-7) $(T - A) \cap (T - B) \subseteq T - A \wedge B$ (intersection)

(-8) $A \notin T - A \wedge B \Rightarrow T - A \wedge B \subseteq T - A$ (conjunction)

Somewhat intermediate between expansion and contraction is the operation of *revision*. The revision of a theory T by a sentence A, $T * A$, should be the result of adding A to T while removing all sentences from T which are inconsistent with A.

Basic postulates for revision

(*1) $T * A = Cn(T * A)$ (closure)

(*2) $A \in T * A$ (success)

(*3) $T * A \subseteq T + A$ (inclusion)

(*4) $\neg A \notin T \Rightarrow T + A \subseteq T * A$ (vacuity)

(*5) $\bot \in T * A \Rightarrow \neg A \in Cn(\emptyset)$ (consistency)

(*6) $Cn(A) = Cn(B) \Rightarrow T * A = T * B$ (extensionality)

Supplementary postulates for revision

(*7) $T * A \wedge B \subseteq T * A + B$ (conjunctive inclusion)

(*8) $\neg B \notin T * A \Rightarrow T * A + B \subseteq T * A \wedge B$ (conjunctive vacuity)

Isaac Levi has suggested that revisions should be defined in terms of contractions and expansions: to revise T by A, one firsts retracts $\neg A$ from T and then expands by A. The idea may be formally expressed by the equation

$$T * A = T - \neg A + A \qquad \text{(Levi identity)}$$

Conversely, one may start with a theory of revisions and introduce contractions as follows:

$$T - A = T * \neg A \cap T \qquad \text{(Harper identity)}$$

The idea here is that one may retract A from T by first revising to include $\neg A$ — so A, being inconsistent with $\neg A$ will have been removed — and then intersecting with the original theory T, thus deleting all sentences that have been added to T in the process of revising by $\neg A$. Given the Levi identity and the Harper identity, it can be shown that the two sets of postulates support each other.

Theorem 1 (Gärdenfors/Makinson) *If a revision function $*$ is defined by the Levi identity from a contraction function satisfying the postulates (-1) to (-4) and (-6) to (-8), then the function $*$ satisfies (*1) to (*8).*

*If a contraction function $-$ is defined by the Harper identity from a revision function satisfying the postulates (*1) to (*8), then the function $-$ satisfies (-1) to (-8).*

Note first that recovery is not needed to verify the revision postulates for the first part of the theorem. Second, Despite the pleasant appearance of duality between contraction and revision postulates, the two sets of postulates do not correspond to each other in a one-to-one fashion.

Obviously, the logic of theory change is a theory about certain kinds of *processes*: tansitions from one theory to another, changed, one. Dynamic logic provides a general framework for reasoning about processes. In dynamic logic one considers programs, or, more generally, actions, $\alpha_0, \alpha_1, ...$, and introduces program-indexed modal operators $\square_\alpha$ for each program $\alpha \in \{\alpha_0, \alpha_1, ...\}$. Instead of $\square_\alpha$ one usually writes $[\alpha]$. For sentences of the form

$$[\alpha]A$$

read "after each computation of the program α (on some precondition) the postcondition A obtains."

It seems natural to explore the prospects for a special kind of dynamic logic where the programs stand for contraction or revision programs $-A_0, -A_1$ $..., *A_0, *A_1, ...$ for each sentence A_i of the language. I call such a dynamic logic an *update logic*.[2]

2 Update logic

The language of update logic extends a basic sentential language with connectives $\bot, \neg, \wedge, \vee$ and $\rightarrow$ by a unary connective $\square$ and a binary connective $[-]$, the *contraction operator*. Instead of the "Polish" $[-]AB$ I shall write

$$[-A]B$$

— read: B holds after contracting by A. The set of atomic formulae will be denoted by 'ATM' and 'FML' will stand for the set of all formulae.

An *expansion operator* (or "strict test") $[+]$ may be introduced by definition:

$$[+A]B := \square(A \rightarrow B) \qquad\qquad \text{D+}$$

It is easy to verify that if $\square$ behaves as in a normal modal logic — as will be stipulated in a moment — , then expansion programs have all the properties that characterise simple additions to a theory. In particular, expansions are monotonic in the following sense:

$$\square B \rightarrow [+A]B.$$

---

[2]The ideas and results presented here have first appeared in the author's unpublished PhD thesis [4]; the research for the relevant parts of the thesis has been carried out in early 1987. Independent research along similar lines is reported in Rao and Foo [3] and van Benthem [18].

As usual, the "necessity" operators $\Box$ and $[-]$ may be supplemented by corresponding "possibility" operators:

$$\Diamond A := \neg\Box\neg A \qquad\qquad\qquad\qquad\qquad D\Diamond$$

$$\langle -A \rangle B := \neg[-A]\neg B \qquad\qquad\qquad\qquad\qquad D\langle\rangle$$

Remark The language of update logic is of a simpler type than the language of propositional dynamic logic. In particular operations on programs, like sequencing (;), choice ($\sqcup$) or iteration (*) are missing here. Such operations could be introduced, though without much conceptual gain. Their introduction would require a considerably more complicated definition of the set of formulae and, in the presence of the star operation, a complete reworking of the completeness argument below. $\lhd$

For an axiomatisation of update logic we start with a basic system **UK** axiomatised as follows.

All classical tautologies

$$[-A](B \to C) \to ([-A]B \to [-A]C) \quad \text{(normality)} \qquad\qquad K$$

$$\Box A \leftrightarrow [-\top]A \qquad\qquad\qquad\qquad\qquad T$$

$$\frac{B}{[-A]B} \quad \text{(necessitation)} \qquad\qquad\qquad\qquad RN$$

$$\frac{A \leftrightarrow B}{[-A]C \to [-B]C} \quad \text{(extensionality)} \qquad\qquad\qquad C6$$

$$\frac{A,\ A \to B}{B} \quad \text{(modus ponens)} \qquad\qquad\qquad MP$$

Without proof I record two unsurprising facts about **UK**:

$$\frac{B \to C}{[-A]B \to [-A]C} \qquad\qquad\qquad\qquad\qquad RM$$

$$[-A]B \wedge [-A]C \leftrightarrow [-A](B \wedge C) \qquad\qquad\qquad\qquad C/M$$

We now extend **UK** by axioms and rules concerning the specific behaviour of update programs. The following idempotency laws are introduced for the sake of simplifying derivations.

$\Box[-A]B \to [-A]B$ (left reduction)   CL$_r$

$[-A]\Box B \leftrightarrow [-A]B$ (right identity)   CR

Remark Left expansion i.e.

$$[-A]B \to \Box[-A]B,$$

has some unwelcome consequences. A principle that quickly spells havoc in the AGM theory (and which is unattractive on its own) is monotonicity for contractions:

$$T \subseteq T' \Rightarrow T - A \subseteq T' - A \tag{1}$$

((1) is a crucial stepping stone towards trivialising systems of theory change; see e.g. [10].) A special case of (1) is

$$T - A \subseteq T + B - A \tag{2}$$

(Indeed, if theories are closed under a compact consequence operation, then (1) and (2) are equivalent.) But given left expansion we can derive an update formula expressing (2) (cf. the translation scheme below), viz.

$$[-A]C \to [+B][-A]C,$$

as follows:

1. $[-A]C \to .B \to [-A]C$ **K**
2. $\Box[-A]C \to \Box(B \to [-A]C)$ 1, RM
3. $[-A]C \to \Box[-A]C$ left expansion
4. $[-A]C \to [+B][-A]C$ 2, 3, D+.

Left expansion expresses a "reflective closure" requirement on theories: if B holds in a theory after contracting by A, then a sentence expressing that fact holds in the theory. It is well known that such reflective closure conditions issue in a budget of paradoxes when combined with plausible conditions on theory change.[3]◁

The next group of postulates is a translation of the AGM principles for contraction into the language of update logic according to the following rules.

a. Let $\star$ stand for either $+$ or $-$.

$$\text{Translate } A \in T \star A_1 \cdots \star A_n \text{ as } \begin{cases} [\star A_1] \cdots [\star A_n]A, & \text{if } n \geq 1; \\ \Box A & \text{otherwise.} \end{cases}$$

b. English 'not, 'and', 'or' and 'if ... then ...' are rendered by their Boolean cousins $\neg$, $\wedge$, $\vee$ and $\rightarrow$.

The labels of the translations bear the numbers of the corresponding AGM postulates. There is no schema C1 since the postulates of **UK** give sufficient expression to the requirement that the output of an update program should be deductively closed.

$[-A]B \rightarrow \Box B$ (inclusion)   C2

$\neg \Box A \wedge \Box B \rightarrow [-A]B$ (vacuity)   C3

$[-A]A \rightarrow [-B]A$ (success)   C4

$\Box B \rightarrow [-A](A \rightarrow B)$ (recovery)   C5

Postulate (-4) resists translation into the language of update logic. But (C4) appears to come close enough to what (-4) is intended to require: A survives contraction by A only if A survives *any* contraction of the original theory; it seems reasonable to expect that only logical truths possess such an immunity to retraction. Finally, the two supplementary postulates:

$[-A]C \wedge [-B]C \rightarrow [-A \wedge B]C$ (intersection)   C7

$\neg[-A \wedge B]A \wedge [-A \wedge B]C \rightarrow [-A]C$ (conjunction)   C8

I shall refer to the system **UK**+{C2 – C5} as '**UL**'.

---

[3]See e.g. Fuhrmann [5].

3 Revisions and conditionals

Suppose now that we had taken the revision operator, [∗], as primitive (together with a box, □, and an adequate set of truth-functional connectives) and consider the update logic **UL*** defined as follows.

All classical tautologies

$$[*A](B \to C) \to ([*A]B \to [*A]C) \qquad\qquad \text{K*}$$

$$\Box(B \to C) \to (\Box B \to \Box C) \qquad\qquad \text{K}\Box$$

$$\frac{B}{[*A]B} \qquad\qquad \text{RN*}$$

$$\frac{B}{\Box B} \qquad\qquad \text{RN}\Box$$

$$\frac{A \leftrightarrow B}{[*A]C \leftrightarrow [*B]C} \qquad\qquad \text{R6}$$

$$\frac{A,\ A \to B}{B} \qquad\qquad \text{MP}$$

$$\Box[*A]B \to [*A]B \qquad\qquad \text{RL}_r$$

$$[*A]\Box B \leftrightarrow [*A]B \qquad\qquad \text{RR}$$

$$[*A]A \qquad\qquad \text{R2}$$

$$[*A]B \to [+A]B \qquad\qquad \text{R3}$$

$$\Diamond A \wedge [+A]B \to [*A]B \qquad\qquad \text{R4}$$

$$[*A]\bot \to [*B]\neg A \qquad\qquad \text{R5}$$

The reader will no doubt have recognized the schemas R2 to R6 as translations of the corresponding AGM postulates for revisions. Similarly, the schemas

$$[*A \wedge B]C \rightarrow [*A](B \rightarrow C) \hspace{4cm} \text{R7}$$

$$\langle *A\rangle B \wedge [*A](B \rightarrow C) \rightarrow [*A \wedge B]C \hspace{3cm} \text{R8}$$

are translations of AGM's supplementary revision postulates. The next four theorems show that, in a certain sense, it does not matter which update operator is chosen as primitive: **UL** and **UL*** are equivalent *modulo* the two identities

$$[*A]B \leftrightarrow [-\neg A][+A]B \hspace{4cm} \text{LI}$$

$$[-A]B \leftrightarrow \Box B \wedge [*\neg A]B. \hspace{4cm} \text{HI}$$

In view of CR, LI may be simplified to

$$[*A]B \leftrightarrow [-\neg A](A \rightarrow B).$$

In the derivations below LI will be used in this simplified form (that is, in tacit conjunction with CR). I shall extend the use of 'LI' and 'HI' to also denote the definitions that result from the object language identities LI and HI upon replacing the double-arrow $\leftrightarrow$ by the identity sign $:=$.

Theorem 2 *Let* $\mathbf{UL}^{LI}$ *be the extension of* **UL** *by the schema LI, taken as a definition. Then*

$$\mathbf{UL}^* + \{HI\} \subseteq \mathbf{UL}^{LI}.$$

Proof. K* and RN* follow from K and RN (together with **K**-principles).
K$\Box$ and RN$\Box$ are — by way of T — special cases of K and RN.
RL and RR follow immediately from CL and CR respectively.
For R2 one needs to show that $[-\neg A](A \rightarrow A)$ which may be obtained using RN.
Applying LI to R3 reveals an instance of C2: $[-\neg A](A \rightarrow B) \rightarrow \Box(A \rightarrow B)$.
Similarly, R4, i.e. $\neg\Box\neg A \wedge \Box(A \rightarrow B) \rightarrow [-\neg A](A \rightarrow B)$ is an instance of C3.
For R5, $[-\neg A](A \rightarrow \bot) \rightarrow [-\neg B](B \rightarrow \neg A)$, use C4 and RM.
R6 follows from C6.
Ad HI: $[-A]B \leftrightarrow \Box B \wedge [-A](\neg A \rightarrow B)$.

1.	$[-A]B$	hypothesis
2.	$\Box B$	1, C2
3.	$[-A]B \rightarrow [-A](A \vee B)$	**K**, RM
4.	$[-A](\neg A \rightarrow B)$	1, 3, **K**
5.	$[-A]B \rightarrow \Box B \wedge [-A](\neg A \rightarrow B)$	$1 \rightarrow 2,\ 1 \rightarrow 4$

6.	$\Box B$	hypothesis
7.	$[-A](A \rightarrow B)$	6, C5, CR
8.	$[-A](\neg A \rightarrow B)$	hypothesis
9.	$[-A](\neg A \vee A \rightarrow B)$	7, 8, **K**
10.	$[-A]B$	9, **K**
11.	$\Box B \wedge [-A](\neg A \rightarrow B) \rightarrow [-A]B$	$6 \wedge 8 \rightarrow 10$
12.	$[-A]B \leftrightarrow \Box B \wedge [-A](\neg A \rightarrow B)$	5, 11 — as required. $\Box$

Theorem 3 $\mathbf{UL}^* + \{\mathrm{HI}, \mathrm{R7}, \mathrm{R8}\} \subseteq \mathbf{UL}^{LI} + \{\mathrm{C7}, \mathrm{C8}\}.$

Proof. Ad R7: We need to show that

$$[-\neg(A \wedge B)](A \wedge B \rightarrow C) \rightarrow [-\neg A](A \wedge B \rightarrow C).$$

1.	$[-\neg(A \wedge B)](A \wedge B \rightarrow C)$	hypothesis
2.	$\Box(A \wedge B \rightarrow C)$	1, C2
3.	$\Box(A \wedge B \rightarrow C) \rightarrow [-A \rightarrow B](A \rightarrow B \rightarrow .A \wedge B \rightarrow C)$	C5, CR
4.	$\Box(A \wedge B \rightarrow C) \rightarrow [-A \rightarrow B](A \wedge B \rightarrow C)$	3, **K**
5.	$[-A \rightarrow B](A \wedge B \rightarrow C)$	2, 4
6.	$[-(A \rightarrow B) \wedge \neg(A \wedge B)](A \wedge B \rightarrow C)$	1, 5, C7
7.	$\neg A \leftrightarrow (A \rightarrow B) \wedge \neg(A \wedge B)$	**K**
8.	$[-\neg A](A \wedge B \rightarrow C)$	6, 7, C6
		— as require

Ad R8: We need to show that

$$\neg[-\neg A](A \rightarrow \neg B) \wedge [-\neg A](A \wedge B \rightarrow C) \rightarrow [-\neg(A \wedge B)](A \wedge B \rightarrow C).$$

1.	$\neg[-\neg A](A \rightarrow \neg B)$	hypothesis
2.	$[-\neg A](A \wedge B \rightarrow C)$	hypothesis

3. $\neg A \leftrightarrow (A \to \neg B) \wedge \neg A$ **K**

4. $\neg[-(A \to \neg B) \wedge \neg A](A \to \neg B)$ 1, 3, C6

5. $[-(A \to \neg B) \wedge \neg A](A \wedge B \to C) \to$
       $\to [-A \to \neg B](A \wedge B \to C)$ 4, C8

6. $[-A \to \neg B](A \wedge B \to C)$ 3, C6

7. $[-\neg(A \wedge B)](A \wedge B \to C)$ 6, **K**, C6 — as required. $\square$

Theorem 4 *Let* $\mathbf{UL}^{*HI}$ *be the extension of* $\mathbf{UL}^*$ *by the schema HI, taken as a definition. Then*

$$\mathbf{UL} + \{\mathrm{LI}\} \subseteq \mathbf{UL}^{*HI}.$$

Proof. For K we combine the K$\square$-instance

$$\square(B \to C) \to (\square B \to \square C)$$

with the K*-instance

$$[*\neg A](B \to C) \to ([*\neg A]B \to [*\neg A]C).$$

Applying classical principles we obtain from the two

$$\square(B \to C) \wedge [*\neg A](B \to C) \to (\square B \wedge [*\neg A]B \to \square C \wedge [*\neg A]C))$$

whence, using HI,

$$[-A](B \to C) \to ([-A]B \to [-A]C).$$

For RN we need to show that $B/\square B$ and that $B/[*\neg A]B$. The former is given by RN, the latter by RN*.
For T observe first that one direction, $[-\top]A \to \square A$, is an instance of C2 (which will be derived next). (Thus our axiomatisation of **UL** is slightly redundant.) For the other direction we need to show that

$$\square A \to \square A \wedge [*\bot]A.$$

But $[*\bot]A$ holds unconditionally, for from $\bot \to A$ we get $[*\bot]\bot \to [*\bot]A$ by RM* (K* and RN*) and the antecedent is an instance of R2.
For C2 one needs to show that $\square B \wedge [*\neg A]B \to \square B$ which is trivial.
Ad C3: We need to show that

$$\neg\square A \wedge \square B \to \square B \wedge [*\neg A]B.$$

1. $\neg\Box A \wedge \Box B$ hypothesis
2. $\neg\Box A \wedge \Box(\neg A \to B)$ 1, K
3. $\neg\Box A \wedge \Box(\neg A \to B) \to [*\neg A]B$ R4
4. $[*\neg A]B$ 2, 3
5. $\Box B \wedge [*\neg A]B$ 1, 4 — as required.

Ad C4: It will suffice to show that

$$[*\neg A]A \to [*\neg B]A.$$

1. $[*\neg A]A$ hypothesis
2. $[*\neg A]\neg A$ R2
3. $[*\neg A]\bot$ 1, 2, K
4. $[*\neg B]A$ 3, R5, K — as required.

Ad C5: We need to show that

$$\Box B \to \Box(A \to B) \wedge [*\neg A](A \to B).$$

1. $\Box B$ hypothesis
2. $\Box(A \to B)$ 1, K
3. $[*\neg A](\neg A \vee B)$ R2, K
4. $\Box(A \to B) \wedge [*\neg A](A \to B)$ 2, 3 — as required.

Ad C6: It suffices to show that

$$\frac{A \leftrightarrow B}{[*\neg A]C \leftrightarrow [*\neg B]C}$$

which follows immediately from R6.

Ad LI: We need to show that

$$[*A]B \leftrightarrow \Box(A \to B) \wedge [*\neg\neg A](A \to B).$$

Left to right:

1. $[*A]B$ hypothesis
2. $\Box(A \to B)$ 1, R3
3. $[*A](A \to B)$ 1, K
4. $\Box(A \to B) \wedge [*\neg\neg A](A \to B)$ 2, 3, K, R6.

Right to left:

1. $[*\neg\neg A](A \to B)$ hypothesis
2. $[*A]A \to [*A]B$ 1, **K**, K
3. $[*A]B$ R2, 2. □

Theorem 5 $\mathbf{UL} + \{\mathrm{LI}, \mathrm{C7}, \mathrm{C8}\} \subseteq \mathbf{UL}^{*HI} + \{\mathrm{R7}, \mathrm{R8}\}.$

Proof. Ad C7: It will suffice to show that

$$[*\neg A]C \wedge [*\neg B]C \to [*\neg(A \vee B)]C.$$

1. $[*\neg A]C$ hypothesis
2. $[*\neg B]C$ hypothesis
3. $\neg A \leftrightarrow (\neg A \vee \neg B) \wedge \neg A$ **K**
4. $\neg B \leftrightarrow (\neg A \vee \neg B) \wedge \neg B$ **K**
5. $[*\neg A \vee \neg B](\neg A \to C$ 1, 3, R7
6. $[*\neg A \vee \neg B](\neg B \to C$ 2, 4, R7
7. $[*\neg(A \wedge B)](\neg(A \wedge B) \to C)$ 5, 6, **K**
8. $[*\neg(A \wedge B)]\neg(A \wedge B) \to [*\neg(A \wedge B)]C$ 7, **K**
9. $[*\neg(A \wedge B)]C$ 8, R2 — as required.

Ad C8:

1. $\neg[-A \wedge B]A$ hypothesis
2. $[-A \wedge B]C$ hypothesis
3. $\neg[-A \wedge B](\neg(A \wedge B) \to A)$ 1, **K**
4. $\neg[*\neg(A \wedge B)]A$ 3, LI
5. $[*\neg(A \wedge B)](\neg A \to C) \to [*\neg(A \wedge B) \wedge \neg A]C$ 4, R8
6. $[*\neg(A \wedge B)](\neg A \to C) \to [*\neg A]C$ 5, **K**, R6
7. $[*\neg(A \wedge B)](\neg A \to C) \to [-A](\neg A \to C)$ 6, LI, **K**, R6
8. $[-A \wedge B](\neg A \to C) \to [*\neg(A \wedge B)](\neg A \to C)$ **K**, LI
9. $[-A \wedge B](\neg A \to C) \to [-A](\neg A \to C)$ 7, 8
10. $\Box C$ 2, C2
11. $[-A](A \to C)$ 10, C5, CR
12. $[-A \wedge B](\neg A \to C) \to [-A](\neg A \vee A \to C)$ 9, 11, **K**
13. $[-A \wedge B]C \to [-A]C$ 12, **K**
14. $[-A]C$ 2, 13. □

If reference to theories is omitted by deleting all boxes, $\Box$, in the theorems of **UL*+R7, R8**, one obtains Lewis' "official" logic of *counterfactual conditionals*. This system **VC** is axiomatised in Lewis [13, p. 132] as follows (using Segerbergs simple and suggestive $\beth$ instead of Lewis' box-arrow):

0. $A > B := \neg(A \beth \neg B)$

1. All classical tautologies

2. $$\frac{B_1 \wedge \cdots \wedge B_n \to B}{(A \beth B_1) \wedge \cdots \wedge (A \beth B_n) \to A \beth B}(n \geq 1)$$

3. $$\frac{A \leftrightarrow B}{A \beth C \to B \beth C}$$

4. $$\frac{A , A \to B}{B}$$

5. $A \beth A$

6. $\neg A \beth A \to B \beth A$

7. $A \wedge B \beth C \to A \beth (B \to C)$

8. $A > B \to (A \beth (B \to C) \to A \wedge B \beth C)$

9. $A \beth B \to (A \to B)$

10. $A \wedge B \to A \beth B$

Theorem 6 *The logic* **VC** *is the $\Box$-free fragment of* **UL*+R7, R8.**

Proof. Consider the $\Box$-free fragment of **UL*+R7, R8**, writing $A \beth B$ instead of $[*A]B$:

All classical tautologies

K. $A \beth (B \to C) \to (A \beth B \to A \beth C)$

RN. $B / A \beth B$

R6. $A \leftrightarrow B \;/\; A \sqsupset C \rightarrow B \sqsupset C$

MP A , $A \rightarrow B \;/\; B$

R2. $A \sqsupset A$

R3. $A \sqsupset B \rightarrow (A \rightarrow B)$

R4. $A \wedge (A \rightarrow B) \rightarrow A \sqsupset B$

R7. $A \wedge B \sqsupset C \rightarrow A \sqsupset (B \rightarrow C)$

R8. $(A > B) \wedge (A \sqsupset (B \rightarrow C)) \rightarrow A \wedge B \sqsupset C$

For the inclusion **VC⊆UL***+R7, R8(without □) it suffices to observe the following facts: K follows from 2, RN follows from 2 and 6, R4 is equivalent to 10, and R5 follows from 6 and 2. For the other direction of inclusion we note that 2 may be derived using RN and K and that R2 and R5 give 6. □

4 Semantics

A *(general) frame* is a structure

$$\langle W, P, C \rangle$$

with W a non-empty set of points (or worlds), $P \subseteq 2^W$ (a set of propositions) and C a family of binary relations on W, one for each proposition in P, i.e.

$$C = \{C_X \subseteq W^2 : X \in P\}.$$

We require that the set of propositions satisfies the following conditions:

(i) $W \in P$,

(ii) if $X \in P$, then $W \setminus X \in P$,

(iii) if $X, Y \in P$, then $X \cup Y \in P$,

(iv) if $X, Y \in P$, then $\{v \in W : \forall w (C_X v w \Rightarrow w \in Y)\} \in P$.

It follows from (i) and (ii) that $\emptyset \in P$ and from (i) and (iii) that if $X, Y \in P$, then $X \cap Y \in P$.

A *valuation* V on a frame $\mathcal{F}$ maps atomic formulae into propositions, i.e. members of P. We extend V to a forcing relation $\models$ between points in W and formulae. Read $(\mathcal{M}, a) \models B$ as "The formula B holds at the point a in a model $\mathcal{M} = \langle F, V \rangle$". Reference to models will usually be suppressed (thus writing $a \models B$ when it does not matter which particular model is under consideration). I use vertical double bars to denote the proposition associated with a formula:

$$\|A\| := \{x \in W : x \models A\}.$$

For atomic formulae we put

$$\|A\| = V(A).$$

For Boolean compounds the definition of $\models$ continues in the usual way, i.e.

$$\|\top\| = W, \quad \|\neg A\| = W \setminus \|A\|, \quad \|A \vee B\| = \|A\| \cup \|B\|.$$

For modal formulae we define:

$$a \models [-A]B \text{ iff } \forall x : C_{\|A\|}ax \Rightarrow x \models B,$$

$$a \models \Box A \text{ iff } \forall x : C_W ax \Rightarrow x \models A.$$

A formula A is *true in a model* $\mathcal{M}$ iff A holds at all points in $\mathcal{M}$. Notation: $\mathcal{M} \models A$.

A is *true on a frame* $\mathcal{F}$ iff A is true in all models $\mathcal{M} = \langle F, V \rangle$ on $\mathcal{F}$. Notation: $\mathcal{F} \models A$.

A is true in a class $\mathcal{X}$ of frames (A is *valid* (in $\mathcal{X}$)) iff A is true on each frame in $\mathcal{X}$. Notation: $\mathcal{X} \models A$.

Remark In a model a theory $T = \{A_1, \ldots, A_n\}$ may be represented by the intersection of all propositions corresponding to members of T^4, i.e.

$$\|T\| = \|A_1\| \cap \cdots \cap \|A_n\|.$$

---

[4]Note that $\|T\|$ may not always be in the set of propositions, P, because P is not generally closed under infinite intersections.

A contraction operation on theories thus represented would be a world-relativised mapping

$$c(\|T\|, \|A\|, a) \mapsto \|T'\| \tag{3}$$

$(a \in W; \|T\|, \|T'\| \subseteq W; \|A\| \in P)$. When contextually fixing the input theory $\|T\|$ (say, by bringing $\|T\|$ into an index position to c and then suppress that index), we may rewrite (3) as

$$c(X, a) \mapsto Y$$

$(a \in W; X \in P; Y \subseteq W)$. Thus the function c may be thought of as taking a proposition at a world to deliver a contracted theory. In defining frames and models we have preferred a relational over a functional notation:

$$C_X a x \quad \text{iff} \quad x \in c(X, a).$$

Despite these motivating remarks, a relation C_X $(X \in P)$ is a rather abstract tool, not biased towards any particular interpretation. So one may wish to look for more natural representations of C_X.

One such representation is contained in van Benthem [18]. A "flow of information" is a structure $\langle I, \sqsubseteq \rangle$, where I is a set of information states and $\sqsubseteq$ a partial order on I. To contract a state $a \in I$ by some proposition $\|A\| \subseteq I$ one would go back along the $\sqsubseteq$-paths from a to the first state of information where A fails (i.e. which is not contained in $\|A\|$). Van Benthem's truth condition for a "downdating"-operator $[-A]$ is: $a \models [-A]B$ iff

$$\forall y : (y \sqsubseteq a \text{ and } y \not\models A \text{ and } \neg \exists z : y \sqsubset z \sqsubseteq x \text{ and } z \not\models A) \Rightarrow y \models B.$$

Thus, for each $X \subseteq I$, we may put

$$C_X := \{\langle x, y \rangle \in I^2 : y \sqsubseteq x \text{ and } y \notin X \text{ and } \neg \exists z : y \sqsubset z \sqsubseteq x \text{ and } z \notin X\}.$$

Note first that in a flow of information structure theories are represented by points in the domain, not by sets of points in the domain. Thus, for a realistic representation of theories, models on such structures ought to be partial. Second, on pain of triviality, $\square$ can no longer be identified with $[-\top]$ but needs independent modelling (if it is wanted). $\triangleleft$

Theorem 7 (Soundness and completeness) *Let $\mathcal{K}$ be the class of all frames. Then $\mathcal{K} \models A$ iff A is a theorem of* **UK**, *for all formulae A.*

Proof. Soundness is an easy exercise. For the completeness part of the proposition we define a canonical model for an update logic L, extending **UK**, as follows:

$$\mathcal{M}_L = \langle W_L, P_L, C_L, V_L \rangle$$

where W_L is the set of all maximally L-consistent set of formulae. Let $|A| := \{x \in W_L : A \in x\}$.

(P) $P_L := \{|A| : A \in \text{FML}\}$;

(C) C_L is a set of relations $C_{|A|} \subseteq W_L{}^2$ (subscript L to $C_{|A|}$ omitted!), for each $|A| \in P_L$ such that
$C_{|A|}ab$ iff $[-A]B \in a \Rightarrow B \in b$, for every $B \in \text{FML}$;

(V) $V_L(A) := |A|$, for every $A \in \text{ATM}$.

These definitions do not unduly depend on the choice of formulae representing truth-sets. For, if $A \dashv\vdash B$, then $|A| = |B|$ and (by C6) $[-A]C \in a$ iff $[-B]C \in a$ whence $C_{|A|} = C_{|B|}$.

Conditions (i) to (iii) on frames are clearly satisfied. It remains to show that canonical models satisfy condition (iv), i.e.

$$\text{if } |A|, |B| \in P_L, \text{ then } \{v \in W_L : \forall w(C_{|A|}vw \Rightarrow w \in |B|)\} \in P_L.$$

It will suffice to prove for an arbitrary $a \in W_L$ that

$$[-A]B \in a \text{ iff } \forall x : C_{|A|}ax \Rightarrow B \in x \tag{4}$$

The left-to-right direction is trivial. So assume the RHS. Then B is a member of every maximally L-consistent extension of $X = \{C : [-A]C \in a\}$, whence $X \vdash B$, i.e. there are $C_1 \ldots C_n \in X$ such that

$$C_1 \wedge \cdots \wedge C_n \to B \in L.$$

But $[-A]C_i \in a$ $(1 \leq i \leq n)$. So, using the schema C,

$$[-A](C_1 \wedge \ldots \wedge C_n) \in a.$$

Thus, by closure of a under RM, $[-A]B \in a$ — as required.

A simple induction on the complexity of formulae shows that in $\mathcal{M}_L$

$$a \models A \text{ iff } A \in a.$$

The base is given by definition (V). In the inductive step for $[-]$ we need to show that

$$[-A]B \in a \text{ iff } \forall x : C_{\|A\|}ax \Rightarrow x \models B.$$

By the inductive hypothesis the RHS reduces to

$$\forall x : C_{|A|}ax \Rightarrow B \in x$$

which by (4) is equivalent to $[-A]B \in a$.

Now pick any non-theorem A of $\mathbf{L}$ and consider any $\mathbf{L}$-consistent set $X \subseteq \text{FML}$ such that $A \notin X$. By Lindenbaum's lemma X may be extended to a set $x \in W_L$ with $A \notin x$; thus $\mathcal{M}_L \not\models A$ whence A is not valid in $\mathcal{K}$. $\square$

Semantic representations of extensions of **UK** may be obtained by imposing further conditions on frames. For each postulates CX considered above, we can find a corresponding condition (cx) on frames. Proofs of these correspondences, listed below, proceed by showing that CX can be verified in an arbitrary model on any frame satisfying (cx) (soundness) and by showing that a canonical model for a logic including CX satisfies the condition (cx) (completeness); the details are routine and, hence, omitted. Two abbreviations will help stating the modelling conditions more succinctly:

$$C_{XY}ab := \exists x : C_X ax \text{ and } C_Y xb \qquad C_X(a) := \{b : C_X ab\}.$$

(cl$_r$) $C_X \subseteq C_{WX}$

(cr) $C_{XW} = C_X$

(c2) $C_W \subseteq C_X$

(c3) $C_W(a) \not\subseteq X \Rightarrow C_X \subseteq C_W$

(c4) $C_X(a) \subseteq X \Rightarrow X = W$

(c5) $C_X(a) \cap X \neq \emptyset \Rightarrow C_X \subseteq C_W$

(c7) $C_{X \cap Y} \Rightarrow C_X \cup C_Y$

(c8) $C_{X \cap Y}(a) \not\subseteq X \Rightarrow C_X \subseteq C_{X \cap Y}$

5 Concluding remarks

Decidability Update logics can be shown *decidable* using filtrations. Ordinary filtrations suffice for logics not including C8. In the presence of C8 a generalised filtration technique, due to Strevens, will work. Details are readily extracted from [17] where Strevens filtrations are introduced in the context of models for conditional logics.

From conditionals to updates In section three we have used an update logic to reconstrue Lewis' preferred logic of conditionals. (This result echoes, in a fully formalised setting, an earlier result of Gärdenfors [8].) But one may also take the reverse route, taking principles for conditionals and reinterpret them as principles about updating. As an example consider the distribution of disjuncts over conditionals:

$$A \vee B \sqsupset C \to (A \sqsupset C) \wedge (B \sqsupset C) \qquad\qquad \text{SDA}$$

This principle is not usually included in logics of conditionals but it has been defended by Nute [16]. There is a route from SDA to a rather unattractive contraction principle characterising full meet contractions,[5]

$$T - A \wedge B = T - A \cap T - B \qquad\qquad \text{(-I)}$$

Rewriting the instance

$$\neg A \vee \neg B \sqsupset C \to (\neg A \sqsupset C) \wedge (\neg B \sqsupset C)$$

of SDA as

$$[*\neg A \vee \neg B]C \to [*\neg A]C \wedge [*\neg B]C$$

we may expand both sides of the arrow by $\Box C$:

$$\Box C \wedge [*\neg A \vee \neg B]C \to \Box C \wedge ([*\neg A]C \wedge [*\neg B]C),$$

---

[5]Cf. [9, Sec. 4.3].

whence, by HI, we obtain

$$[-A \wedge B]C \rightarrow [-A]C \wedge [-B]C$$

which translates to

$$T - A \wedge B \subseteq T - A \cap T - B.$$

(The converse direction of inclusion is given by (-7).)

Alternative modellings As remarked earlier, the semantics in terms of indexed relations are general but, perhaps, less natural than other modellings of updating. Various alternatives to the semantics presented here remain to be explored. Prominent among such alternatives — and closely related to the already mentioned proposal of van Benthem — would be semantics in terms of systems of spheres (see [13] and [11]).

Extensions The language of update logic may be extended to include other relevant operators. One may, for example, generalise on the existing operators by considering contractions not by single sentences but by sets of sentences. Such *multiple contractions* are investigated (in the AGM framework) in [4], [12], and [15] (see also [7]).

Foo and Rao [3] include in their logic of belief revision operators expressing that some belief is justified in view of certain other beliefs. This enriched language allows some interesting observations concerning the differences between foundationalist and coherentist approaches to theory change. In a similar way the — at heart foundationalist — theory of base contractions offered in [6] may be recast in a suitably chosen modal language.

References

[1] Alchourron, C., P. Gärdenfors, D. Makinson, On the logic of theory change: Partial meet functions for contraction and revision, *Journal of Symbolic Logic*, 50 (1985), pp. 510 – 530.

[2] Chellas, B.F., Basic conditional logic, *Journal of Philosophical Logic*, 4 (1975), pp. 133 – 153.

[3] Foo, N.Y., A. Rao, Formal theories of belief revision

[4] Fuhrmann, A., *Relevant Logics, Modal Logics, and Theory Change*, PhD thesis, Australian National University, Canberra, 1988.

[5] Fuhrmann, A., Reflective modalities and theory change, *Synthese*, 81 (1989), pp. 115 – 134.

[6] Fuhrmann, A., Theory contraction through base contraction, *The Journal of Philosophical Logic*, forthcoming.

[7] Fuhrmann, A., R. Niederée and H. Rott, On multiple contractions, forthcoming.

[8] Gärdenfors, P., Conditionals and changes of belief, *Acta Philosophica Fennica*, 30 (1978).

[9] Gärdenfors, P., *Knowledge in Flux. Modeling the Dynamics of Epistemic States*, Cambridge, Mass. (MIT Press), 1988.

[10] Gärdenfors, P., Variations on the Ramsey test: More triviality results, *Studia Logica*, 46, pp. 319 – 325.

[11] Grove, A., Two modellings for theory change, *Journal of Philosophical Logic*, 17 (1988).

[12] Hansson, S.O., New operators for theory change, *Theoria*, forthcoming.

[13] Lewis, D., *Counterfactuals*, Oxford (Blackwell), 1973/1986 (2nd ed.).

[14] Makinson, D., How to give it up: A survey of some formal aspects of the logic of theory change, *Synthese*, 62 (1985), pp. 347 – 363.

[15] Niederée, R., Multiple contractions: a further case against Gärdenfors' principle of recovery, this volume.

[16] Nute, D., *Topics in Conditional Logic*, Dordrecht (Reidel), 1980.

[17] Segerberg, K., Notes on conditional logic, *Studia Logica*, 48 (1989), pp. 157 – 168.

[18] van Benthem, J., Semantic parallels in natural language and computation, in M. Garrido, ed., *Logic Colloquium Granada 1988*, Amsterdam (North-Holland), 1989.

Discourse Representation Theory and Belief Dynamics

Nicholas Asher

Center for Cognitive Science, University of Texas
and IMS, Stuttgart

1. Introduction

Discourse Representation Theory, DRT, is a theory of discourse semantics that analyzes the meaning of texts in terms of each constituent sentence's contribution to an overall discourse meaning. Following the views of Lewis (1969) and Stalnaker (1976), DRT paints an essentially dynamic picture of discourse meaning. But it has developed so far only a strictly cumulative view of discourse meaning. DRT has taken a similar, dynamic view of belief and other attitudes, analyzing them in terms of their contribution to an agent's overall cognitive state. But the DRT approach has also given only a strictly cumulative view of how newly acquired attitudes affect the overall cognitive state. Indeed, there are interesting connections and parallels to be drawn between the processes of attitude formation and discourse interpretation.[1] But the simple, cumulative view of discourse interpretation and attitudes must change if DRT is to do justice to the facts of textual interpretation, as well as belief dynamics. Interpretation is not always cumulative-- at least not for all discourses, and the dynamics of the adjustment of an agent's attitudes in the face of newly acknowledged facts is certainly not always cumulative. The aim of this paper is to explore the possibility of constructing a theory of discourse interpretation and belief formation that incorporates an account of belief revision within the DRT framework.

In exploring a DR-theoretic view of belief revision, one has to come to grips with the work of Gardenfors and also Alchourron and Makinson on belief revision. These philosophical logicians have set the currently dominant paradigm for thinking about belief revision, as the essays in this volume will show. DRT and Gardenfors's dynamic view of belief have much in common. Gardenfors's (1988) theory, which I shall take as representative of this paradigm, construes propositions as functions from belief states to belief states. DRT's view of propositions as a function from contexts to contexts is strikingly similar. Moreover, if one takes these contexts to result from an agent's processing of information, then the two views

---

[1] I have explored this to some extent in Asher (1989).

have very much the same epistemic theory of propositions. DRT's theory of attitudes is a special instance of the more general view: in the theory of belief the relevant contexts are cognitive states. Another point of similarity is that both Gardenfors and DRT theorists take cognitively relevant information to have a logical structure, to which cognitive states are sensitive. It is interesting that the leading ideas of the two theories are so strikingly similar, though the motivations of the two theories are quite different. Gardenfors's views arise from considerations about Bayesian revision, whereas DRT is motivated by problems in the semantics of discourse.

The two views differ considerably, however, on what structure cognitively relevant information and what structure cognitive states have. Gardenfors assumes only a propositional structure for cognitively relevant information, and he considers belief states to be closed under classical logic. His theory is equivalent to one in which mental states are modelled as sets of possible worlds.[1] DRT's view of belief states and the procedure of updating them subscribes to: a particular view of the structure of information, partiality and non-monotonicity. The last two concepts are familiar to those working in semantics and philosophical logic. By the first, I mean that cognitively relevant information is structured in a way such that: (i) predicates and arguments are distinguished, (ii) cognitively relevant information has a logical complexity of at least that of first order logic, (iii) predicates in different attitudinal states may share arguments without being about any particular real individual in the world. The second code word concerns the underlying logic of belief states and their updates: this logic can be seen as partial in an essential way. Further, any realistic updating procedure, I will argue, must also incorporate a non-monotonic element.

These key concepts, a particular view of the structure of information, partiality and non-monotonicity, all have important consequences for belief revision. Gardenfors's theory already offers postulates of belief revision that are interesting to consider from within DRT. The emphasis on partiality and non-monotonicity in the DRT framework suggests an approach to revision that will differ from that provided by the Gardenfors axioms. Once one takes the underlying logic of belief revision to be non-monotonic (or a particular kind of non-monotonic logic), then one must reject some elements of the Gardenfors approach.

---

[1]See for example Spohn (1988).

2. DRT, Verbal Interpretation and Belief Formation

To motivate the use of the DRT framework, I shall devote much of this paper to giving a DR-theoretic perspective on cumulative interpretation and the expansion of one's beliefs with newly acquired beliefs. Although cumulative, these tasks within DRT are already non-trivial. I will first investigate the logic of this view of updating and then explore its consequences for revision.

To make this more precise, let me introduce some DRT terminology. Let me begin with a representation of the information that an agent might glean from a simple text. Such representations in DRT are known as *Discourse Representation Structures* or *DRSs*. These structures may be derived by a mechanical construction procedure from discourses, but that is not my concern here. I'll just suppose that this is done by magic. DRT also offers a theory of how these simple information state DRSs may interact with a background representation of an agent's total cognitive state, the result being first a full interpretation of a text and second, if the information state is accepted, a new belief of the agent. I'll sketch some of this story shortly.[1]

A DRS is a pair of sets, one containing a set of discourse referents and the other a set of conditions-- recursively defined property ascriptions to discourse referents. A DRS gets classical truth conditions when we define what is called in the DRT literature *a proper embedding* of a DRS in a standard Tarskian model. Very roughly, f is a proper embedding of a DRS $K = <U, Con>$ in a model $M = <D, [\![ ]\!]>$, written $[K]_{f, M}$, iff f is a function from the discourse referents in U into D such that all the conditions in Con are satisfied. The notion of embedding encourages us to think of DRSs as models themselves-- partial models of the information content of a discourse. Unlike the traditional notion of embedding in model-theory, however, research in DRT has led to view the DRS partial models as having a rather different kind of structure from the standard Tarskian models, as I will explain below.

The definition of a proper embedding has been extended to intensional models. In intensional models, embedding functions are defined relative to indices like worlds and times. I will assume that something like this is in place. (For details see Asher (1986, 1987, 1989)). The DRT approach to semantics is dynamic in that it construes the content of a sentence as a function augmenting or otherwise altering the context of interpretation. The interpretation of a discourse proceeds by interpreting each sentence S_{n+1} relative to the context created by the interpretation of the previous n sentences and then updating the context with the content of S_{n+1}.

The DR-theoretic perspective on semantics leads naturally to a dynamic view of belief. The basic connection between the analysis of belief and the analysis of discourse is that the

---

[1]For details see Asher (1989).

structures that DRT posits to represent the information content of discourse serve also to specify the structure of cognitively relevant information to which agents may bear attitudes like belief, fear and so on. The theory of belief has focussed to date on the dynamic updating of structures representing agent's cognitive states with information derived from verbal information. The theory posits that information states are represented as DRSs and that these structures may be used to construct more complex structures that partially specify an agent's total cognitive state. In this paper I shall deal only with belief states, and I will represent them using only DRSs.[1]

Embedding functions can be used to determine a set of worlds in which all of the agent's beliefs are true. Thus, DRT is compatible with the more traditional view of belief states that models these as sets of possible worlds. But DRT also refines the possible worlds view by using DRSs to describe a complex, internal structure of belief states. This structure affects the way belief states may be updated with new information. The assumptions DRT makes concerning the structure of belief states complicates considerably the view of belief updating.[2] One wants to know if these complications are worth it. What does a DR-theoretic view of information and belief dynamics add over and above the view of states as sets of possible worlds (or as supervaluations across total theories)? I will try to provide some answers to this question here.

Part I: Updating

The type of belief updating Gardenfors calls *expansions* would appear to have a very simple analogue in DRT: just add the new information state to the old structure and return a new DDRS representation of a the new, updated cognitive state. As soon as we make some suppositions about the structure of cognitive states, however, things are no longer so simple. DRT has concentrated on three problems relevant to belief updating: 1) the problem of determining the reference of anaphoric pronouns, 3) temporal anaphora, 3) the problem of definite reference anaphora. I also mention a fourth, because it is so important in real belief revisions: the updating of relations between concepts. I turn to describing each one of these tasks very briefly.

---

[1]For details concerning the other structures called *delineated DRSs*, see Asher (1986, 1987, 1989).
[2]One problem with DRT here is that we have many levels on which to define update functions. DRS structures vs. contents vs. embedding functions. If we think of DRSs as information states, we may think of them according to a 4 valued semantics as has become fashionable with information states. But that concerns the propositional part, and those questions seem separate from the other questions of quantifier constructions, which is what DRT started out with.

1. Pronominal Anaphora

Anaphoric pronouns pose a problem for verbal interpretation, for a connection must be made between the pronoun and some other noun phrase in the discourse in order to assign the sentence in which the pronoun occurs a well-defined semantic interpretation. Consider the following sentence.

(1) She is very smart.

How would we update our belief state with this information? We would have to know to whom the *she* referred in the context, and in the case of anaphoric pronouns that requires a representation of the prior discourse or conversation. On the approach DRT takes to pronominal interpretation, DRSs serve to represent the context of interpretation, and the pronoun introduces a discourse referent that must be appropriately related to some other discourse referent already introduced into the context. The appropriate relation for simple pronominal anaphora is identity.[1] While every noun phrase introduces a discourse referent, not every discourse referent can be anaphorically related to one introduced by a pronoun. Chomsky and his followers have much studied syntactic constraints on anaphora, such as those having to do with the phenomenon of "disjoint reference," but the semantics and the logical structure of information also play an important role in restricting the possibilities for anaphora. Spelling out how these constraints work within an account of getting from a natural language discourse to an information structure has been one of DRT's principal contributions to the analysis of anaphora.

For instance, the structure of the DRS constructed from (2) and its embedding conditions forbids an anaphoric link between *a donkey* and the second occurrence of *it* in (2), while it is permitted in the first:

(2) Many men who own a donkey beat it. It is unhappy.

Imagine that an agent incorporates the information content of the first sentence of (2) into his beliefs. He then will use this previously incorporated information to interpret the second statement and in particular to try to find the antecedent of the pronoun. Suppose now that the agent wishes incorporate the second sentence of (2). To get a determinate proposition, the agent will again have to find an appropriate antecedent for the pronoun within the context of interpretation. When faced with the second sentence, he must decide how to interpret the pronoun before he can decide what to incorporate.

The semantic constraints on anaphora, the principal of which is called *accessibility*, forbid the intended anaphoric link between *a donkey* and the second occurrence of *it*. These constraints exploit the configuration of the DRS-- in particular, the positions of discourse

---

[1]But other expressions with an anaphoric element like *another* may bear different relations to antecedents. *Another N* should introduce a constraint that the discourse referent it introduces be disjoint from a discourse referent introduced by the appropriate antecedent NP.

referents in the structure of the DRS.[1] The way these constraints are realized technically in the DRS construction procedure is by first constructing a DRS without solving the equations that are introduced by the anaphoric NPs and then using the DRS structure to inform their solution. Let us assume that the DRS for the first sentence of (2) has already been completed. It is of the form,

(K2.1)

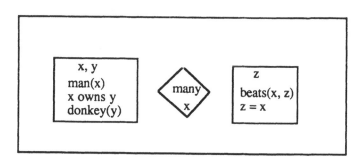

The form of this DRS patterns after the structure of a sentence in the language of generalized quantifiers. If D(A, B) is the generalized quantifier sentence with D the determiner, A the restrictor and B the nuclear scope, then in the above the little DRS on the left of the ◊ is the restrictor, the diamond itself determines a determiner and the box on the right the nuclear scope.[2] The DRS for the second sentence looks like this:

(K2.2)

$$
\boxed{\begin{array}{l} z \\ \text{unhappy}(z) \\ z = [] \end{array}}
$$

The pronoun has introduced an equation that is not complete. We need to find a discourse referent x such that we can replace z = [] by z = x. But this cannot be done within the DRS (K3.2) alone according to the constraints on anaphora resolution. (K2.2) must be added to the context created by previous discourse before the equation can be solved. The context of interpretation here is just the DRS (K2.1). But according to the semantic constraints of anaphora resolution, "updating" or adding the information in (K2.1) to that of (K2.1) also produces no solution to the anaphoric equation.

The semantic constraints on anaphora are sensitive to whether a discourse referent is introduced by a definite noun phrase or not and to whether or not one discourse referent is

---

[1]For proper definitions of these concepts, I must refer the reader to Asher & Wada (1989).
[2]For a detailed discussion of such DRSs, the reader should refer to Kamp and Reyle (1990).

introduced prior to the introduction of another. Were we to formalize the constraints in a rigorous way, we would need a variety of special purpose predicates--Def() and Indef(), which tell us whether a discourse referent was introduced by a definite or an indefinite noun phrase, and precedes(x, y), which means that x is introduced into the DRS prior to y. Other special predicates essential for describing anaphoric updating are the predicate denoting the set of all accessible discourse referents to a discourse referent x, Acc(x) and the predicate Disref(x) denoting the set of all discourse referents that syntactically are determined to be disjoint with respect to x. As expected, disjoint reference may only be determined relative to Syn(K). Another predicate tells us about the order of discourse referents; precedes(x, y) means that x is introduced into the DRS prior to y. I will use these predicates in formulating some postulates for belief updating at the end of this section on updating. For a proper understanding of these concepts and the constraints themselves, which I cannot go into here, the reader is invited to read Asher and Wada (1989).

Any plausible theory of text interpretation must be sensitive to rules about anaphoric processing. But the role of pronouns in a story about belief updating from verbal information is also not to be overlooked. Anaphora resolution affects belief updating, when one updates one's beliefs by incorporating information expressed within natural language discourse. It may very well be that the agent has incorporated the information contained in some sentences of a discourse into his beliefs. DRT models this information as a DRS and hypothesizes that the same sort of structure may serve to model the agent's newly acquired belief. But further sentences in the discourse may contain pronominal elements that depend for their interpretation on the structure of the DRS representing the context of interpretation. This means that in incorporating the new information into his beliefs, the agent must follow the contraints on relations between discourse referents imposed by anaphora resolution. A theory belief dynamics that overlooked the interpetation of pronouns would not be insensitive to the role pronouns play in developing quite particular and determinate sorts of connections between newly accepted beliefs with previously held ones. In overlooking such conditions, one would risk not getting the truth conditions of the new beliefs completely right.

But there is a much more intimate connection between an agent's background beliefs and the way anaphora may affect the updating of beliefs. The structure of the information in the context of interpretation determines which equations representing anaphoric linkings are permitted, which are required and which are not permitted. But one cannot, practically, leave anaphora constrained but unresolved. Information with too much ambiguity in it is not terribly useful; typically whenever possible, agents try to and do resolve pronouns even when the constraints do not determine a unique antecedent. To do this, the agent must rely on world knowledge and default inferences.[1] Suppose one is trying to interpret the following sort of text.

(3.a) The Vice-President entered the President's office. He was nervous and clutching his briefcase.

There is an inference needed here to find the anaphoric antecedent of the personal pronoun. To solve this sort of example (about which DRT in fact has little to say) one must appeal to a good deal of world knowledge, and make some default inferences in order to arrive at the presumed intended antecedent, the Vice-President. We come to a quite different conclusion in discourse (4.a):

(4.a) The Vice-President entered the President's office. He was sitting at his desk.

These inferences can be overturned in the proper context.[2]

(4.b) The Vice-President entered the President's office. He was nervous and clutching his briefcase. After all, he couldn't fire the man without making trouble for himself with the chairman of the board. But if he didn't do something now, the company would fall apart, and everyone would blame him for the disaster.

In (4.b) new information overturns the reference identification made with less information in (3). In processing such examples, we see a much more intimate dependence between text processing and the beliefs of an agent. These examples clearly indicate that the agent is using his beliefs about what typpically happens to reason non-monotonically to likely anaphoric antecedents in the text. The agent must often make some decisions by default, and these default inferences get incorporated as part of the new information state that results from the processing of (4.b). Thus, the agent may revise his interpretation as he acquires new information without rejecting the previously accepted information. He may reject only his previous interpretation of that information.

Anaphora Resolution and Formalizing DRSs as Partial Models

How can we set up the reasoning about anaphora in a perspicuous way? We need to do this properly, or a formal characterization of updating will elude us. DRT gives us a way. Let us take DRSs to be models of a certain sort. DRSs have been suggested to be "partial models" in various works in the DRT literature. We must be careful, though. DRSs are not to be understood as models, partial or complete, in the ordinary sense. Since the truth conditional content of a DRS is to be understood in terms of the embedding functions, discourse referents are not to be understood as elements of a domain in a model in the usual way. Further, DRSs

---

[1]To get a procedure for resolving anaphora we resorted in Asher & Wada (1989) to several non-monotonic constraints to compute salience and finish the anaphora resolution. There are many others that we did not know enough about to include.

[2]The examples (4) are drawn from Asher (1984).

may contain contradictory information. So we must suppose the existence of absurd, or incoherent models along with coherent ones. With these caveats out of the way, however, we may take DRSs to be models and their universes to be a fixed domain of objects of a certain, peculiar kind. Further we define:

Let K and K' be DRSs. Then $K + K' = <(U_K \cup U_{K'}), (Con_K \cup Con_{K'})>$

If ψ is a condition then $K + \{\psi\} = <U_K, (Con_K \cup \{\psi\})>$

Recall that DRSs as contexts permitted, required or did not permit certain anaphoric equations. Now that we are understanding DRSs as models, we can say that DRSs *verify* or *refute* certain anaphoric equations. Suppose x is introduced by an anaphoric pronoun and suppose a given context $\underline{K} + K$ verifies (written ⊢+) x = y for some particular y and that $\underline{K} + K$ refutes (written ⊢-) x = z for all z ≠ y in $\underline{K}$. If $\underline{K} + K \vdash+ x = y$, we should delete the condition x = [] and enter the equation, x = y, into the DRS K as part of the updating procedure; if $\underline{K} + K \vdash- x = z$, then x = z should not entered be into the DRS. This indicates that updating a DRS with new information will not be *just* a matter of addition.

Because we only have to do reasoning about anaphoric connections on the domain of the context, we are only interested in the verification of equations and other formulae about the objects declared in the partial model. We are not interested in the verification of formulae concerning objects in the domain of the total model in doing updating. When we apply DRT to a text with anaphoric pronouns, the constraints typically forbid all but a few candidate equations involving elements of the domain of the context (See Asher and Wada (1989)). In many cases, the theory does not determine the issue in the sense that the DRS verifies one equation and refutes all the others. Sometimes, it refutes all but one equation, but this occurs usually only in highly artificial texts. Thus, a given DRS may neither verify nor refute a particular equation about elements in its universe. The underlying logic of DRSs *qua* models then is partial both in the sense that these models do not determine the truth value of every formula of the (restricted) condition language and in the sense that they do not determine the truth value of every formula that concerns itself only about the elements in DRS's universe. A DRS K determines relative to an embedding function f only a partial extension and antiextension even for the identity predicate on the image of f on the universe of K. That is, it is not the case that relative to f $K \vdash+ x = y$ iff f(x) = f(y) for x, y ∈ U_K and $K \vdash- x = y$ iff f(x) ≠ f(y) for x, y ∈ U_K.

Since we are interested in verifying or refuting a restricted set of equations, it might suffice to look at the atomic diagram of each DRS, the list of atomic conditions verified (i.e., contained) in it. But in order to state the anaphoric restrictions as constraints on models, we need a much more general definition. Further, a more general definition of verification is needed to make sense of the other uses of DRSs. The most natural verification definitions to adopt resemble that for the strong Kleene semantics or a supervaluational approach.[1] In taking either a Kleene, or supervaluation scheme, $\vdash_+$ and $\vdash_-$ define a traditional support relation between a partial model and a formula.[2] The language at issue here is just the language of DRSs. This language contains names for discourse referents, names for DRS predicates, and devices for denoting DRSs and complex conditions. Let us suppose that the formulas of the language are defined as follows:

Let R denote a DRS predicate and let 'x' and 'y' denote discourse referents. Then 'R(x, y)' denotes a DRS condition and is an atomic condition formula.

If U is a set of names of discourse referents and C a set of names for conditions, then the pair $<U, C>$ (graphically sometimes written as a box with the elements of U at the top) denotes a DRS.

If K and K' denote DRSs, then $K \rightarrow K'$, $\neg K$, $K \vee K'$ denote DRS conditions.

If K and K' denote DRSs and x is a discourse referent declared in U_K, then K many K' also denotes a DRS condition.

In defining the supervaluation verification scheme, we may proceed very simply. Note that any DRS K may be extended to a maximal consistent DRS K'; K' is a *maximal extension* of K. Bearing in mind that our partial models are simply DRSs, we may define the supervaluation scheme $\vdash_{+s}$ and $\vdash_{-s}$ as follows.

DEFINITION: Let K, K' be DRSs. $K \leq K'$ iff $U_K \subseteq U_{K'}$ and $Con_K \subseteq Con_{K'}$.

DEFINITION: Let ψ denote any DRS condition and Θ any DRS.

$K \vdash_{+s} \psi$ iff $\forall \underline{K}$ if $\underline{K}$ is a maximal extension of K, then ψ denotes a condition of $\underline{K}$

$K \vdash_{-s} \psi$ iff $\forall \underline{K}$ if $\underline{K}$ is a maximal extension of K, then $\neg\psi$ is a condition of $\underline{K}$

$K \vdash_{+s} \Theta$ iff $\forall \underline{K}$ if $\underline{K}$ is a maximal extension of K, then $\Theta \leq \underline{K}$

$K \vdash_{-s} \Theta$ iff $\forall \underline{K}$ if $\underline{K}$ is a maximal extension of K, then it is not the case that $\Theta \leq \underline{K}$.

---

[1] A general difficulty with any of these logics is their use in a doxastic setting. The closure principles of a doxastic context are notoriously weak; certainly not all tautologies or theorems of first order logic are part of our beliefs nor are our beliefs closed under logical equivalence. A move to a Kleene valuation does not help as much as one would like, since it seems equally clear that our beliefs are not closed under strong Kleene consequence or strong Kleene logical equivalence either. We could avoid this situation for such contexts by restricting the form of the conditions to be verified or refuted. In this section the language of identity without quantifiers and without connectives is sufficient. But this will not be true for other forms of belief updating. I mention this as an issue to be solved for a general theory of updating. As it is rather orthogonal to the issues I am presently concerned with, however, I will ignore its effects here.

[2] One is not forced to either of these traditional partial valuation schemes by considerations concerning anaphora, however. Understanding DRSs as partial models allows for the possibility of incoherent states in the following sense: there are states (models) K such that $K \vdash \perp$. The possibility of incoherent information states allows us to countenance a four valued semantics that extends the Kleene valuation scheme. This might yield quite a different logic of updating. But as far as I can see, this now fails to correspond in any sensible way to the truth conditional view of content.

Here is the Kleene recursive truth definition for our language and DRS partial models, written $\Vdash_k$, $\vdash_k$. We need one auxillary definition.

DEFINITION: K' is an *elementary extension* of K just in case K is isomorphic to K'', for some K''
$\leq$ K.

DEFINITION:

Let φ be an atomic condition formula.

$K \Vdash_k \varphi$ iff denotes a condition of K

$K \vdash_k \varphi$ iff $\neg\varphi$ denotes a condition of K

Let φ be a formula of the form $\neg\psi$.

$K \Vdash_k \varphi$ iff $K \vdash_k \psi$

$K \vdash_k \varphi$ iff $K \Vdash_k \psi$

Let φ be a formula of the form $\psi \vee \zeta$.

$K \Vdash_k \varphi$ iff $K \vdash \psi$ or $K \vdash \zeta$

$K \vdash_k \varphi$ iff $K \vdash_k \psi$ and $K\vdash_k \zeta$

Let φ be a formula of the form $\psi \rightarrow \zeta$.

$K \Vdash_k \varphi$ iff if $K' \Vdash_k \psi(\bar{y}/\bar{z})$, then $K' \Vdash_k \zeta(\bar{y}/\bar{z})$, where $\bar{z} \in U_\psi$ and $\bar{y} \in U_{K'}$
for all possible sequences $\bar{y}$ with y_i having the same type as z_i and where K' is
an elementary extension of K.

$K \vdash_k \varphi(x)$ iff $K \Vdash_k \psi$ and $K\vdash_k$.

Let φ be a formula of the form ψ many ζ.

$K \Vdash_k \varphi$ iff for many y in $U_{K'}$, $K' \Vdash_k \psi(y/z)$ & $K' \Vdash_k \zeta(y/z)$, where $z \in U_\psi$
and y has the same type as z and where K' is an elementary extension of K.

$K \vdash_k \varphi(x)$ iff for many y in $U_{K'}$, $K' \Vdash_k \psi(y/z)$ & for not many y' in $U_{K'}$,K'
$\Vdash_k \psi(y'/z)$, where $z \in U_\psi$ and y has the same type as z and where K' is an
elementary extension of K.

Let $\Theta = $ <U, C> denote a DRS and f be a function from discourse referents denoted by
some constant in U into U_K. Then

$K \Vdash_k \Theta$ iff $K \Vdash \zeta$ for each formula $\zeta \in C_{f(\Theta)}$

$K \vdash_k \Theta$ iff $K \vdash_k \zeta$ for at least one formula $\zeta \in C_{f(\Theta)}$

I will use $\Vdash$ and $\vdash$ without subscripts when I do not mean to choose the Kleene or the supervaluation scheme. Notice the interpretation of the arrow here; it is a universal implication rather than simple implication. The Kleene satisfaction definition runs up against the following difficulty when DRSs are taken to model belief states. It is possible that one may believe φ or ψ without believing φ or believing that ψ. On the Kleene truth definition, however, this is not possible; all complex beliefs are supported by beliefs in simpler constituents.[1] One could perhaps maintain that this is an appropriate view of the rational beliefs of a solipsist, but I find it implausible as a view of ordinary belief. Often agents accept information in the form of a disjunction without believing in one or the other disjunct. One might make a similar argument about the $\rightarrow$ complex condition as well, but I find it much less plausible to suppose that one could believe a universal generalization without believing instantiations of it to arbitrary individuals. It should be noted that this difficulty does not affect the supervaluation definition of consequence for partial models.

To get a more satisfactory satisfaction definition, we need only to change the clauses for disjunctions above to the following:

Let φ be of the form $\psi \vee \zeta$.

$K \Vdash_{k*} \varphi$ iff $K \Vdash_{k*} \psi$ or $K \Vdash_{k*} \zeta$ or $\psi' \vee \zeta' \in K$, where ψ', ζ' are alphabetic variants of φ, ψ.

$K \Vdash_{-k*} \varphi$ iff $K \Vdash_{-k*} \psi$ and $K \Vdash_{-k*} \zeta$

This revision makes sense since our models may contain complex conditions as elements. A belief state in which the agent believed $p \vee q$ without believing either of the disjuncts would be just so modelled. As far as I can tell allowing for models in which one believes a disjunction without believing the disjuncts does not affect the conception of validity, which is perhaps somewhat curious.

The supervaluation definition of verification and refutation determines the following relation to the notion of truth conditional content given by embedding functions. Let M range over models for DRSs, the models into which DRSs are to be properly embedded.

$K \vDash_s \psi$ iff $\forall f, M [K]_{f, M} \rightarrow \exists g \supset f [K + \psi]_{g, M}$

$K \vDash_s \psi$ iff $\forall f, M [K]_{f, M} \rightarrow \neg \exists g \supset f [K + \psi]_{g, M}$

So, for example, suppose $K \vdash x = y$. This will happen only if $x, y \in U_K$. By the definition $K \vdash x = y$ iff $\forall f, M [K]_{f, M} \rightarrow \exists g \supset \psi f [K + \psi]_g, M$ iff $\forall f([K]_{f, M} \rightarrow f(x) = f(y))$. On the other hand suppose $K \vdash x = y$. $K \vdash x = y$ iff $\forall f, M [K]_{f, M} \rightarrow \neg \exists g \supset \psi f [K + \psi]_{g, M}$ iff $\forall f([K]_{f, M} \rightarrow f(x) \neq f(y))$, as expected. The Kleene valuation for $\vdash$ yields a less perfect correspondence with the possible worlds view of content:

$K \vdash \psi$ only if $\forall f, M [K]_{f, M} \rightarrow \exists g \supset f [K + \psi]_{g, M}$

$K \vdash \psi$ iff $\forall f, M [K]_{f, M} \rightarrow \neg \exists g \supset f [K + \psi]_{g, M}$

So far I have only defined the monotonic core logic of DRSs. I now must turn to thinking more precisely about the non-monotonic elements which played a role in anaphora

---

[1] Halpern and Moses (1984) discovered allowing such ungrounded "dishonest formulas" in modal epistemic logics could lead to difficulties in systems with introspection. Their example of a dishonest formula was much more complex: $K(Kp \vee Kq)$. Introspection is not assumed here!

resolution. The role that anaphora resolution suggests for non-monotonic logic in updating is one of filling in the blanks in the valuation left by the Kleene truth definition concerning the equations about the individuals in the domain of the DRS. These blanks must be filled in to complete the anaphora resolution process. Thus, DRSs may be thought of having a monotonic, partial "core" logic surrounded by a "non-monotonic periphery." As anaphora resolution puts little demands on the form of non-monotonic logic to be used, I shall not specify a particular system. But I shall require that the non-monotonic consequence relation have the following properties (exemplified for instance by the non-monotonic inheritance systems of Thomason, Horty and Touretsky.[1] Let > be a quantifier so that $A >_x B$ means something like *A's are normally B's.* For simplicity, let us think of the non-monotonic language as a first order language augmented by the quantifier >. (There is always an easy translation from a first order language into the language of DRSs, should we need that).

(a) $\models$ is a conservative extension of $\vdash$. For φ a formula of first order logic, $\models \varphi$ iff $\vdash \varphi$ and if $\Gamma \vdash \varphi$, then $\Gamma \models \varphi$.

(b) Default MP. $A(t), A >_x B \models B(t)$. But not $\neg B(t), A(t), A >_x B \models B(t)$

(c) Default specificity. $A > B, B > C, A > \neg C, A(t) \models \neg C(t)$ and not $\models C(t)$.

I will also assume that the non-monotonic logic has the following negative property:

(d) Not: $A > B, B > C, A > \neg C \models B > \neg A$.

I will call any non-monotonic logic yielding a consequence relation with such properties a *reasonable non-monotonic consequence relation*. The last stricture may be somewhat controversial, but it is crucial if we are to allow for the possibility of atypical A's who are normal B's and so have C. To give a concrete example, it seems reasonable to assume that penguins are birds, birds fly and penguins do not fly and to suppose that the bare plural gives us instances of generic quantification. But it does not seem reasonable to suppose that birds are not penguins. It does not help to say that birds are not typically penguins or that birds are normally not penguins. Finally, since I will talk about partial models that *verify* certain statements non-monotonically, I require connections between the notion of a model M and the notion of logical consequence. I will say that $M \models \varphi$ iff $Th(M) \models \varphi$.

The definitions of verification, both for the core logic and non-monotonic periphery, imply that updating a DRS with new information refines the Stalnaker-Gardenfors view of belief updating, on which the new information state is the set of worlds that is the intersection of the worlds modelling theold belief state with those worlds that verify the new information. Where the new information contains no discourse referents common with the cognitive state and where no non-monotonic inferences are performed, the truth conditional content of the

---

[1]Were I to develop a non-monotonic logic along the lines of Veltman (1989) or Asher & Morreau (1990), there could be a correspondence between the relation non-monotonic consequence, $\vdash\hspace{-0.4em}\sim$, and one defined using the embedding definition and intensional model for DRT.

DRS updating procedure is just what the Stalnaker-Gardenfors view predicts. But DRT updating may very well diverge from the received view when these assumptions do not hold.

2. Temporal Anaphora

As Barbara Partee already pointed out in (1973), the problem of determining temporal reference is very similar in flavor to the problem of pronominal anaphora resolution. The temporal anaphoric problem to be solved is to locate the event or state described in the information being given within the temporal structure of events that the agents believes to have occurred. Suppose, for example, that an agent accepts the information,

(8) Alexis went to school.

The task of the agent agent is to locate this event of Alexis's going to school among the other events he believes to have occurred. The grammatical rules of tense require that the event must have come before the time of utterance and time of acceptance. But can we be any more definite than that? A set of complex rules determines temporal reference within a text In many cases, which DRT has examined in considerable detail, the grammatical features of tense help determine the location of the event in the temporal ordering. So in a story like,

(9) Jean rentra a la maison. D'abord, il mangea un repas modeste, et apres il fuma sa
     pipe.

the grammatical rules strongly suggest a linear ordering of the three events presented in this discourse. But many times, the agent must rely on knowledge or beliefs of the agent about events and processes to come to an interpretive decision about the relative order of events mentioned in a discourse. Consider the following very similar discourse to (9) (due to Hinrichs):

(10) He turned the switch . The light reflected harshly off the bare, antiseptic walls.

Let us assume that the agent has updated his beliefs with the information content of the first sentence. Without knowing more, he would probably assume that the event described in the next sentence followed the event described in the previous one. But one can easily imagine contexts or continuations of (10) in which the second sentence reports a state co-occurring with the event of turning on the switch-- say for example a context in which the agent has just turned a switch to launch a missile and the second sentence reflects his mood. Here a context tells us how to interpret the connection. Continuations can also force us to revise a previously accepted temporal connection. To go back to example (8), if Alexis went to school and nothing more is said, then a recipient may very well infer that she got there before classes started. The interpreter may even go futher; i.e., if he knows about the particular context of utterance in which I wrote down the assertion, he may infer that she got there before 8:35 am. But of course such inferences can be defeated-- for instance, if (8) continues as follows:

(11) Alexis went to school. She got there late, however.

We can also look at the problem of temporal anaphora from the perspective of partial logic. The language of temporal anaphora is somewhat more complex than the language of pronominal anaphora. The temporal equations one must prove are not just in the language of identity and the predicates about syntactic and semantic structure. One has now also formulas involving the temporal order-- using the notions of precedence and overlap, $<$ and $\cdot$. But unlike pronominal anaphora, temporal anaphora exploits only the purely semantic information in a straightforward, unextended DRS. Typically, the grammar of tense introduces certain temporal equations between eventualities (events and states) or between eventualities and times. These equations put constraints on how the eventualities can be arranged in a temporal order. Solving temporal anaphoric relations requires the interpreter to determine, as far as possible, a complete temporal ordering. So in updating one ordering of events (in one's antecedent beliefs or in prior processing of text) with events described by new information, one has to figure out how to fit the new events into the extant ordering.

A DRS, considered again as a model, verifies or refutes certain equations about the events in its universe. Because of the way DRSs are constructed for temporal discourse, we can be sure that the axioms of $<$ and $\cdot$ are respected; temporal anaphoric equations will be entered in a DRS only if they are compatible with these axioms. Typically, the constraints of the grammar of tense do not determine a linear ordering for the events introduced in a DRS. They verify or refute only a few of many possible temporal equations.. So DRSs once again must be thought of as partial models, with the truth conditions of the formulas of the temporal language being specified by the strong Kleene or some other, partial, valuation scheme.

As with pronominal anaphora, we cannot leave temporal anaphora constrained but unresolved. We have to avoid ambiguity as much as possible in textual interpretation. To be maximally useful, newly accepted information must be as fully as possible integrated with the old. Useful information does not come in little independent packages, which like little bricks one can simply add to the edifice of one's beliefs; rather it is like a molten liquid needing a particular mold in order to acquire a fully definite content. To further determine the ordering of events in a DRS, agents rely on default principles, as in the case pronominal anaphora, to establish a more determinate ordering of events. Temporal anaphora distinguishes itself from pronominal anaphora in that there are degrees of determinacy that the interpretation process confers. But as with pronominal anaphora, the picture seems to be one in which there is no simple updating of a belief set with new information.

There is also a new development. The problems of temporal anaphora are already difficult when we consider only the relations between events in a given text. One could call this the *interpretive* aspect of temporal anaphora. But an agent's updating his beliefs with information from an interpreted text also requires him to integrate the events posited by this information within the temporal structure of his beliefs. This second task, which I'll call the *purely doxastic* aspect of temporal anaphora, takes place without the benefits of textual cues. Clearly dates, times etc.. must serve as useful organizing signposts, as do the axioms for < and . But the purely doxastic aspect of temporal anaphora relies only on semantic information. It has no counterpart in pronominal anaphora, which usually relies a good deal on syntactic information. For the purely doxastic aspect of temporal anaphora, agents must rely on default reasoning even more heavily to eliminate ambiguity.

3. Definite Reference Identification

The third example of a problem requiring a dynamic approach to semantics and belief is the problem of definite reference identification. In accepting and interpreting verbally or perceptually given information, one must decide whether this is information about one or more of the individuals about which one already has information. Like temporal anaphora, this problem has both an interpretive and a purely doxastic aspect. The failure to pay attention to it in theories of belief has led to many puzzles about belief. The interpretive aspect of definite reference identification issues from the following constraint (first precisely formulated within a dynamic framework by Heim (1982)): any definite to be felicitously used must be identified with some salient antecedent in the context. One might take here the context to be either the DRS constructed from the text processed, plus perhaps a more complex structure encoding the shared beliefs of the participants. If one finds an appropriate antecedent for the definite, then one should indicate this in the resulting cognitive state. If not, that should perhaps also be indicated. The doxastic aspect of definite reference identification follows a similar principle: if an agent receives information about an individual i and accepts it, then incorporating such information requires that one identify i with some an already existing conceptual object in one's belief state if i is familiar, distinguish i from other objects if i is unfamiliar. The rationale for this principle is the same as that for temporal and pronominal anaphora: the more highly integrated the information, the more efficient and useful it is.

DRT has represented belief states in terms of a complex structure involving DRSs as constituents. But the basic issues about updating do not require these complexities here. The interpretive aspect of definite reference identification can be understood in purely semantic terms. Let $\underline{K}$ represent the background belief state state. In general we want to verify of some individual $y \in U_{\underline{K}}$ that $x = y$ and $\underline{K} \vdash x = z$ for all $z \in U_{\underline{K}}$ such that $z \neq y$. In pictorial form, we want to update the DRS on the left representing the given belief state with the new information state in S represented by a DRS. The result will be a DRS representing the updated belief state, and it will have a particular form.

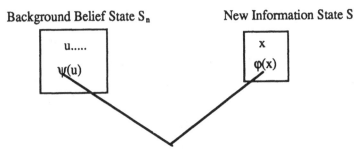

Background Belief State S_n New Information State S

If $S_n + S \vdash u = x$ and for all distinct discourse referents $u_i \in US_n$ such that u_i is a distinct discourse referent from u and $S_n + S \vdash u_i = x$

Then: Belief State S_{n+1}

| u, x, . . . |
| $\psi(u)$ |
| $\varphi(x)$ |
| $x = u$ |

Suppose that we can refute a particular equation but not arrive at a unique determination. We might also want to insert negative information.

If $\psi(u)$ & $\varphi(x) \vdash u \neq x$, then:

Belief State S_{n+1}

| u, x, . . . |
| $\psi(u)$ |
| $\varphi(x)$ |
| $x \neq u$ |

Once again we can imagine that for either aspect of the problem, the DRS context plays the role of partial model-- refuting certain identifications but not necessarily uniquely determining the issue. In general we have to appeal to default rules to solve definite reference anpahora.

We can specify a few cases of the general problem. Let us first briefly consider the problem of definite reference identification with definite descriptions. Definite descriptions can be anaphoric in two ways-- either the antecedent is introduced in the context created in the processing of a text or is presupposed to exist in the beliefs of the recipient. The semantics of definite descriptions gives us the following axiom.

$\varphi(y)$ & $y \in U_K$ & the($\varphi(z)$) $\vdash z = y$.

To resolve definite reference, $\underline{K} + K$ must verify for some discourse referent $y \in U_K$ that $\varphi(y)$ and refute $\varphi(z)$ for all other possible candidates z. The constraints on definite reference will lead us to reject a DRS (model) in which φ is verified of more than one object if the description is not a plural one. The key difference between descriptions and on other sorts of anaphoric expressions is that we exploit the content of the conditions introduced by the description, and that content can be arbitrarily complex. Because descriptions can be arbitrarily complex, we will need the model theory for the full DRS language sketched earlier.

Once again a partial monotonic core logic with a non-monotonic periphery is appropriate. In many situations, the information in $\underline{K}$ + K won't be sufficient to verify $\varphi(y)$ for some y and refute $\varphi(z)$ for all other z. At best then the information in the context only does not decide whether φ applies or not to elements of the context's universe. In those situations in which the information in $\underline{K}$ + K is not sufficient to verify $\varphi(y)$ for some y and refute $\varphi(z)$ for all other z, we will seek to fill in the gaps by appealing to non-monotonic principles of reasoning. If we look at proper names, an especially simple sort of definite, then we can see how these principles of default reasoning might work in more detail.

Typical principles for definite reference identification exploit mutual beliefs about the commonality of reference; i.e., we assume that for each referring expression α there is an object of the appropriate type to which all believe α refers. So upon accepting some information about α, an agent will typically update his beliefs by identifying the discourse referent introduced by α in the report with the one that has the condition named(x, α) in his background belief state. Here is an example. Suppose that the agent A is a typical American and knows a good deal about (American) football and suppose that agent B says:

(11) The Giants won't make the playoffs this year, because their offensive line is too inexperienced. In fact they'll be very lucky to have a winning season.

Let's suppose that A agrees with this gloomy assessment of the Giants's prospects. Then he will first form the DRS for this new information, which looks roughly like this (the discourse referents expressed by capital letters are plural discourse referents denoting groups of individuals; e in the DRS below is an event discourse referent):

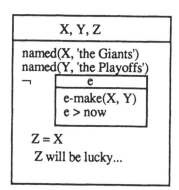

Now he must integrate. He already knows lots about football, so there must be a discourse referent in his background belief state that represents the team as well as the playoffs. In integrating the new information into his belief state, he will identify those discourse referents introduced by *the Giants* and *the playoffs* in the new information state with the appropriate ones in the DRS representing his background belief state. Thus, the updated belief state will look something like this according to DRT:

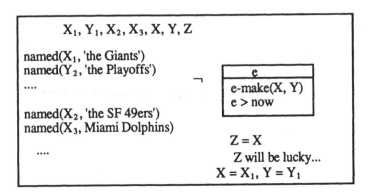

DRT supposes that principles like these guide agents' encoding of new verbal information within belief states.[1] The one for proper names that I have mentioned is idiotically simple minded. Another at about the same level of sophistication is: suppose that you learn that α has some property φ. If your background beliefs contain a proposition attributing to α' a property φ' incompatible with φ, then you should not add $\alpha \doteq \alpha'$ to your cognitive state, unless $\alpha \doteq \alpha'$ is implied by $\varphi(\alpha)$. This principle too (call it *) seems reasonable. But both are beliefs about belief updating, which though well-grounded in experience, admit of exceptions. They may be thought of as non-monotonic rules open to counterexample. Thus, mistakes in updating of an interesting sort can occur when an agent exploits such a non-monotonic rule in a situation which is a counterexample to it.

There are two ways in which updating with definite reference identification with proper names can go wrong. One can incorporate contradictory information without knowing that it is contradictory; and one's default rules for updating can lead one astray. Mistakes in updating of the first kind can occur even if the agent is ideally rational and logically omniscient. When such mistakes occur we have belief puzzles of a classical kind like the one described by Kripke (1979). One question that arises in Kripke's story and which DRT formalism helps to answer is, what is Pierre's doxastic predicament? Pierre's story well-known, so I will only sketch the details. Growing up in France, Pierre forms a belief about a city named *Londres*. He looks at picture books and the like and decides that the town he sees in the pictures is beautiful. He takes the town to be called 'Londres'. Knowing that Pierre at this stage of his life is a

---

[1] Agents not only use such rules in updating their own beliefs, but they also apply them to updating their representations of the cognitive states of other agents, but I won't go into that here.

monolingual French speaker, we might write down the relevant portion of Pierre's belief state after he forms his belief as follows in the DRS formalism.

```
┌─────────────────────┐
│ u, ...              │
├─────────────────────┤
│ named(u, 'Londres') │
│ beautiful(u)        │
└─────────────────────┘
```

Later in life, Pierre finds himself by mysterious circumstances suddenly in a seedy part of London, where he learns English without the benefit of a French English dictionary. His direct experience convinces him that London is a very ugly city. Yet he does not retract the former belief, because of the way he adds his new belief to his cognitive state. Naturally, Pierre employs the principle * and distinguishes between discourse referents. In effect he supposes that there are two towns, with incompatible properties. Thus, after the London update, Pierre's cognitive state looks like this:

```
┌────────────────────────────────────────────────┐
│   u, x                                          │
├────────────────────────────────────────────────┤
│ named(u, 'Londres')     named(x, 'London')      │
│ beautiful(u)            ┌──────────────┐        │
│                       ¬ │ beautiful(x) │        │
│                         └──────────────┘        │
└────────────────────────────────────────────────┘
```

One thing that is missing from the picture above is anything indicating that u and x stand for the same object. More precisely, what is missing is information that would force any proper embedding of the DRS to map both u and x onto London. Let us assume that such a mechanism is in place (See Asher (1986) (1989), Kamp (1985)). As soon as such a mechanism is in place, however, the belief state depicted above becomes inconsistent. Pierre's logical omniscience has not prevented him from landing in contradiction. One might think that is because the principles he relied on for updating his cognitive state were default assumptions, open as he most likely knows to counterexample but which he did not suspect in the cases he used them. Without a dictionary Pierre was rational to suppose that reports about *Londres* and reports using the word *London* were about two different cities. But in fact Pierre's reasoning is valid monotonically. His belief state is inconsistent even without the identification -- in virtue of the referential meaning of *Londres* and *London*.

A different difficulty besets the Count Almaviva at the end of the marriage of Figaro. This is a puzzle that does not hinge on the consistency of the prior belief state. The Count goes wrong by using default rules. He is hiding watching his wife and Susanna, her maid. The first is wooed by Cherubino and the second by Figaro, two servants the Count considers scoundrels. The trick is that the Contessa is dressed like Susanna and Susanna like the Countess. The Count acquires true perceptual beliefs, but he mixes up the Contessa and Susanna. Perhaps he uses the incautious rule: if the person is wearing X's clothes then that person is X. Thus the count moves from a correct belief state to one that cannot be correct, by using (incautious) non-monotonic reasoning. In fact he ends up believing an inconsistency by applying his non-monotonic rules. But then that was the aim of the ruse.

Once one posits a structure for cognitive states like that exhibited by DRSs, then many variations on the Pierre puzzle become possible. One variation on the Pierre puzzle is to think about cases where principles for identifying discourse referents fail. A similar story to Pierre's can be told about concepts. That is, one can easily imagine an agent who fails to identify two concepts-- like for instance *furze* and *gorse* or *Linden* and *lime*. The treatment of such cases proceeds along exactly the same lines as the treatment of Pierre; the only change is that one must now postulate discourse referents for concepts. When one reflects on these cases it becomes evident that belief updating must not only resolve questions about the identity of individuals but also about the identity of concepts.

4. Concept Integration

Once we countenance discourse referents for concepts-- something which is natural in connection with the extension of puzzles like that of Pierre, we invite a natural extension of questions about updating to abstract, higher order objects in general. With definite reference identification, we saw that individual objects had to be properly identified in order to update the belief state appropriately. With temporal anaphora, we saw that events had to be located within the temporal flow of events in order to update the belief state appropriately. When we introduce concepts or propositions, the proper updating of a belief state will depend upon how the various concepts or propositions are related to each other.

A research project in DRT that ought to be pursued is to explore links between concepts and between propositions by looking carefully at why and how questions. Why and how questions, as Sylvain Bromberger noticed long ago, may be fruitfully understood as a plea by the speaker for help in connecting or integrating propositions or concepts. But the dynamic perspective of belief updating also helps us think about this problem. Consider the following example. Suppose I am flying my airplane through bad weather and am descending through a cloud deck with the temperature below freezing. All of a sudden I hear a loud thunk on the nose. I then observe that ice has formed along the leading edges of the wings. This observation explains to me the noise: ice was slung off the propeller and hit the fuselage.

Updating my belief state with the last observation led me to reorganize my belief state in a particular way. What before was simply a dangling, unrelated observation about a noise now fits into a pattern of expectations that is generated by my accepting this additional piece of information about ice forming on the wing. One way to imagine how one might begin to handle such a phenomenon in doxastic updating is to see such unrelated propositions as terms in a relation whose other term is missing or needs to be supplied to complete and integrate the belief state. My belief state contained in effect an implicit why question in it-- a why question might just be so represented. Such uncompleted or questioning belief states in updating would then serve a similar, though not entirely analogous role to those conditions introduced by pronouns and demand, when possible, a completion or filling in.

This last bit of talk is especially vague and metaphorical, and I shall not pursue it here any further. Nevertheless, I do not believe that we can make sense of updating in general unless we take account of phenomena like these. Even if we do not have a theory of such updating, however, we can at least glean from it the same lessons about updating that our other phenomena have indicated. To understand such updating we will need to rely on a more refined structure for cognitive states. That structure will be most likely a higher order structure quantifying over propositions. Such a structure will obey the dictates of a partial logic; not all the links required for an explanation will be given explicitly by the previous belief state or by the new material, and so one will need to appeal to defaults yet again to finish the updating process. This is certainly the case in the example I cited. In constructing the explanatory link, I appeal to all sorts of default assumptions that are encoded into general rules about ice formation on propellers and noises.

A second, perhaps more tractable connection between propositions should be mentioned. Clearly one way in which propositions are related to each other within a cognitive state is through patterns of reasoning. Thus, some propositions will *justify* other propositions by being used as premises in a particular pattern of reasoning. While the patterns of reasoning used here are certainly incomplete, keeping track of supporting premises will be useful, both for the monotonic core and the non-monotonic completion. It also seems that this is certainly something that agents do. This is more apparent with revision than updating, but the point is simple enough. If in the face of new information I must correct my prior belief that φ, then I will be inclined to remove or correct those beliefs dependent on φ as well. For instance, suppose in entering a village that I know has a hamburger stand belonging to the McA chain, I see a woman eating a hamburger. I infer that she bought the hamburger at McA's and so I conclude McA's is open. But now if I then ask the person how her McA hamburger is and she tells me, "Oh this is a hamburger I cooked myself," I will have to correct first my belief that she bought the hamburger at McA's. But I will also, if rational, remove the belief that is dependent solely on this one, namely that McA's is open. Such corrections are possible only if the agent somehow keeps track of the inferential dependencies among the propositions that he believes. The mechanisms for revision and correction already developed will handle monotonic inferential dependencies. As the example shows, however, it will be also extremely important to keep track of such dependencies arising from non-monotonic reasoning. Here one needs an additional mechanism. I will capture these dependencies here by encoding them with a particular predicate, *because*, whose arguments may be DRS conditions or DRSs. To simplify matters, I will restrict those arguments to those DRSs and DRS conditions in which *because* does not figure as a predicate. If a belief state non-monotonically implies a certain conclusion φ and it is a fact of the non-monotonic logic that φ is a non-monotonic consequence of ψ and the model verifies ψ, then because(ψ, φ) is verified. With all this said, we now give the satisfaction conditions for our new predicate within the semantic framework elaborated above:

$$\mathcal{M} \vdash \text{because}(\varphi, \psi) \text{ iff } \mathcal{M} \vdash \varphi \& \mathcal{M} \vDash \psi \& \mathcal{M} \vdash \varphi >_x \psi \&$$
$$\text{for all } \zeta, (\mathcal{M} \vdash \varphi \& \zeta >_x \neg\psi \rightarrow \text{not } \mathcal{M} \vDash \zeta).$$

We will use this notion of encoding inferences later when we define a DR-theoretic notion of revision.

5. Formalization of Updating in DRT

Let me sum up where we have come so far. Each of the four problems mentioned, pronominal and temporal anaphora, definite reference identification, and concept integration, reveals a particular complexity of updating beliefs. The lessons learned from working on these problems is that the procedure of belief updating relies on a certain conception of structure of information, and that the appropriate logic for belief updating which addresses these problems combines a partial, monotonic logic core with a non-monotonic *completion*.

DEFINITION: If $\mathcal{M}$ is a partial model, then the *completion* of $\mathcal{M}$ is that extension $\mathcal{M}'$ of $\mathcal{M}$ such that $\mathcal{M}' \vdash+ \varphi$ iff $\mathcal{M} \vDash \varphi$ and $\mathcal{M}' \vdash- \varphi$ iff $\mathcal{M} \vDash \neg\varphi$.

The reason for this combination of logics becomes clear when we see how the updating process can go awry. Pierre, for instance, formed his beliefs and updated them reasonably, but his peculiar situation-- in particular, the discontinuity of his French and English existences-- lead him very far astray in his interpretation. Mozart's Count Almaviva actually takes true information and updates his belief state so that he ends up believing an inconsistency. Thus, the update procedure does not in general preserve truth. The underlying non-monotonic reasoning used in the process of updating may force the agent to revise his beliefs without rejecting the verbal information originally accepted. He may reject only the interpretation of that information that was part of the original updating process.

I have defined a partial valuation on DRS models for all DRS conditions. To fill in the gaps in a partial model, I assumed a default logic defined on top of such partial models. Restricting myself just to phenomena that DRT has studied in detail and with these assumptions, I can formalize the update procedures. This will make an explicit comparison with Gardenfors's notion of expansion possible.

The Gardenfors postulates give a general characterization of expansion. They apply to sets of sentences. So let S, S' range over sets of sentences, while A ranges over sentences of a propositional language. Each set of sentences in Σ is assumed to be closed under logical consequence.

Gardenfors Postulates for Addition:

(A0+) for $S \in \Sigma$, $S \vdash A$ iff $A \in S$.

(AI+) $S + A \in \Sigma$

(AII+) $A \in S{+}A$

(AIII+) $S \subseteq S + A$

(AIV+) $A \in S \rightarrow S + A = S$

(AV+) $S \subseteq S' \rightarrow S + A \subseteq S' + A$

(AVI+) $S{+}A$ is the smallest belief set satisfying AI+ - A5+

What we want is a general characterization of UPDATE like Gardenfors's postulates for addition. UPDATE is a partial function from partial models and DRSs to partial models. Thus it can be thought of as a variant of the Gardenfors notion of expansion, though unlike expansion, UPDATE can fail. First the language of UPDATE. The language will include terms (at least variables) for DRSs (information states), conditions (properties), discourse referents (individuals), and two 1-place predicates on DRSs, U and Con, the usual truth functional connectives and quantifiers, and distinguished predicates $\cdot$, $<$, and $=$. Now for some special predicates concerning updating itself. Let K_0 be some subDRS of K_1 or let $K_0 \doteq K_1$. UPDATE*(K, K_1, K_0) is the the resulting transformation of K_1 after updating K with K_0. I will also write UPDATE*$(K, K, K_0) = $ UPDATE(K, K_0) to denote the resulting transformation of K after updating K with K_0. We need to have such a complex update function because our models are complex structures, and updating may affect various portions of this structure in different ways. Define Comp(K, K') be the DRS $\langle U, Con \rangle$ $U \subseteq U_K$, Con $\subseteq$ Con$_K$ where K is a subDRS of K' and K' is not a subDRS of any other DRS. The second argument of Comp(K, K') gives the DRS context of K; i.e. K is a subDRS of K'. Thus Comp(K', K) may verify more than just the information in K might suggest, because the information in superordinate DRSs to K in K' will also be available. Finally, define a predicate $\approx$ on DRSs such that $K \approx K'$ iff K and K' are isomorphic up to those discourse referents declared in U_K and $U_{K'}$.

We will define a function, UPDATE , by means of a series of constraints on the partial models that result from applying the function in particular circumstances. I will ignore here the updating of belief states with respect to temporal information since that is more complicated than updating with reference to pronominal anaphora and definite reference identification, and the latter are complicated enough already.

UPDATE is the smallest function satisfying the (A1)-(A7) postulates.

(A1) Idempotence:

$K_0 \leq K$ & UPDATE $*(K, K_1, K_1) \approx K_0 \Rightarrow$ UPDATE$* (K, K, K_1) = K$.

(A2) Success:

$K \Vdash+ \varphi$ or Comp$(K_1, K_1) \Vdash+ \varphi \Rightarrow$ UPDATE$* (K, K, K_1) \Vdash \varphi$.

(A3) Absolute Anaphoric Constraints for Pronominal Anaphors:

(i) $\text{Syn}(K_0) \Vdash \mathbf{y} \in \text{Disref}(\mathbf{x})$ & $\mathbf{x} \in U_{K_1} \Rightarrow$ UPDATE $(K, K_1, K_0) \Vdash \mathbf{x} = \mathbf{y}$.

(ii) $\text{Syn}(K_0) \Vdash \text{precedes}(\mathbf{x}, \mathbf{y})$ & Main clause$(\mathbf{y})$ & Indef$(\mathbf{y})$

$\Rightarrow$ UPDATE$*(K, K_0, K_0) \Vdash \mathbf{x} = \mathbf{y}$

(iii) $K + K_0 \Vdash+ \mathbf{y} \notin \text{Acc}(\mathbf{x})$ and $\mathbf{x} \in U_{K_1} \Rightarrow$ UPDATE$*(K, K_1, K_0) \Vdash \mathbf{x} = \mathbf{y}$.

(A4) Non-monotonic Completion for Pronominal Anaphors:

Suppose: $v \in U_{K_1}$ & $K_1 \Vdash+ v = []$ & $x \in U_K$ & $\forall u \in U_K$ $(u \neq x \rightarrow$

UPDATE$*(K, K_1, K_0) \Vdash u = v)$ & not(UPDATE$*(K, K_1, K_0) \Vdash x = v)$

Then: UPDATE$*(K, K_1, K_0) \Vdash x = v$.

(A5) Anaphoric Constraint for Definites:

Suppose: $v \in U_{K_1}$ and $\text{Syn}(K_1) \Vdash \text{Def}(v)$ & $K_1 \Vdash \varphi(v)$ and $x \in U_K$ and $K \Vdash \varphi(x)$

Then: UPDATE$*(K, K_1, K_0) \Vdash x = v$.

Now we can take care of the rest of the non-monotonic completions in one fell swoop with a strengthened "non-monotonic success" axiom, which I split into two parts.

(A6) Non- Monotonic Success.

(i) UPDATE$*(K, \text{Comp}(K_1, K_0), K_0) \models\approx \zeta \Rightarrow$ UPDATE$*(K, K_1, K_0) \models\approx \zeta$.

(ii) UPDATE$*(K, K_1, K_0) \models\approx \zeta \Rightarrow$ UPDATE$*(K, K_1, K_0) \Vdash \zeta$.

(A7) Updates of Conceptual Links.

Suppose: UPDATE$*(K, K_1, K_0) \Vdash \varphi$ & ψ and UPDATE$*(K, K_1, K_0) \Vdash \varphi >_x \zeta$ and

not(UPDATE$*(K, K_1, K_0) \Vdash \varphi$ & $\psi >_x \neg\zeta)$

Then UPDATE$*(K, K_1, K_0) \Vdash \text{because}(\varphi, \zeta)$.

These rules encode formally the results of our preceding, informal discussions about updating. (A1) - (A2) are counterparts to three of the Gardenfors postulates for expansions-- namely (A+II-A+ IV). Let us define a Gardenfors belief state counterpart to DRS K to be simply the theory of K, Th(K). We can easily show that A+II, the restricted form of III, and IV hold for Gardenfors belief state counterparts. Missing for the notion of UPDATE, however, are the monotonicity postulate (A+V), and the closure postulate A+I. The closure postulate fails, because some DRSs may have incompleted conditions in them (those introduced for instance by anaphoric pronouns); simply adding such conditions to a belief state *does not result* in a new belief state. The conditions must be completed before we get a new belief state. Sometimes they cannot be completed, and then UPDATE fails to yield a new belief state. An example of a case in which UPDATE fails to yield a new belief state is the following. Let K be the empty delineated DRS and let K_0 be the DRS that results from processing the sentence *she is smart.* The incomplete condition introduced by the anaphoric pronoun cannot be completed in this context.

UPDATE also typically adds information beyond that monotonically implied in the DRS representing the new information, the "new DRS" and the background DRS. This information is often non-monotonically implied by that contained in the new DRS and the background DRS. This is the crucial difference between UPDATE and simple Gardenforsian expansion and accounts for the failure to find a correlate of (A+V) for updates. Information that is a non-monotonic consequence may not hold in partial models which expand on the information in K + K_0. We have seen two examples in which postulates for non-monotonic completion of definite reference were exploited to introduce information that would be retracted upon the agent's becoming aware of certain features of his doxastic situation. Exactly what the UPDATE function will look like, however, will depend upon what non-monotonic principles the basic belief state verifies.

FACTS:

UPDATE(K, $K_{\varphi\,\&\,\psi}$) = UPDATE(UPDATE(K, K_φ), K_ψ), where K_ζ is the DRS derived from ζ.

UPDATE(UPDATE(K, K_φ), K_ψ)) ≠ UPDATE(UPDATE(K, K_ψ), K_φ))

Th(UPDATE(K, K_0)) = {ψ: Th(UPDATE(K, K_0))$\mid\approx \psi$}

The first fact follows from the principles of DRS construction. As for the second, let φ and ψ be respectively the sentences, *I met a girl who is nice* and *she is also smart*. As for the third fact, since $\vdash \subseteq \approx$, $\text{Th}(\text{UPDATE}(K, K_0)) \subseteq \{\psi: \text{Th}(\text{UPDATE}(K, K_0)) \approx \psi\}$. Suppose that $\text{Th}(\text{UPDATE}(K, K_0)) \approx \psi$. Then since $\approx$ is a reasonable non-monotonic consequence relation, $\text{UPDATE}(K, K_0) \approx \psi$. By (A7), $\text{UPDATE}(K, K_0) \vdash \psi$, and so $\psi \in \text{Th}(\text{UPDATE}(K, K_0))$.

PART II: Revision in DRT.

With the basic DR theoretic apparatus of updating in place, we may now begin to investigate the more complex notion of belief revision. Clearly though updating beliefs in a DR-theoretic framework is much more complicated than the theories of Stalnaker or Gardenfors would suggest, it still will not do justice to the facts of belief change. We have seen that updating can lead to doxastic difficulties-- witness the Count Almaviva. But agents also recover quickly from these difficulties. The theory so far does not tell us how this might be possible. The slogans of the DRT approach-- structured information, partiality and non-monotonicity now have to be applied to a theory of revision. I do each in turn.

Two sorts of belief revision may be distinguished-- belief revision due to reasoning and belief revision due to the acceptance of new information. Most of the work on belief revision has concentrated on the second sort of belief revision here, and I shall follow suit.[1] I shall also assume, along with most of those working in this area, that the acceptance of information is idealized in the sense that one has in fact decided to accept the new information; so the task of revision is that of revising one's prior beliefs so as to conform with the new information.[2]

1. Local Revision and Structured Information

Belief updating of the sort we looked at cannot be defined when belief states are thought of simply as points without structure or as sets of worlds. In this section, I want to examine more closely possible forms of revision in a highly structured view of beliefs.

---

[1] The first sort of revision does not even arise for most theorists in this area, who like Gardenfors assume a background classical logic or at least an underlying logic with a fixed point in the following sense using Tarski's notation: $\text{Cn}(A) = \text{Cn}(\text{Cn}(A))$, while assuming that belief states are to be identified with such fixed points. These are reasonable assumptions for belief revision, only if one is interested in a language of belief states of relatively restricted, expressive power and only if one idealizes beyond the computational powers of normal agents. Once we take the language of belief states to reflect the self-referential capacities of natural language, then there are arguments that suggest that the logic of belief states should not have a fixpoint, or at the very least that the fixpoint won't be classical. Depending on what sort of approach to the paradoxes, we choose, we will end up with various possibilities. I mention this only because concept updating may force us to a fragment expressively rich enough to generate the paradoxes.
[2] One might also think of modelling more of the process of deliberation by weighting both the new information and previous beliefs. Thus, the acceptance of the new would not be assured. But I will not pursue such complexities here.

Natural language does not directly reflect how agents revise their beliefs. But we can look at how agents help other people revise their beliefs. This may give us some insight into a more sensitive and delicate revision mechanism than is possible to express in a propositional language.

One way in which agents revise the beliefs of others is through the use of constituent negation.[1] The use of constituent negation often follows an explicit verbal statement of a belief by the agent. Here is an example.

(12) Agent A: John and Jane went to the movies together.

Agent B: No, it's not Jane but Susie that went with him to the movies.

The negation in agent B's assertion has a curious scope-- over just a proper name in cleft position in the example above. The truth conditions of what Agent B states appear to be only that Susie went with John to the movies. But these truth conditions do not capture what is special about Agent B's statement. A dynamic, discourse view of meaning and of belief advances a much better thesis about the meaning of Agent B's statement: Agent B is using constituent negation to correct Agent A's belief in a particular way. Informally, I take agent B to be doing the following. He is trying to correct A's belief. His offer of correction or adjustment is not to wipe out the old belief and replace it with a new one but to replace merely one of the individual arguments constitutive of the old belief with a new individual argument. The form of the response of agent B tells A, provided he accepts that information, which argument of which predicate that is constitutive of his belief to revise. Even to state this operation coherently, we must suppose that beliefs have a particular sort of structure; they must have a predicate argument structure or have a list of predicates each with its own arguments, as DRT does. Furthermore this predicate argument structure must be connected to the syntactic constituents from which the DRS is derived. Revision by constituent negation like anaphora exploits the structure DRT assigns to cognitively relevant information.

Revision by constituent negation does not require an explicit statement of the belief requiring revision by agent A. Agent B may offer the revision because he assumes that agent A must have a certain belief in virtue of how he acts. Consider for instance the following exchange after both A and B discover a mess in A's house.

(13) Agent A: I'll spank Judy when I catch her.

Agent B: It wasn't Judy but Frank who made the mess.

I construe this dialogue along the following lines. Agent B assumes that Agent A must have the belief that Judy made the mess or was responsible for it somehow. Agent B believes (perhaps knows) that Frank did it and so takes it upon himself to correct agent A's belief. Again agent B uses the device of constituent negation to correct A's belief. If agent A accepts

---

[1] I would like to thank Hans Kamp for drawing my attention to this phenomenon.

the information offered by agent A, he will revise his belief by shifting the argument of the property equivalent (in some sense) to that denoted by *make a mess*. Given how these beliefs are internalized into the agent's cognitive state, revision by constitutive negation merely alters the internal anchor for some discourse referent that figures as an argument in the agent's belief to be corrected.

As I think the last exchange makes evident, correction by the use of constituent negation does not require that the agent actually express the belief to be corrected in words. Thus, the revision procedure exploits the structure of beliefs, not just the structure of the discourse by means of which we express them. Furthermore, this structure distinguishes at least predicates and arguments.

One can revise predicates that are constitutive of belief just as one can revise arguments.

(14) Agent A: Who was that man who bought the very expensive bottle of wine?

   Agent B: It wasn't a man. It was a woman.

One can also revise properties contributed by verb phrases. Consider the following possible revisions.

(15) They weren't fighting, just playing.

(16) John wasn't searching for seashells on the beach last week. He was planting anti-personnel mines.

On the basis of this data, constituent negation invites the following explanation. Like Lewis and Stalnaker, I suppose a view of a dialogue or conversation as the building up of a common ground. Unlike Lewis and Stalnaker, I assume that the common ground is a structured object-- much like an SDRS. In particular discourse referents and predicate ascriptions to those discourse referents are made explicit, and there is a mechanism for keeping track of conversational turns and what is proposed for inclusion in the common ground and what has already been included. The use of constituent negation then by a conversational partner indicates that the proposition that is a candidate for inclusion in the common ground must be revised before inclusion in the following way. I will suppose that the use of constituent negation for the purposes of belief revision contains two components-- a negated constituent and its positive correlate (usually embedded within a full clause). Positive correlate also indicated by means of the cleft construction. Suppose that the negation has scope over the constituent ψ. Then in translating the constituent ψ into the DRS language, one will come up with a DR-theoretic structure that matches some component or an internal anchor of the component proposition. One must replace this DR-theoretic structure in the candidate proposition with the DR-theoretic translation of the positive correlate.

So far we have not advanced beyond revising predicates and arguments. We have only exploited the weakest assumption concerning belief structure. We should enquire as to whether constituent negation may work to correct more complex beliefs. Consider the following conversation about A's party:

(17) Agent A: Everyone had a terrible time at the party.

    Agent B: No, it wasn't everyone, just Jim and Janet.

Here *everyone* has much the same status as one of the definites. So it appears one can correct the semantic contribution of a quantified noun phrase.

Thus far we have seen that noun phrases and verb phrases may be within the scope of constituent negation. But one also can revise information passed on by a wide variety of determiners through the use of constituent negation: [12]

(18) Agent A: Everyone had a terrible time at the party.

    Agent B: No, not everyone. Only a few people didn't enjoy themselves.

(19) Agent A: Few had a good time at the party.

    Agent B: No, it wasn't few. Most of the guests enjoyed themselves.

(20) Agent A: Some people had a terrible time at the party.

    Agent B: No, there weren't any. All of the guests enjoyed themselves.

(21) Agent A: Each person ate a peach.

    Agent B: No, not everyone. Some ate a pear.

One can also revise information passed on a particular noun phrase by placing for instance head of a relative clause and or a phrase from within a relative clause within the scope of a constituent negation.

(22) Agent A: Everyone who ate the fish hated it.

    Agent B: No, not everyone. Only a few people didn't like it.

    Agent C: And, not the fish. It was the meat that they hated.

The same holds true of modifiers of verb phrases such as adverbs and modals. Finally, were one to pursue in detail the sort of issue outlined under concept integration in the introduction of this paper, one would see that constituent negation also may be used to revise relations between propositions. Consider the following exchange between Agents A and B, which is of a piece with the other examples of constituent negation:

(23) Agent A: Fred teased him.

    Agent B: No, that's not why Sam hit Fred. Fred didn't say anything to Sam. Sam was just jealous of all the attention Fred was getting.

---

[1]There are some oddities, however -- (22) for example:
    (22) Agent A: No one had a good time at the party.
        Agent B: #No, it wasn't no one. Most of the guests enjoyed themselves.
I'm not sure why (22) sounds anomalous-- perhaps just the use of double negation

[2]It appears that (21) isn't quite of the right form. The determiner *each* does not combine well with constituent negation-- perhaps because of its tendency toward having wide scope. But with a determiner taking wide scope we would not be able to exploit constituent negation in the usual way. For it is the entire phrase within the scope of the negation that gives the material to be revised.

There do seem to be certain limits to what elements can fall within the scope of constituent negation. For instance grammar does not allow any ordinary conjunctions to fall within the scope of constituent negation. Nor does it allow full sentences to fall within its scope.

If we take the view that our belief models are built up out of applicative structures that are the translations of syntactic structures in the sense of Montague grammar, something similar (Cresswell (1985)), then we can make sense of constituent negation. Revision by means of constituent negation requires a view of partial models as built up by a series applications of functions to arguments. For instance we might assume, as is traditionally done, that a quantifier contributes a certain applicative structure taking properties of individuals as arguments. Thus, we now have defined a certain function for each element in the language that might be used in building or revising models.

In contrast to Gardenfors's notion of contraction and revision (which one might think of as global notions, as contractions and revisions of an *entire* belief state), the linguistic phenomenon of constituent negation suggests a notion of *local contraction of* a partial model. Let M be a partial model representing the conversation or the last conversational turn, and define a function FOCUS on M that returns a predicative or partial DRS. FOCUS(M) is determined by the constituent negation. The value of FOCUS(M) is the DRS contribution of the phrase in the constituent negation position. FOCUS(M) is well defined only if this structure is part of the partial model M which is its argument. FOCUS(M) is also typically not a partial model itself but rather some sort of structure that when combined with another of the right type yields a DRS or partial model. *Local Contraction of° M* is then defined as the structure $M*$ such that the combination of Focus with $M*$ yields M. Contraction in a system like MG or Cresswell's system would thus be thought of as a form of λ-abstraction: the contraction is an object of type $v \rightarrow (i \rightarrow t)$, where focus is of type v, and the type of propositions is $(i \rightarrow t)$. Because of the way partial models are built up, local contraction is not a function from belief states to belief states. It is a function from belief states to partial structures (λ-abstracted DRSs). When we abstract out the contribution of a noun phrase, for instance what we typically get is a DRS with a marker for a quantifier variable. To make sense, local construction must combined with a *local revision* operation, which replaces the structure of FOCUS(M) with another structure-- that given by the positive correlate of the constituent negation construction. I'll call this TOPIC(M). *Local revision of* a model M, $M\#$, is defined as follows:

$$M\# = M*\{TOPIC(M)\}.$$

Local revision only a partial function from coherent belief states to coherent belief states. Sometimes local revision may take a coherent belief state and yield an incoherent belief state. Unlike more global versions of revision (such as the view of revision suggested by Gardenfors), local revision makes no attempt at guaranteeing consistency. Also unlike the global revision notion, local revision does not appear to have any interesting characterization in terms of postulates. Such postulates would have to be so highly context sensitive, they would end up being just variants of the operational definition on structured belief states.

Constituent negation is a tool with limited applications. For instance, there is no way to use constituent negation to help Pierre out of his difficulties. Notice there how difficult it is to fix his dilemma. We would be puzzled as to how he got into such a state, unless we knew the whole story. The explanation of this according to the perspective I have adopted here is relatively simple. One can't fix Pierre's puzzle by the use of constituent negation; the difficulties cannot be fixed simply by correcting a part of one of his assertions. One has to adopt a different procedure with someone has become hopelessly confused -- an explanation from ground 0 to put everything right. But constituent negation does offer a way to revise beliefs minimally in many situations.

2 Revision and Non-Monotinicity

The notion of local revision that I described in the previous section must, it seems, be treated in a theory that understands belief states as highly structured objects like perhaps the DRSs of DRT. But it goes in a very different direction from what one might call Gardenfors's notion of "global revision." Local revision has no consistency check. It also relies very heavily on linguistic cues. Global revision does not rely on linguistic cues and has a built in consistency check. One might want to ask, what corresponds to Gardenfors's more global notion of revision within the DR-theoretic framework that I have been developing here-- i.e. one that has a consistency check and is independent of a particular linguistic context? Since there are several major differences between the classical and the DR-theoretic conceptions of belief, it seems best to look at how changing the classical conception one respect at a time affects the notion of revision. First let us consider the structured aspect of beliefs in DRT. This can be added to the classical conception without affecting revision, it seems to me. In fact Gardenfors has already done it, but supposing that belief states are to be modelled by sets of sentences. Second, what about partiality? Again at least a limited form of partiality underlies the Stalnaker-Gardenfors view of belief states. Partiality does affect revision, however, insofar as it suggests a need for non-monotonic principles of reasoning. The Stalnaker-Gardenfors view does not consider any such principles. It seems to me that changing the underlying consequence relation to one that incorporates non-monotonic elements has quite dramatic consequences for the classical notions concerning belief revision.

Given what I have said about DRS updating, the following principle holds within this framework. Let L be a first order language augmented by the default quantifier >. Let S be the theory in L of a DR-theoretic belief state, or what I have called a Gardenfors counterpart to a DR-theoretic belief state. Let Σ be the class of all such Gardenfors counterparts. Then:

(A0) $S = \{\varphi : S \approx \varphi\}$.

I.e. belief states are fixed points of the non-monotonic consequence relation. Thus, the background consequence relation will include non-monotonic inferences.

Now let me return to the non-monotonic logic. Since the purpose of this paper is not to develop a default logic, recall my definition of a "reasonable" non-monotonic consequence relation. It must have the following properties.

(a) $\approx$ is a conservative extension of $\vdash$.

(b) Default MP. $A(t),\ A >_x B \approx B(t)$. But not $\neg B(t), A(t),\ A >_x B \approx B(t)$.

(c) Default specificity $A > B, B > C, A > \neg C, A(t) \approx \neg C(t)$ and not $\approx C(t)$.

(d) Not: $A > B, B > C, A > \neg C, B(t) \approx \neg A(t)$.

A reasonable non-monotonic consequence relation may add properties concerning the relation between $>$ and other conditionals. For instance it may allow default transitivity or other forms of reasoning other than those prohibited by (d). It may add other modal operators to the language. It may not, however, incorporate any additional principles validating non-modal or default sentences. Some current theories of non-monotonic reasoning, for instance prioritized circumscription and various versions of default reasoning with ordering mechanisms, Thomason and Horty's nets, might be said to yield reasonable consequence definitions. So do the more expressive, modal theories of Veltman (1989) or Asher and Morreau (1989). But to make the consequence relation precise, I will assume, perhaps unrealistically, that $\approx$ is to be thought of as the smallest consequence relation obeying (a)-(d).

A modest point about revision is this. Whatever we ultimately decide upon as our definition of global revision, the Levi Identity, which Gardenfors has used to define revision, and Gardenfors's postulates for revision, contraction and expansion, are inconsistent with the assumption (A0), where $\approx$ is defined by means of the properties (a)-(d).

I will use the Gardenfors postulates for expansions, contractions and revisions on Gardenfors belief state counterparts. I have already given the axioms for expansion in the first part of this paper (section 3). Here are the Gardenfors postulates for contraction adapted to an underlying non-monotonic logic.

(A-0) $S - A = \{\varphi : S - A \approx \varphi\}$

(A-I) $S - A \subseteq \Sigma$

(A-II) $A \notin S \Rightarrow S - A = S$

(A-III) $S - A \subseteq S$

(A-IV) not $\mathrel{\vdash\mkern-9mu\sim} A \Rightarrow A \notin S - A$

(A-V) $A \in S \Rightarrow S \subseteq (S - A) + A$

(A-VI) $\vdash A \leftrightarrow B \Rightarrow S - A = S - B$

(A-VII) $S - A \cap S - B \subseteq S - (A \& B)$

(A-VIII) $A \notin S - (A \& B) \rightarrow S - (A \& B) \subseteq S - A$

I now give the Gardenfors axioms for revisions and the statement of the revision rule.
Revisions:

(A*0) $S * A = \{\varphi : S * A \approx \varphi\}$

(A*I) $S * A \subseteq \Sigma$

(A*II) $A \in S*A$

(A*III) $S * A \subseteq S + A$

(A*IV) $\neg A \notin S \rightarrow S + A \subseteq S * A$

(A*V) $S * A = \bot$ iff $\vdash \neg A$

(A*VI) $\vdash A \leftrightarrow B \rightarrow S * A = S * B$

(A*VII) $S * A \& B \subseteq (S * A) + B$

(A*VIII) $\neg B \notin (S * A) \rightarrow ((S * A) + B) \subseteq S * (A \& B)$

One of Gardenfors's nice results is that revisions satisfying the axioms above may be defined in terms of additions, contractions and the Levi identity.

The Levi Identity: $S * A = (S - \neg A) + A$.

It is this result that does not go through when one replaces the classical monotonic consequence relation in Gardenfors's theory with a non-monotonic one. In giving countermodels I will often use familiar default scenarios. I would like to and perhaps could use theories that are directly relevant to DRT belief updating, but these would be too complicated to state in our simple default language.

PROPOSITION 1: The Gardenfors postulates for *, + and -, together with the Levi identity and (A0) are inconsistent.

Let $\approx$ be a reasonable non-monotonic consequence relation, and let * be defined by the Levi identity and let $S \in \Sigma$ be a fixed point of $\approx$, i.e., $\{\varphi: S \approx \varphi\} = S$. Let $\underline{B} = \{Bird(t), Bird(x) >x$ Fly(x), Penguin(x) >x $\neg$Fly(x)$\}$, let $S = \{\varphi: \underline{B} \approx \varphi\}$, and let A = Penguin(t). By the definition of $\approx$, $S \supset \{Bird(t), Bird(x) >x Fly(x), Penguin(x) >x \neg$Fly(x), Fly(t)$\}$. By (A-II) and the definition of $\approx$, $S - \neg A = S$. By the Levi-identity, $S * A = S + A$. By (AIII+), $S \subseteq S + A$, but by the definition of $\approx$ again, $\neg$Fly(t) $\in S*A$. But then S*A is inconsistent. By (A*V), $\approx$ $\neg$Penguin(t), which contradicts the fact that $\approx$ is a conservative extension of classical logic. No atomic sentence is a theorem of classical logic.

Note that the proof does not appeal to (A+V), suspect within this framework for other reasons. With the non-monotonic consequence relation made precise, we can also make good on an earlier claim about updating in the presence of a non-monotonic consequence relation.

PROPOSITION 2: (A+V) is inconsistent with (A0).

Let $\underline{B}$ = {bird(x) >x fly(x)}, A = bird(t). Let $\underline{J}$ = {ψ: $\underline{B}$ $\vDash$ ψ} and let $\underline{B'}$ = {bird(x) >x fly(x), bird(t), penguin(t), penguin(x) >x ¬fly(x)}. Let $\underline{H}$ = {ψ: $\underline{B'}$ $\vDash$ ψ}. $\underline{J}$ ⊆ $\underline{H}$, but when we add A to both sets and use default modus ponens, we get incomparable sets, which contradicts (A+V).

Also problematic are principles like (A-III) in this framework:

PROPOSITION 3: (A-III) is inconsistent with (A0).

Let J = {bird(x) $>_x$ fly(x), bird(x) & penguin(x) $>_x$ bird(x), bird(x) & penguin(x) $>_x$ ¬fly(x), bird(t), penguin(t)}. Let S = {φ: J $\vDash$ φ}. Since $\vDash$ is a reasonable non-monotonic consequence relation S $\vdash$ ¬fly(t) and not S $\vdash$ fly(t) by specificity. But suppose A := penguin(t). Then S- A $\vdash$ fly(t). This contradicts (A-III).

Finally, suppose that we strengthen our conception of a reasonable non-monotonic consequence relation so that it is skeptical in case of direct conflicts as Horty, Thomason et. al and Veltman suggest. That is, it is not the case that one infers A(t) or ¬A(t) by default from the following premises: B(x) $>_x$ A(x), C(x) $>_x$ ¬A(x), B(t) and C(t). Now understand (A00) to be just like (A0) except that it exploits such a strengthened, reasonable non-monotonic consequence relation.

PROPOSITION 4: (A*II), (A*III) and (A*V) are inconsistent with (A00).

Suppose that S is the fixed point under a strong reasonable relation $\vDash$ of {B(x) $>_x$ A(x), C(x) $>_x$ ¬A(x), B(t), C(t)}, where A(t), B(t) and C(t) are all atomic formulas, and suppose we revise by ¬B(t). By (A*V), S*¬B(t) must be consistent. By (A*II) S*¬B(t) $\vdash$ ¬B(t), and so S*¬B(t) does not verify B(t). By default modus ponens, (S*¬B(t))*C(t) $\vDash$ ¬A(t). But since $\vDash$ is a strengthened, reasonable non-monotonic consequence relation, not S $\vDash$ ¬A(t). This contradicts (A*III).

The general problem with a non-monotonic version of the Gardenfors theory is this. Sometimes adding new information may simply involve a change in the monotonic core of information of the previous belief state. Provided we can determine when such cases take place if in fact there are changes in belief states that modify the monotonic core without touching the non-monotonic periphery, the Gardenfors postulates work well enough. But sometimes the new information may undermine the assumptions about what is normal that support the non-monotonic inferences. Then in that case, it appears that we suspend the non-monotonic inferences drawn from the old belief state, and instead update the monotonic core and then take non-monotonic closure. For example, if I have the "penguin theory" described earlier as part of my belief state augmented with some natural enough default principles and I learn that Tweety is a bird, I may conclude that Tweety flies. But if I further learn that I am in Antartica rather than in Germany, then all bets are off. I will no longer draw the non-monotonic inferences about Tweety. Not surprisingly, the Gardenfors revision axioms are insensitive to the interplay between the monotonic core and its non-monotonic completion.

One might think that such results only apply to a language with > or some other conditional default operator. One might hope that by eliminating this operator from the language, one could restore the validity of the Gardenfors axioms and the Levy identity, at least for the extensional fragment of L. But even this is not guaranteed, once one has a background non-monotonic consequence relation. As we saw earlier in our updating rules, the language of the equations or formulas required for the updating process might be wholly extensional or very simple, and yet the background consequence relation could be non-monotonic. The same counterexamples would hold, if we took out the default conditionals and built in their information content on the models. For instance, $bird(x) >_x fly(x)$ would be translated as a constraint on updating partial models.

How can we revise the Gardenfors picture to take account of the distinction in the types of reasoning we employ in belief updating and revision? One possible strategy is this: we define revision as Gardenfors suggests on the monotonic core of the belief state and then perform the non-monotonic completion. To put this into practice, we must distinguish the monotonic core and the non-monotonic completion of a Gardenfors belief state counterpart. Let a *modified Gardenfors belief state* then consist in a pair of sets of sentences $<X, |\approx (X)>$, where X is a set of sentences closed under $\vdash$ and $|\sim(X)$ is the fixpoint of X under $|\sim$. To get a sensible theory of modified Gardenfors belief states, we need operations of expansion and contraction for such states,. For a modified Gardenfors belief state counterpart $<X, |\approx(X)>$ and any formula φ,

DEFINITION
$$<X, |\approx(X)> \oplus \varphi = <\vdash(X +\varphi), |\approx (X +\varphi)>$$
$$<X, |\approx(X)> \setminus \varphi = <\vdash(X - \varphi), |\approx(X - \varphi)>$$

Keeping the Gardenfors postulates for *, -, and +, for theories under $\vdash$, we may now define revision in a non-monotonic setting:

DEFINITION: The revision of a modified Gardenfors belief state $<X, |\approx(X)>$ with φ, written
$$REVISE_G(<X, |\approx(X)>, \varphi), =_{df} <\vdash(X * \varphi), |\approx (X * \varphi)>.$$

The revision process as now defined also obeys some postulates that are merely variants of the Gardenfors ones. For two modified Gardenfors belief states $S = <X |\approx(X)>$, and $S' = <X, |\approx(X)>$, I will write $S \subseteq S'$ iff $X \subseteq X'$ and $|\approx(X) \subseteq |\approx(X')$.

PROPOSITION 5:

(G0) $\cup REVISE_G(S, A) = \{\varphi: \cup REVISE_G(S, A) |\approx \varphi\}$.

(G1) $REVISE_G(S, A) \subseteq S$

(G2) A ∈ REVISE$_G$(S, A).

(G3) ¬ A ∉ S → S ⊕ A ⊆ REVISE$_G$(S, A)

(G4) REVISE$_G$(S, A) = ⊥ iff ⊢ ¬A

(G5) ⊢ A ↔ B → REVISE$_G$(S, A) = REVISE$_G$(S, B)

(G6) ¬B ∉ (S * A) → REVISE$_G$(S, A) ⊕ B ⊆ REVISE$_G$(S, A & B)

Missing are the postulates

(G*) REVISE$_G$(S, A) ⊆ S ⊕ A

(G**) REVISE$_G$(S, A & B) ⊆ REVISE$_G$(S, A) ⊕ B.

that correspond to Gardenfors's (A*III) and (A*6) axioms. By separating out the non-monotonic inferences of the belief state, we make it easy to falsify these axioms. To falsify (G*) let S = {A(x) >$_x$ B(x), A(x) &C(x) >$_x$ ¬B(x), A(t), C(t)} Suppose we update with ¬C(t). Then REVISE$_G$(S, ¬C(t)) contains in its non-monotonic part B(t) and S⊕ ¬C(t) contains ¬B(t).

Since modified Gardenfors belief states are not, from our perspective, real belief states, we might like to transfer our findings intox the DR-theoretic viewpoint of belief states. Modified Gardenfors belief states are just pairs of theories; they do not have the fine structure of DR-theoretic belief states and do not support the same analysis of updating. In order to state the appropriate notion of revision, again it seems to me that we would have to distinguish between the core, monotonic partial model and its non-monontonic completions. But this assumption now leads to difficulty. Adding new information cannot, if DRT is right, be represented by means of the expansion operation +. Rather it must, as I have tried to show, be represented by a function UPDATE that is a good deal more complicated and incorporates a non-monotonic completion. But if that is the case, then we cannot easily separate out the non-monotonic completion from the updating of the monotonic core with new information, as required for the definition of revision above. We might be able to limit in relevant ways the non-monotonic completion required for updating and thus distinguish between two non-monotonic completions. But I am wary of doing so, for we might nevertheless be able to construct examples like those used in propositions (1) and (2) just exploiting the non-monotonic update rules.

The DRT view of belief, however, has a much more sophisticated way of keeping track of dependencies through the use of UPDATE. Though giving us a theory that is closed under the non-monotonic consequence relation, UPDATE also keeps track of what follows from what when the non-monotonic completion is called upon. We should capitalize on this in defining a DR-theoretic, global notion of revision, REVISION. But to define REVISION properly, we must do away with the Gardenfors operations of contraction and expansion and define our own proper DR-theoretic ones. Actually only a contraction operation is needed, since we may use UPDATE in place of the notion of expansion. In what follows let B be a DR-theoretic belief state and define: B ⊢ only-because(φ, ψ) iff B ⊢ because(φ, ψ) and for no ζ ≠ φ, B$_0$ ⊢ because(ζ,

ψ). Following Gardenfors, I will suppose that there is a partial ordering $\leq$ on belief states reflecting the degree to which one state is at least as epistemically entrenched as another from the perspective of some third belief state.[1] I shall say that B is maximally$\leq$ with respect to B_0 just in case for all B' , $B \leq$ B' with respect to B_0. $\leq$ is subject to the following constraints:

1. $\{B: B \text{ maximally} \leq \text{ with respect to } B_0 \text{ and } B \rightleftharpoons B_0\} = \{B_0\}$.

2. Suppose $B_0 \vdash \varphi$ and $B_0 \vdash$ only-because(φ, ψ). Suppose also that $B \not\vdash \varphi$ and $B' \not\vdash \varphi$. Then $B \leq$ B' with respect to B_0, if $B \vdash \psi$.

3. For all B and all coherent B_0, $B \leq B_\perp$ with respect to B_0, where $B_\perp$ is the incoherent belief state.

DEFINITION: CONTRACT(B, φ) = <U, Con>,
  such that $U = \cap U_{B_i}$ and $Con = \cap Con_{B_i}$ for all B_i such that:
  (i) B_i is maximally$\leq$ with respect to B;
  (ii) $B_i \not\vdash \varphi$;
  (iii) For all ψ, ζ if $B \vdash$ only-because(ψ, ζ) and if $B \vdash$ not ($\psi \& \neg\varphi >_x \zeta$),
       then not($B_i \vdash \zeta$).

Condition (iii) is novel. It makes sure that the contraction of a belief state removes those non-monotonic inferences that might depend on implicitly assuming φ.

Now we can define a DR-theoretic notion of revision that is general, has a consistency check and has something analogous to the Levi-identity.

DEFINITION: REVISION(B, φ) = <UPDATE(CONTRACT(B, $\neg\varphi$), φ)>

This definition also yields a few Gardenfors-like postulates.

PROPOSITION 6: Let φ range over arbitrary conditions or DRSs.
  (R0) Th(REVISION(B, φ)) = $\{\psi : \text{Th(REVISION(B, } \varphi\text{))} \approx \psi\}$.
  (R1) REVISION(B, φ) $\vdash\!\!+ \varphi$, for φ a completed condition.
  (R2) REVISION(B, φ) = $\perp$ iff φ is not Kleene satisfiable.
  (R3) φ and ψ are strong Kleene equivalent $\rightarrow$ REVISION(B, φ)) $\rightleftharpoons$ REVISION(B, ψ)

[1]For a discussion see Gardenfors (1988).

Note that the counterparts to (A*I), (A*III), (A*IV), (A*VI) and (A*VIII) are missing. I have left out (A*III) and(A*VI) because of arguments like that in proposition 4. We might very well want to use strengthened, reasonable non-monotonic consequence relations. (A*I) fails because REVISION and UPDATE are partial functions. (A*IV) and (A*VIII) fail because of the closure of the theory as a whole under a non-monotonic consequence relation. The difficulties of propositions 1 and 2 do not arise with this definition of revision, because of the more sophisticated mechanism of tracking dependencies between beliefs. If we take for example the scenario of proposition 1, we see that once we attempt to revise the belief state, call it B, with *penguin(t)*, the contraction of B with respect to ¬ *penguin(t)* will remove the conclusion *flies(t)*. So no consistency will result when CONTRACT(B, ¬*penguin(t)*) is updated with *penguin(t)*. Such examples indicate that revision will preserve consistency when mere updating will not. Updating B with *penguin(t)*. will yield inconsistency. Key here is the complex notion of retraction and the mechanism of keeping track of inferential dependencies.

Conclusions

I have sketched a model of belief updating and belief revision motivated by concerns about the logic of belief and belief reports. In this model beliefs are assumed to have a complex structure and to be related together within the cognitive state in quite intricate ways. The structure is built up modified during belief updating and during revision. The model of beliefs is much more complex than that presupposed in the classical theory of belief revision such as propounded by Alchourron, Makinson and Gardenfors. Nevertheless, at least some of the developments of the classical theory may be carried over to this more complex model.

Acknowledgments

I would like to thank M. Morreau for his comments on an earlier draft of this paper.

References

Asher, N. (1984): 'Non-Monotonic Reasoning and the Conceptual Foundations of Linguistic Understanding', *Proceedings of the AAAI Workshop on Non-Monotonic Reasoning*, Mowhonk House, New Paltz, New York, 1984.

Asher, N. (1986): 'Belief in Discourse Representation Theory', *Journal of Philosophical Logic* 15, pp. 127-189.

Asher, N. (1987): 'A Typology for Attitude Verbs and their Anaphoric Properties', *Linguistics and Philosophy* 10, pp. 125-197.

Asher, N. (1989): 'Belief, Acceptance and Belief Reports', *Canadian Journal of Philosophy*.

Asher, N. & Morreau, M (1989): 'A Dynamic Modal Semantics for Default Reasoning and Generics', GMD Workshop on Non-Monotonic Logic, Sankt Augustin, FRG.

Asher, N. & Wada, H. (1989): 'A Computational Account of Syntactic, Semantic and Discourse Constraints on Anaphora', *Journal of Semantics*.

Cresswell, M. (1985): *Structured Meanings*, Cambridge MA: MIT Press.

Gardenfors, P. (1988): *Knowledge in Flux*, Cambridge, MA: MIT Press.

Halpern, J. & Moses, Y. (1984): 'Toward a Theory of Knowledge and Ignorance: A Preliminary Report', *Proceedings of the AAAI Workshop on Non-Monotonic Reasoning*, Mowhonk House, New Paltz, New York, 1984.

Heim, I. (1982): *The Semantics of Indefinite and Definite Noun Phrases*, Ph.D Dissertation, University of Massachussetts at Amherst, Amherst, Mass.

Kamp, Hans (1979) 'Events, Instants and Temporal Reference', in Bauerle, R., Egli, U. and von Stechow, A. (eds.) Semantics from Different Points of View, 376-417, Berlin: de Gruyter.

Kamp H. (1981): 'A Theory of Truth and Semantic Representation', in Groenendijk J., Janssen Th., Stokhof M. eds., *Formal Methods in the Study of Language*, Mathematisch Centrum Tracts, Amsterdam, 277-322. (Also in J. A. G. Groenendijk, et al (eds.), *Truth, Interpretation and Information*, Foris, Dordrecht, 1-41.)

Kamp, H. (1981): 'Evenements, Representations Discursives et Reference Temporelle', *Langages*, 64, 39-64.

Kamp, H (1984/85): 'Context, Thought and Communication', *Proceedings of the Aristotelian Society*.

Spohn, W. (1988): "Ordinal Conditional Functions. A Dynamic Theory of Epistemic States," in Harper W., Skyrms B., *Causation in Decision, Belief, Change, and Statistics*, Dordrecht: Kluwer Academic Press, pp. 105-134.

Veltman, F. (1989): 'Defaults in Update Semantics', DYANA deliverable 2.5a

Multiple Contraction.
A Further Case Against Gärdenfors'
Principle of Recovery

Reinhard Niederée

1 The AGM theory of belief contraction

This paper deals with some issues centered around the so-called postulate of Recovery, which in (Gärdenfors, 1988) has been invoked as part of a theory of belief contraction. This theory, in turn, is embedded into a more general theoretical framework concerning "the dynamics of epistemic states" (resp. theory change), developed by Carlos Alchourrón, Peter Gärdenfors and David Makinson (for short: 'AGM'). In the AGM set-up, epistemic states are construed as *belief sets*, where a belief set simply is a theory in the sense of a deductively closed set of sentences in an appropriate language L. The underlying logic is assumed to comprise the customary connectives $\{\neg, \&, \vee, \rightarrow, \leftrightarrow\}$ in the sense of classical propositional logic, the consequence relation being denoted by $\vdash$. For each set X of propositions its deductive closure is denoted by $Cn(X) := \{A \mid X \vdash A\}$. In particular, Cn is assumed to satisfy *monotonicity* (i.e. if $X \subseteq Y$, then $Cn(X) \subseteq Cn(Y)$) and

$$B \in Cn(K \cup \{A\}) \quad \text{if and only if} \quad (A \rightarrow B) \in Cn(K). \tag{1}$$

A two-placed *contraction function*, $-$, is then introduced that assigns to each belief set K and proposition A a belief set K_A^- which is assumed to result by retracting A from K. In an analogous fashion, belief *revision* and *expansion* are discussed in terms of corresponding revision and expansion functions, the expansion of K w.r.t. A being defined by $K_A^+ := Cn(K \cup \{A\})$. As regards contraction, the following rationality postulates make up the core of the AGM theory. For all sentences A, B and belief sets K:

(K⁻1) K_A^- is a belief set.

(K⁻2) $K_A^- \subseteq K$.

(K⁻3)   If $A \notin K$, then $K_A^- = K$.

(K⁻4)   If not $\vdash A$, then $A \notin K_A^-$.

(K⁻5)   If $A \in K$, then $K \subseteq (K_A^-)_A^+$.

(K⁻6)   If $\vdash A \leftrightarrow B$, then $K_A^- = K_B^-$.

(K⁻7) $K_A^- \cap K_B^- \subseteq K_{A\&B}^-$.

(K⁻8)   If $A \notin K_{A\&B}^-$, then $K_{A\&B}^- \subseteq K_A^-$.

As pointed out in section 4 of (Gärdenfors, 1988), contraction functions satisfying these postulates can be constructed in various ways. In particular, they can be defined in terms of "orderings of epistemic entrenchment": if the latter meet certain requirements (viz. postulates (EE1)–(EE5)), the resulting contraction functions $A \mapsto K_A^-$ will satisfy the above eight postulates; and, conversely, each such contraction function can be represented this way.

2   The Postulate of Recovery

Among the above postulates, it has been the postulate of *Recovery*, (K⁻5), which has primarily been subjected to criticism (see e.g. Makinson, 1987; Fuhrmann, forthcoming). I refrain from reviewing this criticism here. Instead, a simple general observation will be discussed which, I believe, further strengthens the case against this principle. The following simple — not to say trivial — lemma is at the heart of the considerations to follow.

Proposition 1. Assume that $A \in K$. Then, regardless of whether or not B is in K, (K⁻5) together with (K⁻1) implies that

(a) $(B \to A) \in K_{A\lor B}^-$

(b) $A \in (K_{A\lor B}^-)_B^+, \quad \neg B \in (K_{A\lor B}^-)_{\neg A}^+.$

Proof: By recovery, $K \subseteq (K_{A\lor B}^-)_{A\lor B}^+$, whence in particular $A \in (K_{A\lor B}^-)_{A\lor B}^+$, and thus by (K$^-$1), making use of (1), $(A \lor B \to A) \in K_{A\lor B}^-$. By (K$^-$1), then, $(B \to A) \in K_{A\lor B}^-$. (b) is an immediate consequence of (a); it could, in fact, be derived from (K$^-$5) and the above assumptions about the underlying logic alone. ∎

Obviously, the proposition generalizes to disjunctions of arbitrary length. This consequence of Recovery seems hardly acceptable as a general postulate — provided one considers contraction (also) for its own sake and not, say, solely in view of revision, which would amount to treating it as a derived concept, deprived of any independent meaning in its own right (see below). There are several starting-points for making the reservations one has about conditions (a) and (b) more precise.

Drawing on a corresponding distinction in (Harman, 1986), Gärdenfors (1988, p. 35, 66ff.) juxtaposes *foundations* and *coherence* theories of belief change. Indeed, condition (a) appears to be in perfect accord with the attractive but problematic coherentist heuristics of "minimality of change", favoured by Gärdenfors. For, as A was assumed to belong to the initially given belief set K, $B \to A$, too, must belong to K simply because it is a logical consequence of A[1]. A coherentist would thus tend to maintain this belief while retracting $A \lor B$; at least he would not (necessarily) object to the requirement of maintaining it. This is in conflict with the foundationalist position (such a position is advocated e.g. in Fuhrmann (forthcoming); it also underlies various AI procedures for updating databases). A foundationalist stipulates that if beliefs $A_1, \ldots, A_n$ are given up, so too should all beliefs B whose credibility relied on the discarded beliefs in the sense that believing $A_1, \ldots, A_n$ provided the only justification for believing B. In the above situation, for instance, it will sometimes be the case that A's being

---

[1] A different picture emerges if sets of propositions are taken into consideration which are not deductively closed or closed with respect to some weaker than the classical notion of consequence. Indeed, if closure under classical consequence were dropped, it could be the case that $A \in K$, but $B \to A \notin K$. In certain situations of that kind it would then even be impossible to contract K with respect to $A \lor B$ in such a way that (K$^-$5), (K$^-$2) and an approriate version of (K$^-$4) (viz.: if not $\vdash A$, then $A \notin Cn(K_A^-)$) are jointly satisfied. (Consider, for instance, $K = \{A, B\}$, where A, B are logically independent and not $\vdash A \lor B$.)

included in K provides the only reason for $B \to A$ to be included in K. Now, if $A \lor B$ is not a tautology, then this disjunction, and thus A itself, should not be contained in the belief set $K_{A \lor B}^-$ (as required by the above postulates (K⁻1) and (K⁻4)). Accordingly, in such a situation $B \to A$ should not be included therein either, contrary to (a)[2]. This is to say that while the basic set-up of the AGM approach is non-fondationalist, Recovery is even anti-foundationalist.

But one need not necessarily subscribe to the foundationalist perspective to see that (a) and (b) lay bare a serious structural drawback of (K⁻5). Indeed, keeping in mind Proposition 1, the general intuitions underlying Recovery seem to create a paradox. On the one hand, if one first retracts $A \lor B$ and then expands with respect to B, one puts in something *stronger*, as it were, than one retracted (as B implies $A \lor B$). So, if one believes in Recovery, then finding oneself committed to a condition of the kind $A \in (K_{A \lor B}^-)_B^+$ should not come as a surprise. But on the other hand, retracting $A \lor B$ may also be conceived of as a strong way of retracting A *and* B (as together with $A \lor B$, both A and B have to be retracted). Hence, to put in B again is to add, in a way, *less* than one retracted. From this perspective, no doubt, the condition in question, when invoked as a general postulate, is counterintuitive.

3 Multiple contraction and Recovery: An impossibility theorem

To bring this objection into relief, let us explicitly introduce the concept of *(simultaneous) multiple contraction*, i.e. contractions with respect to several beliefs $A_1, \ldots, A_n$ which are to be retracted at the same time. (This is a concept which in view of a general theory of contraction seems to me worth exploring also in its own right.) For notational simplicity, let us consider only the case $n \leq 2$. So assume a single contraction function to be given. The question then arises whether this function can be extended to a multiple contraction function in a reasonable way. We shall use the expression $K_{A,B}^-$ to denote the contraction of K w.r.t. A and B; that is, it will be assumed

---

[2]It goes without saying that under different circumstances instances of (a) could make perfect sense from a foundationalist point of view.

that $K_{A,B}^-$ is a belief set (included in K) which contains neither A nor B (unless A, respectively B, is a tautology).

In certain cases, multiple contraction may easily be reduced to single contraction. (An obvious requirement is $K_{A,A}^- = K_A^-$, for instance.) But the task of multiple contraction cannot generally be reduced to single contraction. For, $K_{A\&B}^-$ is required not to contain the conjunction of A and B (unless $\vdash A\&B$); hence at least A or B have to be dropped, but not necessarily both of them. In $K_{A\vee B}^-$, on the other hand, not only A and B must be eliminated but also their disjunction (provided that not $\vdash A \vee B$); but the latter may well be retained in the contraction of K w.r.t. A and B. This suggests the following weaker postulate:

$$\text{If not } \vdash A \vee B, \quad \text{then} \quad K_{A\vee B}^- \subseteq K_{A,B}^- ,{}^3 \tag{2}$$

where in certain situations equality may hold. If this condition is satisfied (together with the trivial assumptions mentioned before), the multiple-contraction operator will be said to *regularly extend* the single-contraction function considered.

This appears to be a plausible requirement for multiple contraction (provided one is prepared to join the AGM approach in deliberately putting aside most of the specific problems associated with nonmonotonic reasoning[4]). However, one must be very careful at this point. If one added, for instance, the postulate $K_{A,B}^- \subseteq K_A^-, K_B^-$ — or if one introduced in place of (2) the general monotonicity requirement that $K_C^- \subseteq K_{A,B}^-$ whenever $C \in K$, $\vdash A \to C$, $\vdash B \to C$ and not $\vdash C$ — it would follow that always $K_{A\vee B}^- \subseteq K_{B,B}^- = K_B^-$ (except for the trivial exceptions). But this implies that $K_A^- = K_{A\vee(A\&B)}^- \subseteq K_{A\&B}^-$ (substitute $A\&B$ for B and apply (K^-6)). It is pointed out in (Gärdenfors, 1988, pp. 63ff) that this cannot be accepted as a "generally valid rule for contractions": under the assumption of

---

[3] One might add the dual postulate $K_{A,B}^- \subseteq K_{A\&B}^-$. But as it is not needed for the present discussion, I refrain from doing so.

[4] Otherwise (2) would be open to criticism analogous to the one that could be advanced against principle (K^-2). As for (K^-2), consider e.g. some belief set K which contains the two beliefs (a) that x is a bird, and (b) that x is a penguin and (thus) cannot fly. If one retracts (b), one might wish to simultaneously add the new belief that x can fly; but this is blocked by (K^-2). (However, the non-foundationalist and monotonic framework under discussion does not provide the tools for an adequate treatment of such examples, anyway.

(K⁻4) it implies that for no pair A, B of propositions (except for tautologies) $K^-_{A\&B} = K^-_B$ and $B \in K^-_A$ can hold simultaneously. Observe that the above-mentioned (unrestricted) principle $K^-_{A,B} \subseteq K^-_A, K^-_B$ is untenable for the same reason, plausible though it may appear at first sight. (Otherwise the preceding considerations would have challenged the requirement of regularity itself.) For, that postulate implies that $K^-_{A,A\&B} \subseteq K^-_{A\&B}$; but it may be assumed that, as a rule, $K^-_{A,A\&B} = K^{-5}_A$, which again yields the critical condition $K^-_A \subseteq K^-_{A\&B}$. Note in passing that attempts at reducing multiple contraction to single contractions by generally assuming $K^-_{A,B} = K^-_A \cap K^-_B$ or $K^-_{A,B} = (K^-_A)^-_B$ can in the same way be shown to fail.

If one accepts (2), the range of potential postulates for single contraction will be restricted because they have to be compatible with regular extendibility. For this to become a real restriction, further desirable properties of multiple contraction have to be specified. Several such properties are ready at hand. Two of them will be listed now, both of which turn out to be in conflict with Recovery.

- Unless the epistemic situation referred to is extremely poor, one would, for instance, expect that there are propositions A and B along with some belief set K containing A and B such that retracting A and B and putting in B again results in a belief set which does not contain A, that is,

$$A \notin (K^-_{A,B})^+_B. \tag{3}$$

Needless to say that this cannot be made into a general rule. Because of (1), condition (3) is equivalent to

$$(B \to A) \notin K^-_{A,B}, \tag{4}$$

which is in turn equivalent to $(\neg A \to \neg B) \notin K^-_{A,B}$ and thus to

$$\neg B \notin (K^-_{A,B})^+_{\neg A}. \tag{5}$$

A multiple contraction function will be called *non-degenerate* w.r.t. (3) if this is satisfied for some A, B and K such that $A \in K$ and not $\vdash A \vee B$.

---

[5]It suffices to assume that (for sentences A that are no tautologies) $K^-_A \subseteq K^-_{A,A\&B}$, which under the assumption of K⁻6 turns out to be an instance of (2).

- An interesting candidate for a *general* rule is the condition that

$$\text{If} \quad B \notin K, \quad \text{then} \quad K^-_{A,B} = K^-_A, \tag{6}$$

which is a direct counterpart to (K^-3). It implies in particular that if $B, \neg B \notin K$, then

$$K^-_{A,B} = K^-_{A,\neg B} = K^-_A. \tag{7}$$

For the present purpose, a corresponding existential statement will do: A multiple contraction function will be called *non-degenerate* w.r.t. (7) if (7) is fulfilled for some A, B and K such that $A \in K$, $B, \neg B \notin K$ and neither $\vdash A \lor B$ nor $\vdash A \lor \neg B$.

The stage has now been set for the impossibility theorem announced in the heading of this section; it will spell out the 'paradox' mentioned in the beginning of this section:

> **Proposition 2.** Assume a (single-)contraction function, $-$, to be given that satisfies (K^-1), (K^-4), and (K^-5). Then there is no non-degenerate multiple contraction function which regularly extends this single-contraction function, where 'non-degenerate' stands for: non-degenerate w.r.t (3) or (7).

Proof: Ad (3): Because of the presupposed monotonicity of Cn, this is an immediate consequence of Proposition 1(b).

Ad (7): Assume there was a mutiple contraction function that regularly extends $-$, and that (7) was satisfied for some A,B and K which meet the requirements specified above. (2) then readily implies that $K^-_{A\lor B} \subseteq K^-_A$ and $K^-_{A\lor\neg B} \subseteq K^-_A$. But by Proposition 1(a) this entails that both $B \to A$ and $\neg B \to A$ belong to K^-_A, whence $A \in K^-_A$, contradicting (K^-4). ∎

Note that if, for some reason or other, one decided to restrict the range of situations where (2) is assumed to hold[6], the basic spirit of Proposition 2

---

[6] Likewise, one could consider interesting weaker versions of this condition such as

$$\text{if} \quad A \lor B \notin K^-_{A,B}, \text{then} \quad K^-_{A\lor B} \subseteq K^-_{A,B} \tag{8}$$

(which could be derived from more general principles such as: whenever $B \notin K^-_{A_1,\dots,A_n}$ then $K^-_{A_1,\dots A_n,B} = K^-_{A_1,\dots,A_n}$; both principles will be discussed elswhere). In fact, like most monotonicity principles, (2) might be too restrictive in certain situations (this poin could be retained by refining the above arguments and concepts and notions of non-degeneracy accordingly. In fact, even single examples along these lines would suffice to call Recovery into question.

4   Two Remarks

Let me conclude this note on the postulate of Recovery with two remarks. The first one will concern belief revision, the second one the coherentist ideal of minimal change.

Reducing revision to contraction.   A central theme of the AGM theory is the interdefinability of belief revision and belief contraction; for details see Gärdenfors (1988, section 3). Suffice it to mention here that it can be shown that a contraction operator satisfying the principles cited above can be derived from a revision function $*$ (satisfying certain rationality postulates) by means of the so-called Harper identity; and given some revision function that satisfies the above postulates except, possibly, for (K^-5), a corresponding revision function can be derived by means of the the definition

$$K_A^* = (K_{\neg A}^-)_A^+, \tag{9}$$

called the *Levi identity*. The Levi identity is inverse to the Harper identity and allows to represent each revision function both by contractions that satisfy Recovery and by contractions that do not. This fit between contractions and revisions and their relation to concepts such as the notion of 'epistemic entrenchment' lends a particular attractivity to AGM's overall theory of contraction and revision.

However, the foregoing considerations cast a shadow, firstly, on the idea of reducing contraction to revision by means of the Harper identity, as any contraction function defined this way will satisfy Recovery (cf. Gärdenfors, Theorem 3.4); and secondly, on the concept of reducing contraction — and thus, via the Levi identity, revision — to orderings of epistemic

---

has been made by Hans Rott). For, although it appears not to have consequences that are outright fatal (as opposed, for instance, to the principle $K_A^- \subseteq K_{A\&B}^-$ mentioned above), it still narrows down the range of plausible possibilities of determining $K_{A,B}^-$ (which involves dropping $A \vee B$ or $A \leftrightarrow B$) by tying this case to the more restrictive situation where $A \vee B$ has to be retracted.

entrenchment as axiomatized in Gärdenfors (ibid.), since Recovery is also satisfied by all contraction functions defined in terms of epistemic entrenchment (cf. ibid. Theorem 4.30). In fact, various ways of constructing contraction functions discussed in chapter 4 of Gärdenfors' book involve Recovery[7].

One way of circumventing this problem is to partly detach the concept of contraction involved here from its original connotations. This would yield an artificial concept of 'contraction in view of revision' which is no longer liable to the above criticism. Indeed, multiple contraction does not seem to play any particular role in this connection (although it might in a more refined account of revision), nor do the combined contraction-expansion operations in conclusion (b) of Proposition 1 have much to do with the Levi identity. What is special in the case of 'contraction in view of revision' stands out most clearly in the case of conclusion (a): If one is only interested in the revision function defined from a contraction function by the Levi identity, $K^-_{A \vee B}$ would be of interest only as a — more or less artificial — way of representing the revision $K^*_{\neg A \& \neg B}$. Now, as $K^*_{\neg A \& \neg B}$ contains $\neg A \& \neg B$, and thus its logical consequences, it contains $B \to A$, independently of whether or not it was contained in the correspnding contraction. Why, then, care about (a)?

The price to pay for such a move is a loss of potential epistemological impact of the Levi identity (and similarly, of the Harper identity). For, to accept this move is to depart from the idea of reducing revision in a rigid way to an all-purpose contraction function[8]. But as I take it, this would amount to throwing over board a basic constituent of AGM's overall theory of revision and contraction.

Let us now turn to the second remark announced, which primarily deals with contraction itself.

Minimal Change. Already the comparatively weak assumptions invoked in section 3 entail that Recovery will be violated, which means that together with a proposition A certain 'derived' propositions of the type $B \to A$ sometimes have to be dropped, too — as required by the foundationalist and contrary to the coherentist ideal of minimal change. In particuar, the

---

[7]See Lemmas 4.1, 4.7, 4.12, and Theorem 4.31 for maxichoice, full meet, partial meet and safe contraction functions.

[8]Independently of the specific issues treated here, this seems to me a problematic idea, indeed; but this topic lies outside the scope of the present paper.

intuitions underlying (3) seem to be closely related to foundationalist concepts, as they might be taken as referring to situations where a belief A is not 'based' on a belief B (although they do not, of course, directly imply a foundationalist position).

Does this mean that arguments of the type presented above do not only challenge Recovery but also any kind of coherence theory of contraction? I do not think so. To illustrate this a bit further, let us consider the following principle for single contraction:

$$\text{If } A \vee B \notin K_A^-, \text{ then } K_{A \vee B}^- \subseteq K_A^-. \tag{10}$$

As is easily seen, the principle follows from (2) together with (6) and (K$^-$1). Being weaker than those principles, it could, in fact, already be derived from less restrictive assumptions (such as condition (8)[9] in place of (2)), and it appears to be perfectly in line with a 'coherentist' philosophy. In particular, it can be shown to be consistent with the AGM theory of contraction. However, under the assumption of (K$^-$1) it implies together with Recovery that

$$A \vee B \in K_A^- \text{ or } A \vee \neg B \in K_A^- \tag{11}$$

for all belief sets K and propositions A, B such that $A \in K$. To see this, recall that in virtue of Proposition 1 Recovery (together with (K$^-$1)) implies that

$$B \rightarrow A \in K_{A \vee B}^- \text{ and } \neg B \rightarrow A \in K_{A \vee \neg B}^- \tag{12}$$

for all $A \in K$ (regardless of whether or not $(\neg)B \rightarrow A \in K_A^-$, which in itself appears to be quite a counterintuitive principle to assume). Now, suppose that $A \vee B \notin K_A^-$. (10) then readily yields that $K_{A \vee B}^- \subseteq K_A^-$, whence by (12) and (K$^-$1) $\neg B \vee A \in K_A^-$, proving (11).

Condition (11) expresses the naive ideal of minimal change in its purest form. It characterizes so-called maxichoice contraction functions[10] (see Gärdenfors, 1988, section 4.2), and it implies that for all propositions A with $\neg A \in K$ the corresponding revision $K_{\neg A}^* = (K_A^-)_A^+$ contains either B or $\neg B$, that is, $K_{\neg A}^*$ is a complete theory. But this would certainly be an

---

[9]See footnote 6.

[10]In fact, any orderly maxichoice function (as introduced in Alchourrón and Makinson, 1982; see also Gärdenfors, 1988, p. 77) satisfies both Recovery and (10).

undesirable requirement (compare also Gärdenfors, 1988, sections 3.5, 4.2). This means that the coherentist ideal of minimal change must be qualified correspondingly[11]. Note that this does not affect the AGM postulates themselves as they do not entail any such condition, that is, they allow that for certain propositions B both $B \vee A$ and $\neg B \vee A$ may not be contained in K_A^- (because both may be "equally entrenched").

Although this would be in line with a naive ideal of minimal change, Recovery and (10) cannot, therefore, in general be postulated to hold simultaneously. In view of the problematic character of principle (12), which is a consequence of AGM's theory of contraction under discussion, it seems worthwhile to reflect about 'coherentist' theories of belief contraction that do not imply this condition, while, perhaps satisfying principles such as (10).

What, then, about the soundness of the intuitions underlying Recovery? Obviously, Recovery can not be derived from some vague coherentist principle of minimal change alone. (Accordingly, the statement made in section 2 to the effect that Recovery is in line with a coherence theory of contraction, has to be understood in terms of compatibility rather than entailment.) Rather, there seems to be a common intuition that underlies this principle and the analogous principle

$$\text{If } A \notin K, \text{ then } (K_A^+)_A^- = K. \tag{13}$$

Both of these rules have to do with the idea that first carrying out some operation (viz. expansion, repectively contraction) and then carrying out a 'reverse' operation should take us back to the belief set we started with, which in most situations seems a plausible thing to assume. As it happens, (13) proves to be untenable for obvious reasons (cf. Gärdenfors, ibid. p. 62f.), whereras there are interesting contraction operators that satisfy Recovery. In fact, the idea just mentioned should be understood in terms of the successive

---

[11]This particular criticism marks only the tip of the iceberg: Most of the propositions $(\neg)B$ entering this way $K_{\neg A}^*$ would, in fact, be useless, if not even misleading. The concept of 'informational economy' underlying the ideal of minimal change in its most elementary forms does not take into acount that it is not only the number of proposition preserved that counts, but also their 'informational value' (or, to put it differently: their 'utiliy' or 'adequacy', say, in terms of prediction). To what extent AGM's notion of epistemic entrenchment potentially captures this aspect is an interisting question not to be discussed here. (Compare also Fuhrmann, 1988, p. 120ff.)

iteration of operations of theory change in time, a process that will usually involve some kind of control structure based on the explicit knowledge of previous stages (i.e. 'memory') — a concept that lies outside the scope of the AGM approach. In contrast, Recovery and (13), as they stand, refer to the set-theoretic concatenation of single-contraction and single-expansion operators[12]. As is exemplified by the case of (13), and could be further sustained by other observations, such a straightforward translation of principles governing successive theory change into rules concerning the set-theoretic concatenation of single-step operators is highly problematic (let alone a corresponding reduction of successive theory change to the simple case). But it is exactly a translation of that kind to which the undeniable initial plausibility of Recovery appears to be due.

For all these reasons, I do not believe that the above considerations challenging Recovery already suffice to force a foundationalist (respectively, anticoherentist) approach upon us. All in all, the pros and cons of both the purely coherentist (which should mean more than just: non-foundationalist) and the purely foundationalist perspective suggest to strive for a deeper level of analysis that allows for an integration of coherentist and foundationalist intuitions.

Acknowledgements and Note. I should like to thank Hans Rott and André Fuhrmann for their stimulating comments on an earlier draft of this paper. Meanwhile, I have been informed that the issue of multiple contraction has already independently been pursued by Fuhrmann (1988) and Hansson (forthcoming).

References

[1] Alchourrón, C.E., and Makinson, D. (1982). The logic of theory change: contraction functions and their associated revision functions. *Theoria*, *48*, 14–37.

[2] Fuhrmann, A. (1988). Relevant logics, modal logics and theory change. PhD thesis, Australian National University.

---

[12]In the case of Recovery, the statements of the type $A \to B$ contained in K_A^- if $B \in K$ take the part of the memory just mentioned; in the case of (13), memory cannot be mimicked this way.

[3] Fuhrmann, A. (forthcoming). Theory contraction through base contraction. *Journal of Philosophical Logic.*

[4] Gärdenfors, P. (1988). *Knowledge in Flux: Modeling the Dynamics of Epistemic States.* Cambridge, Mass.: Bradford-MIT.

[5] Hansson, S.O. (forthcoming) New operators for theory change. *Theoria.*

[6] Harman, G. (1986). *Change in View: Principles of Reasoning.* Cambridge, Mass.: MIT Press

[7] Makinson, D. (1987). On the status of the postulate of recovery in the logic of theory change. *Journal of Philosophical logic, 16,* 383–394.

Lecture Notes in Computer Science